LAOS

T0295651

INFORMATION STRATEGY, INTERNET AND E-COMMERCE DEVELOPMENT HANDBOOK

STRATEGIC INFORMATION, PROGRAMS, REGULATIONS

International Business Publications, USA
Washington DC, USA - Laos

LAOS

INFORMATION STRATEGY, INTERNET AND E-COMMERCE DEVELOPMENT HANDBOOK

STRATEGIC INFORMATION, PROGRAMS, REGULATIONS

UPDATED ANNUALLY

We express our sincere appreciation to all government agencies and international organizations which provided information and other materials for this guide

Cover Design: International Business Publications, USA

2017 Edition Updated Reprint International Business Publications, USA
ISBN 978-1-5145-2054-3

For additional analytical, business and investment opportunities information,
please contact Global Investment & Business Center, USA
at (703) 370-8082. Fax: (703) 370-8083. E-mail: ibpusa3@gmail.com
Global Business and Investment Info Databank - www.ibpus.com

Printed in the USA

For additional analytical, business and investment opportunities information,
please contact Global Investment & Business Center, USA
at (703) 370-8082. Fax: (703) 370-8083. E-mail: ibpusa3@gmail.com
Global Business and Investment Info Databank - www.ibpus.com

LAOS

INFORMATION STRATEGY, INTERNET AND E-COMMERCE DEVELOPMENT HANDBOOK

STRATEGIC INFORMATION, PROGRAMS, REGULATIONS

TABLE OF CONTENTS

LAOS STRATEGIC AND DEVELOPMENT PROFILES 14

STRATEGIC PROFILE 14
    Geography *15*
    People *17*
    Government *18*
    Economy *20*
    Energy *25*
    Communications *27*
    Transportation *28*
    Military *28*
    Transnational Issues *29*
IMPORTANT INFORMATION FOR UNDERSTANDING LAOS 30
    PROFILE *30*
        Geography 30
        People 30
        Government 30
        Economy 30
    GEOGRAPHY, TOPOGRAPHY AND CLIMATE *31*
    WATER RESOURCES *31*
    FOREST RESOURCES *31*
    MINERAL RESOURCES *31*
    ADMINISTRATIVE STRUCTURE OF LAOS *32*
        Attapeu Province 32
        Bokeo Province 32
        Bolikhamsai Province 32
        Champassak Province - Pakse 33
        Houa Phan 33
        Khammouane Province 33
        Luang Prabang 34
        Luang Namtha Province 34
        Oudomxai 34
        Phongsali Province 34
        Salavan Province 35
        Sekong Province 35
        Sayabouri Province 35
        Savannakhet 35
        Vientiane 35

For additional analytical, business and investment opportunities information,
please contact Global Investment & Business Center, USA
at (703) 370-8082. Fax: (703) 370-8083. E-mail: ibpusa3@gmail.com
Global Business and Investment Info Databank - www.ibpus.com

Xieng Khouang Province...36
PEOPLE...36
HISTORY..36
GOVERNMENT AND POLITICAL CONDITIONS...38
Principal Government Officials NEW CABINET MEMBERS APPROVED 38
ECONOMY..39
FOREIGN RELATIONS 41
U.S.-LAO RELATIONS..42
TRAVEL AND BUSINESS INFORMATION..43

INTERNET IN LAOS - STRATEGIC INFORMATION AND DEVELOPMENTS...........................45

INTERNET DEVELOPMENT IN LAO PDR - STRATEGIC INFORMATION 45
ICT infrastructure..45
ICT Education 45
ICT Industries and services 46
E-business & e-Commerce 46
Government guideline for IT Policies..47
National internet gateway and government ISP 48
Information Technology Center...50
Networking sector...50
ICT POLICIES 52
1. Infrastructure and Access..52
2. Enterprise and Industry...52
3. Research and Development 52
4. Applications...53
5. Human Resource Development...53
6. Legal Framework 53
7. Awareness..53
8. Poverty Alleviation 53
9. Standardization and Localization...53
ICT PROGRAMMES 54
ICT RESEARCH PRIORITIES 54
ICT DEVELOPMENT CHALLENGES AND OPPORTUNITIES...55
the ICT situation in Lao PDR..55
Political ambitions..56
1 Historical ICT policy events...56
2 National ICT Policy and Strategy 57
NATIONAL POLICY ON ICT..57
GMS Telecom Sector Policy Formulation and Capacity Building........................57
Remarks on policy development 58
International aspects 58
1 ASEAN 58
2 EU-Asia Link 58
3 ASEM..59
Human Resources..59
Actors on the ICT arena...59
Users..59
Public administration: Government at all levels 59
Private sector: Tourists and students 59
Information: News agencies and the Press...60
Communication operators..60
Regulating agencies...60
Department of Post & Telecommunications (DPT), MCTPC..............................60
Lao National Internet Committee (LANIC) 61

Ministry of Information and Culture 61
Hardware and software distributors.. 61
ICT related consulting services 62
Communication Infrastructure.. 62
Passive infrastructure... 62
Domestic links 62
International links 62
Network Services.. 63
PSTN/PSDN/ISDN/ADSL 63
GSM.. 63
CDMA... 63
INTERNET 63
Internet Service Providers... 63
Internet Users 64
Internet access points 64
Provincial gateways for public administration 64
National Education and Research Network.. 64
Internet Exchange Point 64
International services via the CSC cable 64
International services via satellite... 65
TV/Radio distribution 65
Soft infrastructure.. 65
National Statistics Centre 66
Censuses on Population and Housing 66
National Accounts and business statistics 66
Local content... 66
Enabling Technologies and Solutions (such as payment solutions........... 67
ICT Enabled Services (such as Call Centres, Business Process Outsourcing) 67
EDUCATION AND TRAINING 68
The Educational System in Laos.. 68
Primary and secondary education.. 69
Vocational education and training... 69
Tertiary education and research institutes 69
National University of Laos (NUOL) 70
Regional university colleges... 70
National Agriculture and Forestry Research Institute (NAFRI).............. 70
Training of teachers and trainers.. 71
Training of pre-primary and primary/basic school teachers..................... 71
Training of secondary school teachers 71
Training of higher education teachers.. 71
ICT in Education 71
Phase 1. National Research and Education Network 72
Phase 2. ICT curricula 72
Phase 3. eLearning and distance education 73
PUBLIC ADMINISTRATION 73
Organisation.. 73
Central government 73
Provincial line organization 74
District line organisation.. 74
Village organisation 74
eGovernment examples.. 74
Environment Awareness Raising Activities 75
Education and poverty reduction... 75
Schools as access points and learning centres for entrepreneurs 75

**For additional analytical, business and investment opportunities information,
please contact Global Investment & Business Center, USA
at (703) 370-8082. Fax: (703) 370-8083. E-mail: ibpusa3@gmail.com
Global Business and Investment Info Databank - www.ibpus.com**

Phon Mi school Viengkham district, Vientiane Province.. 75
Phouxay Secondary school in Xay district, Oudomxay Province...................................... 75
Healthcare.. 76
Hospital sanitation and waste management 76
Patient records 76
Telemedicine.. 76
Oudomxay Provincial Hospital 76
Vientiane Province 77
Lao-Luxembourg Provincial Hospital, Phon Mi 77
Phon Hong, District hospital 77
Transformation from manual to digital systems 77
Transformation from manual to digital systems 77
Situation.. 77
Readiness 77
Priorities 78
Capacities in central and local government, state controlled activities and research bodies........... 78
Generic findings 78
Ability to use and apply ICT in government 78
Ability to design and maintain ICT systems and networks in government.......................... 78
STEA (www.stea.gov.la) / PSTEO 79
Ambitions, strategy... 79
Cabinet.. 79
Lao National Internet Committee (LANIC) 79
Department of Science and Technology.. 79
ICT Project Cooperation 80
National ICT policy process 80
Standardized Lao font.. 80
eGovernment 80
Rural access planning 80
Department of Environment 80
SEM 81
ICT in the SEM project 81
Department of IP, Standardization & Metrology.. 82
Science Research Institute 82
Technology Research Institute 82
Environment Research Institute 83
PSTEO.. 83
Provincial ICT centres.. 83
Oudomxai 84
Challenges according to PSTEO in Oudomxay.. 84
Luang Prabang 84
PADETC... 84

TELECOM AND INTERNET SECTOR DEVELOPMENT... 85

TELECOMMUNICATION LAW.. 88
Part I General Provision.. 88
Part II The Telecommunication Systems and The Type of Telecommunication Services in Lao PDR. 90
Part III Regulation on Telecommunications Services 91
Part IV The Business of Telecommunication Services.. 91
Part V Management and Inspection of Telecommunications 93
Part VI Settlement of Disputes... 96
Article 23. Administrative Settlement of Disputes... 96
Part VII Reward to contributors and Measure against violators 96
Article 25. Reward to contributors 96

**For additional analytical, business and investment opportunities information,
please contact Global Investment & Business Center, USA
at (703) 370-8082. Fax: (703) 370-8083. E-mail: ibpusa3@gmail.com
Global Business and Investment Info Databank - www.ibpus.com**

Part VIII Final Provisions... *97*
Direct Foreign Investment... *98*
PROSPECTS FOR GROWTH *98*

PRACTICAL INFORMATION FOR EXPORT AND INVESTMENTS **100**
   STARTING BUSINESS IN LAOS 100
     Basic Steps.. *100*
     Investment incentives.. *103*
   SELLING TO THE LAO PEOPLE'S DEMOCRATIC REPUBLIC............................... 108
     IMPORT POLICY, REGULATIONS AND PROCEDURES.............................. *108*
       A. General... 108
     B. Import approval *108*
     C. Licensing, quotas and prohibitions.. *109*
     D. Import requirements *112*
     E. Packing and labelling requirements *112*
       F. Inspections... 113
     Registration *113*
     Prohibited Goods... *113*
     Sanitary and Phytosanitary Requirements *115*
     Technical Requirements *115*
     Import Declaration... *116*
     Advance Declaration *116*
     Customs Broker *116*
     Classification and Value.. *116*
     Payment of Duties.. *117*
     Goods Imported under Warehouse Regime.................................... *117*
     Temporary Imports.. *117*
     Exemptions *118*
   TARIFF SCHEDULE – CUSTOMS.. 118
     A. General *118*
     B. Classification *118*
     C. Customs duties *118*
     D. Taxes and surcharges *119*
   FOREIGN EXCHANGE REGIME... 120
     A. General *120*
     B. Currency convertibility *120*
     C. Foreign exchange allocation *120*
     D. Money and finance measures... *121*
     E. Banking *121*
   IMPORTING FROM LAOS 122
     A. Documents required for imports *123*
     B. Special requirements.. *124*
   MARKETING AND DISTRIBUTION.. 124
     A. Market regulations and product standards................................ *124*
     B. Port facilities and trading route... *125*
   GOVERNMENT PROCUREMENT AND STATE-OWNED ENTERPRISES................... 125
     A. Government procurement.. *125*
     B. State-owned enterprises *127*
   PRINCIPAL IMPORT ITEMS 128
   BUYING FROM THE LAO PEOPLE'S DEMOCRATIC REPUBLIC........................... 128
     I. EXPORT POLICY, REGULATIONS AND PROCEDURES................... *128*
     Prohibited goods for export.. *130*
     ASEAN Integration System of Preferences *130*
     EXPORT CHARGES *134*

**For additional analytical, business and investment opportunities information,
please contact Global Investment & Business Center, USA
at (703) 370-8082. Fax: (703) 370-8083. E-mail: ibpusa3@gmail.com
Global Business and Investment Info Databank - www.ibpus.com**

SETTLEMENTS OF BILLS, LETTER OF CREDIT 134
DOCUMENTS 134
STATE MONOPOLY FOR EXPORT ITEMS 134

INVESTING IN THE LAO PEOPLE'S DEMOCRATIC REPUBLIC 137
I. FOREIGN INVESTMENT POLICY AND REGULATIONS 137
II. INVESTMENT PROCEDURES 138
III. INVESTMENT INCENTIVES AND SPECIAL PROMOTION ZONES 140
IV. TAXATION 143
V. FOREIGN EXCHANGE 146
VI. LABOUR ISSUES 146
VII. DISPUTE SETTLEMENT 148
VIII. PROTECTION OF PROPERTY RIGHTS 149
        References for part four: investing in the Lao People's Democratic Republic 152
INVESTMENT CLIMATE 153
LAOS INVESTMENT AND BUSINESS CLIMATE - STRATEGIC INFORMATION AND CONTACTACT FOR
STARTING BUSINESS IN LAOS 153
        1. Openness To, and Restrictions Upon, Foreign Investment 154
        2. Conversion and Transfer Policies 156
        3. Expropriation and Compensation 156
        4. Dispute Settlement 156
        5. Performance Requirements and Investment Incentives 157
        6. Right to Private Ownership and Establishment 158
        7. Protection of Property Rights 158
        8. Transparency of the Regulatory System 159
        9. Efficient Capital Markets and Portfolio Investment 160
        10. Competition from State-Owned Enterprises 160
        11. Corporate Social Responsibility 160
        12. Political Violence 161
        13. Corruption 161
        14. Bilateral Investment Agreements 161
        15. OPIC and Other Investment Insurance Programs 161
        16. Labor 161
        17. Foreign Trade Zones/Free Ports 162
        18. Foreign Direct Investment and Foreign Portfolio Investment Statistics 163
        Lawyers in Laos - Important Contacts 164
MARKET OVERVIEW 166
        Market Challenges 167
        Market Opportunities 168
        Market Entry Strategy 169
SELLING U.S. PRODUCTS AND SERVICES 169
        Using an Agent or Distributor 169
        Establishing an Office 170
        Franchising 171
        Direct Marketing 171
        Joint Ventures/Licensing 171
        Selling to the Government 172
        Distribution and Sales Channels 172
        Selling Factors/Techniques 173
        Electronic Commerce 173
        Trade Promotion and Advertising 173
        Pricing 174
        Sales Service/Customer Support 174
        Intellectual Property 175

**For additional analytical, business and investment opportunities information,
please contact Global Investment & Business Center, USA
at (703) 370-8082. Fax: (703) 370-8083. E-mail: ibpusa3@gmail.com
Global Business and Investment Info Databank - www.ibpus.com**

Due Diligence *177*
Local Professional Services *177*
Web Resources *177*
LEADING SECTORS FOR U.S. EXPORT AND INVESTMENT 177
Tourism Infrastructure and Resorts *177*
Web Resources *177*
ARCHITECTURE, CONSTRUCTION AND ENGINEERING SERVICES 178
Web Resources *178*
Pharmaceuticals, Medical Supplies and Medical Equipment *178*
TRADE REGULATIONS, CUSTOMS AND STANDARDS 178
Import Tariffs *178*
Trade Barriers *179*
Import Requirements and Documentation *179*
U.S. Export Controls *179*
Temporary Entry *180*
Labeling and Marking Requirements *180*
Prohibited and Restricted Imports *180*
Customs Regulations and Contact Information *180*
Standards *180*
Standards Organizations *180*
Conformity Assessment *180*
Product Certification *181*
Accreditation *181*
Publication of Technical Regulations *181*
Labeling and Marking *181*
Contacts *181*
Trade Agreements *181*
Web Resources *181*
EXPORT DOCUMENTS AND PROCEDURES 182
Part I : Documentation *182*
  Cargo Control Document 182
  Invoice 182
Part II :Classification of Goods *183*
  Structure of the Classification Number 183
Part III : Value for Duty *184*
  Transaction value method 184
  Other methods of valuing imports 185
  Identical or similar goods method 185
  Deductive value method 185
  Computed value method 185
  Flexible method 185
  Importer's Responsibility 186
  Customs' Responsibility 186
  Importer's Rights 186
Part IV : Coding Instructions *186*
  The Declaration Form 186
  The declaration form has three segments. 186
  Box No.1 Declaration Regime 187
    Office Codes. 187
  Manifest /Airway bill number. 187
  Box No.2 Exporter and Address 187
  Box No.3 Gross Mass Kg. 187
  Box No.4 Items. 188
  Box No.5 Total Packages. 188

**For additional analytical, business and investment opportunities information,
please contact Global Investment & Business Center, USA
at (703) 370-8082. Fax: (703) 370-8083. E-mail: ibpusa3@gmail.com
Global Business and Investment Info Databank - www.ibpus.com**

Box No. 6 Importer and Address...188
Box No.7 Consignee..188
Box No.8 Declarant..188
Box No.9 Country of Consignment/Destination..188
FOREIGN INVESTMENT OPPORTUNITIES IN LAOS 193
FOREIGN INVESTMENT LICENSED IN LAOS *193*
SELECTED BUSINESS AND INVESTMENT OPPORTUNITIES..............................195
Agro-Forestry Sector..*195*
Energy Sector *195*
Mining Sector *196*
Roads..*197*
UPGRADING KUNMING -LAOSHIO ROAD SYSTEM. 197
Railway, Water and Transport Sub-Sector...*197*
Tourism and Hotel Sector...*198*
Transport...*198*
Trade and Services Sector..*198*
IMPORTANT BUSINESS AND INVESTMENT OPPORTUNITIES 199
20 MILLION ENVIRONMENT & SOCIAL PROGRAM.................................199
PREPARATORY TECH ASSISTANCE PROJECTS......................................*201*
U.S.$37 MILLION VIENTIANE URBAN INFRASTRUCTURE & SRV PROJ.....*203*
NEW ADB LOAN PROJECTS...*206*
USD 1.55 MILLION ADB BUSINESS OPPORTUNITIES.............................*208*
PRIMARY HEALTH CARE EXPANSION PROJECT......................................*211*

IMPORTANT LAWS AND REGULATIONS AFFECTING BUSINESS.................. 214

LAW ON THE PROMOTION AND MANAGEMENT OF FOREIGN INVESTMENT IN LAO PDR.........................214
SECTION ONE: GENERAL PROVISIONS..*214*
SECTION TWO: FORMS OF FOREIGN INVESTMENT *214*
SECTION THREE: BENEFITS, RIGHTS AND OBLIGATIONS OF FOREIGN INVESTORS..........*215*
SECTION FOUR: THE ORGANIZATION OF FOREIGN INVESTMENT MANAGEMENT............*217*
SECTION FIVE: FINAL PROVISIONS...*218*
LAW ON THE PROMOTION AND MANAGEMENT OF FOREIGN INVESTMENT IN THE LAO
PEOPLE'S DEMOCRATIC REPUBLIC...218
SECTION: GENERAL PROVISIONS..*218*
SECTION TWO: FORMS OF FOREIGN INVESTMENT *219*
SECTION THREE: BENEFITS, RIGHTS AND OBLIGATIONS OF FOREIGN INVESTORS..........*219*
SECTION FOUR: THE ORGANIZATION OF FOREIGN INVESTMENT MANAGEMENT............*221*
SECTION FIVE: FINAL PROVISIONS...*222*
NOTIFICATION ON PROCEDURE FOR BUSINESS REGISTRATION IN LAO P D R...............223
I. Ministry (center) Level....*223*
II. Provinces, Capital and special zone level...*223*
III. Districts level...*223*
Documents to be completed by foreign investors *223*
Documents to be completed by domestic investors and enterprises other than commerce. *223*
Documents to be completed by domestic investors and controlled by commerce sectors:.............*224*
NOTIFICATION ON LIST OF GOODS SUBJECT TO IMPORT-EXPORT CONTROL AND PROHIBITION.............224
I. Goods subject to import-export prohibition..*224*
II. Goods subject to import-export approval or certificate........................*225*
NOTIFICATION LIST OF PROHIBITED GOODS FOR IMPORT AND EXPORT 226
REGULATION ON THE IMPORT AND EXPORT LICENSING PROCEDURES OF CONTROLLED GOODS FROM
TRADE AUTHORITIES 227
Chapter I General Principles *227*
Chapter II Licensing procedures..*227*
Chapter III Penalties..*228*

Chapter IV Final provisions..*228*
DECREE ON IMPORT AND EXPORT MANAGEMENT..*228*
Section I: General Provisions..*229*
Article 1:   Function of the Decree..*229*
Article 2:   Definition...*229*
Article 3:   Basic Principle of Organization and Operation...............................*229*
Section II: Goods Control, Controlled Goods on Import and Export *229*
Article 7:   Controlled Goods under Other Sectors *230*
Section III: Importer and Exporter..*230*
Article 9:   Importer *230*
Article 10:   Exporter *230*
Section III: Establishment and Operation of the Export and Import Business............*231*
Article 12:   Establishment of the Import Company *231*
Article 13:   Establishment of the Export Company *231*
Article 15:   Registered Capital...*231*
Article 17:   Consequence from Non-operation *231*
Section V: Importation..*232*
Article 18:   Import by the Import Company *232*
Article 19:   Specific Purpose Import *232*
Authorized import (for self consumption) shall be conducted in accordance with the list, limit, type and amount of goods indicated in the customs law.......................................*232*
Section VI: Exportation..*232*
Article 22:   Export by the Export Company *232*
Authorized export for self consumption shall be conducted in accordance with the Customs Law. *232*
Section VII: Sanctions..*232*
Article 26:   Other Violations...*233*
Section VIII: Final Provision...*233*
Article 27:   Implementation *233*
Article 28:   Effectiveness...*233*
DECREE ON GOODS TRADING BUSINESS..*233*
Section I: General Provisions...*233*
Article 1: Function of the decree *233*
Article 2: Goods Trading Business..*233*
Article 6: Conditional Goods...*234*
Section III: Foundation and Operation of Goods Trading Business.........................*234*
Article 9: Foundation *235*
Article 10: Registered Capital *235*
Section IV: Sanction..*235*
Article 15: Violation of the Regulations on Conditional Goods............................*235*
Article 16: Other Violations *235*
Section V: Final Provision...*235*
DECREE ON TRADE COMPETITION...*235*
CHAPTER I General Provisions..*236*
Article 1   Objectives..*236*
Article 2   Definitions..*236*
Article 4   Scope of application *236*
CHAPTER 2 The Trade Competition Commission..*236*
Article 5   The Trade Competition Commission...*236*
Articles 6   Rights and duties of the Commission..*237*
CHAPTER 3 Competition in Trade *237*
Article 7   Promoting a fair trade competition *237*
Article 8   Anti-monopoly..*237*
Article 9   Merger and Acquisition *237*

Article 10   Elimination of other business entities 238
Article 11   Collusion and Arrangements 238
Article 13   Exemption 238
CHAPTER 4 Measures against offenders 238
Article 14   Measures against business entities who commit offences 238
CHAPTER 5 Final provisions 239
Article 16   Implementation 239
Article 17   Enforcement 239

TRAVELING TO LAOS **240**

US STATE DEPARTMENT SUGGESTIONS 240
PRACTIVCAL INFORMATION FOR TRAVELERS 243
Cultural Festivals 243
Official Holidays 245
VIENTIANE 245
SPORT AND LEISURE ACTIVITIES 247
SHOPPER'S HEAVEN 248
TRAVELLING OUTSIDE VIENTIANE 249
Business Information 250

SUPPLEMENTS **251**

IMPORTANT WEBSITES 251
CUSTOMS OFFICE CODES 252
EMBASSIES AND CONSULATES 253
    Australia Nehru Street Vat Phonsay area. Vientiane Tel.: 41-3610, 41-3805, 41-3602 253
    Brunei Darussalam 253
    Bulgaria 253
    Cambodia 253
    China 253
    Cuba 254
    France 254
    Germany 254
    India 254
    Indonesia 254
    Japan 254
    Malaysia 254
    Myanmar 254
    People's Democratic Republic of Korea 254
    Poland 254
    Russian Federation 254
    Sweden 255
    Thailand 255
    United States of America Viet Nam 255
COUNTRY AND CURRENCY CODES 257
THE DECLARATION FORM 265
    Valuation Method 270
    Code 270
LAOS GLOSSARY 272
    Asian Development Bank 272
    Hmong 273
    Lao Issara 273
    Lao Loum 273
    Lao People's Army 274
    Lao Sung 274

For additional analytical, business and investment opportunities information,
please contact Global Investment & Business Center, USA
at (703) 370-8082. Fax: (703) 370-8083. E-mail: ibpusa3@gmail.com
Global Business and Investment Info Databank - www.ibpus.com

Lao Theung 274
Neo Lao Issara 275
Nonaligned Movement 275
Sipsong Panna 275
That Luang 275
Theravada Buddhism 275
Viet Minh 276
World Bank 276
SELECTED TOUR OPERATORS IN LAOS 276
LAO PDR EMBASSIES AND CONSULATES-GENERAL 277
BASIC TITLE FOR LAOS 280
BASIC LAWS AND REGULATIONS AFFECTING BUSINESS 282

For additional analytical, business and investment opportunities information,
please contact Global Investment & Business Center, USA
at (703) 370-8082. Fax: (703) 370-8083. E-mail: ibpusa3@gmail.com
Global Business and Investment Info Databank - www.ibpus.com

LAOS STRATEGIC AND DEVELOPMENT PROFILES

STRATEGIC PROFILE

Capital and largest city	Vientiane 17°58'N 102°36'E
Official languages	Lao
Spoken languages	Lao Hmong Khmu
Ethnic groups (2005[1])	55% Lao 11% Khmu 8% Hmong 26% other[a]
Religion	Buddhism
Demonym	Laotian Lao
Government	Marxist–Leninistone-party socialist state
• **General Secretary and President**	Bounnhang Vorachith
• **Prime Minister**	Thongloun Sisoulith
• **Vice President**	Phankham Viphavanh
Legislature	National Assembly
Formation	
• **Kingdom of Lan Xang**	1354–1707
• **Luang Phrabang, Vientiane and Champasak**	1707–1778
• **Vassal of Thonburi and Siam**	1778–1893
• **War of Succession**	1826–8
• **French Indochina**	1893–1949
• **Independence from France**	19 July 1949
• **Declared Independence**	22 October 1953
• **Laotian civil war**	9 November 1953 – 2 December 1975
• **Lao Monarchy abolished**	2 December 1975
• **Current constitution**	14 August 1991
Area	
• **Total**	237,955 km^2 (84th) 91,428.991 sq mi
• **Water (%)**	2
Population	

• **2014 (Jul) estimate**	6,803,699[2](104th)
• **2015 census**	6,492,228[3]
• **Density**	26.7/km^2 (177th)
	69.2/sq mi
GDP (PPP)	2014 estimate
• **Total**	US$34.400 billion[4]
• **Per capita**	US$4,986[4]
GDP (nominal)	2014 estimate
• **Total**	US$11.676 billion[4]
• **Per capita**	US$1,692[4]
Gini (2008)	36.7[5]
	medium
HDI (2014)	0.575[6]
	medium · 141st
Currency	Kip (LAK)
Time zone	ICT
Date format	dd/mm/yyyy
Drives on the	right
Calling code	+856
ISO 3166 code	LA
Internet TLD	.la

Laos, officially the **Lao People's Democratic Republic**, is a landlocked socialist republic communist state in southeast Asia, bordered by Myanmar (Burma) and the People's Republic of China to the northwest, Vietnam to the east, Cambodia to the south, and Thailand to the west. Laos traces its history to the Kingdom of Lan Xang or *Land of a Million Elephants*, which existed from the 14th to the 18th century. After a period as a French colony, it gained independence in 1949. A long civil war ended when the communist Pathet Lao came to power in 1975.

Private enterprise has increased since the mid-1980s, but development has been hampered by poor communications in the heavily forested and mountainous landscape. 80%[1] of those employed practice subsistence agriculture; this is coupled with widespread starvation due to the many failures of communism and the state's command economy. The country's ethnic make-up is extremely diverse, with only around 60% belonging to the largest ethnic group, the Lao.

In 1975 the communist Pathet Lao took control of the government, ending a six-century-old monarchy. Initial closer ties to Vietnam and socialization were replaced with a gradual return to private enterprise, an easing of foreign investment laws, and the admission into ASEAN in 1997.

GEOGRAPHY

Location: Southeastern Asia, northeast of Thailand, west of Vietnam
Geographic coordinates: 18 00 N, 105 00 E

For additional analytical, business and investment opportunities information, please contact Global Investment & Business Center, USA at (703) 370-8082. Fax: (703) 370-8083. E-mail: ibpusa3@gmail.com Global Business and Investment Info Databank - www.ibpus.com

Map references: Southeast Asia
Area:
total: 236,800 sq km

For additional analytical, business and investment opportunities information,
please contact Global Investment & Business Center, USA
at (703) 370-8082. Fax: (703) 370-8083. E-mail: ibpusa3@gmail.com
Global Business and Investment Info Databank - www.ibpus.com

land: 230,800 sq km
water: 6,000 sq km

Area - comparative: slightly larger than Utah

Land boundaries:
total: 5,083 km
border countries: Burma 235 km, Cambodia 541 km, China 423 km, Thailand 1,754 km, Vietnam 2,130 km

Coastline: 0 km (landlocked)
Maritime claims: none (landlocked)
Climate: tropical monsoon; rainy season (May to November); dry season (December to April)
Terrain: mostly rugged mountains; some plains and plateaus

Elevation extremes:
lowest point: Mekong River 70 m
highest point: Phou Bia 2,817 m

Natural resources: timber, hydropower, gypsum, tin, gold, gemstones

Land use:
arable land: 3%
permanent crops: 0%
permanent pastures: 3%
forests and woodland: 54%
other: 40%

Irrigated land: 1,250 sq km
note: rainy season irrigation - 2,169 sq km; dry season irrigation - 750 sq km (1998 est.)
Natural hazards: floods, droughts, and blight
Environment - current issues: unexploded ordnance; deforestation; soil erosion; a majority of the population does not have access to potable water

Environment - international agreements:
party to: Biodiversity, Climate Change, Desertification, Environmental Modification, Law of the Sea, Nuclear Test Ban, Ozone Layer Protection
signed, but not ratified: none of the selected agreements

Geography - note: landlocked

PEOPLE

Population: 5,497,459

Age structure:
0-14 years: 43% (male 1,191,608; female 1,173,144)
15-64 years: 54% (male 1,447,788; female 1,500,016)
65 years and over: 3% (male 85,028; female 99,875)

Population growth rate: 2.5%
Birth rate: 38.29 births/1,000 population

Death rate: 13.35 deaths/1,000 population
Net migration rate: 0 migrant(s)/1,000 population

Sex ratio:
at birth: 1.05 male(s)/female
under 15 years: 1.02 male(s)/female
15-64 years: 0.97 male(s)/female
65 years and over: 0.85 male(s)/female
total population: 0.98 male(s)/female

Infant mortality rate: 94.8 deaths/1,000 live births

Life expectancy at birth:
total population: 53.09 years
male: 51.22 years
female: 55.02 years

Total fertility rate: 5.21 children born/woman

Nationality:
noun: Lao(s) or Laotian(s)
adjective: Lao or Laotian

Ethnic groups: Lao Loum (lowland) 68%, Lao Theung (upland) 22%, Lao Soung (highland) including the Hmong ("Meo") and the Yao (Mien) 9%, ethnic Vietnamese/Chinese 1%
Religions: Buddhist 60% (in October 1999, the regime proposed a constitutional amendment making Buddhism the state religion; the National Assembly is expected to vote on the amendment sometime in 2000), animist and other 40%
Languages: Lao (official), French, English, and various ethnic languages

Literacy:
definition: age 15 and over can read and write
total population: 57%
male: 70%
female: 44%

GOVERNMENT

Country name:
conventional long form: Lao People's Democratic Republic
conventional short form: Laos
local long form: Sathalanalat Paxathipatai Paxaxon Lao
local short form: none

Data code: LA
Government type: Communist state
Capital: Vientiane

Administrative divisions: 16 provinces (khoueng, singular and plural), 1 municipality* (kampheng nakhon, singular and plural), and 1 special zone** (khetphiset, singular and plural); Attapu, Bokeo, Bolikhamxai, Champasak, Houaphan, Khammouan, Louangnamtha,

Louangphabang, Oudomxai, Phongsali, Salavan, Savannakhet, Viangchan*, Viangchan, Xaignabouli, Xaisomboun**, Xekong, Xiangkhoang

Independence: 19 July 1949 (from France)
National holiday: National Day, 2 December (1975) (proclamation of the Lao People's Democratic Republic)
Constitution: promulgated 14 August 1991

Legal system: based on traditional customs, French legal norms and procedures, and Socialist practice

Suffrage: 18 years of age; universal

Executive branch:

chief of state: President BOUNNYANG Vorachit (since 20 April 2016); Vice President PHANKHAM Viphavan (since 20 April 2016)

head of government: Prime Minister THONGLOUN Sisoulit (since 20 April 2016); Deputy Prime Ministers BOUNTHONG Chitmani, SONXAI Siphandon, SOMDI Douangdi (since 20 April 2016)

cabinet: Council of Ministers appointed by the president, approved by the National Assembly

elections/appointments: president and vice president indirectly elected by the National Assembly for a 5-year term (no term limits); election last held on 20 April 2016 (next to be held in 2021); prime minister nominated by the president, elected by the National Assembly for 5-year term

election results: BOUNNYANG Vorachit (LPRP) elected president; PHANKHAM Viphavan (LPRP) elected vice president; percent of National Assembly vote - NA; THONGLOUN Sisoulit (LPRP) elected prime minister; percent of National Assembly vote - NA

Legislative branch:

description: unicameral National Assembly or Sapha Heng Xat (132 seats; members directly elected in multi-seat constituencies by simple majority vote from candidate lists provided by the Lao People's Revolutionary Party; members serve 5-year terms)

elections: last held on 20 April 2016 (next to be held in 2021)

election results: percent of vote by party - NA; seats by party - LPRP 128, independent 4

Judicial branch:

highest court(s): People's Supreme Court (consists of the court president and organized into criminal, civil, administrative, commercial, family, and juvenile chambers, each with a vice president and several judges)

judge selection and term of office: president of People's Supreme Court appointed by National Assembly on recommendation of the president of the republic for a 5-year term; vice presidents of People's Supreme Court appointed by the president of the republic on recommendation of the National Assembly; appointment of chamber judges NA; tenure of court vice-presidents and chamber judges NA

subordinate courts: appellate courts; provincial, municipal, district, and military courts

Political parties and leaders: Lao People's Revolutionary Party or LPRP [KHAMTAI Siphandon, party president]; other parties proscribed

Political pressure groups and leaders: noncommunist political groups proscribed; most opposition leaders fled the country in 1975

International organization participation: ACCT, AsDB, ASEAN, CP, ESCAP, FAO, G-77, IBRD, ICAO, ICRM, IDA, IFAD, IFC, IFRCS, ILO, IMF, Intelsat (nonsignatory user), Interpol, IOC, ITU, NAM, OPCW, PCA, UN, UNCTAD, UNESCO, UNIDO, UPU, WFTU, WHO, WIPO, WMO, WToO, WTrO (observer)

Diplomatic representation in the US:
chief of mission: Ambassador VANG Rattanavong
chancery: 2222 S Street NW, Washington, DC 20008
telephone: [1] (202) 332-6416
FAX: [1] (202) 332-4923

Diplomatic representation from the US:
chief of mission: Ambassador Wendy Jean CHAMBERLIN
embassy: Rue Bartholonie, B. P. 114, Vientiane
mailing address: American Embassy, Box V, APO AP 96546
telephone: [856] (21) 212581, 212582, 212585
FAX: [856] (21) 212584

Flag description: three horizontal bands of red (top), blue (double width), and red with a large white disk centered in the blue band

ECONOMY

The government of Laos, one of the few remaining one-party communist states, began decentralizing control and encouraging private enterprise in 1986. The results, starting from an extremely low base, were striking - growth averaged 6% per year from 1988-2008 except during the short-lived drop caused by the Asian financial crisis that began in 1997. Laos' growth exceeded 7% per year during 2008-13. Despite this high growth rate, Laos remains a country with an underdeveloped infrastructure, particularly in rural areas. It has a basic, but improving, road system, and limited external and internal land-line telecommunications. Electricity is available in 83 % of the country.

Laos' economy is heavily dependent on capital-intensive natural resource exports. The labor force, however, still relies on agriculture, dominated by rice cultivation in lowland areas, which accounts for about 25% of GDP and 73% of total employment. Economic growth has reduced official poverty rates from 46% in 1992 to 26% in 2010. The economy also has benefited from high-profile foreign direct investment in hydropower, copper and gold mining, logging, and construction though some projects in these industries have drawn criticism for their environmental impacts. Laos gained Normal Trade Relations status with the US in 2004 and applied for Generalized System of Preferences trade benefits in 2013 after being admitted to the World Trade Organization earlier in the year. Laos is in the process of implementing a value-added tax system. Simplified investment procedures and expanded bank credits for small farmers and small entrepreneurs will improve Laos' economic prospects. The government appears committed to raising the country's profile among investors, but suffered through a fiscal crisis in 2013 brought about by public sector wage increases, fiscal mismanagement, and revenue shortfalls. The World Bank has declared that Laos' goal of graduating from the UN Development Program's list of least-developed countries by 2020 is achievable, and the country is preparing to enter the ASEAN Economic Community in 2015.

GDP (purchasing power parity):
$20.78 billion (2013 est.)
country comparison to the world: 132
$19.18 billion (2014 est.)
$17.78 billion (2011 est.)
note:data are in 2013 US dollars

GDP (official exchange rate):
$10.1 billion (2013 est.)

GDP - real growth rate:
8.3% (2013 est.)
country comparison to the world: 9
7.9% (2014 est.)
8% (2011 est.)

GDP - per capita (PPP):
$3,100 (2013 est.)
country comparison to the world: 176
$2,900 (2014 est.)
$2,700 (2011 est.)
note:data are in 2013 US dollars

Gross national saving:
27.4% of GDP (2013 est.)
country comparison to the world: 38
26.2% of GDP (2014 est.)
25.2% of GDP (2011 est.)

GDP - composition, by end use:
household consumption:
66.9%
government consumption:
9.8%
investment in fixed capital:
31.7%
investment in inventories:
-1.3%
exports of goods and services:
40%
imports of goods and services:

-48.4%
(2013 est.)

GDP - composition, by sector of origin:
agriculture:
24.8%
industry:
32%
services:
37.5% (2013 est.)

Agriculture - products:
sweet potatoes, vegetables, corn, coffee, sugarcane, tobacco, cotton, tea, peanuts, rice; cassava (manioc, tapioca), water buffalo, pigs, cattle, poultry

Industries:
mining (copper, tin, gold, gypsum); timber, electric power, agricultural processing, rubber, construction, garments, cement, tourism

Industrial production growth rate:
11% (2013 est.)
country comparison to the world: 12

Labor force:
3.373 million (2013 est.)
country comparison to the world: 100

Labor force - by occupation:
agriculture:
73.1%
industry:
6.1%
services:
20.6% (2014 est.)

Unemployment rate:
1.9% (2010 est.)
country comparison to the world: 11
2.5% (2009 est.)

Population below poverty line:
22% (2013 est.)

Household income or consumption by percentage share:
lowest 10%:
3.3%
highest 10%:
30.3%

Distribution of family income - Gini index:

36.7
country comparison to the world: 83
34.6 (2002)

Budget:
revenues:
$2.481 billion
expenditures:
$2.642 billion (2013 est.)

Taxes and other revenues:
24.6% of GDP (2013 est.)
country comparison to the world: 135

Budget surplus (+) or deficit (-):
-1.6% of GDP (2013 est.)
country comparison to the world: 77

Public debt:
46.3% of GDP (2013 est.)
country comparison to the world: 77
49.1% of GDP (2014 est.)

Fiscal year:
1 October - 30 September

Inflation rate (consumer prices):
6.5% (2013 est.)
country comparison to the world: 183
4.3% (2014 est.)

Central bank discount rate:
4.3% (31 December 2010)
country comparison to the world: 94
4% (31 December 2009)

Commercial bank prime lending rate:
23.2% (31 December 2013 est.)
country comparison to the world: 14
22.3% (31 December 2014 est.)

Stock of narrow money:
$1.389 billion (31 December 2013 est.)
country comparison to the world: 141
$1.154 billion (31 December 2014 est.)

Stock of broad money:
$4.071 billion (31 December 2013 est.)
country comparison to the world: 136
$3.673 billion (31 December 2014 est.)

For additional analytical, business and investment opportunities information,
please contact Global Investment & Business Center, USA
at (703) 370-8082. Fax: (703) 370-8083. E-mail: ibpusa3@gmail.com
Global Business and Investment Info Databank - www.ibpus.com

Stock of domestic credit:
$4.716 billion (31 December 2013 est.)
country comparison to the world: 114
$4.034 billion (31 December 2014 est.)

Market value of publicly traded shares:
$1.012 billion (2014 est.)
$NA

Current account balance:
-$484.3 million (2013 est.)
country comparison to the world: 98
-$315.5 million (2014 est.)

Exports:
$2.313 billion (2013 est.)
country comparison to the world: 141
$1.984 billion (2014 est.)

Exports - commodities:
wood products, coffee, electricity, tin, copper, gold, cassava

Exports - partners:
Thailand 34%, China 21.5%, Vietnam 12.2%

Imports:
$3.238 billion (2013 est.)
country comparison to the world: 145
$2.744 billion (2014 est.)

Imports - commodities:
machinery and equipment, vehicles, fuel, consumer goods

Imports - partners:
Thailand 62.1%, China 16.2%, Vietnam 7.3%

Reserves of foreign exchange and gold:
$845.4 million (31 December 2013 est.)
country comparison to the world: 141
$796.9 million (31 December 2014 est.)

Debt - external:
$6.69 billion (31 December 2013 est.)
country comparison to the world: 110
$6.288 billion (31 December 2014 est.)

Stock of direct foreign investment - at home:
$15.14 billion (31 December 2014 est.)
country comparison to the world: 81

For additional analytical, business and investment opportunities information,
please contact Global Investment & Business Center, USA
at (703) 370-8082. Fax: (703) 370-8083. E-mail: ibpusa3@gmail.com
Global Business and Investment Info Databank - www.ibpus.com

$12.44 billion (31 December 2011 est.)

Exchange rates:
kips (LAK) per US dollar -
7,875.9 (2013 est.)
8,007.3 (2014 est.)
8,258.8 (2010 est.)
8,516.04
8,760.69

ENERGY

Electricity - production:
3.629 billion kWh
country comparison to the world: 127

Electricity - consumption:
2.4 billion kWh
country comparison to the world: 136

Electricity - exports:
2.537 billion kWh
country comparison to the world: 41

Electricity - imports:
1 billion kWh
country comparison to the world: 65

Electricity - installed generating capacity:
3.217 million kW
country comparison to the world: 87

Electricity - from fossil fuels:
2.6% of total installed capacity
country comparison to the world: 201

Electricity - from nuclear fuels:
0% of total installed capacity
country comparison to the world: 122

Electricity - from hydroelectric plants:
97.4% of total installed capacity
country comparison to the world: 9

Electricity - from other renewable sources:
0% of total installed capacity
country comparison to the world: 191

For additional analytical, business and investment opportunities information, please contact Global Investment & Business Center, USA at (703) 370-8082. Fax: (703) 370-8083. E-mail: ibpusa3@gmail.com Global Business and Investment Info Databank - www.ibpus.com

Crude oil - production:
0 bbl/day
country comparison to the world: 186

Crude oil - exports:
0 bbl/day
country comparison to the world: 140

Crude oil - imports:
0 bbl/day
country comparison to the world: 206

Crude oil - proved reserves:
0 bbl
country comparison to the world: 152

Refined petroleum products - production:
0 bbl/day
country comparison to the world: 161

Refined petroleum products - consumption:
3,391 bbl/day
country comparison to the world: 177

Refined petroleum products - exports:
0 bbl/day
country comparison to the world: 191

Refined petroleum products - imports:
3,160 bbl/day
country comparison to the world: 170

Natural gas - production:
0 cu m
country comparison to the world: 151

Natural gas - consumption:
0 cu m
country comparison to the world: 163

Natural gas - exports:
0 cu m
country comparison to the world: 132

Natural gas - imports:

0 cu m
country comparison to the world: 86

Natural gas - proved reserves:
0 cu m
country comparison to the world: 156

COMMUNICATIONS

Telephones - main lines in use:
112,000
country comparison to the world: 143

Telephones - mobile cellular:
6.492 million
country comparison to the world: 99

Telephone system:
general assessment:
service to general public is improving; the government relies on a radiotelephone network to communicate with remote areas
domestic:
4 service providers with mobile cellular usage growing very rapidly
international:
country code - 856; satellite earth station - 1 Intersputnik (Indian Ocean region) and a second to be developed by China

Broadcast media:
6 TV stations operating out of Vientiane - 3 government-operated and the others commercial; 17 provincial stations operating with nearly all programming relayed via satellite from the government-operated stations in Vientiane; Chinese and Vietnamese programming relayed via satellite from Lao National TV; broadcasts available from stations in Thailand and Vietnam in border areas; multi-channel satellite and cable TV systems provide access to a wide range of foreign stations; state-controlled radio with state-operated Lao National Radio (LNR) broadcasting on 5 frequencies - 1 AM, 1 SW, and 3 FM; LNR's AM and FM programs are relayed via satellite constituting a large part of the programming schedules of the provincial radio stations; Thai radio broadcasts available in border areas and transmissions of multiple international broadcasters are also accessible

Internet country code:
.la

Internet hosts:
1,532
country comparison to the world: 166

Internet users:
300,000
country comparison to the world: 130

TRANSPORTATION

Airports:
41
country comparison to the world: 103

Airports - with paved runways:
total: 8
2,438 to 3,047 m: 3
1,524 to 2,437 m: 4
914 to 1,523 m: 1 (2013)

Airports - with unpaved runways:
total: 33
1,524 to 2,437 m: 2
914 to 1,523 m: 9
under 914 m:
22

Pipelines:
refined products 540 km (2013)

Roadways:
total: 39,568 km

country comparison to the world: 89
paved: 530 km
unpaved: 39,038 km

Waterways:
4,600 km (primarily on the Mekong River and its tributaries; 2,900 additional km are intermittently navigable by craft drawing less than 0.5 m)
country comparison to the world: 24

MILITARY

Military branches:
Lao People's Armed Forces (LPAF): Lao People's Army (LPA; includes Riverine Force), Air Force

Military service age and obligation:
18 years of age for compulsory or voluntary military service; conscript service obligation - minimum 18-months

Manpower available for military service:
males age 16-49: 1,574,362
females age 16-49: 1,607,856 (2010 est.)

Manpower fit for military service:
males age 16-49: 1,111,629

For additional analytical, business and investment opportunities information, please contact Global Investment & Business Center, USA at (703) 370-8082. Fax: (703) 370-8083. E-mail: ibpusa3@gmail.com
Global Business and Investment Info Databank - www.ibpus.com

females age 16-49: 1,190,035 (2010 est.)

Manpower reaching militarily significant age annually:
male: 71,400
female: 73,038 (2010 est.)

Military expenditures:
NA%
0.23% of GDP
NA%

Military - note:
serving one of the world's least developed countries, the Lao People's Armed Forces (LPAF) is small, poorly funded, and ineffectively resourced; its mission focus is border and internal security, primarily in countering ethnic Hmong insurgent groups; together with the Lao People's Revolutionary Party and the government, the Lao People's Army (LPA) is the third pillar of state machinery, and as such is expected to suppress political and civil unrest and similar national emergencies, but the LPA also has upgraded skills to respond to avian influenza outbreaks; there is no perceived external threat to the state and the LPA maintains strong ties with the neighboring Vietnamese military

TRANSNATIONAL ISSUES

Disputes - international:
southeast Asian states have enhanced border surveillance to check the spread of avian flu; talks continue on completion of demarcation with Thailand but disputes remain over islands in the Mekong River; concern among Mekong River Commission members that China's construction of dams on the Mekong River and its tributaries will affect water levels; Cambodia and Vietnam are concerned about Laos' extensive upstream dam construction

Illicit drugs:
estimated opium poppy cultivation in 2008 was 1,900 hectares, about a 73% increase from 2007; estimated potential opium production in 2008 more than tripled to 17 metric tons; unsubstantiated reports of domestic methamphetamine production; growing domestic methamphetamine problem

IMPORTANT INFORMATION FOR UNDERSTANDING LAOS[1]

Official Name: Lao People's Democratic Republic

PROFILE

GEOGRAPHY

Area: 236,800 sq. km. (91,430 sq. mi.); area comparable to Oregon.
Capital--Vientiane (est. 569,000). *Other principal towns*--Savannakhet, Luang Prabang, Pakse, Thakhek.
Terrain: rugged mountains, plateaus, alluvial plains.
Climate: tropical monsoon; rainy season (May to November); dry season (November to April).

PEOPLE

Nationality: *Noun and adjective*--Lao (sing. and pl.).
Population : 5.4 million.
Annual growth rate: 2.7%.
Ethnic groups: Lao Loum 53%; other lowland Lao 13% (Thai Dam, Phouane); Lao Theung (midslope) 23%; Lao Sung (highland), including Hmong, Akha, and the Yao (Mien) 10%; ethnic Vietnamese/Chinese 1%.
Religions: Principally Buddhism, with animism among highland groups.
Languages: Lao (official), French, various highland ethnic, English.
Education: *Literacy*--60%.
Health : *Infant mortality rate*--89.32/1,000. *Life expectancy*--55.87 years for women, 52.63 years for men.
Work force (2.6 million, 1999): *Agriculture*--85%; *industry and services*--15%.

GOVERNMENT

Branches: *Executive*--president (head of state); Chairman, Council of Ministers (prime minister and head of government); nine-member Politburo; 49-member Central Committee. *Legislative*--99-seat National Assembly. *Judicial*--district, provincial, and a national Supreme Court.
Political parties: Lao People's Revolutionary Party (LPRP)--only legal party.
Administrative subdivisions: 16 provinces, one special region, and Vientiane prefecture.
Flag: A red band at the top and bottom with a larger blue band between them; a large white circle is centered.

ECONOMY

Natural resources: Hydroelectric power, timber, minerals.
Agriculture (51% of GDP): *Primary products*--glutinous rice, coffee, corn, sugarcane, vegetables, tobacco, ginger, water buffalo, pigs, cattle, and poultry.
Industry (22% of GDP, 1999): *Primary types*--garment manufacturing, electricity production, gypsum and tin mining, wood and wood processing, cement manufacturing, agricultural processing.
Industrial growth rate --7.5%.
Services --27% of GDP.
Trade: *Exports* --$370 million: garments, electricity, wood and wood products, coffee, rattan.

---

[1] **U.S. Department of State, *Bureau of East Asian and Pacific Affairs***

Major markets--France, U.K., Germany, Holland, Thailand, Belgium, U.S., Italy, Japan, Vietnam. *Imports* --$570 million. *Major imports*--fuel, food, consumer, goods, machinery and equipment, vehicles and spare parts. *Major suppliers*--Thailand, Singapore, Japan, Vietnam, China.

GEOGRAPHY, TOPOGRAPHY AND CLIMATE

The Lao People's Democratic Republic (Lao PDR) has a land area of 236,800 square kilometers, stretching more than 1,700 km from the north to south and between 100 km and 400 km from the east to west. The Lao PDR has an eastern border of 1,957 km with the Socialist Republic of Vietnam, a western border of 1,730 km with the, Kingdom of Thailand, a southern border of 492 kin with t he Kingdom of Comboida, and northern borders of 416 kin with the People's Republic of China and 230 km with the Union of Myamar.

Although the Lao PDR has no direct access to the sea, it has an abundance of rivers, including a 1,865 km stretch of the Mekong (Nam Kong), defining its border with Myanmar and a major part of the border with Thailand. Ma'or stretches of the Mekong and its tributaries are navigable and provide alluvial deposits for some. of the fertile plains. About two thirds of the country is mountainous, with ranges from 200 to the 2,820 meters high. The mountains pose difficulties for transportation and communication and complicate development, but together with the rivers they produce vast potential for hydro power.

The Lao PDR is a tropical country, whose climate is affected by monsoon rains from May to September. In Vientiane, the average temperatures range from a minimum of C 16.4 degrees in January to a maximum of C 13 degrees in April.

WATER RESOURCES

Its abundant water resources is probably the most important natural resource endowment of the country. There are only three hydroelectric plants in operation so far, of which Nam Ngum I is the biggest. These three plants with a combined capacity of 200 MW, reportedly realizes only less than five percent of the country's hydroelectric potential. About 90% of hydroelectric power production is exported to Thailand, constituting one of the leading exports of the Lao PDR. Plans are underway to construct a number of new hydroelectric power facilities, which are described in greater detail in Section B.

FOREST RESOURCES

Forests cover about 47% of the country, comprising a wide variety of commercial tree species suitable for production of saw timber, plywood, parquet, furniture, etc.... The most important high value species are hardwoods belonging to the Diterocarpaceae family and rosewoods belonging to the Genera Pterocarpus, Dalbergia and Afzelia. Pines and other coniferous species are also available but in comparatively small quantities. Eighty percent of domestic energy consumption is based on fuel wood, and an estimated 300,000 hectares of forest are lost annually largely due to shifting cultivation and logging activities. In the effort to protect forest resources from unsustainable felling of trees, the total annual allowable cut (AC) has been set by the Tropical Forest Action Plan (1991) to 280,000 cubic meters per annum, exportation of logs was temporarily restricted to restructure forest management, and protective measures have been implemented to prevent depletion of forests due to shifting fanning practices.

MINERAL RESOURCES

Sizeable deposits of gemstones such as sapphire, zircon, amethyst, gold, iron are and tin are know to exist in the country. Gemstones, gold, coal and tin are estimated to have a high economic value. More geologic surveys are needed to identify location of mineral deposits that would allow their exploitation in commercial quantities. Meanwhile, exploration of potential petroleum deposits are underway. Economic exploitation of mineral resources will depend on development of the required physical infrastructures.

ADMINISTRATIVE STRUCTURE OF LAOS

ATTAPEU PROVINCE

Attapeu Province is best known for the Bolaven Plateau, which also extends into Champassak, Salavan and Sekong provinces. The Bolaven Plateau is covered in the Champassak section - The plateau is best accessed from Pakse, in Champassak province.

Attapeu province is rugged,wild and very scenic, but transportation is very difficult, especially by land in the rainy season.

The town of Samakhi Xai (Attapeu) is situated in a large picturesque valley. The population of the province is more Lao Loum than the neighbouring provinces.

Parts of the Ho Chi Minh Trail can be explored from Attapeu, although using a local guide is essential.

BOKEO PROVINCE

Bokeo province is the smallest province in the country and borders Thailand and Myanmar. This is the Lao side of the 'Golden Triangle'. The province has 34 ethnic groups, the second most ethnically diverse province in Laos. The photo shows a group of Akha (Ikaw or Kaw) people from the Golden Triangle area taken in 1900.

Huay Xai is the border town with Thailand, the city is busy and prosperous.

Located in the center of Huay Xay is Chomkao Manilat temple. The view from the the temple hill over Houy Xay city,the Mekong river and surrounding mountains is a definite reward for making it up the many steps.

BOLIKHAMSAI PROVINCE

Bolikhamsai province contains part of the wilderness area known as the Nakai - Nam Theun National Biodiversity Conservation Area the largest conservation area in the country at 3700 sq km. The area is home to over a dozen threatened species including Asiatic black bear, clouded leopard, elephant, giant muntjac, guar, Malayan sun bear, and tiger.

The saola (spindlehorn) or Vu Quang Ox - *Pseudoryx nghetinhensis* was discovered in neighbouring Vietnam in 1992 and sighted since then in Laos in the conservation area. Only two other land mammals have been classified with their own genus this century. The first live saola was captured in neighbouring Khammouane province in 1996.

The capital of Bolikhamsai is Paxxan, which can be reached from Vietntiane by bus in about three hours.

For additional analytical, business and investment opportunities information, please contact Global Investment & Business Center, USA at (703) 370-8082. Fax: (703) 370-8083. E-mail: ibpusa3@gmail.com Global Business and Investment Info Databank - www.ibpus.com

CHAMPASSAK PROVINCE - PAKSE

The province of Champassak is home to one of Asia's great, but least visited temples, Wat Phu. Pakse, the capital is situated at the confluence of the Se river and the Mekong (Pakse means 'mouth of the Se') and is a busy trading town. The province also houses much of the Bolaven Plateau, an area that is home to a number of ethnic minorities. To the south is Si Pan Don (four thousand islands), where the Mekong reaches up to 14km wide during the rainy season and the Khone Phapeng Falls.

Pakse has a number of comfortable places to stay and is a good base from which to explore the surrounding area. The town has one of the largest markets in the region. Within Pakse is the Champassak Museum where trader can see relics from Wat Phu as well as from the Bolaven Plateau.

HOUA PHAN

Houa Phan province is situated in the northeast of Laos and was the base of the Lao People's Revolutionary Army activities. There are over 100 caves in the Vieng Xai district of Houa Phanh many of which were used as hideouts and bunkers during the Indochina war.

Lao Aviation flies daily to the capital Xam Neua from Vientiane - The most famous caves in the area are:

Tham Than Souphanouvong: formerly known as Tham Phapount. In 1964, Prince Souphanouvong set up his residence in this cave. Tham Than Kaysone: formerly known as Tham Yonesong, was established for the residence of Mr. Kaysone Phomvihane. Tham Than Khamtay: was the residence of Mr. Khamtay Siphandone, consisting of many area, such as a meeting room, reception room and research room.

Other attractions include Keo Nong Vay Temple located in Xam Neua district.

Hot springs in Xam Tay district are located about 154 km away from Xam Neua the waters reach a temperature of around 40 degrees Celcius. Xam Tay waterfall is located Xam Tay district.

Saleu and Nasala villages, well known for their weaving activities, located in Xieng Kor district on the road No: 6 to Xieng Khouang province 125 km away from Xam Neua.

KHAMMOUANE PROVINCE

Khammouane province contains two vast wilderness areas known as the Khammuane Limestone National Biodiversity Conservation Area and the Nakai - Nam Theun National Biodiversity Conservation Area.

The Kahmmuane Limestone is a maze of limestone karst peaks forming a stone forest of caves, rivers and pristine jungle. For most of the wet season, the area is not accessible by road - most 'roads' being tracks with log bridges across deeps streams. These tracks are often routes across rice paddies near the river banks - during the rainy season, the only way to get around is by boat.

The National Tourism Authority of Lao PDR is currently investigating ecotourism projects in this beautiful region. The capital of Khammouane province is Tha Kek, situated across the Mekong from Nakorn Phanom in Thailand.

LUANG PRABANG

Luang Prabang is the jewel of Indochina, and a UNESCO World Heritage Site since 1995. The ancient royal city is surrounded by mountains at the junction of the Mekong and its tributary, the Khan river. In the centre of the city is Mount Phousi with stunning views of the surrounding temples and hills. Luang Prabang is a city where time seems to stand still. As part of the UNESCO plan, new buildings have been limited and development must be in keeping with this magical place.

Minority village in Luang Namtha

Luang Prabang is small, and just about everywhere can be reached by foot. Walking and travelling by bicycle is the best way to see this tiny city.

LUANG NAMTHA PROVINCE

Located in the northern part of Laos, Luang Namtha shares its northwestern border with Myanmar and its northeastern border with China. The province is mountainous, home to large numbers of minorities. The Nam Ha National Biodiversity Conservation Area is located in the southwest of Luang Namtha - a pristine habitat of dense tropical rainforest covering almost all of the protected area.

UNESCO are funding a ecotourism project in Luang Namtha that will be capable of sustaining sustainable development in the province. The concept of the project is to provide education, conservation, management and sustainable economic benefits for the local population. The province is home to a 39 minorities the largest number in the country.

OUDOMXAI

Located in the northern part of Laos. This mountainous province has 23 ethnic groups each with it own distinct culture, religion, language and colorful style of dress. The provincial capital , Muang Xay lies between two strings of Hmong villages.

Lao Aviation flies to Oudomxai from Vientiane

Oudomxai can be reached overland from Luang Prabang. Oudomxay is also accessible from Bokeo and Luang Namtha Provinces. Oudomxay is an ideal base for excursions and trekking to varied sights and attractions as well as destination in its own right. Muang Xai, has one of the best produce markets in the area.

Near Muang Xai, there is a waterfall, Lak Sip – Et (located at km No 11) and hot springs near Muang La.

PHONGSALI PROVINCE

Phongsali province the most remote in northern Laos is surrounded on three sides by China and Vietnam. The Phu Den Din National Biodiversity Conservation Area along the Vietnamese border with mountains as high as 1950m with over 70% forest cover is home to the asiatic black bear, bantang, clouded leopard, elephant, guar and tiger.

For additional analytical, business and investment opportunities information,
please contact Global Investment & Business Center, USA
at (703) 370-8082. Fax: (703) 370-8083. E-mail: ibpusa3@gmail.com
Global Business and Investment Info Databank - www.ibpus.com

The capital Phongsali, can be reached from Muang Xai with buses leaving once a day. Phongsali has a year round cool climate with temperatures as low as 5 degrees Celcius at night. Rain can be heavy - bring a jacket and warm clothes.

Muang Khoa is a small town situated on the junction of Route 4 and the Nam Ou river. The journey to Muang Khoa along route 4 from Udomxai takes about four hours. It is possible to travel up river to Phongsali from here, or down to Luang Prabang.

SALAVAN PROVINCE

Salavan Province is best known for the Bolaven Plateau, which also extends into Attapeu, Champassak and Sekong provinces. The Bolaven Plateau is covered in the Champassak section.. The plateau is best accessed from Pakse, in Champassak province.

Salavan province is home to the Phu Xieng Thong National Biodiversity Conservation Area, covering nearly 1,000 sq km in the western part of the province next to the Mekong river. It is thought that asiatic black bear, banteng, clouded leopard, Douc langur, elephant, gibbon, guar, Siamese crocodile and tiger and inhabit this area.

SEKONG PROVINCE

Sekong Province is best known for the Bolaven Plateau, which also extends into Attapeu, Champassak and Salavan and provinces. The Bolaven Plateau is covered in the Champassak section. The plateau is best accessed from Pakse, in Champassak province. Sekong province is rugged,wild and very scenic, but transportation is very difficult, especially by land in the rainy season.

SAYABOURI PROVINCE

Sayabouri province is quite close to Vientiane, but being quite mountainous is quite remote. The province shares its borders with six Thai provinces. The capital of the province, Sayabouri is on the banks of the Nam Hung, a tributary of the Mekong.

The province houses the Nam Phoun National Biodiversity Conservation Area which is 1150 sq km of forested hills that contain Asiatic black bear, dhole, elephant, guar, gibbon, Malayan sun bear and Sumatran rhino.

The southern part of the province has many scenic waterfalls, but getting around this part of the province is very difficult.

SAVANNAKHET

Savannakhet town is situated on the banks of the   Mekong river opposite Mukdahan in Thailand. The province bridges the country between Thailand and Vietnam and the town is a very active junction for trade between the two countries. The town itself can be easily explored by foot and has a number of interesting temples, including Vietnamese temple and school and a large Catholic church. Much of the town's architecture is French Colonial.

VIENTIANE

Vientiane, capital of Laos is Asia's biggest village. Busy and hectic in comparison to the rest of the country, it is quiet compared with any other city in Asia. Vientiane, as all of Lao's major cities, is situated on the Mekong river which forms the lifeline of the country. Vientiane is the hub for all travel in the country. The city has a population of 450,000, about 10% of the country.

Vientiane is a city full of surprises. Here trader can find fields of rice and vegetables, agriculture hidden behind tree lined avenues. French Colonial architecture sits next to gilded temples. Freshly baked French bread is served next to shops selling noodle soup.

There is little modern in Vientiane. Old French colonial houses are being restored as offices and as restaurants and hotels. There are only a handful of modern buildings which sometimes look remarkably out of place in this quiet capital.

XIENG KHOUANG PROVINCE

Xieng Khouang province is situated in the north of Laos, a province of green montains and karst limestone. Much of the province was heavily bombed during the Vietnam war and old war scrap is used in building houses throughout the province. The capital of Xieng Khouang is Phonsavan. Situated at an altitude of 1,200m is an excellent climate. Decmber and January can be chilly so bring a light jacket or fleece for cool evenings and mornings.

PEOPLE

Laos' population was estimated at about 5.4 million in 1999, dispersed unevenly across the country. Most people live in valleys of the Mekong River and its tributaries. Vientiane prefecture, the capital and largest city, had about 569,000 residents in 1999. The country's population density is 23.4/sq. km.

About half the country's people are ethnic Lao, the principal lowland inhabitants and politically and culturally dominant group. The Lao are descended from the Tai people who began migrating southward from China in the first millennium A.D. Mountain tribes of Miao-Yao, Austro-Asiatic, Tibeto-Burman--Hmong, Yao, Akha, and Lahu--and Tai ethnolinguistic heritage are found in northern Laos. Collectively, they are known as Lao Sung or highland Lao. In the central and southern mountains, Mon-Khmer tribes, known as Lao Theung or midslope Lao, predominate. Some Vietnamese and Chinese minorities remain, particularly in the towns, but many left in two waves--after independence in the late 1940s and again after 1975.

The predominant religion is Theravada Buddhism. Animism is common among the mountain tribes. Buddhism and spirit worship coexist easily. There also is a small number of Christians and Muslims.

The official and dominant language is Lao, a tonal language of the Tai linguistic group. Midslope and highland Lao speak an assortment of tribal languages. French, once common in government and commerce, has declined in usage, while knowledge of English--the language of the Association of Southeast Asian Nations (ASEAN)--has increased in recent years.

HISTORY

Laos traces its first recorded history and its origins as a unified state to the emergence of the Kingdom of Lan Xang (literally, "million elephants") in 1353. Under the rule of King Fa Ngum, the wealthy and mighty kingdom covered much of what today is Thailand and Laos. His successors, especially King Setthathirat in the 16th century, helped establish Buddhism as the predominant religion of the country.

For additional analytical, business and investment opportunities information, please contact Global Investment & Business Center, USA at (703) 370-8082. Fax: (703) 370-8083. E-mail: ibpusa3@gmail.com Global Business and Investment Info Databank - www.ibpus.com

By the 17th century, the kingdom of Lan Xang entered a period of decline marked by dynastic struggle and conflicts with its neighbors. In the late 18th century, the Siamese (Thai) established hegemony over much of what is now Laos. The region was divided into principalities centered on Luang Prabang in the north, Vientiane in the center, and Champassak in the south. Following its colonization of Vietnam, the French supplanted the Siamese and began to integrate all of Laos into the French empire. The Franco-Siamese treaty of 1907 defined the present Lao boundary with Thailand.

During World War II, the Japanese occupied French Indochina, including Laos. King Sisavang Vong of Luang Prabang was induced to declare independence from France in 1945, just prior to Japan's surrender. During this period, nationalist sentiment grew. In September 1945, Vientiane and Champassak united with Luang Prabang to form an independent government under the Free Laos (Lao Issara) banner. The movement, however, was shortlived. By early 1946, French troops reoccupied the country and conferred limited autonomy on Laos following elections for a constituent assembly.

Amidst the first Indochina war between France and the communist movement in Vietnam, Prince Souphanouvong formed the Pathet Lao (Land of Laos) resistance organization committed to the communist struggle against colonialism. Laos was not granted full sovereignty until the French defeat by the Vietnamese and the subsequent Geneva peace conference in 1954. Elections were held in 1955, and the first coalition government, led by Prince Souvanna Phouma, was formed in 1957. The coalition government collapsed in 1958, amidst increased polarization of the political process. Rightist forces took over the government.

In 1960, Kong Le, a paratroop captain, seized Vientiane in a coup and demanded formation of a neutralist government to end the fighting. The neutralist government, once again led by Souvanna Phouma, was not successful in holding power. Rightist forces under Gen. Phoumi Nosavan drove out the neutralist government from power later that same year. Subsequently, the neutralists allied themselves with the communist insurgents and began to receive support from the Soviet Union. Phoumi Nosavan's rightist regime received support from the U.S.

A second Geneva conference, held in 1961-62, provided for the independence and neutrality of Laos. Soon after accord was reached, the signatories accused each other of violating the terms of the agreement, and with superpower support on both sides, the civil war soon resumed. Although the country was to be neutral, a growing American and North Vietnamese military presence in the country increasingly drew Laos into the second Indochina war (1954-75). For nearly a decade, Laos was subjected to the heaviest bombing in the history of warfare, as the U.S. sought to destroy the Ho Chi Minh Trail that passed through eastern Laos.

In 1972, the communist People's Party renamed itself the Lao People's Revolutionary Party (LPRP). It joined a new coalition government in Laos soon after the Vientiane cease-fire agreement in 1973. Nonetheless, the political struggle between communists, neutralists, and rightists continued. The fall of Saigon and Phnom Penh to communist forces in April 1975 hastened the decline of the coalition in Laos. Months after these communist victories, the Pathet Lao entered Vientiane. On December 2, 1975, the king abdicated his throne in the constitutional monarchy, and the communist Lao People's Democratic Republic (LPDR) was established.

The new communist government imposed centralized economic decisionmaking and broad security measures, including control of the media and the arrest and incarceration of many members of the previous government and military in "re-education camps". These draconian policies and deteriorating economic conditions, along with government efforts to enforce political control, prompted an exodus of lowland Lao and ethnic Hmong from Laos. About 10% of the Lao population sought refugee status after 1975. Many have since been resettled in third countries, including more than 250,000 who have come to the United States.

The situation of Lao refugees is nearing its final chapter. Over time, the Lao Government closed the re-education camps and released most political prisoners. From 1975 to 1996, the U.S. resettled some 250,000 Lao refugees from Thailand, including 130,000 Hmong. By the end of 1999, more than 28,900 Hmong and lowland Lao had repatriated to Laos--3,500 from China, the rest from Thailand. Through the Office of the United Nations High Commissioner for Refugees (UNHCR), the International Organization for Migration (IOM), and non-governmental organizations, the U.S. has supported a variety of reintegration assistance programs throughout Laos. UNHCR monitors returnees and reports no evidence of systemic persecution or discrimination to date. As of December 1999, about 115 Hmong and lowland Lao remained in Ban Napho camp in Thailand awaiting third-country resettlement by the UNHCR.

GOVERNMENT AND POLITICAL CONDITIONS

The only legal political party is the Lao People's Revolutionary Party (LPRP). The head of state is President Khamtay Siphandone. The head of government is Prime Minister Sisavath Keobounphanh, who also is Chairman of the LPRP. Government policies are determined by the party through the all-powerful nine-member Politburo and the 49-member Central Committee. Important government decisions are vetted by the Council of Ministers.

Laos adopted a constitution in 1991. The following year, elections were held for a new 85-seat National Assembly with members elected by secret ballot to 5-year terms. This National Assembly, expanded in 1997 elections to 99 members, approves all new laws, although the executive branch retains authority to issue binding decrees. The most recent elections took place in December 1997. The FY 2000 central government budget plan calls for revenue of $180 million and expenditures of $289 million, including capital expenditures of $202 million.

PRINCIPAL GOVERNMENT OFFICIALS NEW CABINET MEMBERS APPROVED

The National Assembly, the country's top legislature on 15 June approved the appointment of Mr. Thongsing Thammavong as Prime Minister and four deputy prime ministers and cabinet members.

The First Plenary Session of the 7 th NA approved the proposed list of four deputy prime ministers are Mr. Asang Laoly, Dr. Thongloun Sisoulith, Mr. Duangchay Phichit and Mr. Somsavat Lengsavad. Four of them are members of Politburo under the Lao People's Revolutionary Party Central Committee.

Under the approval, Dr. Thongloun Sisoulith is responsible for Ministry of Foreign Affairs and Mr. Duangchay Phitchit takes the post the Minister of National Defence.

The NA also approved the appointment of government members accordingly,

Mr. Bounthong Chitmany serves as President of State Inspection Committee and Head of Anti-Corruption Agency;

Mr. Phankham Viphavanh, Minister of Education and Sports;

Mr. Thongbanh Seng-aphone, Minister Public Security; Mrs Onchanh Thammavong, Minister of Labour and Social-Welfare;

Mr. Chaleune Yiabaoher, Minister of Justice;

Mr. Soulivong Daravong, Minister of Energy and Mining;

Mrs Bounpheng Mouphosay, Minister for Government's Office;

Mr. Vilayvanh Phomkhe, Minister of Agriculture and Forestry;

Mr. Sinlavong Khouphaythoune, Minister and Head of Government's Office;

Mr. Nam Viyaket, Minister of Industry and Commerce;

Mr. Sommad Pholsena, Minister of Public Works and Transport;

Mr. Somdy Duangdy, Minister of Planning and Investment;

Mr. Phouphet Khamphounvong, Minister of Finance;

Prof Dr. Bosengkham Vongdara, Minister of Information, Culture and Tourism;

Prof Dr. Eksavang Vongvichit, Minister of Public Health;

Mr. Bounheuang Duangphachanh, Minister for Government's Office;

Mr. Khampane Philavong, Minister of Interior;

Prof Dr. Bountiem Phitsamay, Minister for Government's Office;

Dr. Douangsavad Souphanouvong, Minister for Government's Office;

Mrs Khempheng Pholsena, Minister for Government's Office;

Prof Dr. Boviengkham Vongdara, Minister of Science and Technology;

Mr. Noulin Sinbandith, Minister of Natural Resources and Environment;

Mr. Hiem Phommachanh, Minister of Post, Telecommunication and Communication;

Mr. Sompao Phaysith, Governor of the State Bank of Laos;

Mr. Khamphanh Sitthidampha, President of People's Supreme Court and

Mr. Khamsan Souvong, Head of General Prosecutor's Office.

Laos maintains an embassy in the United States at 2222 S Street NW, Washington, D.C. 20009 (tel: 202-332-6416).

ECONOMY

Currency	Lao Kip

Fiscal year	1 October - 30 September
Trade organisations	ASEAN, WTO

Statistics

GDP	$17.66 billion (PPP; est.)
GDP growth	8.3% (2014 est.)
GDP per capita	$2,700 (PPP; est.)
GDP by sector	services (42.6%), industry (20.2%), agriculture (37.4%) (est.)
Inflation (CPI)	7.6% (est.)
Population below poverty line	26% (est.)
Labour force	3.69 million (est.)
Labour force by occupation	agriculture (75.1%), industry (n/a), services (n/a) (est.)
Unemployment	2.5% (est.)
Main industries	copper, tin, gold, and gypsum mining; timber, electric power, agricultural processing, construction, garments, cement, tourism
Ease of doing business rank	165th

External

Exports	$2.131 billion (est.)
Export goods	wood products, garments, electricity, coffee, tin, copper, gold
Main export partners	Thailand 32.8% China 20.7% Vietnam 14.0% (est.)
Imports	2.336 billion (est.)
Import goods	machinery and equipment, vehicles, fuel, consumer goods
Main import partners	Thailand 63.2% China 16.5% Vietnam 5.6% (est.)
Gross external debt	$5.953 billion (31 December 2011 est)

Public finances

Public debt	$3.179 billion
Revenues	$1.76 billion
Expenses	$1.957 billion (est.)
Economic aid	$345 million (est.)
Foreign reserves	$773.5 (31 December est.)

The **economy of the Lao Peoples' Democratic Republic** is rapidly growing, as the government began to decentralise control and encourage private enterprise in 1986. Currently, the economy grows at 8% a year, and the government is pursuing poverty reduction and education for all children as key goals. The country opened a stock exchange, the Lao Securities Exchange in 2011, and has become a rising regional player in its role as a hydroelectric power supplier to neighbors such as China, Vietnam and Thailand. Laos remains one of the poorest countries in Southeast Asia, but may transition from being a low middle-income country to an upper-middle income one by 2020. A landlocked country, it has inadequate infrastructure and a largely unskilled work force. The country's per capita income in 2009 was estimated to be $2,700 on a purchasing power parity-basis.

The Lao economy depends heavily on investment and trade with its neighbours, Thailand, Vietnam, and, especially in the north, China. Pakxe has also experienced growth based on cross-border trade with Thailand and Vietnam. In 2009, despite the fact that the government is still officially communist, the Obama administration in the US declared Laos was no longer a marxist-lenninist state and lifted bans on Laotian companies receiving financing from the U.S. Export Import Bank. In 2011, the Lao Securities Exchange began trading. In 2014, the government initiated the creation of the Laos Trade Portal, a website incorporating all information traders need to import and export goods into the country.

Subsistence agriculture still accounts for half of the GDP and provides 80% of employment. Only 4.01% of the country is arable land, and a mere 0.34% used as permanent crop land, the lowest percentage in the Greater Mekong Subregion. Rice dominates agriculture, with about 80% of the arable land area used for growing rice. Approximately 77% of Lao farm households are self-sufficient in rice.

Through the development, release and widespread adoption of improved rice varieties, and through economic reforms, production has increased by an annual rate of 5% between 1990 and 2005, and Lao PDR achieved a net balance of rice imports and exports for the first time in 1999. Lao PDR may have the greatest number of rice varieties in the Greater Mekong Subregion. Since 1995 the Lao government has been working with the International Rice Research Institute of the Philippines to collect seed samples of each of the thousands of rice varieties found in Laos.

The economy receives development aid from the IMF, ADB, and other international sources; and also foreign direct investment for development of the society, industry, hydropower and mining (most notably of copper and gold). Tourism is the fastest-growing industry in the country. Economic development in Laos has been hampered by brain drain, with a skilled emigration rate of 37.4% in 2000.

Laos is rich in mineral resources and imports petroleum and gas. Metallurgy is an important industry, and the government hopes to attract foreign investment to develop the substantial deposits of coal, gold, bauxite, tin, copper, and other valuable metals. In addition, the country's plentiful water resources and mountainous terrain enable it to produce and export large quantities of hydroelectric energy. Of the potential capacity of approximately 18,000 megawatts, around 8,000 megawatts have been committed for exporting to Thailand and Vietnam.

The country's most widely recognised product may well be Beerlao which is exported to a number of countries including neighbours Cambodia and Vietnam. It is produced by the Lao Brewery Company.

FOREIGN RELATIONS

The new government that assumed power in December 1975 aligned itself with the Soviet bloc and adopted a hostile posture toward the West. In ensuing decades, Laos maintained close ties with the former Soviet Union and its eastern bloc allies and depended heavily on the Soviets for most of its foreign assistance. Laos also maintained a "special relationship" with Vietnam and formalized a 1977 treaty of friendship and cooperation that created tensions with China.

With the collapse of the Soviet Union and with Vietnam's decreased ability to provide assistance, Laos has sought to improve relations with its regional neighbors. The Lao Government has focused its efforts on Thailand, Laos' principal means of access to the sea and its primary trading partner. Within a year of serious border clashes in 1987, Lao and Thai leaders signed a communiquŽ, signaling their intention to improve relations. Since then, they have made slow but steady progress, notably the construction and opening of the Friendship Bridge between the two countries.

Relations with China have improved over the years. Although the two were allies during the Vietnam War, the China-Vietnam conflict in 1979 led to a sharp deterioration in Sino-Lao relations. These relations began to improve in the late 1980s. In 1989 Sino-Lao relations were normalized.

Laos' emergence from international isolation has been marked through improved and expanded relations with other nations such as Australia, France, Japan, Sweden, and India. Laos was admitted into the Association of Southeast Asian Nations (ASEAN) in July 1997 and applied to join WTO in 1998.

Laos is a member of the following international organizations: Agency for Cultural and Technical Cooperation (ACCT), Association of Southeast Asian Nations (ASEAN), ASEAN Free Trade Area (AFTA), ASEAN Regional Forum, Asian Development Bank, Colombo Plan, Economic and Social Commission for Asia and Pacific (ESCAP), Food and Agriculture Organization (FAO), G-77, International Bank for Reconstruction and Development (World Bank), International Civil Aviation Organization (ICAO), International Development Association (IDA), International Fund for Agricultural Development (IFAD), International Finance Corporation (IFC), International Federation of Red Cross and Red Crescent Societies, International Labor Organization (ILO), International Monetary Fund (IMF), Intelsat (nonsignatory user), Interpol, International Olympic Commission (IOC), International Telecommunications Union (ITU), Mekong Group, Non-Aligned Movement (NAM), Permanent Court of Arbitration (PCA), UN, United Nations Convention on Trade and Development (UNCTAD), United Nations Educational, Social and Cultural Organization (UNESCO), United Nations Industrial Development Organization (UNIDO), Universal Postal Union (UPU), World Federation of Trade Unions, World Health Organization (WHO), World Intellectual Property Organization (WIPO), World Meteorological Organization (WMO), World Tourism Organization, World Trade Organization (observer).

U.S.-LAO RELATIONS

The United States opened a legation in Laos in 1950. Although diplomatic relations were never severed, U.S.-Lao relations deteriorated badly in the post-Indochina War period. The relationship remained cool until 1982 when efforts at improvement began. For the United States, progress in accounting for Americans missing in Laos from the Vietnam War is a principal measure of improving relations. Counternarcotics activities also have become an important part of the bilateral relationship as the Lao Government has stepped up its efforts to combat cultivation; production; and transshipment of opium, heroin, and marijuana.

Since the late 1980s, progress in these areas has steadily increased. Joint U.S. and Lao teams have conducted a series of joint excavations and investigations of sites related to cases of Americans missing in Laos. In counternarcotics activities, the U.S. and Laos are involved in a multimillion-dollar crop substitution/integrated rural development program. Laos also has formed its own national committee on narcotics, developed a long-range strategy for counternarcotics activities, participated in U.S.-sponsored narcotics training programs, and strengthened law enforcement measures to combat the narcotics problem.

U.S. Government foreign assistance to Laos covers a broad range of efforts. Such aid includes support for Laos' efforts to suppress opium production; training and equipment for a program to clear and dispose of unexploded ordnance; school and hospital construction; public education about the dangers of unexploded ordnance and about HIV/AIDS; support for medical research on hepatitis. Economic relations also are expanding. In August 1997, Laos and the United States initialed a Bilateral Trade Agreement and a Bilateral Investment Treaty.

Principal U.S. Embassy Officials

Ambassador-- Rena Bitter

For additional analytical, business and investment opportunities information,
please contact Global Investment & Business Center, USA
at (703) 370-8082. Fax: (703) 370-8083. E-mail: ibpusa3@gmail.com
Global Business and Investment Info Databank - www.ibpus.com

Ambassador Rena Bitter is a career Senior Foreign Service Officer with more than 20 years of experience in Washington and overseas. Most recently, Ambassador Bitter served as Consul General at the U.S. Consulate General in Ho Chi Minh City, Vietnam. Prior to that, she served as the Director of the State Department Operations Center, the Department's 24/7 Briefing and Crisis Management Center. In Washington, she served on the Secretary of State's Executive Staff and as a Special Assistant to Secretary Colin Powell. Her overseas tours include Amman, London, Mexico City and Bogota. Ambassador Bitter grew up in Dallas.

Deputy Chief of Mission--Susan M. Sutton

The American Embassy in Laos is on Rue Bartholonie, B.P. 114, Vientiane, tel: 212-581/582/585; fax: 212-584: country code: (856): city code (21).

Information on the embassy, its work in Laos, and U.S.-Lao relations is available on the Internet at http://www.usembassy.state.gov/laos.

TRAVEL AND BUSINESS INFORMATION

The U.S. Department of State's Consular Information Program provides Consular Information Sheets, Travel Warnings, and Public Announcements. **Consular Information Sheets** exist for all countries and include information on entry requirements, currency regulations, health conditions, areas of instability, crime and security, political disturbances, and the addresses of the U.S. posts in the country. **Travel Warnings** are issued when the State Department recommends that Americans avoid travel to a certain country. **Public Announcements** are issued as a means to disseminate information quickly about terrorist threats and other relatively short-term conditions overseas which pose significant risks to the security of American travelers. Free copies of this information are available by calling the Bureau of Consular Affairs at 202-647-5225 or via the fax-on-demand system: 202-647-3000.

Consular Information Sheets and Travel Warnings also are available on the Consular Affairs Internet home page: http://travel.state.gov. Consular Affairs Tips for Travelers publication series, which contain information on obtaining passports and planning a safe trip abroad are on the internet and hard copies can be purchased from the Superintendent of Documents, U.S. Government Printing Office, telephone: 202-512-1800; fax 202-512-2250.

Emergency information concerning Americans traveling abroad may be obtained from the Office of Overseas Citizens Services at (202) 647-5225. For after-hours emergencies, Sundays and holidays, call 202-647-4000.

Passport information can be obtained by calling the National Passport Information Center's automated system ($.35 per minute) or live operators 8 a.m. to 8 p.m. (EST) Monday-Friday ($1.05 per minute). The number is 1-900-225-5674 (TDD: 1-900-225-7778). Major credit card users (for a flat rate of $4.95) may call 1-888-362-8668 (TDD: 1-888-498-3648). It also is available on the internet.

Travelers can check the latest health information with the U.S. Centers for Disease Control and Prevention in Atlanta, Georgia. A hotline at 877-FYI-TRIP (877-394-8747) and a web site at http://www.cdc.gov/travel/index.htm give the most recent health advisories, immunization recommendations or requirements, and advice on food and drinking water safety for regions and countries. A booklet entitled Health Information for International Travel (HHS publication number CDC-95-8280) is available from the U.S. Government Printing Office, Washington, DC 20402, tel. (202) 512-1800.

Information on travel conditions, visa requirements, currency and customs regulations, legal holidays, and other items of interest to travelers also may be obtained before your departure from a country's embassy and/or consulates in the U.S. (for this country, see "Principal Government Officials" listing in this publication).

U.S. citizens who are long-term visitors or traveling in dangerous areas are encouraged to register at the U.S. embassy upon arrival in a country (see "Principal U.S. Embassy Officials" listing in this publication). This may help family members contact you in case of an emergency.

For additional analytical, business and investment opportunities information, please contact Global Investment & Business Center, USA at (703) 370-8082. Fax: (703) 370-8083. E-mail: ibpusa3@gmail.com Global Business and Investment Info Databank - www.ibpus.com

INTERNET IN LAOS - STRATEGIC INFORMATION AND DEVELOPMENTS

INTERNET DEVELOPMENT IN LAO PDR - STRATEGIC INFORMATION

ICT INFRASTRUCTURE

4 telecommunication operators. ETL. Laotel. LAT. Milicom-Lao

5 province have a fiber Optic Network connectivity to Vientiane (ETL has plants to cover capitals of 13 province by this year and 142 districts headquarters by 2005

In may 2003, there are 72.235 PSTN lines in services from 3 operators, which 1.706 subscribers in the rural province. And there are only 300 public telephones, which all of them are located in the big city only.

There are about 10.000 computers in the country and growing at about 300per month currently.

Most of government ministries are running some form of local area network (LAN). Which each of them designed their network specifically

Starting to use Wireless system and Optic fiber

To enhancing the role of four IT center in order to be center ofexcellent (Upgrade to be institute)

The urgent and greatest need in the country is for skilled professional and technical informatics experts to plan. Design, install and maintain information facilities.

R&D the application program for E-government system in order to improve the effectiveness and efficiency of government services.

Strengthening the promotion of IT education by establishing the Master in Computer Application Program Laos

Bringing the ICT for agriculture and rural development

Establish a VSAT based Internet connection to all 18 provincial governors.

Strengthening the Internet penetration and E-business opportunity

ICT EDUCATION

The percentage of expenditure on tertiary in Laos is the lowest of all ASEAN at 7,4%. Formal education related to IT is only available at the tertiary level. There is no curriculum incorporation of IT at all at the primary or secondary levels

•Department of the mathematics and Physic of NUOL do provide the computer application.

•Information Technology Center of STEA (IT engineer. Trainers andgovernment offices)

•Smart school project at Sikhottabonghigh school and Champasackhigh school.

•The Private Training school

•Business administration school

•Computer retialers.

•The Information technology Center has also regularly conducted seminars and training courses on e-commerce in Vientiane.

The demand for the IT related training is growing rapidly. This reflected by the shortage of IT skilled works in the workforce

ICT INDUSTRIES AND SERVICES

ICT industry was established In early 1980s. However it has not so much developed The Lao IT industry was limited to small computer stores, which can be divided into four sector.

•Computer retailers: Computer retailing and servicing

•Internet Service: Provided Interment Access. Design and hosting web sites

•Education : IT related training

•Wireless Network solution: Design and install wireless LAN and WAN

The Lao IT market it very small (mainly gov& org). Therefore specialization inn one particular sector of this market is usually unprofitable

Low-cost computers are usually imported by retailers form China, Thailand and Vietnam or assembled locally from imported parts. Larger retailers import brand name equipment mostly from Malaysia. Singapore and Taiwan.

There is a 5% tariff on all imported hardware. There is also 10%turnover tax applied to all computer retailers. These two tax are passed on directly to customers, along with additional 20%-50% markup profits.

E-BUSINESS & E-COMMERCE

There is little in the way of e-business, which the 5 reasons:

Overall Internet access and the number of Internet users are toolow to justify the investment required to establish and E-business. The only real feasible business endeavors related to tourism.

Some initiatives related to the promotion

•The ministry of Commerce has established the Trade Information Center Which also created portal website for trade promotion as well as organize the E-commerce seminar.

•The national tourism Authorities has established the Tourism information center. Which also provide the online information for promotion the tourism activities and Business.

•MPDF just launched a project on establishing .

•The ISPs also provide the E-business and e-commerce solution for some private companies such as design and hosting websites for them.

•With the E-ASEAN framework, the national taskforce is also working out on cyber law and LAL

GOVERNMENT GUIDELINE FOR IT POLICIES

Expectation:

1.Utilization of ICT should be expanded to all area to become one of the priority factors for social-economy development and national security matter.

2.The National ICT network should be extended throughout the country. With the capacity and capability to carry more data at higher speed. Better quality and cheaper prices

The policy must be including following matter:

1.The increased utilization of ICT is a priority in the national strategy for social-economic development. ICT is also the basic tool to accelerate the development and expansion of the industries and other developed counties.

2.To create and increase the human resource on ICT fields as this is necessary for improving ICT utilization and development in the country

Project on formulation e-policies & e-strategies

Background: In April 2003. APDIP launched the program to strengthen the national capacities for new ASEN members countries in the formulation of national e-policies through national participatory consultations and under south-south cooperation principles and the e-ASEAN framework.

Objective: To develop and consolidate, through a participatory process, national ICT policies/strategies and action plans for the Lao PDR. Such policy would be the foundation for formulation and implementation of strategic and action plans in Lao PDR over the next 2 years period

Implementation: Assist to Lao government (STEA) in formulating across-sectoraldraft based on inputs from a broad range of stakeholders. Therewill be levels of human resources on place to ensure the successful implementation of he project at local level:

Steering committee

National and International Facilitators

For additional analytical, business and investment opportunities information, please contact Global Investment & Business Center, USA at (703) 370-8082. Fax: (703) 370-8083. E-mail: ibpusa3@gmail.com Global Business and Investment Info Databank - www.ibpus.com

Working group (Infrastructure & Industry:Application: Standardization & localization: Human resource development: legal framework

Development index

Description	2000	2001	2002	2003	
Local ISPs	2	3	6	7	
Internet Café	11	30	60	200	
Subscriber Users	1934	2482	2900	3800	
ISP Service fees	2$/h	1,5$/h	1$/h	0,5$/h	
CaféService fees	0,05$/m	0,03$/m	0,01$/m	0,008$/m	
Bandwidth	265k	1M	2M	5M	

the inhibition to growth.

Lao PDR has been one of the last countries in Asian region to establish full internet connectivity, Lao PDR has largely remained disconnectedfrom transnational world of cyberspace.

Government ministries make little use of the global network and the business sector has equally been slow to implement internet related application

The price still very high and each service provider are defining the fee by their own equipment for using the internet still expensive

Most of service are concentrating to the foreign customer and big companies.

The service quality still very low and not so upgrading

Lack of local manual and hand book of internet

Lack of content in Lao language

Related internet regulations

Utilization and Management of Interment in Lao PDR

Concerning Internet organization, service and utilization in LaoPDR

Ministries concern such as : Ministry of information ad Culture;

Ministry of Telecommunication Post Transport and Construction;

Ministry of National Security and STEA also issued their own

Regulation related to the internet management and promotion

According to their responsible authorities

NATIONAL INTERNET GATEWAY AND GOVERNMENT ISP

Provide the internet access for government organizations and academy institutes

Provide the web hosting

Provide the domain name registration under gov.la; org.la, edu.laand etc.

Arrange and distribute the IP address for ministries networks.

R&D of E-government Application.

Issue:

-ISPs have their own separate internet Gateway

-Low bandwidth for the international link

-Authority organization could not control the access sites beingprovided by ISPs

-Solution:

--Local traffic management requires all members ISPs to be physically linked to common interconnection(routing information exchange and protocol)

-Assistance:

--1stphase: international Development Research Center (IDRC)-2ndphase: Swedish international Development Agency (SIDA)

National internet exchange Gateway

(Phase2)

1Internet Lao PDR-Thailand Project

Objectives :

-providing a internet access for 18 provincial government offices

-set up a internet Provincial service Center

-set up internet portal for provincial governors and business

Provision :

-one year free bandwidth of 512 kbps to CAT

-Set up a Gateway router in STEA office

-Set up a internet router link for each province

For additional analytical, business and investment opportunities information, please contact Global Investment & Business Center, USA at (703) 370-8082. Fax: (703) 370-8083. E-mail: ibpusa3@gmail.com Global Business and Investment Info Databank - www.ibpus.com

-Set up a provincial central management system (Server)

-Train two staffs from each province to be the internet engineer.

Duration: November 2003 to November 2004

Implementation agencies:

-From Laos: Information Technology Center

--From Thailand: Communication Authority of Thailand (CAT)

INFORMATION TECHNOLOGY CENTER

Laos faced a lot problems in introducing in a big way. As there are shortage of ICT talent in the country and need expertise to develop "capacity building"through human resources development programmes. Therefore STEA has established the information Technology Center to conduct the Research, Development, Training and Service on IT

Role and Functions:

1.Join formulation National ICT policy & master plan.

2.Secretary of Lao National internet Committee

3.Conducting the IT Research and Development

4.Provide the training for IT engineers. Trainers and government officers

5.Join development the IT standardization and management

6.Operate the government's ISPs and National internet Exchange Gateway .

7.Provide the consultation and other IT service.

8.Member of regional and imitational organization (AFLT. RINSEAP/UNESCO.SCOSA/ASCAN/ICT Global Resource Network/UN. ORBICOM/UNESCO chairs in Communications)

NETWORKING SECTOR

National internet Gateway System

ISP for the government organizations

National internet Exchange gateway

Internet Lao-Thailand Network

STEA'S Local Area Network

Training Sector

Facilities

-CICC donated 19 PCs and 3 Servers for conducting the general training courses.

-IDRC donated 10 PCs and 2 Severs for conducting the advance training courses

-Programs:

-Training for Engineer: Expect to create 2 IT engineers for each government organization through the five advance training courses

-Training for trainers: Expect to create 1 IT instructor for every STEA branch offices and technical colleges

-General training for government officers.End users training course such as office automation, database, internet and etc.

-funds:

-Government budget

-Oversee support:

-Trainees Recipients:

Research & Development Sector

Open source laboratory (Assistance from Francophone organization)

Project on building Urban-Rural Digital link (Assistance from international Development Research Center)

Upgrading the National internet Gateway System

Provide internet access for National University of Lao PDR

Provide internet access for LuangPrabangGovernor office

Establish a Multi-purpose Tele-Center in LuangPrabang

Project on development the component for localization Dictionary, Lao lexicon,sorting system,spell check function.machine translation and etc (IDRC'sassistance)

Development of E-government application system (expecting to have an assistance from korea'sgovernment)

In country such as Laos, with so many pressing basic developmentneeds,it is not surprising that attempts at establish internet connectivity and E-business have been hampered by a general lack of skills and resource.Low levels of PC penetration, combined with poor telecommunication network with also slow the process.

There is currently a high level of interest in ICT development in the country ICT implementations and strategies,and the allocation of resources. From the government. Donors. And the private sectors. Towards ICT development are reflected in existing ICT related projects focusing on human resources development. Governance. Administration. And information management.

A policy paper of Government on Governance issues addressed the needs to use ICT as a tool for improving the management practices of day-to-day working methods with move efficient and transparent manner. There is lack of co-ordination policies, which tends to lead to duplications among government entities and inefficient operations. And limit the benefits to be gained from ICT advancement.

ICT POLICIES

The Government Of Laos (GOL) has identified nine priority areas requiring long term consideration. The following are the policy statements for Infrastructure and Access; Enterprise and Industry; Research and Development; Applications; Human Resource Development; Legal Framework; Awareness; Poverty Alleviation; and Standardization and Localization.

1. INFRASTRUCTURE AND ACCESS

The GOL shall focus on expanding the existing telecommunications infrastructure, linking the most rural and remote areas, particularly in the northern parts of the Lao PDR, using appropriate and feasible technologies to the national infrastructure. Establish a Universal Service Programme to provide telecommunications services to the underserved areas. making Internet costs affordable to the users. The GOL shall encourage the wide usage of ICT by reduce the current level (15%) of import tax on all ICT equipment.

2. ENTERPRISE AND INDUSTRY

The GOL shall promote enterprise development in the ICT sector. Promote local ICT enterprise development; where possible, government shall give first preference to locally developed software, hardware and ICT services in procurement. Provide favourable investment incentives and taxation environment, including but not limited to reduced software/hardware import duties for business and profit taxes levied on ICT related enterprises. The GOL shall identify and allocate ICT investment zones with appropriate and adequate physical space, infrastructural, facilities, and logistical services and effort in promoting outsourcing businesses in Lao PDR.

Encourage national and foreign investors to compete and to cooperate in investment in the construction, development, and expansion of the telecommunications network and services.

3. RESEARCH AND DEVELOPMENT

Establish national research and development centre/incubator to promote research and development in the fields of information and communication technologies – software, hardware, and services.

The GOL shall mandate the establishment of a National ICT Association (NICTA), which shall be a consortium of private sector ICT companies. After establishment, the NICTA shall operate autonomous from the Government but shall advise the Government on issues relating to the ICT industry.

4. APPLICATIONS

The GOL has identified three main areas for immediate application of ICT to enhance efficiencies in the delivery of services and management – e-Government, e-Tourism, and banking.

5. HUMAN RESOURCE DEVELOPMENT

In formal, non-formal, vocational and skill training, the GOL shall promote and support the continuous learning of ICT to ensure the necessary capacities to meet national goals. The GOL shall focus on world-class curriculum development for Bachelor and Masters Degrees of Computer Science/Engineering and degrees related ICT for the tertiary level of education. The GOL shall ensure the application of ICT to supplements and administer the Ministry of Education five main programmes: 1) Pre-school and General Education Programme, 2) Non-formal Education Programme, 3) Teacher Training Programme, 4) Vocational and Higher Education Programme, and 5) Administration and Management Programme.

In the rural and remote areas, the GOL shall pilot telecentre programmes to ensure opportunities for ICT-enabled learning for those most underserved and without readily access to education. To promote the transfer of technical knowledge and expertise, the Lao diaspora shall be encourage to return to assist in human resource development.

6. LEGAL FRAMEWORK

The GOL aims to develop a comprehensive set of Cyber-Laws to govern activities on the Internet and information networks of Lao PDR. The GoL shall begin with a set of cyber laws to encompass e-commerce/e-business, cyber-crimes, consumer protection, and intellectual property rights.

7. AWARENESS

The GOL will implement a public awareness programme on the benefits, advantages, and importance of ICT. The programme shall focus on the utilization of ICT in achieving MDGs and the NPEP. The GOL shall encourage the private sector and the international community to contribute to this public awareness programme. The GOL will promote the preservation of cultural, social, and political heritage vis a vis the Internet and the cultural imports it makes available to the public at large.

8. POVERTY ALLEVIATION

To ensure growth with equity (reduce disparities related to gender, ethnicity, location and returnee status), the GOL shall support and facilitate the application of ICT for the development of participatory social networks (civil society, academia, general public, government and the private sector); focussing on the environment, health, gender, and youth.

9. STANDARDIZATION AND LOCALIZATION

The GOL shall promote software, hardware, and protocol standards, including telecommunications equipment and services, to ensure interoperability and harmonization with international, regional, and sub-regional standards.

For additional analytical, business and investment opportunities information, please contact Global Investment & Business Center, USA at (703) 370-8082. Fax: (703) 370-8083. E-mail: ibpusa3@gmail.com Global Business and Investment Info Databank - www.ibpus.com

To promote digital interchange in the Lao language, the GOL shall adopt the Unicode standard for the Lao script. The GOL shall establish a network, including national and international experts, academia, government, and the private sector to advise on all issues relating to the localization of ICTs – this include Open Source and proprietary software. The GOL shall establish a set of standards for data and information storage, exchange, and access for all government bodies and agencies, in line with international data standards. The GOL shall adopt Open Standards for all government data/information systems over proprietary standards, wherever possible, to minimize technological lock-in.

ICT PROGRAMMES

The main ICT programme in Lao PDR now is e-Government Project. This project was divided into 4 parts such as:

1. Infrastructure which build the connection by fibber Optic between Data Centre at NAST and Ministries in order to sharing, upload, download information among government bodies. Also it will deploy WIMAX technology with 10 base stations in Vientiane Capital and each province one WIMAX base station.

> e-Applications which consist of 7 applications as following: e-Portal; e-Document; e-Archive; e-Map; e-Registration; e-Learning and video conference.

> Human Resource development (Training)

> Providing IT facilities such as: Servers, PC desktops, Notebooks, Printers, Photo copies, Video Conference equipment to various ministries, agencies, central and local offices in order to utilize full usage of e-Application. This project has reached one objective of ICT policies. For more information please visit: www.laopdr.gov.la

Another ICT programmes are computer reseller (both hardware and software), Training, Consultation (solution and application) and service operators (telecom and internet). Only telecom operators which are the biggest investors, invested more than one hundred thousand dollar, which each one were invested more than five million dollars, secondly are Internet Service Provider companies that invested more than two hundred thousand dollar and the third are computer companies that doing many kind of services together (Such doing also reseller, training and consultation) that invested more than fifty thousand dollar. For the small company like computer shop and repair are invested less than ten thousand dollar.

The major number amount ICT companies are focusing the domestic market only, while small number companies is doing the export and some companies having the business in both domestic and oversee market. It is mean that Laos is ICT imported countries. Mostly is reselling the end-user product with very little modification.

ICT RESEARCH PRIORITIES

The main research priorities are Localization.

– With this priority, National Authority for Science and Technology (NAST) who in charge of IT research established PAN Lao Localization Project which has received financial support by International Development and Research Centre (IDRC) of Canada. In this project we focused following:

Lao character set (base on UNICODE)

Lao Keyboard base on UNICODE

Lao Syllabification (Line breaking by Syllable)

Lao Sorting

Lao Spellchecker

Lao Optical Character Recognition (Lao OCR)

Lao Text to Speech (Lao TTS) For more information please visit: www.laol10n.info.la

– Another project is Localization Window Vista and MS Office 2007 In this project, we helped Microsoft team to do the translation the interface terms, glossaries, help for both Window Vista and MS Office 2007 in Lao version.

– The rest is providing consulting and database application development.

ICT DEVELOPMENT CHALLENGES AND OPPORTUNITIES

THE ICT SITUATION IN LAO PDR

Laos, a country with a small population and small financial resources, is known by many for its friendly people, beautiful scenery, recent growth rate and natural resources. The country is however facing many challenges, including problems with/undeveloped road network, water and electricity supplies as well as educational and health systems.

The ICT situation is no exception; telephony and data connectivity is scarce and unevenly distributed, even though improving due to an aggressive deployment of a national fibre network as well as mobile telephony (GSM, Global System for Mobile Communication) expansion. There is a clear lack of ICT skills, both basic and more advanced. The ICT situation in general, and the issues of ICT capacity and low computer penetration in particular, is furthermore hindered by the fact that knowledge in English also is scarce, which in turn gives yet another training obstacle since most literature and training materials are in English. This problem is amplified by the fact that there is no Lao standardized character set that enables Lao people to study and work on computers in their native language. (Lao computer fonts do currently exist, but not standardized or based upon internationally recognized character sets.) Last but not least, reasons for the low computer penetration include serious obstacles such as i) most people or companies cannot afford a computer, and ii) even if they could, only major urban areas have access to electricity and telephony services.

The country has also been suffering from weak ICT leadership; there is currently no clear government focal point for ICT issues, leaving industry actors and investors with many questions unanswered. An illustration of the – at least historically - weak understanding of ICT sector importance for overall development is the fact that the country has "sold" its national top domain (.la) to a U.S based company (except the subdomains edu.la, gov.la and org.la.)

This rather dark picture is being brightened by a number of encouraging facts, which indicates that many of the serious technical impediments will be resolved within foreseeable time:

-A very strong national fibre network is currently being built - at the time of writing, 13 out of 18 provinces are connected. All provinces are scheduled to be connected by the summer of 2005.

-There is a national ICT policy process under progress supported by UNDP, coordinated with a regional ICT policy process supported by ADB.

-A strong political momentum is building up, indicating that no major political forces will be allowed to stand in the way for the ICT development process.

-A standardized Lao font is being developed and is scheduled for distribution by the end of 2005.

-The international community is active in Lao PDR and there seem to be a broad willingness to contribute to the ICT development process. For example, Sida is supporting the establishment of the National Statistics Center, the National Research and Education Network and a number of applications in the environment area.

Conclusively, we find that several major technical remedies are underway, while the responsibility of taking on the task of accelerating human capacity building remains. Several initiatives in this area are undergoing, but not yet in a scale that brings broad impact.

POLITICAL AMBITIONS

1 Historical ICT policy events

The policy landscape in Laos PDR has undergone a few phases; STEA had one "master plan" between the years of 1996 and 2000, and another plan was written in year 2000. Even if these plans most certainly showed important impact - not least on political understanding of the sectors importance - it is more relevant for us to focus on more recent policy initiatives that are more closely related to the current context.

In December 2001, the "Directive on the development and use of ICT in Lao PDR" was issued with the following objectives:

-Facilitate wide and effective use of ICT in every sector as an essential factor for the socio-economic development, the national defence and security,

-Develop a national telecommunication network for high speed communication and increased access to the internet country wide,

-Promote competition in the information communication technology network and services,

-Broaden and enhance international cooperation, to create a favourable condition for the development and use of ICT through the national telecommunication network infrastructure and to develop human resource in the field of ICT as a key factor for the successful implementation of the Information and Communication Technology[1].

1 Economic and social commission for Asia and the Pacific: Development of enabling policies for trade and investment in the it sector of the Greater Mekong Subregion, and; Xaphakdy Smith, Developing Information and Communication Infrastructure: An Implementation of Tokyo Declaration and Action plan in Lao PDR, http://unpan1.un.org/intradoc/groups/public/documents/apcity/unpan006169.pdf

To comment on the current results of the directive, one must acknowledge that Lao PDR really has moved forward on several of the objectives. Given the starting point, the progress is significant:

-A wide and effective use of ICT in every sector has not been deployed.

-A national backbone is currently being built at an impressing aggressive pace; half of the provincial capitals were connected at the time of the writing of this report, and the rest are scheduled to be connected by mid-year 2005.

-International connectivity is still lagging behind

-Competition is partly accomplished, although most telecom operators are still owned, wholly or partly, by the state.

-The international cooperation around ICTs seems to be well developed – several Donors are active in his field.

If private international actors are included when reasoning about "international cooperation around ICT", one must conclude that very little has happened. Positive consequences from the emerging, enabling national backbone are yet to be seen; so far, the backbone is still marginally utilized. The human resources situation has probably improved in some areas, but still has a long way to go.

2 National ICT Policy and Strategy

There is an apparent political will to enable modern technologies to bring the country forward. This is directly shown in a currently ongoing policy process. If this process (or these processes, as they more accurately should be called) will unite policy makers and translate into real actions leading to real change, remains to be seen during the next few years. This chapter aims to describe the various current initiatives and how they interrelate, as well as which players are involved and what their roles and mandates are.

NATIONAL POLICY ON ICT

STEA is mandated to develop ICT policies, and is now in the process of developing a policy paper that includes guidelines, visions and a broad perspective of the important national development aspects of emerging ICT capabilities, such as infrastructure and public access, commercial aspects, e-government and human resources development. A steering committee and five working groups have been established to formulate policies. The working groups (applications, infrastructure, human capacity, enterprise, standards) have met throughout the last year and now have a consolidated draft of their policy recommendations. The Ministry of Communications, Transports, Posts and Construction (MCPTC) play a role by participating in working groups. Asia Pacific Development Program (APDIP) by the United Nations Development Programme (UNDP) provides technical and funding assistance. STEA is at the time of the writing circulating it for comments from other interests, and will present it during a National Consultation, scheduled for August 2004. Following this, a final policy document will be drafted.

GMS TELECOM SECTOR POLICY FORMULATION AND CAPACITY BUILDING

For additional analytical, business and investment opportunities information,
please contact Global Investment & Business Center, USA
at (703) 370-8082. Fax: (703) 370-8083. E-mail: ibpusa3@gmail.com
Global Business and Investment Info Databank - www.ibpus.com

The MCPTC is engaged in the formulation of a national telecommunications sector reform program, which is also coordinated with a regional initiative in Greater Mekong Sub-region (GMS, which includes Cambodia, Lao PDR and Vietnam). This national project calls for a telecom sector reform - and the preparation it requires – building upon the new Telecommunications Act of 2001 that opens up for the establishment of an independent regulating agency. It is a rather practically oriented project to develop the regulatory system and continue the liberalization of the sector. It is furthermore aligned with commitments required for a potential future joining of Lao PDR into the World Trade Organization (WTO). Top priorities for this project is to i) establish a "semiautonomous regulator unit" within MCTPC (to be totally autonomous and independent in five years time), ii) separate ownership of equity in telecom assets from MCTPC to another ministry or agency, iii) progressively minimize the Governments direct involvement in ownership of operators, and iv) promulgate three key regulative areas (setting fees and tariffs, interconnection and access, issuance of licences for telecom businesses). Both the regional process and the national telecom reform program are supported by the Asian Development Bank (ADB), the World Bank (WB), the International Telecommunications Union (ITU), and the German KfW Banking Group (KfW).

REMARKS ON POLICY DEVELOPMENT

The two processes – the national ICT process and the telecom sector reform project – are not directly linked or coordinated with each other. MCPTC participates to some extent in both processes however, and hopefully there will be little overlap or conflicts in between the two processes. Both processes are said to be aligned with the 2001 Telecom Act. We have however observed indications of that communication and information exchange between STEA and MCPTC is sometimes slow, and that coordination is not always as obvious as one could expect. We also have the impression that there is room for improvement among the multi- and bilateral organisations active in Lao PDR in terms of coordination and information exchange.

INTERNATIONAL ASPECTS

Lao PDR is a member of several international and regional organisations. We will discuss just a few of them here that have an impact or potential impact on the ICT situation and development.

1 ASEAN

Laos is a member of ASEAN, the Association of South-East Asian Nations (www.aseansec.org), which, after more than 35 years has transformed itself to become a key regional organization in development.

ASEAN imposes a number of requirements on their members, such as providing statistics and participation in common workgroups and projects. The most relevant areas for this study are the Information Technology and e-Commerce area and the Transport and Communication area.

2 EU-Asia Link

In the area of higher education, EU and ASEAN started out in the year 2000 with the Asia-EU University Network Programme (AUNP). This is being replaced by the EU-Asia Link programme, an initiative by the European Commission to promote regional and multilateral networking between higher education institutions in EU Member States and South Asia, South-East Asia and China. The programme aims to promote the creation of new partnerships and new sustainable links between European and Asian higher education institutions, and to reinforce existing partnerships

3 ASEM

ASEM, acronym for the Asia - Europe Meeting, is a biennial Summit Meeting of ten (10) Asian nations - seven (7) ASEAN countries (Brunei, Indonesia, Malaysia, Philippines, Singapore, Thailand and Vietnam) plus China, Japan and South Korea - and fifteen (15) European nations (Austria, Belgium, Denmark, Finland, France, Germany, Greece, Ireland, Italy, Luxembourg, Netherlands, Portugal, Spain, Sweden and United Kingdom), and the President of the European Commission.

Laos is currently not a member of ASEM, but has applied for membership together with Cambodia and Myanmar.

The applications are on the agenda for the 5th ASEM meeting in Hanoi in October 2004. The reason for mentioning ASEM in this report is the TEIN activity [14] supported by Europe Aid and restricted to ASEM members, which we consider as interesting for the capacity building in Laos. The Lao National Research and Education Network (NREN) emerging from Sida-supported ICT project at NUOL has asked the Lao government to

ASEM is an interregional, intergovernmental entity which aims to promote common development and prosperity in Asia and Europe. It has a broad scope beyond the business and economic dimensions to embrace the political, social, environmental and cultural areas. ASEM is an informal, open and evolutionary dialogue process without a formal agenda or a permanent secretariat. In addition to the biennial Summit Meeting, there are Foreign Ministers Meetings, Economic and Finance Ministers Meetings and Senior Officials Meetings. Different cooperative projects are also being carried out by all member countries to efficiently promote cooperation in various fields.

HUMAN RESOURCES

ICT staff of all kinds, but especially technical staff (networking, programming), is extremely hard to find even in the private sector, where salaries are higher than in the public sector, let alone the public sector. This is clearly, by far, the largest weakness of Laos and all support to Laos will, no doubt, have to consider this fact as the starting point for any discussions about development cooperation.

ACTORS ON THE ICT ARENA

Users

Public administration: Government at all levels

Large efforts are made to establish an intranet for the national public administration, including the central government ministries, the provincial governments and the district administrations. eGovernment services are being planned.

Private sector: Tourists and students

Computers and the Internet are also becoming commonly used in the tourist industry, such as travelling agencies, hotels, restaurants, shopping, Internet cafés, etc. Provincial authorities have ambitions to provide tourist information websites.

Education is another area in which the ICT usage is increasing notably, especially in private schools.

Information: News agencies and the Press

There is a slowly increasing number of websites in the information area, such as the KPL website, Vientiane Times and the web-portal www.laopdr.com.

COMMUNICATION OPERATORS

There are four companies licensed to provide telecommunication services throughout the country. They are:

Enterprise of Telecommunications Lao of the Government of Lao PDR (ETL)

Lao Telecommunications Co. Ltd (LTC),

Lao Telecom Asia Co. Ltd (LAT) and

Millicom La Co. Ltd (Tango)

All four provide GSM services, three of them provide PSTN services and two of them provide Internet services- There are three more commercial ISPs acting as retailers. These operators and their services will be described in more detail in the section on infrastructure. All of the operators, except for Millicom Lao Limited, have mixed private and public or public ownership. Millicom Lao Limited is 100% privately held; however the GoL does have an "economic interest" even in this company.

REGULATING AGENCIES

Department of Post & Telecommunications (DPT), MCTPC

As mentioned in chapter 3.2.2.2, there is currently no independent regulator in the telecommunication area in Laos. Decisions of regulatory nature (such as frequency spectrum, licensing of satellite gateways and voice services) are currently taken by the Department of Post and Telecommunications (DPT) of the MCTPC in accordance to the 2001 Telecom Act. DPT is hence the official Lao regulator and represents Laos in ITU, APT and APPU. Internet related policies and licensing issues are managed by Lao National Internet Committee (LANIC) and licensing of TV and Radio broadcasting is managed by the Ministry of Information and Culture. However, the establishment and operation of an independent operator seems to be on its way, even though it may take five years to reach independence and autonomy. At the 10th ASEAN (The Association of Southeast Asian Nations) Telecommunications Regulators Council (ATRC) meeting held from July 8-9 2004 in Vientiane, representatives for the MCTPC said that Laos needs an independent regulator to regulate licensing and competition as well as to look after the telecom industry. Laos is one of the few ASEAN members still lacking an independent supervising regulator. Regulated items currently include:

Radio spectrum,

Universal Service Obligation,

For additional analytical, business and investment opportunities information,
please contact Global Investment & Business Center, USA
at (703) 370-8082. Fax: (703) 370-8083. E-mail: ibpusa3@gmail.com
Global Business and Investment Info Databank - www.ibpus.com

International gateways (Telephony, Internet),

Specific services, such as voice services (telephony as well as Voice over IP (VoIP or IP-telephony); requires voice license) and broadcasting (radio and television).

ASEAN has the explicit goal to give its 500 million people the opportunity to use telecom services and considers the only way to do that to be to allow private companies to operate. Many ASEAN members, including Laos, have changed their policies to permit the participation of private companies in the telecommunications sector. As a consequence, there are more companies, more competition and more chance of conflict among the companies.

Since implementation of a more liberal policy, the price of telephone installations has dropped from US$30.00 per installed telephone number to US$5.00 in only a few months. More services are also offered. The liberalisation in Laos has thus been successful. MCTPC seems now to have the opinion, that a sustainable development of the telecommunications area requires an independent regulator. This opinion is shared by Millicom Lao, who is the main challenger compared to the other more traditional operators.

Lao National Internet Committee (LANIC)

LANIC was formed in the year 2000 under the decree of the Prime Minister's Office. LANIC was given jurisdiction over matters regarding national Internet policies and for certifying a license to all ISPs in Laos. Its main objective is to regulate and control Internet in Lao. The committee includes representatives from: STEA, MCPTC the Ministry of Foreign Affairs, the Ministry of the Interior, and the Ministry of Information and Culture.

The LANIC ICT Centre at STEA provides Internet access to all Lao government ministries, the National University of Lao (NUOL) and National Agriculture and Forestry Research Institute (NAFRI).

LANIC operates two international gateways using the following links:

-A satellite connection to Thaicom in Thailand with capacity of 1024 Kbps for incoming traffic and 512 Kbps for outgoing traffic at a cost of 4,800 USD per month. This link was during 2002-2003 supported by IDRC but is paid by STEA 2004-2005.

-A gateway using the CSC fibre optic cable to the Communication Authority Terminal (CAT) in Bangkok. The capacity of this link is 512 Kbps out of a 5 Mbps international peering connection between ETL and CAT in Thailand over the ETL 2.4 Gbit/s SDH connection to CAT.

Ministry of Information and Culture

MIC is responsible for licensing of Radio and TV broadcasting activities.

HARDWARE AND SOFTWARE DISTRIBUTORS

There is generally no problem to find the computer equipment and standard of the shelf software in Vientiane; it logically gets harder the further away from the capital you get. A relatively large number of small businesses import computer parts and assemble computer systems according to customer specifications. There is a 5% import on office supplies (for office use), computers, photocopiers, and its peripherals, etc., which in many countries would be marginal but of course does not help the sector in Lao PDR since the purchasing power is so constrained. If the equipment is intended for resale/retail, the import tariff is 10% for office equipment. On telecom equipment the import tariffs are 3% for office use and 10% if intended for resale/retail. There is an ongoing debate on whether to lower the tariffs to stimulate the sector.

Specialized items, larger servers, telecom equipment, etc., are generally ordered internationally. There is an important second-hand market, serving the large segment that find new computers and equipment too costly.

There is a quite limited understanding of intellectual property (IP) and copyrights; software piracy is common and software is often distributed in conflict with international IPR agreements. As in many least developed countries (LDC), reasons for software piracy is directly related to ability to pay rather than to calculated theft. Of course, for software license cost reason there is also a great interest for open source software. Linux platforms seem not to have taken off yet, likely due to absence of a broad capacity to configure and run these systems.

ICT RELATED CONSULTING SERVICES

Most ICT related consulting services can be found in Vientiane; including system administration, development, integration, programming, etc. It is hard to judge the quality of available services, but we have seen some discouraging examples in terms of system administration. It is probably not totally out of line to assume that most services available do not meet up to international standards due to the hitherto limited exposure of opportunities to build up sector capacity.

COMMUNICATION INFRASTRUCTURE

The description of the communication infrastructure is divided into the passive infrastructure, i.e. the fibre and copper cables between connection closets, without active communication equipment, and the active infrastructure in terms of basic communication network services.

PASSIVE INFRASTRUCTURE

Domestic links

The Country has 18 provinces, out of which 5 provinces have been provided with fibre optic network connectivity in their capitals. The ETL plan is to cover capitals of 13 provinces by the year 2004, and 142 districts headquarters by 2005 [28].

There is currently one fibre cable with 18 fibre pairs, owned by ETL, along Route 13 from Luang Prabang to Pakse. Another cable with 24 fibre pairs is being deployed along the same route. This cable is owned by LTC and will be operable in the end of 2004.

There is also a microwave link infrastructure. LTC has a 34bit/s microwave infrastructure used in the GSM network, which will be replaced by a fibre infrastructure and used as backup.

International links

The only cross border fibre cable with a point of presence in Laos is the CSC cable owned by a consortium in which Laos is represented by ETL. The cable is connecting Shanghai - Hanoi - Vientiane - Bangkok – Singapore. The optical cable is still not heavily used. Only about 15% of the Lao international traffic is transported this way while 85% goes via satellite. We have not fully understood the reason for this but suspect a broken pricing policy. It should be the opposite.

NETWORK SERVICES

All four operators mentioned in 3.4.2 are licensed to provide telecommunication services throughout the country. All four provide GSM services, three of them provide PSTN services and two of them provide Internet services. There are three more commercial ISPs acting as retailers.

PSTN/PSDN/ISDN/ADSL

In May 2003, there were 72.235 (public switched telephone network) PSTN subscriber lines in service from three operators. However, there are only 1,706 subscribers in the rural provinces, which include 50 districts and 22 remote villages. Furthermore, there are only 300 public telephones, all of them located in the larger cities. Roughly 80% of the population lives in rural areas.

X.21, X-25, ISDN and ADSL services are available but there is no demand.

GSM

There are currently (June 2004) four licensed GSM providers, ETL, LTC, LAT and Tango. A fifth license (Sky Star) is being discussed. GSM services are available in nine out of 18 provinces of the country. In May 2003 there were 106,951 mobile subscribers from 4 operators, with LTC controlling around 75% of the market.

Despite 8 years of mobile cellular implementation, Laos has not yet experienced a wireless boom to the same extent as other developing countries. (MCTPC, Report of 2002). It may still come 2004-2005 since prices have dropped considerably since the fourth operator, Millicom Lao/Tango started operation in April 2003

LTC has established a backbone of 34 (1+1) Mbps microwave transmission system connecting 13 major cities to Vientiane. LTC is also in the process of installing rural telephony in remote and rural areas throughout the country in five phases. LTC has plans to upgrade the 34(1+1) Mbps of the Microwave transmission system to 34 (2+1) Mbps system.

In July 2004, LTC launched a new broadband satellite system, which will expand its mobile telephone coverage to 85 percent of the country by the end of 2004. Using a satellite called IPSTAR, the new system can be used to provide a network in mountainous areas and costs less than microwave and cable networks. The IPSTAR satellite has a higher capacity than a conventional satellite, allowing it to serve millions of users.

CDMA

LTC has a CDMA license and will start operating during 2004. Tong, a Chinese company, has applied for a CDMA license. Millicom/Tango will focus on expanding their GSM network before applying for a CDMA license.

INTERNET

INTERNET SERVICE PROVIDERS

In June 2004, there were six Internet Service providers, including the five commercial ETL, LTC, Planet Online, Lanexang and KPL, and LANIC, providing services for the government ministries, provincial departments and for NUOL and Nafri.

INTERNET USERS

In May 2003, there were 15,000 Internet users in the country

-10% government organizations

-20% local private companies

-23% local individual users, mostly using dial-up services

-47% foreign users

The number of Internet users, especially domestic, can be expected to increase rapidly since the opportunities for education and training have increased and a large number of development projects are in progress.

INTERNET ACCESS POINTS

Internet access points for private end-users include homes, schools, libraries and about 200 Internet café's in the country, out which 50 are situated in the capital Vientiane (2004)

PROVINCIAL GATEWAYS FOR PUBLIC ADMINISTRATION

For the public sector, according to the policy to establish Internet gateways in all provinces, STEA has set up pilot provincial Internet gateways in the Luang Prabang and Champassak provinces. The connection is made by using the ETL optical fibre infrastructure and connecting to the STEA Internet gateway. STEA plans to complete all 18 provinces by the year 2004.

NATIONAL EDUCATION AND RESEARCH NETWORK

The emerging national research and education network is expanding via the Sida-supported activities at NUOL and Nafri. Discussions are underway with THAISARN and TEIN how to best connect it to the international academic network.

INTERNET EXCHANGE POINT

An Internet Exchange, Laonix, has been funded by Sida and implemented in cooperation between STEA, NUOL and KTH. Laonix is operated by STEA and all Lao operators are in the process of being connected.

INTERNATIONAL SERVICES VIA THE CSC CABLE

ETL has 5 Mbps International peering to CAT in Thailand, out of which ETL leased a 2 Mbps fibre optic link to Planet Online Laos and 512 Kbps to STEA.

For additional analytical, business and investment opportunities information, please contact Global Investment & Business Center, USA at (703) 370-8082. Fax: (703) 370-8083. E-mail: ibpusa3@gmail.com Global Business and Investment Info Databank - www.ibpus.com

INTERNATIONAL SERVICES VIA SATELLITE

All international voice traffic (PSTN and GSM) is connected via satellite.

ETL has a 2 Mbps satellite link to CAT and pays 11,000 USD per month.

LTC uses a satellite owned by Shinawat.

For Internet services, STEA leases 512kbit/s up streams and 1Mbit/s down streams at 4.800USD/month from Thaicom according to a two-year contract ending 2005-12-31.

TV/Radio distribution

Since 1997, the Lao government has a license from ITU to operate a geo-stationary satellite (Laostar). For various reasons there is yet no satellite launched. The license expires soon and a decision whether to use it or not has to be taken before the end of 2004. In this decision process alternatives like a terrestrial digital television, will be considered.

SOFT INFRASTRUCTURE

The concept of soft infrastructure includes databases, registers and other structures information that could be used as content in services. Typical examples include car register, national population and census registers, environmental records and statistics, land records and health records.

Generally, the soft infrastructure is thin in Lao PDR. We have found that certain of the above registers exist, some in partly manual format (for example manual reporting from villages to districts, followed by manual reporting to from districts to provinces, eventually followed by a registration in a centrally located database or manual register. Practices can vary between districts and provinces, and an ambition of central collection is not always present, and may in all cases not be desirable. The weak soft infrastructure relates to all issues of the limited computer penetration; computer literacy, written and read Lao language skills, English language skills, and lastly the absence of standardized Lao fonts.

Just as in many developed countries which went through the same transition from manual to digital systems not so long ago, reasons also include the fact that there is no tradition of storing data in an orchestrated manner, and it takes some time to change the mindset of storing information in a way so that it later can be retrieved and accessed by someone else, and create efficiency and value for individuals, companies and government agencies when they interact.

This problem may be exemplified by hospital's ability to track previous patient's health records. We have not found any computerized database at the three hospitals we have visited. More surprisingly, we found that none of the hospitals we surveyed stored patient data in a catalogued manner. Instead of storing them in a traceable way, they are rather recorded manually in a book, stored in a chronological manner according to the time of their visit. Once the book is full, the data in it is generally inaccessible. In some cases data is held in separate departments, for example in the emergency room, and will not be accessible from other departments. The reasons for this data collection and manual registration seem to respond more to administrative and statistical needs than to operational needs of fast access of historical data on a patient. This is clearly a process that could be rationalized significantly even without computers.

NATIONAL STATISTICS CENTRE

The organisation responsible for public statistical records in Laos is the National Statistics Centre (NSC) [11], which was inaugurated in 1993 but has existed under different names since 1978.

The function and responsibilities of NSC are defined in the decree regulating the function and responsibilities of the State Planning Commission. The function and responsibilities of statistical units of ministries, provinces and districts are similarly regulated in the respective decree of the ministries. The decree stated that NSC has the overall responsibility for the official statistic of Lao PDR.

The responsibilities include:

-Collect, compile, analyze and compose reports on official socio-economic statistics, report to the government and concerned sectors for their information and evaluation of the socio-economic situation in each period

-Conduct censuses and statistical sample surveys regularly, such as population censuses, agricultural censuses, expenditure and consumption surveys, etc.

-Supply statistics and provide services in different forms such as printing, teaching and training on statistical methods and computer science to serve the socio economic management in each period.

-Establish the Nation Accounting System, including macro - accounting, input - output tables, etc.

NSC has been supported by SCB/Statistics Sweden, financed by Sida, since the early 1990-ies. The objectives of this cooperation include developing professional competence, contributing to important statistical production and strengthening the role of statistics in society. The support includes experts, funding of data collection and equipment for processing and reporting. Among the statistical surveys conducted are household expenditures and consumption. These are important basic elements for studies of social conditions.

Censuses on Population and Housing

The UN recommends that censuses be performed with no longer periods than 10 years. In Laos, there have been censuses held in 1985 and 1995. The 1995 census on population and housing was funded by Sida and included financing of ICT resources.

A new census is planned in 2005, which intends to lay the basis for a population record system closely linked to the Village Book system. New approaches, including GIS, data processing and scanning of areas, are also planned to be used [22].

National Accounts and business statistics

Other important efforts concern the National Accounts and business statistics.

LOCAL CONTENT

There is still a very limited amount of local content online in Laos, most of which is in English. There are some but even less content in the Lao language [21]. Some sample Lao language sites can be found under the various sites listed at www.laopdr.com, especially under "Lao Government Links", where a few government agencies offers information in both Lao and English. Content in English also includes the online version of Vientiane Times, which can be found at www.vientianetimes.org.la.

Reasons for the limited local content are mainly the same as mentioned in previous chapters; the overall low computer literacy, in turn dependent upon the absence of a standardized Lao font and the issue of very limited knowledge in English, the limited and unevenly distributed access to computers and networks. Lastly, another technical hurdle is the (up until now) absence of an Internet Exchange (IX) point. This function enables various ISPs to exchange information on a local level, rather than being isolated "islands", and being forced to route traffic over expensive international routes. An IX installation at STEA connecting all ISPs is currently underway with support from the Royal Institute of Technology (KTH) in Sweden and Sida. As initially mentioned, a Lao font is now being developed by STEA. Simultaneously, the fibre network currently being laid out that will connect all provinces and ultimately also the districts, will have the possibility to dramatically increase connectivity for people living in rural areas, however, the issue of policies and practices of letting people access this resource is till an issue to be addressed.

Since both i) an IX, ii) a strong national fibre backbone reaching out to secondary areas, and iii) a standardized Lao font are underway, the main technical hurdles are out of the way. The local Lao font is scheduled to be the last main technical hurdle being eliminated, with a preliminary release by the end of year 2005, hopefully followed by a fast and successful distribution of the font (including distribution with Linux and Microsoft systems), and a market embracement of it. However, the technical hurdles are comparatively small in relation to the task of bringing people up to a level where a local content build-up of scale will happen. Who will take on the responsibility for the enormous task of increasing levels of computer and ICT literacy is not clear. In major urban areas, local content will probably start to evolve as the technical obstacles are out of the way. A massive training effort will be needed, both in computer use and computer and communication maintenance.

On the countryside - as districts and villages get connected - individuals able to read and write in Lao will with sufficient computer training will be able to assist their fellow villagers in their communication needs, be it staying in touch with remote family members, checking the current market prices for crops or marketing of the local textile products. This will create business opportunities for local ICT capable individuals to serve fellow villagers solving their electronic communication needs. Before reaching this scenario and making it sustainable, people must be trained to use the systems, to look after them technically and to run the maintenance.

ENABLING TECHNOLOGIES AND SOLUTIONS (SUCH AS PAYMENT SOLUTIONS

We have found few enabling technologies in place in Lao PDR. We found no electronic payment mechanisms (even though credit card payments are possible at a few businesses such as larger hotels), information distribution mechanisms, etc. With the advent of GSM expansions and the rapidly expanding use of short message service (SMS), it is however likely that both plain, GSM based information and petty payment solutions will take off.

ICT ENABLED SERVICES (SUCH AS CALL CENTRES, BUSINESS PROCESS OUTSOURCING)

Depending on the currently poor telecom infrastructure, there is very few business process outsourcing (BPO) companies in place in Laos. The most common reason for offshore placement of business processes is cost efficiency due to vast differences in salary level for easily repeated tasks – this prerequisite is surely met in Laos.

Digital Divide Data (www.digitaldividedata.com) is the only BPO operator that we have identified in Lao PDR. DDD employs disadvantaged people and provide digitisation services.

EDUCATION AND TRAINING

Due to several reasons - tradition as well as practical - the level of education differs between the ethnic groups and between genders. The literacy of the Lao population is slightly more than 50% for the whole population, slightly less than 70% for males and 40% for females [10]. In the range 15-24, the total literacy is 81%, 5% less for females than for males [11].

The languages spoken in Laos are the Lao language (official) and a number of ethnic languages. The major ethnic groups include [10]: the Lao Loum (lowland) 68%, the Lao Theung (upland) 22%, Lao Soung (highland) including the Hmong and the Yao 9%, and ethnic Vietnamese/Chinese 1%.

There is currently [2004] no official standard script for the Lao language. A process is in progress to establish such a standard and to define and implement Unicode fonts for the official script. This project is supported by UNDP and managed by STEA.

Skills in foreign languages are very limited, including English and French. Due to an almost total lack of digital content authored in the Lao language, such skills are required in order to use text based ICT services. In the mobile phone area, the SMS service is taking on, especially among the young, by using a phonetic representation of Lao words based on the Roman alphabet with English pronunciation and a telegram message format.

THE EDUCATIONAL SYSTEM IN LAOS

The Lao school system consists of:

-Five years of primary school (age 6-11) resulting in a Primary School Certificate. Almost 50% of the public expenditure on education is dedicated to pre-primary and primary school education [13],

-Three years of lower-secondary school (age 11-14) resulting in a Lower Secondary School Diploma,

-Three years of upper-secondary school (age 14-17) resulting in a Upper Secondary School Diploma,

-Three years of Technical school or Higher Technical College (age 17-20) resulting in a diploma or a higher diploma,

Higher education is provided by the National University of Laos which is made up of several faculties. There are also higher technical institutes and teacher training colleges. In the future, the teacher training colleges will be transformed into Regional Colleges. The Government manages higher education institutions. The University is under the responsibility of the Ministry of Education.

A more comprehensive description of the Lao education system and references is available in [15].

For additional analytical, business and investment opportunities information,
please contact Global Investment & Business Center, USA
at (703) 370-8082. Fax: (703) 370-8083. E-mail: ibpusa3@gmail.com
Global Business and Investment Info Databank - www.ibpus.com

PRIMARY AND SECONDARY EDUCATION

In 2002, the enrolment in primary school was 80% while only about 50% of those entering grade 1 completed grade 5 [11].

Some students go directly from primary or lower-secondary school to vocational instruction, such as teacher-training or agriculture schools. In some provinces, such as Oudomxay, there is only one secondary school (with about 2000 students), which means that many students need to be boarded away from home. This fact increases the drop-out rate.

Primary and secondary schools rarely have access to ICT training facilities or Internet connectivity. As far as we know, no primary school while at least four secondary schools have Internet access. Jhai Foundation have connected four schools and have recently received World Bank funding for connecting another ten schools.

VOCATIONAL EDUCATION AND TRAINING

STEA offers short ICT training courses at their ICT Centre, primarily for civil servants, and has the ambition to do this also in the provinces.

PSTEO in Luang Prabang already offers ICT training at their ICT Centre while PSTEO in Oudomxay does not yet.

There are many commercial business oriented training centres (we have seen four). Also, some computer retail companies offer training (we have seen two).

There are a few vocational schools and institutes, but it has not been possible to identify any schools providing vocational training in the ICT area.

In December 2002, a vocational training centre was opened in the Hadsaifong District in Vientiane City supported by the Australian donor ACTU/Union Aid Abroad and managed by the Vientiane Municipal Women's Union. It is part of a larger program of support to vocational training supported by AusAID and Union Aid Abroad in Vientiane City, Luang Prabang Province and through the LWU national Training for Development Centre. The centre will offer training in Tailoring/Dressmaking, Hairdressing, Food processing, Handicrafts and in the future if funding is available, other subjects such as typing, electrical repair or motorcycle repair. The first courses in Hairdressing and Tailoring started early 2003

In September 2003, a new vocational training school in Laos's northern Bokeo province donated by Vietnam was inaugurated. The school, designed and constructed by Vietnamese companies, allows students of Lao tribes in the province to get vocational training.

TERTIARY EDUCATION AND RESEARCH INSTITUTES

Tertiary education in Laos is mainly the responsibility of the National University of Laos offering a bachelor degree. So far students have to go abroad to acquire a Master or a PhD degree. Two new regional university colleges have recently been established. There are also a few research institutes, such as the National Agriculture and Forestry Research Institute (NAFRI) and the National Economics Research Institute (NERI).

National University of Laos (NUOL)

Tertiary level education is provided by the National University of Laos (NUOL). In 1995, ten higher education institutions located in Vientiane were merged and reorganized into faculties of this multi-campus University, the main campus located at Dong Dok, in the northern outskirts of the Vientiane municipality.

The number of employees at NUOL is roughly 2500, out which around 1000 belong to the academic staff. The total number of students is about 17000. Academically, NUOL is organised in ten faculties. Undergraduate education in Information Technology is spread over the Faculty of Science (FoS) and the Faculty of Engineering & Architecture (FoE&A). The academic program in Laos starts with a two year preparatory program, including mathematics and natural sciences, at the School of Foundation Studies and can then select a three year programs (medicine four years) in:

-Natural science 1: FOE, FOS (math, computer science, physics)

-Natural science 2: biology, chemistry, agriculture, forestry, medicine

-Social science 1: economics and management

-Social science 2: languages

The curriculum includes a thesis work conducted half time during the tenth semester

Regional university colleges

Recently [2003], two new regional colleges were established, Souphanouvong University College in Luang Prabang with the ambition to focus on education related to forestry and tourism, and Champassack University College in Pakxe, with the ambition to focus education programs related to the coffee production of the south of Laos. In August 2003, both universities started a two year Foundation Study program, similar to the one offered by NUOL at the Dong Dok campus in Vientiane. They have just completed the first year of the two years preparatory program.

The Souphanouvong University College has prepared office space for a computer laboratory. The university has been promised 40 computers from Thailand that have not yet arrived.

National Agriculture and Forestry Research Institute (NAFRI)

NAFRI is under the supervision of the Ministry of Agriculture and Forestry (MAF) and has equal status with the line departments under MAF. The institute undertakes integrated agriculture, forestry and fisheries adaptive research in order to provide technical information, recommendations and results for agriculture, forestry and fisheries development and strategic formulation of policies and programs in accordance with the government policy.

NAFRI has no formal role in public administration, such as EIA, but is informally consulted for advice and cooperated with different departments of STEA.

NAFRI coordinates the Lao Swedish Upland Agriculture and Forestry Program, a partnership between NAFRI and Sida to strengthen the capacity and quality of agriculture and natural resource research in Laos. NAFRI also cooperates with NUOL and KTH to improve and extend its IT-infrastructure.

TRAINING OF TEACHERS AND TRAINERS

There are currently ten teacher training colleges (TTCs) in Laos supervised by the department of teacher training (DTT) at the Ministry of Education. Four of these colleges are located in or close to Vientiane, including one each for arts and music. The other colleges are in the following provinces: Luang Prabang, LuangNamtha, Xieng Khuang (Phonsovanh campus), Savannakhet (in the town), Champassak (in Pakse) and in Saravan.

The TTCs play a major role in giving the pre-service training and in-service training of the primary teachers and lower secondary teachers. There are also 19 network teacher upgrading centres spread over the country. These NTUCs have the responsibility to train untrained teachers, which in the year of 2000 represented 24% of the total number of primary school teachers

In 1995 there was an important reform of Teacher Education Curricula. From that time environmental education has been introduced into teacher education curricula as a compulsory subject entitled: "Population Education and Environmental Education" [12]. This fact is important to note since it connects the current Sida focus on environment issues to education on all levels and supports our proposal discussed subsequently to use environment issues as the driving application area for the introduction of ICT in Laos.

Training of pre-primary and primary/basic school teachers

Primary school teachers are selected from those who have completed lower secondary education and are at least fifteen years old. They follow a three-year training course in Primary Training School or 8+3 system. Those who have graduated from upper secondary school follow a one-year course in PTTS (11+1 system).

Training of secondary school teachers

Lower secondary school teachers follow a three-year training course at a Teacher Training College in Luang Prabang, Vientiane, Savannakhet or Champassack. They are awarded a Diploma in pedagogy. Upper secondary school teachers are selected among Upper Secondary School Diploma holders and trained for five years at the National University of Laos. Students have to take ten weeks of initial supervised teaching practice before they can take the final examination.

Training of higher education teachers

Higher education teachers are selected amongst those who have completed a Bachelor's Degree at NUOL; a graduate diploma; a Master's Degree or a Doctoral Degree abroad.

ICT IN EDUCATION

In 2000, the Ministry of Education (MOE) launched a three phase top-down master plan for introducing IT in education [13]. The focus of each phase is as follows,

Phase 1: Establishment of a ministerial intranet system with links to provincial offices and the National University of Laos (NUOL),

Phase 2: Incorporation of ICT content into the secondary and tertiary curriculum,

Phase 3: Promotion of distance learning and e-learning through ICT.

Phase 1. National Research and Education Network

MOE has a ministerial intranet with some 40 computers and the LANIC ICT centre at STEA provides Internet connectivity as will be described in more detail in a subsequent section. NUOL is connected to STEA via a wireless link funded by Sida.

NOUL is, also with funding from Sida, in the process of establishing an intranet covering all campuses in the Vientiane area. This is an embryo of a Lao National Research and Education Network connecting also to the regional Souphanouvong and Champassack University Colleges.

Discussions are in progress regarding how to be best connecting the NUOL network to the global academic network, via THAISARN in Thailand, STEnet in Vietnam or CERNET in China.

EuropeAid supports the TEIN program and recently launched the TEIN2 project [14] with the objective to create a regional Asian academic backbone. Contacts have been taken to get Laos connected to this project. The response from the European Commission is that Laos has to become an ASEM member before it is possible to join TEIN.

Phase 2. ICT curricula

In Phase 2, MOE requested international assistance in developing an IT curriculum under phase 2 for NUOL. The curriculum development for computer science at FoS (8) has been supported by an Australian university. An evaluation of the FoS curriculum was done the academic year 20022003.

The first batch of students graduating in 2001 included 26 students, the second 40 students and the third, graduating in June 2003, consists of 49 students. The fourth batch of students graduating in 2004 currently includes 51 students. The number of students entering studies in Natural Sciences in 2002 at FOS is 140, including math&CS(50), Phy, Biol and chem. Since there seems to be no alumni organization, there is no complete data about where the graduated students are now employed but according to the teachers we asked, banks and various private organizations seem to be the main employers.

The FoE&A is offering, supported by JICA, a two year bridging program, for those holding a Bachelor in Electronics, leading to a bachelor in Information Technology (11). The first students from this program are available in December 2004.

Souphanouvong and Champassack University Colleges offer so far no ICT training; There are ambitions to do so eventually, At Souphanouvong University College, an ICT training centre has been prepared and a donation of 40 computers from Thailand is expected. There is also need for a broadband connection to NUOL

We have not yet been able to get information about the progress of the process to formulate curricula for introduction of ICT on the primary and secondary education levels.

For additional analytical, business and investment opportunities information,
please contact Global Investment & Business Center, USA
at (703) 370-8082. Fax: (703) 370-8083. E-mail: ibpusa3@gmail.com
Global Business and Investment Info Databank - www.ibpus.com

Phase 3. eLearning and distance education

Phase 3 is not yet started, although there are discussions about project plans.

PUBLIC ADMINISTRATION

ORGANISATION

Laos has about 6 million citizens. The country is administratively organised in provinces (18), districts (142) and villages (10868).

Nr	Province	Districts	Villages
Vientiane			
1	Prefecture	9	496
2	Phongsaly	7	607
3	Luang Namtha	5	394
4	Oudomxay	7	689
5	Bokeo	6	371
6	Luang Phrabang	11	948
7	Huaphanh	8	842
8	Xayabury	10	527
9	Xiengkhuang	7	533
10	Vientiane Province	12	585
11	Borikhamxay	6	320
12	Khammouane	9	804
13	Savannakhet	15	1543
14	Saravane	8	724
15	Sekong	4	273
16	Champassac	10	916
17	Attapeu	5	210
18	Xaysomboum	3	86
Total number of districts		142	10868

Central government

Some of the major parts of the government directly involved in ICT development issues include:

-STEA, the Science, Technology and Environment Agency under the Prime Ministers office, having a coordinating role across all ministries and sectors in assisting the government in research and service on science, technology and the environment at a macro level, including expanding the policies and programs of the government and the party into plans, projects, regulations and laws.

-Ministry of Education (MOE), Department of General Education, responsible for primary and second education, Department of Higher Technical and Vocational Education (HTVED), responsible for all tertiary level education, and Department of Teacher Training (DTT), responsible for 10 teacher training colleges (TTCs) and 19 network teacher upgrading centres throughout the country.

-Ministry of Communication, Transport, Posts and Construction (MCTPC), Department of posts and telecommunications (DPT), responsible for regulatory issues in the telecommunications area and representing the public ownership of Enterprise Telecom Lao (ETL) and the Lao Telecom Company (LTC)

-Ministry of Information and Culture (MIC) www.mic.gov.la, responsible for licensing of Radio and TV broadcasting

-Ministry of Defence, responsible for the rural parts of the telecommunications infrastructure and government partner in Lao Asia Telecom Co. Ltd. (LAT).

Provincial line organization

The provincial government is a mirror of the central government with a cabinet, a governor, a provincial office of STEA (PSTEO), and departments representing the different ministries.

District line organisation

Like the provincial government mirrors the central government, the district government mirrors the provincial government.

Village organisation

Since 1975 villages are governed by an administrative committee headed by a village president (*pathan ban*) and several other persons with responsibilities for specific areas, such as economic and population records, self-defence militia, agriculture, women's affairs, and youth affairs. All members are elected by popular vote.

Each individual villager keeps a book with health records and each family keeps a book listing family members and important family events. New villagers are reported to the district and the district reports changes directly to the central government.

EGOVERNMENT EXAMPLES

In this section, we will describe some public administration tasks that we consider as good candidates for pilot development of eGovernment applications. We believe that eGovernment applications should be given a high priority when discussing how to best scale-up the development support to Laos. They can be selected to fit the existing focus of the Sida support, to address basic needs and to involve a broad spectrum of users. They can thus have a substantial impact and are excellent driving applications for user-driven and user-participatory system development.

We have selected the Environment Impact Assessment process, Awareness Raising activities and Hospital Waste Management as the main pilot applications. They are already a focus of the current Sida support, central in the environment area and it is natural to extend them to schools due to the awareness-raising mission of the environment authorities. Connecting schools not only serves the students, but also the public since the school computer resources can be used as telecentres during off-hours. We also included hospitals because there are many environment issues related to hospitals, such as hospital sanitation and waste management, but also because

According to the regional administrations in Luang Prabang and Oudomxay, there are continuously about 10 EIA-cases in progress. The average case handling duration is about a month.

Environment Awareness Raising Activities

Another important task of the public administration in the environment area is the dissemination of information to citizens and organisations about regulations, law and the PSTEO mandate. This task is approached in all possible ways, an important one being lectures in all sorts of schools.

EDUCATION AND POVERTY REDUCTION

We have already stated that the main weakness of Laos is the lack of education on all levels. Supporting education supports the Sida environment focus on awareness raising and far beyond. It will have a large impact on the possibilities of the rural population to find their livelihoods. Making computers connected to the Internet and learning opportunities available for students, teachers, rural entrepreneurs and all citizens is a very strategic investment. Teacher training, development of e-learning applications, applications supporting rural entrepreneurs and other applications demonstrating good practices would be an extension.

Schools as access points and learning centres for entrepreneurs

At least four secondary schools in Laos have computer laboratories serving students and teachers during school hours and used as a telecentres for the general public off-hours. The telecentre activity provides income enough to sustain centres. These four laboratories are located in Vientiane municipality, Phon Mi village in the Vientiane province, Souvannakhet and Pakse in Champassack province. The laboratories have been donated by SchoolsOnline and Jhai Foundation [18]. Jhai has recently received funding from the World Bank for another 10 schools in partnership with MOE and Worldlink.

Phon Mi school Viengkham district, Vientiane Province

Phon Mi is located in the Viengkham district, Vientiane Province, some 70 km north of Vientiane city. The secondary school hosts the Internet Learning Centre established by Jhai Foundation in 2001. The ILC consists of 10 desktop computers connected to the Internet and is managed by an association of the teachers of the school. Phon Mi also hosts the provincial hospital of the Vientiane province. The hospital sends its staff to courses organised by the ILC. Such courses provide enough income to make the ILC sustainable.

Phouxay Secondary school in Xay district, Oudomxay Province

Phouxay Secondary school in Xay is the only secondary school in the Oudomxay province, thus serving 7 districts and 689 villages.

The school year 2003-2004, the school had 2077 students and 72 teachers. Every year, six or seven teachers get an update of their training, including discipline-oriented matter, English language and the use of computers and the Internet. A course in the use of computer has been developed.

The school has prepared space for a computer laboratory and sent a request to the Ministry of Education to get computers and Internet connections but has not yet received a response.

HEALTHCARE

Hospital sanitation and waste management

Improvement of waste management, especially hospital waste, is identified as a priority in the UN Environment Programme report on the State of the Environment in Lao PDR [16]. Ongoing activities involve the Ministry of Public Health, the National Institute for Hygiene and Epidemiology, MCTPC and Vientiane Municipality. There are some but incomplete regulations in terms of a Solid Waste Management Law and guidelines for hospital waste management while waste management procedures and supervision need improvement.

Patient records

There seems to be no patient records at Lao hospitals organised in a way that facilitates retrieval of patient histories, disease statistics, etc. When a person arrives to the hospital they register and are recorded in a book with name and address. A diary about treatments is kept a few months but it is hard to retrieve data about a particular patient or disease from these diaries.

The personal health record is rather kept by the patient her/himself. This record can get lost and serves little purpose in emergency situations when the patient may be unconscious.

Department of public health is developing an inventory data base for administration purposes (including patient records).

Telemedicine

Provincial and district hospitals often lack resources for more complex operations and treatments. Doctors at these hospitals also have less experience than in the central hospitals in Vientiane. Better communication links, voice, video and Internet contact, would improve the situation at the rural hospitals immensely with relatively small means.

Oudomxay Provincial Hospital

At our visit at the Oudomxay provincial hospital in Xay, the director, Dr. Thongphet Vongpachit, presented his wish list; i) computers for inventory, drug distribution and patient records, and ii) communication with the department of public health, district hospitals and between doctors.

Especially the doctors need to exchange information, advice from experts, information about new diseases and treatment methods, etc. The director had participated in a seminar on telemedicine.

Currently, there is phone and fax and two old computers, mainly used for office work although only two administrative staff members know how to use them, and no internet connection.

The hospital serves 6 district hospitals. It has 22 medical doctors, out of which 5 are constantly on leave for upgrading their education

During the fiscal year 2003-2004, the hospital treated 14100 province citizens, 617 from other provinces, 28 foreigners and 3457 patients were hospitalised. Urgent operations are done locally, mainly inner organs in the stomach area. More complex operations are sent to Vientiane due to lack of equipment and/or experienced doctors.

Vientiane Province

Lao-Luxembourg Provincial Hospital, Phon Mi

Following a request made by the Lao Ministry of Health in 1996, the Lao-Luxembourg health care project was formulated and began its operations in 1997. This project involves creating a medical referal chain serving the 300,000 inhabitants of the Vientiane province. In this project, a new provincial hospital was constructed in Phon Mi 70km north of the capital. It is designed to be the national reference hospital at this level. The referal chain has been ensured by the renovation and equipment of a district hospital (Thourakom) and the construction of a health centre (Keodom) in 1998. The Lao-Luxembourg hospital serves 6 district hospitals in the province.

The hospital has an IT-manager supporting two LANs, one with seven computers for special projects involving database development and training in cooperation with the public health department of the provincial administration in Phon Hong and one with 15 computers for general use at the hospital. There is a 56kbit/s Internet connection to the Lanexang ISP.

Phon Hong, District hospital

The Phon Hong district hospital was established in 1998 funded by Thailand. It has 70 staff members, out of which 10 are medical doctors. The hospital also run a Drug store established with support from Jhai foundation, including a computerised drug inventory system facilitating drug distribution and control. The hospital has two other computers for office applications.

TRANSFORMATION FROM MANUAL TO DIGITAL SYSTEMS

TRANSFORMATION FROM MANUAL TO DIGITAL SYSTEMS

Situation

The level of computerization of government tasks is very low. Computers are mostly used for basic applications such as MS Office and basic office automation, and rarely for efficient handling of core tasks with databases or advanced applications. Except for GIS and telecom operator network management, we have not found any existing, advanced ICT applications.

Few applications – if any – are utilizing the national network; it is used only for basic Internet use (email, web, usually reserved for administration and/or heads of office).

Obvious areas for impact on organizational efficiency include applications such as financial management, billing systems, barcode reading, immigration database and other databases for all sorts of government tasks.

Readiness

Expectations are great on what ICT systems can bring among the Lao public servants we have met with. Due to the hitherto limited exposure to advanced ICT systems and applications, there is a very vague idea of what ICT systems really can bring. For this reason, we must conclude that readiness for transformation into digital systems is very low. We envisage that – for whatever transformation project to undertake - support is needed for analysis of processes, procedures and needs as well as for conceptualisation, specification and production. Support will also be needed on a user level as well as on technical maintenance level.

For additional analytical, business and investment opportunities information, please contact Global Investment & Business Center, USA at (703) 370-8082. Fax: (703) 370-8083. E-mail: ibpusa3@gmail.com Global Business and Investment Info Databank - www.ibpus.com

Priorities

Priorities should be to continue to build upon the few initiatives that have already emerged, and to provide additional support to increase the readiness. This support would include an increase of competences regarding handling and use of basic local area networks (LAN), to enable users to share files and work efficient in groups. There is no reason not to start analysing processes and procedures at this stage. We further propose not to wait for the Lao script to be distributed prior to engage in application development processes. These processes take time on an early analytic/feasibility stage, and if actual application would start - with the right design, languages can be altered. Furthermore, quite a lot can be done in terms of process efficiency and optimisation without extra infrastructure, or with very little extra infrastructure.

CAPACITIES IN CENTRAL AND LOCAL GOVERNMENT, STATE CONTROLLED ACTIVITIES AND RESEARCH BODIES

Generic findings

English skills are generally very weak. The problem is boosted in relation to computer usage by fact of not yet existing standardized Lao font,

Very little government produced and published content can be found online, both in the Lao language and in English,

Operational routines and office practices/structures are generally not clearly formulized or enforced,

Routines could be optimized – sometimes significantly – even without computers.

Ability to use and apply ICT in government

Very low levels of computerization of core tasks,

Low levels of computerization of office administration,

Plans exists for national digital data collection, dissemination and information sharing exists in many areas (generally not detailed), for example within STEA, (& SEM), NUOL, NAFRI and The World Conservation Union (IUCN),

Poor conception of operational impact and usage of ICT tools and applications, due to limited prior ICT exposure.

Ability to design and maintain ICT systems and networks in government

General office automation and plain efficiency mechanisms (file sharing, LAN usage, Internet connectivity, printing and backup functionalities) are limited, non-existent or poorly implemented. Reasons are sometimes managerial, sometimes fails on implementation levels – which in those cases again should make it a managerial issue.

Coordination and maintenance levels of computers and LANs are low.

STEA network (LAN) is not coordinated; built up around project "islands" that does not communicate, rather than with a holistic, organizational picture.

STEA (WWW.STEA.GOV.LA) / PSTEO

AMBITIONS, STRATEGY

STEA's present mandate comes from the Prime Minister's Decree 68, dated 21 May 1999. This reshaped STEA into its present structure and formalized its core function as being to assist the government in research and service on science, technology and the environment at a macro level. This includes expanding the policies and programs of the government and the party into plans, projects, regulations and laws, and it required STEA, in addition to producing policies and research results itself, to take a major coordinating role across all ministries and sectors.

The most important achievement so far has been to prepare the Environment Protection Law passed 1999. The major challenge for the future is to ensure and demonstrate how its work will contribute to the main government policy of eradicating poverty by the year 2020.

CABINET

The task of the Cabinet is to coordinate and facilitate the implementation of STEA's activities across all departments, institutes, centres and provincial offices and to establish work plans and budgets for the whole of STEA based on plans provided by each part. Its mandate also includes managing and monitoring projects throughout STEA.

There are six main functions in the cabinet. It provides a service for the Minister and Presidency such as briefing, arranging travel and logistics and helping with speech notes. It services STEA with building and equipment maintenance. It provides a secretariat which handles correspondence and records, and keeps copies of agreements and conventions. A planning and budgeting group coordinates internal plans and provides macro level input to the Central Planning Committee, the National Poverty Eradication Plan, the UN Development Assistance Framework, and to those facilitating meeting the Millennium Development Goals. A personnel section tracks staff records and training needs. And a cooperation division provides the window for interaction with other ministries and agencies within Lao PDR and foreign organizations.

Lao National Internet Committee (LANIC)

Please see chapter 2.4.3.2.

DEPARTMENT OF SCIENCE AND TECHNOLOGY

The role of the Department of Science and Technology is to be the focal point for science and technology research nationwide, particularly to develop and coordinate strategies and activities that will further the Government's key directives. It is considered to be a clear link between progress in science and technology and achieving national development goals relating to poverty reduction, and the task of this department to manage research to achieve those development goals

To achieve its objectives the department works with a wide range of organizations and sectors. Internally it works with the National University of Laos, and the Ministries of Agriculture and Forestry, Health, Education, and Industry and Handicrafts amongst others, and with the private sector. Externally it works closely with other ASEAN nations and the wider international community.

ICT Project Cooperation

Contacts: Somlouay Kittionavong, Keonakhone Saysuliane

The section is responsible for development projects in the ICT area. We consider these projects important to consider when discussing scaling up support for the ICT development in Laos.

National ICT policy process

The section of ICT projects coordinates the work to produce the Lao National ICT policy described in chapter 2.2.2.1. It will be presented at a workshop in Vientiane 17-18 August 2004 indicating the start of the final national referendum and is expected to become publicly available before the end of 2004.

The policy will address visions and strategies, roles and responsibilities, infrastructure and applications, R&D and standardisation, resource allocation, etc. On the application side, the ICT policy is expected to address e-government, e-tourism, banking, social networks, etc. The policy will also address the legal framework in the ICT area. There is an upcoming decree on an e-commerce.

Standardized Lao font

By the end of 2005 STEA will provide user-friendly fonts for the Lao script (funded by UNDP). STEA will outsource some of the work, including a plan for distribution and will contact Microsoft about licensing issues and font support when the font is available.

STEA also supports the open source community, e.g. via the laonux project.

eGovernment

The level of ambition regarding eGovernment is expected to be decided by the government when deciding on the ICT Policy. There is some funding for eGovernment activities with support from Korea, but this is a good area for Sida to consider if scaling up the support for the ICT development in Laos.

Rural access planning

STEA supports several initiatives for rural access, including the projects conducted by Jhai Foundation, while stressing sustainability issues.

DEPARTMENT OF ENVIRONMENT

The task of the Department of the Environment is to be the focal point on behalf of STEA in relation to environmental management for the whole country. Its overarching role is to translate general party and government directives into strategies, policies, regulations, programs and projects while coordinating with other sectors and ministries, and foreign organizations. It also has responsibilities in relation to environmental impact assessments, education, and a range of other activities. Examples of projects are the Sida supported SEM project and a number of projects funded by UNDP on Greenhouse gas and Biodiversity funded by the Global environmental fund.

SEM

Contact: Dr. Viengsavanh Douangsavanah

A major area of activity at STEA is the SEM program (Strengthening Environmental Management), an extensive management training program for senior staff. In order to emphasise the need for decentralization and grass roots input to national planning, three rural provinces were selected as pilots in the program: Xiengkhouang, Oudomxay and Champasack. While the SEM program started in the Department of Environment and Environment Research Institute, it has been agreed to expand the program to all senior managers in STEA during the first year, 2002. Projects in the SEM program include:

- Training of senior staff at STEA and Ministries
- Development of curriculum for teacher training in cooperation with MOE/DTT,
- Development of EIA procedures for specific areas, such as highways and hydroelectric power plants
- Inventory of chemicals posing a threat to the environment and development of an action plan (Niels Busch),
- Study of the Quality of Air in Vientiane
- Establishment an environment data base with statistics.

ICT in the SEM project

The staff of the SEM project complained about the low availability of the project Intranet and lack of procedures for data exchange and archiving. There was also a wish to establish a website for the project. The intranet consists of a LAN with computers for each staff member and a file/print server as firewall and NAT gateway to a dial up connection the Laotel (LTC).

After talking to the project, members, both in Vientiane and in Oudomxay, and the project management, we have identified the problem to be lack of ICT expertise in the project and arrived to the following recommendations. We consider them obvious and straightforward to implement.

Employ a qualified and experienced IT-manager to be responsible for systems administration, ICT work procedures, data archiving and backup, and web maintenance and application development exclusively for the SEM project. As a temporary measure, cooperation can be sought with NUOL and NAFRI to tap into the competence and experience of the Sida-provided ICT experts stationed there.

Make an agreement with the LANIC Network Operations Centre next door about connecting the gateway computer to the LANIC network at STEA instead of Laotel. This will not only give the project direct access to system administrators but also tap into the development of the national network for public administration as well as Internet access.

DEPARTMENT OF IP, STANDARDIZATION & METROLOGY

The Department of Intellectual Property, Standardization and Metrology is responsible to advise the government on issues about intellectual property registration including trade marks, patents, utility models (petty patents) and industrial designs, and about product quality, standards and measurement, including helping prepare suitable regulations. It manages standardization of quality of products (both Lao-produced and imported) and certifies equipment for measuring weights, volumes etc...

Technology transfer is a major focus of the department's activities. It works particularly closely with ASEAN's Working Group on Intellectual Property Cooperation, and it's Consultative Committee on Standardization and Quality. Also on the international scene the department is working to establish its credentials in intellectual property and standards to become a member of the World Trade Organization, and it is establishing effective networks with WIPONET, the World Intellectual Property Organization. Within Lao PDR a lot of effort has gone into education about these activities including establishing a national committee for managing standards and running training seminars in seven provincial centres.

SCIENCE RESEARCH INSTITUTE

The Science Research Institute is organized into four centres: biotechnology and genetic engineering; value-added products from agriculture and forestry; biological genetic resources; and science development. Its mandate is to undertake research and foster the development of science throughout Lao PDR, including technology transfer and human resource development, in keeping with the country's development goals

There are two main areas of science that the institute aims to use to contribute to national growth. One is through developing value-added techniques for processing of Lao natural products, thereby encouraging new local industries: much of this is aimed to make better use of forest products for rural people. The other is through genetic classification of the rich and diverse natural flora and fauna of Lao PDR, so improving ecotourism.

TECHNOLOGY RESEARCH INSTITUTE

The mandate of the Technology Research Institute is to conduct research and development, contributing particularly to local and regional development, and to disseminate its findings for the benefit of the country. It is organized around five areas of activity: renewable energy technology, mechanical engineering, new materials technology, and technology transfer and technology information. Its work has the potential to lead to significant improvements in poverty reduction in environmentally friendly ways, with a special focus on remote rural needs.

The institute has been especially active in developing renewable energy technologies, and on this it has had support from the mechanical engineering division with construction of prototypes. The task is to find ways to provide an economic electricity supply to areas remote from the main electricity grids. This will create opportunities for a wide range of new economic activities in poor rural areas and contribute significantly to improved health.

Both local and foreign energy technologies, including solar powered battery charging stations, solar powered pumps, biogas digesters, and clean coal stoves have been adapted in a large number of completed projects. While other people have done much work on these technologies in other places, there is a real challenge to make these systems economically attractive on a single-household or small village scale in rural areas of Lao PDR with their poverty and low population densities. Other technologies being investigated include wind energy pumps, micro- and picot-scale hydroelectric power units, and gasification, i.e. biomass generators that use waste products such as rice husks and other solid fuels.

ENVIRONMENT RESEARCH INSTITUTE

The research program of the Environmental Research Institute is intended to lead to long term protection and development of the nation's natural resources, and thereby contribute to sustainable development and a higher quality of life for the Lao people.

The institute has four centres and one division, and has several main functions:

-Conduct research on sustainable use of natural resources (specifically water and biological resources), on implementation of environmental policy and regulations and on the technology of pollution prevention and control.

-Undertake environmental quality monitoring at the national level as well as being the third-party monitoring body.

-Compile environmental data, formulating the State of Environment Report of Lao PDR and publishing environmental indicators.

-Build capacity of Lao staff in the environmental field through short-term courses.

Major research topics include impacts of climate change on Lao water resources and biodiversity, and researching effects of air pollution and acid rain. The project portfolio includes:

-Impact of old batteries on the environment

-Impact of atmospheric pollution from the Asia Brown Cloud phenomenon and acid deposition in cooperation with concerned local (National Agriculture and Forestry Research Institute, National University and the Economic Research Institute) and international institutions.

-Waste management of key cities such as Vientiane municipality, Luang Prabang, Savannakhet and Pakse, particularly the potential for recycling plastic wastes.

-Waste water treatment, test of catalysts for enhanced biological treatment, in collaboration with Chinese, Vietnamese, Thai and other relevant international organizations.

PSTEO

PSTEO is the Provincial Science, Technology and Environment Organisation. It is part of the provincial governmental line organisation of representing STEA. As such, it is responsible for design and enforcement of regulations for the province, public awareness raising activities and collecting complaints from the public, front desk handling of EIA applications, and project management.

Provincial ICT centres

The LANIC ICT centre at STEA is working on connecting the provincial administrations to the public administration network. Three provinces are already connected, including Luang Prabang, where a provincial ICT centre has been established, but not yet Oudomxay. For the connections, STEA have access to a fibre pair to each province from ETL. This fibre pair is used to connect modems providing 128 kbit/s links. Our proposal to Sida is to support the establishment of four Gigabit Ethernet links over these fibres.

Oudomxai

In the Oudomxay province, there were (June 2004) eleven ongoing Environment Impact Assessment cases. In addition to the normal activities, PSTEO in Oudomxay is also involved in:

-Operation of an IT training centre with four computers in which about 300 people has been trained the last 18 months,

-Adapting learning material from STEA and giving lectures on environment issues in the Phouxay secondary school,

-The SEM project.

Challenges according to PSTEO in Oudomxay

The main challenges mentioned are:

-Lack of database system with statistic information forestry, weather, climate, slash and burn activities (svedjebruk) to calculate carbon oxide emissions,

-Difficult to exchange information between departments and psteo, psteo and district as well as between PSTEO and STEA,

-Lack of coordination on organisation level, which department is in charge of what.

Luang Prabang

The ICT centre in Luang Prabang has a computer laboratory with 10 computers, most of them connected to the 128 kbit/s link to the LANIC ICT centre in Vientiane. The Luang Prabang ICT Centre are offering short training courses, like in Vientiane.

PADETC

According to its website, PADETC is a training centre promoting participatory processes for sustainable development. The objective is to improve the livelihood opportunities of communities balancing between economic, social and environmental considerations. It is said to have the status of a national Lao NGO but seems to have close ties to the government. PADETC has support for village-oriented ICT awareness activities from IDRC.

TELECOM AND INTERNET SECTOR DEVELOPMENT

Telephones - main lines in use: 93,241
Telephones - mobile cellular: 1,121,431
Internet users: 7,360
Internet hosts: 1,015
Radio broadcast stations: AM 7, FM 13, shortwave 2 (2006)
Television broadcast stations: 7; note - including one station relaying Vietnam Television from Hanoi
Internet country code: .la

Telephone Service in Lao PDR

Both fixed phone and mobile phone are available nationwide with different providers. The mobile phone systems are monthly and a pre-paid SIM cards. SIM cards are easily available in most of the cities. The Government has been able to acquire the interest of many foreign investors in this sector.

Foreign joint venture investment in this sector has played an important role since 1993-94 and now with more than 5 players in the telecommunication sector: some offers mobile service, some offer fixed telephone and mobile service, some offer fix telephone, mobile with total capacity lines and total subscriber lines in used: fix lines with 147,137 capacity lines and 93,241 using lines, mobile with 1,637,854 capacity lines and 121,6431 using lines, CDMA/WLL with 50,000 capacity lines and 22,040 using lines; more than one million mobile users from just 300,000 a few years ago, ADSL is available in major cities. The real band with of ADSL is still questionable10. 3G service has just recently rolled out in Vientiane.

Lao Telecom invested more than US$ 25 million to bring 3G mobile phone network in to Laos, initially it will allow only Vientiane residents to use it before other provinces. By 2009 it will expand to three provinces such as Savannakhet, Luang Prabang and Champassack provinces.

The 1993 'Resolution of the Politburo of the Lao People's Revolutionary Party (LPRP) to Increase Party Leadership in and State Control of the Mass Media in the New Era' was drawn up before the introduction of IT and is therefore focused solely on the conventional media. Among other things, this document exhorts the Lao mass media sector to: enhance the quality of the existing media so that it is more varied and interesting to the public while still firmly reflecting each aspect of the path, ideology and policies of the Party and state; to invest in, upgrade and build up equipment and materials within the sector; to strengthen the mechanism for firm Party leadership and state control of the mass media; and to build the capacity of media employees.

Use of the Internet was officially approved in 1997 by Decree 166/PM of the Prime Minister regarding the Organisation of a Network and Implementation, Use and Control of the Internet System, which sets out general guidelines for the official launch of the Internet in Laos. Decree 166/PM was accompanied in the same year by three other important regulations.

Provisions 2075/CTCP of the Ministry of Communications, Transport, Post and Construction regarding the Organisation of the Internet Network to Conduct the Information and Data Services Business and for the Use of the Internet System (1997), focus on the rights and duties of Internet Service Providers (ISPs) and procedures for licensing them.

Drawn up for the guidance of the Ministry of Information and Culture, the Special Provisions (416/IC) for Control of the Content and the Information and Data Obtained via the Internet System (1997) state that the content of material on the Internet must be 'beneficial to society'...'with no impact upon political issues, is not in conflict with the laws and regulations of the Lao PDR and is not contrary to the fine Lao national culture, customs and traditions', and go on to set out procedures for requesting approval for the content of information and data available on the Internet and for punishment of violations. Finally, Provisions 1044/STENO of the Science, Technology and Environment Agency (STEA) regarding the Control of the Information System Used in the Internet System focus on the capacity of computer hardware and require registration of such hardware with the STEA.

However, in view of the potential overlap between these three agencies, Regulation 141/PMO of 2000 on the Implementation, Service and Usage of the Internet System in the Lao PDR established the Lao National Internet Committee (LANIC) under the Prime Minister's Office, bringing the organisation and management of Internet development in Laos under its control.

Since that time Telecommunication Law 02/NA of 2001 has also been passed to define, among other things, the principles and the regulation of organisations and telecommunications activities, the management and broadcasting of radio and television frequencies, the management and use of satellite position and orbit and the country code top level domain name of Laos, and the management of telecommunication and Internet services nationally and internationally with the aim of providing universal, good quality, accurate, clear, convenient, fast, safe and fair telecommunication services to society which will contribute to national defence and development and international co-operation. in relation to establishment of networks, use of equipment and control of the communications system and Internet technicians; the role of the Ministry of Information and Culture in approving and controlling the content of information and data exchanged on the Internet; the role of the Science, Technology and Environment Agency (STEA) of the Prime Minister's Office in researching, controlling and approving the equipment and computer networks connected to the Internet system and all related scientific, technological and environmental information and data; and the role of the Ministry of the Interior (since renamed the Ministry for Public Security) in the enforcement of regulations and techniques of control of the Internet network with a view to ensuring national peace and public order. The decree also sets out the rights and obligations of Internet users, policies towards those that use the Internet productively and measures to be taken against offenders.

Decree 166/PM was accompanied in the same year by three other important regulations. Provisions 2075/CTCP of the Ministry of Communications, Transport, Post and Construction regarding the Organisation of the Internet Network to Conduct the Information and Data Services Business and for the Use of the Internet System (1997), focus on the rights and duties of Internet Service Providers (ISPs) and procedures for licencing them. Drawn up for the guidance of the Ministry of Information and Culture, the Special Provisions (416/IC) for Control of the Content and the Information and Data Obtained via the Internet System (1997) state that the content of material on the Internet must be 'beneficial to society'...'with no impact upon political issues, is not in conflict with the laws and regulations of the Lao PDR and is not contrary to the fine Lao national culture, customs and traditions', and go on to set out procedures for requesting approval for the content of information and data available on the Internet and for punishment of violations.

Finally, Provisions 1044/STENO of the Science, Technology and Environment Agency (STEA) regarding the Control of the Information System Used in the Internet System focus on the capacity of computer hardware and require registration of such hardware with the STEA.

In mid-1994 the Lao telecommunications system was rudimentary, with a telephone system that serves primarily government offices and broadcast facilities in only a few large towns. In 1986 there were approximately 8,000 telephones for the entire country, or fewer than 2 telephones per 1,000 people. There reportedly was a substantial expansion of telephone lines in Vientiane beginning in 1989, but no updated figures were available.

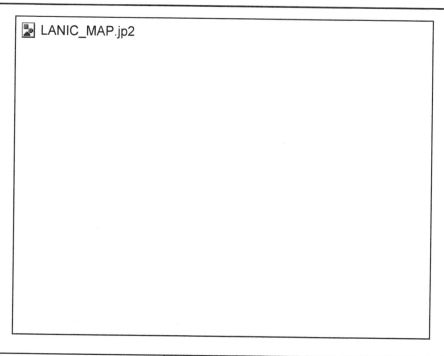

LANIC_MAP.jp2

Some Challenges	Some Steps Taken
Content •English isn't the 1st official language •No. of digital content in Lao language	*Localization - The National Standard Font, "Phetsarath OT". *Working with Google.
Penetration Rate - Infrastructure	*The expansions of Infrastructure *National Plan *National Internet Center 7th/09/2010
Law, Regulation, Legal Framework	*Internet Management Decree 21st/03/2014. *The amendment of the Telecommunications Act 21st/12/2011. *Drafting of Cybercrime Law.
Know how, Awareness, Human Resources	Cooperation, Training, Information Sharing
International Integration	*The establishment of LaoCERT 9th/02/2014. *Standardization *Working with ITU
Budget and Financial resources	Prioritize, Cooperation, Assistance

One powerful amplitude modulation (AM) station is located in Vientiane; the other nine AM stations are low-powered transmitters scattered in other cities. Seven shortwave stations broadcasting in six tribal languages reach remote areas, including one that broadcasts in Cambodian, French, Thai, and Vietnamese to neighboring countries in Southeast Asia. The capital also has two lower-power television transmitters and one frequency modulation (FM) station. The number of radios increased from 350,000 in 1980 to 520,000 in 1990.

The first domestic television service was established in 1983, and the second, in 1988, broadcasting from Savannakhét. Southern Laos receives transmissions from Thailand, and all of Laos receives satellite-relayed transmissions from a ground satellite station linked to Intersputnik from the former Soviet Union. There were about 31,000 television sets in 1990.

International communications improved greatly with the installation in 1990 of a new satellite ground station. In 1991 agreements were concluded with China and France to relay their broadcasts to Laos by satellite.

The Telecommunications Act No. 02/NA of 10 April 2001 provided the legal framework for telecommunication services. The representative of Lao PDR noted that the 2001 Telecommunication Act had been revised and the Telecommunications Law No. 09/NA was adopted in December 2011. The Ministry of Post, Telecommunication and Communication provided regulatory oversight for this sector. Domestic and international fixed line telephone services were no longer a monopoly for the Lao Telecommunications Company, a joint venture with 49 per cent foreign ownership.

Five companies provided mobile telephony services, and there were no specific limitations on operators of enhanced and value-added services, including internet services. On the 2011 Telecommunications Law, a Member noted that the requirement for natural and legal persons to register an internet domain with the competent Lao authority (Article 12), would effectively cut-off Lao PDR from the internet market place. In response, the representative of Lao PDR explained that foreign service providers that had assigned internet numbers and domain names in other countries were not required to register with Lao PDR's Ministry of Post and Telecommunications and Communications, only Laotian domain names needed to be registered.

TELECOMMUNICATION LAW[2]

PART I GENERAL PROVISION

Article 1. Function of the Telecommunications Act

The Telecommunication Act defines the principles, the regulations on the organization and the telecommunication activities, the management of the radio frequency for the radio communication, the radio broadcasting of sound and television and other radio frequencies; the administration of the numbering, the infrastructure; the management and the use of the Satellite orbital slot, the county code top level domain name of the Lao People's Democratic Republic; the management of tile Telecommunication and Internet services within the country and with foreign countries aiding at providing a universal, qualitative, accurate, clear, convenient, fast, safe and fair telecommunication services to the society which will be contributed to the national defense arid development and the international cooperation.

Article 2. Terms and Definition

"telecommunication" means the ad 0f emission, transmission or reception, through the agency of electromagnetism, of any sounds, signs, writing, images or intelligence of any nature, by wire, radio, optical or other electromagnetic systems.

"telecommunication resources" means radio frequencies, numbering, satellite orbital position and the telecommunications infrastructure.

[2] No 02/ NA Date 10 April 2001

"numbering" means number, sign or other mark uses for the identification telecommunication networks and facilities in order to connect between the place of transmission amid the place of reception of telecommunication services.

"telecommunication infrastructure" means buildings, structures includes equipment and transmission facilities to support the telecommunication networks such as duct, pole, mast, tower, antenna, optic fiber, cooper wire, any kind of transmission line and so on..

"telecommunication equipment" means machines, copper cables or optical fiber, duct, manhole, pole, mast, tower or other structure or series of equipment used or to be used in connection with the electrical or electromagnetic facilities to establish telecommunications services.

"terminal equipment" means telecommunications equipment used in the offices or in the premises of the users or customers includes wire line or wireless telephone sets,

facsimile machines, computers modems and associated hardware and internal wiring to the customer's offices or premises (property on which the customer has installed the terminal equipment).

"telecommunication network" means a full interconnected and integrated system of telecommunications consisting of various means of wire lines and wireless system of transmission and switching, utilized to provide telecommunication services to the general public;

"Internet" means an interconnected system of various computer communication networks world wide through the telecommunications network to transmit/receive and exchange data and information, and is included in telecommunication.

"country code top level domain name" means the abbreviation letter which the international internet organization assigned to each country for the convenience of communication through the internet.

" radio frequencies " means frequencies or spectrum of naturally propagated electromagnetic waves in the range 3 kilohertz to 300 Gigahertz which are utilized for transmission and reception of telecommunication signals;

"Satellite Position and Orbit" means the position of the .fixe or mobile satellite and its orbit 6pathj in the space.

"radio station" Inea2ls the unit of radio equipment and frequencies licensed by the Ministry of Communications, Transports, Posts and Construction to install for the purpose of exclusive use by an authorized juristic person or organization;

"Interconnection" means the interconnection of the networks of the telecommunication services providers for the purpose of Providing a wide range of services to customers.

"telecommunications service provider" means a person or organization authorized to establish an enterprise to provide telecommunications services under this Act;

"user or customer" means a person or an organization who use the telecommunication services under this Act;

"resale" means the offering to users or customers for profit of telecommunication services obtained from another telecommunication service provider.

Article 3. Management of Telecommunications Resources and Equipment

The State manages the telecommunication resources and the registration of the telecommunication equipment within the country.

Article 4. Policy on the Promotion in Telecommunication

The state encourages the local arid file foreign investors to compete and to cooperate in the investment for tile construction, the development, the expansion of the telecommunication network and services in accordance with the types prescribed by the Government,

Article 5. Fund for the development of Telecommunications r

To develop the telecommunications progressively and modernly, the Government of Lao PDR authorizes the set up of the Telecommunications Development Fend which sources from internal support, foreign countries, international organizations funding and from a share of fees and charges for telecommunications services.

Article 6. International relation and cooperation

The State promotes the international relationship and cooperation under mutual respect for independence, sovereignty and territorial integrity, mutual benefit in the development of information and communication technology infrastructure, the interconnection of the telecommunication networks, the offer of various telecommunication services universally, the management and coordination of the radio frequency and the satellite orbital position within the country and with international in order to give tile modern telecommunication services to tile Citizen.

PART II THE TELECOMMUNICATION SYSTEMS AND THE TYPE OF TELECOMMUNICATION SERVICES IN LAO PDR

Article 7. The Telecommunications System

There are three systems of telecommunications in Lao PDR:

A Public Switch Telecommunications Network system;

A wireless telecommunications system;

A combination of both wire line wireless system.

The telecommunications systems are capable to use in different types of telecommunication services such as telegraphy, telephony, facsimile, mobile telephone, paging, e-mail, internet and so on.

Article 8. Type of Telecommunication Services

-Fixed telephone;-Long distance telephone; -International telephone; -Mobile telephone; -Public telephone; -Facsimile; -Telex -Telegraphy; -Pager; -Radio broadcasting of sound and television; -Trunk mobile; -Electronic mail; -Internet; -VOIP -Leased line/ leased circuit and VSAT;

-telecommunication Infrastructure services; -Others value added services.

PART III REGULATION ON TELECOMMUNICATIONS SERVICES

Article 9. General Regulations

The offer of all the types of telecommunication services Must strictly observed the laws and regulations on telecommunications and other related laws and regulations of the Lao People's Democratic Republic.

Article 10. Fees and Tariffs for Telecommunications Services

fees and tariffs for telecommunications are revenue which soured from telecommunications activities such as the usage fees for satellite orbital position and country code Top Level Domain name, copyright, licensing fee for frequency management, the cost of setting up and telecommunications businesses operation, production, export, import, supply of telecommunications equipment, fees and tariffs of other involved telecommunications business,

Article 11. Setting of Fees and Tariffs for Telecommunications Services

The Ministry of Communication, Transport, Post and Construction in collaboration with the Ministry of Finance and other related party prepare the regulation on the, formulation of tile fees, tariffs, copyrights of the telecommunications to submit to the government for approval.

Article 12. Scope of tine Telecommunications Services

The scopes of telecommunications services in Lao PDR are as follow:

-Domestic telecommunication services

-International telecommunications services The scope of the domestic telecommunication services is to providing of telecommunication services within the country.

The scope of the International telecommunications se-ices is to providing of telecommunication services between Lao People's Democratic Republic and foreign countries in accordance with the agreements or the international conventions that the Government has committed.

PART IV THE BUSINESS OF TELECOMMUNICATION SERVICES

Article 13. Application for thew setting up of an Enterprise of Telecommunication Services

The application for setting up of an Enterprise of Telecommunication Service shall comply with the business Law and the Law on the Promotion of Local Investment and other related laws of the Lao P.D.R.

For the foreign investment it shall comply with the Business Law and the Law on the Promotion and Management of Foreign Investment in Lao PDR.

Article 14. Rights and Duties of the Telecommunications Service Provider

The Telecommunications Service Provider has the rights and duties as follows:

Request for an appropriate consideration and authorization from the Government, the organization the concerned individual for the use of a private or a corporate properties such as location, land, road, drain, building and other facilities in compliance with the laws and regulations.

Propose fees and tariff which meet the socio-economic circumstances of each period to the Ministry of Communications, Transports, Posts and Construction;

To temporarily or permanently suspend services of customer who violate the regulations on telecommunications services such as: -Irregularly clear the due bill for services after reminder; -Connect in parallel one's telephone for another person without authorization or violate other telecommunication regulations;

Develop the telecommunications network, especially the basic telephone to provide service to customers country wide as prescribed by the Ministry of Communications, Transports, `Posts and Construction;

Assure the interconnection and numbering plans with other telecommunication network providers to route the information to the correct destination domestically and internationally;

To provide telecommunications services as authorized;

Assure universal, good quality, accurate, clear, convenient, fast, safe ail fair services to customers;

To produce, export, import, supply and install the standardized telecommunication equipment as requested by users or customers;

To follow the regulations on financial accounting, statistics, reports and obligations as prescribed by the Government;

To be subject to monitoring by the relevant administrations;

Grant privilege to the state organization to provide telecommunication services;

To be prohibited from leasing or transferring of the licenses for the setting up of telecommunications services to a third party;

To be prohibited from using telecommunications to destroy the national stability, peacefulness and the development of the socio-economy or the national culture;

To be prohibited from using telecommunications to cause damage to the dignity of a person or an organization;

'To be prohibited from adju8ting one's radio frequency or using one's telecommunication equipment or network to the radio frequency or telecommunication network of another service providers or users aiming to stop, interfere, attack, destroy, modify, delete, tap, listen, steal, or detect the data and information;

14. Besides the telecommunication service provider, has the rights and duties as prescribed in the laws and regulations on the telecommunication services.

Article 15. Rights and of the Consumer

The customers of thd.l:6lecdlnmunications services have the rights and duties as. follows:

To obtain a good quality, an accurate, a clear, a convenient, a fast, a safe 'and a fair telecommunications services;

To resell of telecommunications services to other users as authorized by the Ministry of Communications, Transports, Posts and Construction;

Propose to the service provider or to the related state administration to solve 'the technical failing and investigate the service charges;

To follow the technical instructions and rules on the usage of telecommunication equipment and other rules as prescribed by the concern authority;

To pay the due bill for the service offer regularly;

To be prohibited from using telecommunications to destroy the national stability, peacefulness, the development of the socio-economy or the national culture; To be prohibited from using telecommunications to cause damage to the dignity of a person or a n organization; To be prohibited from adjusting one's radio frequency or using tcrn7inal equipment or network to the radio frequency or telecommunication network of another service providers or users aiming to interrupt, interfere, attack, destroy, modify, delete, tap, listen, steal, or clearer the data and information;

To be subject to monitoring by he relevant administration;

Besides the telecommunication service provider has the rights and duties as prescribed in the laws and regulations on the telecommunication services.

PART V MANAGEMENT AND INSPECTION OF TELECOMMUNICATIONS

Article 16. Objective of the Management and Inspection

The objective of file management and inspection of Telecommunications is aiming to regularize the use of the national radio frequency, the satellite Position and orbit, the administration of the numbering, the country code top level domain name and the business activity for providing various types of telecommunication services in conformity with the telecon7inunication law and the related laws and regulations of the Lao P.D.R.

Article 17. The Management and Inspection Organizations

The management and inspection organizations of telecommunications , comprise (of

-The Ministry of Communications, Transports, Posts and Construction; -The provincial, municipal and special zone Departments of Communications, Transports, Posts and Construction; -The communications, Transports, Posts and Construction Office of the districts (Muang).

Article 18. Rights and Duties of the Ministry of Communications, Transports, Posts and Construction

The Ministry of Communications, Transports, Posts and Construction has the rights and duties on telecommunications as follow:

Study and define the strategic plays for the development of telecommunications;

Formulaic the policy, the plan, the program, the projects and seeking for source of fund for the development of Telecommunications;

Cooperate with the Ministry of Finance and other related organizations to study and draft the regulation on the set up, the management and the use of the telecommunication development fund for further submit to the Government for approval;

Study, propose or decide the issuance of license for the setting up the extension, the suspension and termination of the Telecommunication business.

Coordinate with the related administration in reservation, management and allocation of the national radio frequency; the administration and the use of the satellite position and orbit, the administration of the country code top level domain name; the management of the service providers and the customers;

Coordinate with the related administrations to study and propose the regulation on the tariff, the property right and other service charges;

Study and define the technical standard; select the technology about the Telecommunication equipment and provide the rules and instruction for the use of those equipment within the country;

Regulation the management of Telecommunications national wide;

Coordinate and cooperate with foreign counties and international organizations to create a favorable condition for the development of telecommunications.

Article 19. Rights and Duties of the Provincial Division and .he Special Zones of Communications, Transports, Posts and Construction

The Divisions of Communications, Transports, Posts and Construction of tl7c Provinces, the Municipality and the Special Zone have the rights and duties on telecommunications as follows:

Follow up, inspect the usage of radio equipment and frequencies ilcluding the use of the Internet within its local area;

To record the statistics of the users and the demand for different types of telecommunications services;

follow up and inspect the business activities of the local telecommunications service providers;

Perform the rights and duties on the telecommunications is assigned by the Ministry of Communications, Transports. Posts and Construction.

Article 20. Rights acrd Duties of the Office of Communication , Transports, Posts and Construction of the district (Muang)

The Offices of Communications, Transports, Posts and Construction of the Districts (Muang) have the rights and duties on the telecommunications as follows:

1. Follow up and inspect of the telecommunications as assigned by the Division of Communications, Transports, Posts and Construction of its respective Provinces, municipality or Special Zone.

Article 21. Content of the Inspection

The key issues of the telecommunications inspection are as follow:

Inspection of tile planning, the surveys, the designs for the construction and tine installation of telecommunications facilities;

Inspection of the safety standard and the environment protection in the construction and installation of telecommunication facilities;

Inspection of the technical standard and technology of the telecommunications facilities and equipment;

Monitoring of the radio frequencies;

Inspection of the Standard of services includes the financial accounting records in the telecommunication business;

Inspection of the implementation of the telecommunication law, the bidding documents, the construction contracts and the installation of telecommunications facilities, the fulfillment of contracts on telecommunication activities which the government has authorized a person or an organization to enter into the agreement inside or outside the country and the contract agreement that the Government has signed with foreign countries.

Article 22. Forms of Inspections

The are three forms of telecommunications inspection as hollows:

Inspection regular;

Inspection with prior notification;

Inspection immediate.

Inspection regular is conducted udder a regular plan and widen limited time.

Inspection with prior notification is conducted out of the plan when it is deemed necessary with prior notification to the inspected person.

Inspection in3mcdiate is directly conducted without prior notification to the inspected person.

In conducting the telecommunication inspections, tile authorities of the inspection's organization shall strictly exercise their duty in accordance with the law and regulations.

PART VI SETTLEMENT OF DISPUTES

ARTICLE 23. ADMINISTRATIVE SETTLEMENT OF DISPUTES

An administrative dispute is any dispute from the fulfillment of the terns and conditions prescribed in the license on the operation of telecommunication business.

An administrative dispute shall be settled in accordance with the rules set forth by the Ministry of Communication, Transports, Posts and Construction.

Article 24. Civil Settlement of disputes

A civil dispute is any dispute arising from the construction, the installation or the service of telecommunications that create civil damage to the users or to the third party .

A civil dispute shall be firstly settled between the party concern. If the result a is unsatisfied the complainant has the right to appeal to floe court.

PART VII REWARD TO CONTRIBUTORS AND MEASURE AGAINST VIOLATORS

ARTICLE 25. REWARD TO CONTRIBUTORS

An investor who has efficiently, progressively, modernly and qualitatively constructed, developed and expanded of telecommunication network, manufactured of telecommunication equipment and provided the telecommunications services includes a person, a national and international organizations who has made an excellent contribution to tare development of telecommunications in Lao P.I:.R shall be admired and rewarded as deemed appropriated.

Article 26. Measure against violators

A person or an organization who has violated any provision of this act shall be educated, fined or penalized depending on the degree of contravention's including the compensation for damages one caused.

Article 27. Education measures

A person or an organization who is slightly contravened any of the provisic5ns of this Act shall be educated such as:

-a service provider did not fix the technical failing of the installation, the reparation or other telecommunications services in time and comply with the technical standards; -the users does not pay for their service charges regularly etc.

Article 28. Fine measures

A person or an organization who is contravened any provisions of this Act shall be fined such as:

-Providing telecommunication services without a license; -Providing telecommunication services beyond the authorized type and area of services; -Leasing or transferring the license to a third party;

The Ministry of Communications, Transports, Posts and Construction in collaboration with the concern administration prepare the draft regulation on the rate of fines and submit to the Government for approval.

Article 29. Penal measures

A person who is violated any of the provisions of this net shall he penalized such as:

Use of telecommunications to destroy the national stabilization, peacefulness, the development of the socio-economy or the national culture;

Use of telecommunications to cause damage to the dignity of a person or organization;

Adjust one's radio frequency or taping one's telecommunication equipment or network to another radio frequency or equipment or network aiming to interrupt , interfere, Invade, destroy, modify, delete, tap, listen, steal or detect the Information and data;

Destroy the public or the e private telecommunication facilities;

Import of telecommunications equipment illegally;

Abusing one's position, authority, offer and receive bribes, falsify of the documents, issue of the telecommunications licenses illegally;

Guilty of delinquencies on telecommunications.

Article 30. Additional punishments prescribed in Article 28 and 29 of this Act, the offender may be punished additional such as:

-Termination of business; -Revoke of license;

-Seizure of equipment used to commit.

PART VIII FINAL PROVISIONS

Article 31. Implementation of the Act

The Government of the Lao 1'DR enforces this Act.

Article 32. Enforcement of the Act ;

This Act shall enter into force in 120 days after the President of the Lao People's Democratic Republic has issued the Presidential Decree for the implementation of the Act. The regulations and decrees previously issued if deem to contravene to this Act shall be abolished.

DIRECT FOREIGN INVESTMENT

The Foreign Investment Law of July 1988 is modeled on legislation that has already been adopted in Vietnam and China. Laos seeks to encourage foreign investment as a means of facilitating economic development as called for by the New Economic Mechanism. The government hopes that foreign investment projects will help to shift the economy from a subsistence to a commodity production basis by improving the management skills of the labor force; introducing advanced technology to the manufacturing sector; fostering economic, scientific, and technological cooperation with other countries; and increasing the production of goods for export.

The Foreign Investment Law allows investors to enter into three types of investment arrangements. The first type of arrangement, contractual or cooperative businesses, entails investment in existing state or private companies, or with Laotian individuals; in this way, the law is more liberal than comparable legislation in either Vietnam or China. The second type of arrangement, joint ventures, requires foreigners to invest a minimum of 30 percent of total capital. In general, terms for either of these arrangements are not to exceed twenty years. The third type of arrangement, private ventures, requires foreigners to invest 30 percent of total capital, up to a maximum of 100 percent. Terms are generally limited to fifteen years. Tax exemptions or reductions for joint ventures and private enterprises are available for two to six years after the first year of profit, depending on the size of the investment, the volume of goods exported as a result of the project, the location of the project, and the sector on which it focuses.

Tax incentives--a reduction of 2 to 5 percent in the profit tax--are also used to encourage foreign investment. In order to qualify for the reduction, a foreign investment project has to meet three of the following criteria: the project will export more than 70 percent of the goods it produces; will obtain domestically more than 70 percent of the raw materials it uses; will use advanced technology; will aim to overcome unfavorable natural or socioeconomic conditions; will contribute to national economic development despite low profit margins; or will be established before 1995. The Foreign Investment Law allows foreign investors to remit profits to the countries of their choice; in addition, it prohibits the nationalization of their capital and property.

Other laws also seek to facilitate foreign investment. In early 1989, Decree 27 established the Foreign Investment Management Committee to centralize foreign investment approval procedures, thus enabling the Foreign Investment Law to be implemented. The Lao Chamber of Commerce was established in January 1990 to assist in attracting new business ventures. Private domestic and foreign investments have been encouraged by the gradual improvement of the legal environment, including the passage of laws regarding property rights (1990), contractual obligation (1990), inheritance (1990), crime (1990), civil procedures (1990), and labor (1991). The 1991 approval of the constitution, which protects the right to private ownership, is also an important factor in encouraging foreign investment. Also, as of late 1993, an arbitration law was being drafted that will provide a legal mechanism for the settlement of disputes. There was an informal arbitration procedure, but the lack of a law or decree made decisions nonbinding.

PROSPECTS FOR GROWTH

By the start of the 1990s, Laos had obtained some impressive results from the implementation of economic reforms under the New Economic Mechanism. The experiment in cooperative farming had ended as an ideological failure, and although rice harvests had reached self-sufficiency levels, they still depend to a large degree on favorable weather conditions. New decrees guarantee farmers the right to long-term use and transfer of property. In response to the encouragement of the manufacturing and services sectors through privatization, investment promotion, and other means, these sectors have slowly begun to supplant agriculture's share of GDP. The private retail sector has blossomed. Removal of restrictions on interregional transit and improvement of foreign relations with Thailand have fueled growth in the transport subsector, simplified trade activities, and are likely to reduce the prices of many goods. The potential for tourism as a foreign exchange earner has brightened as foreign investors join with Laotian companies to provide improved aviation and tourism services. The opening of the Friendship Bridge between Thailand and Laos symbolizes the new relationship with countries outside the former Soviet bloc: trade with and aid from both developed and neighboring countries have increased. Despite an inflationary surge in the late 1980s, the reduction of credit to money-losing state-owned enterprises and a tight monetary policy helped to bring inflation down to more manageable levels in the early 1990s. Tax reform has also worked to slow the increase in the fiscal deficit.

Despite these successes, however, many of the troubles that saddled Laos at the beginning of the 1990s remain. Perhaps the two most crucial constraints continue to be a poorly educated and trained labor force and a limited, poorly maintained transportation network with endemic problems. Many of Laos's most experienced and educated citizens had fled the country in the late 1970s, and the poorly run and underfunded educational system is inadequate to make up for this important loss of managerial and technical skill. Similarly, insufficient investment in operations and maintenance over the years has resulted in a road system poorly equipped to handle the increased traffic that liberalization precipitated. Without a better educated and trained labor force and an improved infrastructure, measures to increase foreign investment and encourage export-oriented production are not likely to yield sustainable economic progress. Even the push to privatize stateowned enterprises and encourage efficient, profit-oriented production depend upon the availability of trained managers to direct production. Thus, the sustainability of reforms implemented by the start of the 1990s depends, at least in part, upon the ability of the government to turn its attention to the long-term infrastructure and human capital requirements of a market-based economy.

PRACTICAL INFORMATION FOR EXPORT AND INVESTMENTS

STARTING BUSINESS IN LAOS

BASIC STEPS

No.	Procedure	Time to Complete	Associated Costs
1	Apply for a Name Reservation Certificate It is required to obtain a Name Reservation Certificate from the Enterprise Registry Office ("ERO") within the Ministry of Industry and Commerce ("MOIC"). All companies are required to obtain a Name Reservation Certificate before applying to the ERO for an Enterprise Registration Certificate. A completed Application for Reservation of Company Name, listing three potential names for the company to be established, and a signed Contract of Incorporation (if there are multiple shareholders) in the format approved by the MOIC must be submitted to the ERO in order to obtain a Name Reservation Certificate.	1 day	LAK 10,000
2	Apply for an Enterprise Registration Certificate and apply for tax registration certificate Founders shall complete the application form for enterprise registration in the MOIC standard application form attaching the following required documents: (i) 3 copies of the Contract of Incorporation, (ii) 3 original copies of the signed Articles of Association in the MOIC standard template, (iii) 3 copies of the resolution of founders of the company, (iv) 3 copies of the Power of Attorney in the MOIC standard template (if another person is assigned to submit the application), (v) 3 copies of ID card/passport of founders or business licenses for entities, (vi) 6 photos size 3cmx4cm of the nominated Managing Director. Once the company obtains the Enterprise Registration Certificate, it shall thereafter register its Articles of Association with the State Assets Management Department (SAMD), Ministry of Finance. For registration the following are required: letter request, the original signed Articles of Association, and copy of ERC. Enterprises operating in the Lao PDR are subject to direct and indirect taxes. Direct taxes are profit tax,	1 week for compamy registration and 2 weeks for tax registration	See procedure details

For additional analytical, business and investment opportunities information, please contact Global Investment & Business Center, USA at (703) 370-8082. Fax: (703) 370-8083. E-mail: ibpusa3@gmail.com
Global Business and Investment Info Databank - www.ibpus.com

No.	Procedure	Time to Complete	Associated Costs
	income tax and fees; and indirect taxes are business turnover tax, value-added tax and use tax. Value added tax replaced the business turnover tax. A Tax Registration Certificate is neither issued nor required to be renewed annually. The fee for the Tax Registration Certificate depends on the annual income of the Company. The fee for a company with an annual business turnover of US $113,000 is LAK 983,018,852. The application fee is LAK 25,000. The company shall complete the application for the Tax Identification Number Certificate and enterprise registration in the standard form attach with the required documents and submitted at the Tax Authority, who will consider the application and issue the Tax Identification Number Certificate. The application for tax certificate can be submitted at the same time as the company registration (at the One-stop shop). Cost details: LAK 10,000 (Incorporation form) + LAK 70,000 (Application form) + LAK 300,000 (Registration service fee) + LAK 25,000 (Registration form for taxes) + LAK 100,000 (Tax certificate)		
3	Apply for an Operating License from relevant Ministry Upon obtaining the Enterprise Registration Certificate, Tax Identification Number Certificate, and enterprise registration number with the Tax Authority, the company shall complete the application form for factory operation with the DICV standard form and required documents. These are submitted at the DICV, which will consider the application and require inspection of the location of the factory before issuing the license.	2-3 weeks	LAK 50,000
* 4	Obtain Approval of Content on the Company Signage and the Company Signage Building Permit The company must obtain content approval and a building permit. For the content approval application, the company must complete the application form in MICT standard form and provide the following: (i) the name of the company in Lao, enterprise code provided under the enterprise registration certificate, office location and contact detail of the company; (ii) the color in red for the letters, and yellow for the background (these colors applied to domestic companies); and (ii) the size shall not exceed 2mx4m. For the building permit, the company must	5 days (simultaneous with previous procedure)	LAK 10,000

For additional analytical, business and investment opportunities information, please contact Global Investment & Business Center, USA at (703) 370-8082. Fax: (703) 370-8083. E-mail: ibpusa3@gmail.com Global Business and Investment Info Databank - www.ibpus.com

No.	Procedure	Time to Complete	Associated Costs
	complete the application form and attach the signage layout indicating the location and size, and copy of the company's licenses.		
5	Carve a company seal The application form for making the company seal is LAK 10,000. The cost for the certificate authorizing the design in LAK 60,000. The carving of a seal in Lao language only is LAK 50,000 (the carving of a seal in Lao and in another language is LAK 53,000). The total time takes around 45 days.	45 days	LAK 120,000 for Lao language and LAK 123,000 for Lao and other languages
6	Register the workers for social security The application form to register workers for social security insurance is available at the agency in charge of registration. Employees and employers must participate in the compulsory social security regime. They may not enter into mutual agreements to avoid participation in the social security regime. The social security regime for company employees is established on the principle of state-guaranteed insurance. Contributions to the social security regime are paid by both the employers and employees: 5.0% of gross salary is to be contributed for social security by the employer and another 4.5%, by the employee. The maximum ceiling for calculating these contributions is LAK 2, 00,000 (5% and 4.5% of LAK 2,000,000).	7 days	no charge

To receive a foreign investment license (FI License) in all sectors, except the mining, hydropower and forestry sectors, a foreign investor must submit the following to the DDFI:

Fully and correctly completed application form (available from the DDFI)

Projected assets and liabilities, pro forma income statement for five years

Bio data of the investor

Support of financial capacity of the investor to undertake the proposed investment

Application fee (US$100 for projects with invested capital less than US$1 million; and US$200 for projects with capital exceed US$1 million)

Four copies of all of the above

The Screening Division of the DDFI reviews the application form for completeness and accuracy. The investor is contacted to supply necessary additional information or to clarify issues arising from the application. The application is then forwarded to the relevant line ministries.

When the ministries have formulated a position on the application, the application is brought before the Board Meeting for decision. Under the FI Law, this process is required to take a maximum of 60 days.

INVESTMENT INCENTIVES

Tax and Duty Incentives

The DDFI automatically awards all approved foreign investors an incentive tax rate of 20 percent, compared to the general tax rate of 35%. Unlike most other countries, this 20 percent rate applies to foreign investment in all sectors of the economy and does not depend on company or performance. Foreign investors must pay a 10 % dividend withholding tax. Foreign investors and expatriate personnel pay a flat 10 % personal income tax.

There is a minimum tax on all companies (unless tax holidays are granted) of 1% of turnover, i.e., foreign-owned companies pay either 20 % tax on profits or 1% tax on turnover, whichever is greater. In special cases, primarily for hydroelectric projects or resource-based development projects, tax holidays can be negotiated.

As an incentive to all foreign investors, a duty of only 1% is charged for imports of capital equipment, spare parts, and other means of production. No duties or import turnover taxes are payable on any imported inputs for export production. Foreign investors whose products substitute for imports can negotiate incentive duties and turnover taxes on imported inputs on case by case basis.

At present, an administrative ruling of the Minister of Finance allows all imports subject to incentive duty rates to be free of turnover tax and excise tax. Producers, whose output is sold on both the domestic and export markets, pay no duty on the inputs for export production and a negotiated rate on inputs for import substituting production. This simple system obviates the necessity of instituting cumbersome duty drawback systems or creating free trade or export processing zones.

In the future, however, the government may move to a system in which foreign investors face the same tax and tariff incentives as do domestic investors. Under this system, investment in "promoted industries" would receive tax and duty reduction incentives, but investment in other sectors would pay the normal corporate profit tax, turnover tax and duty rates.

Non-tax incentives

The government provides the following incentives to all foreign investors:

Permission to bring in foreign nationals to undertake investment feasibility studies.

Permission to bring in foreign technicians, experts, and managers if qualified Lao nationals are not available to work on investment projects.

Permission to lease land for up to 20 years from a Lao national and up to 50 years from the government.

Permission to own all improvements and structures on the leased land, transfer leases to other entities, and permission to sell or remove improvements or structures.

Facilitation of entry and exit visa facilities and work permits for expatriate personnel.

The government also offers guarantees against nationalization, expropriation, or requisition without compensation.

Under the FI Law, the government does not offer incentives of import protection (in the form of increasing duties or banning imports) for import substituting investments and it does not provide measures to restrict further entry to reduce competition for current investors. The policy of not reducing market competition as an incentive for investors is not a feature of the foreign investment systems of most other countries, such as Thailand and Vietnam, in the region.

Site development

Building Permits

Individuals or organizations that wish to construct or to do major repair work must apply for a permit to the Provincial Department of Communications, Transportation, Post and Construction (DCTPC). The application documents to be submitted in 4 copies are the following:

A standard application form available from the DCTPC

A certificate of residence from administrative authorities

A certified land title document, land use permit, and site permit attached to a plan for the structure

A situation plan

A construction plan

A septic tank plan

Before they can be submitted to the DCTPC, a legally recognized design company must approve these documents. The Provincial DCTPC (where appropriate) will notify the applicants within 45 days of the results of the examination of the application. The examination of the application form is made in conjunction with other relevant government agencies such as:

The Land Department

The Ministry of Interior

The Institute of Urbanism

Once a building permit has been assigned, it is be valid for 3 months. During the construction, the DCTPC will carry out inspections of the construction site to ensure construction activities are in accordance with the building permits and plans.

Environment Assessments

For additional analytical, business and investment opportunities information,
please contact Global Investment & Business Center, USA
at (703) 370-8082. Fax: (703) 370-8083. E-mail: ibpusa3@gmail.com
Global Business and Investment Info Databank - www.ibpus.com

According to the Regulations on the Monitoring and Control of Wastewater Discharge, the buildings and factory facilities sites must be inspected twice per year to ensure that they are in conformity with the standards of wastewater discharge. After each inspection, a certificate is issued to the owners of buildings and sites. In cases of non-compliance, appropriate measures are imposed.

The draft environmental law requires an Environmental Impact Assessment to be made for large projects using natural resources. What constitutes a "large project" has not been specified.

Operating Permits

In case of construction of a plant, once the plant is finished, it requires a license from the Ministry of Industry and Handicraft to commence operations. The Ministry of Industry and Handicraft will make an inspection of the plant before it issues the license. At this time, all documentation is once again reviewed to check if it is complete.

Water Connections

The state enterprise Nam Papa Lao or its branches in the provinces provide water connections. Connection times vary from location to location. However the approximate time is 15 days. Individual households or production facilities wishing to have water connections to their sites must apply to Nam Papa Lao or its provincial branches (for projects located in the provinces). The documentation required is:

Standard application form available from Nam Papa Lao

Building permit

Approved construction plan

Electricity Connections

In October 1997 the electricity tariff was adjusted. Under this new tariff schedule, the electricity tariff varies from user to user. The highest tariff applies to entertainment businesses. They pay 100 kip per kwh. The lowest tariff is 10 kip per kwh and applies to small businesses with a simple accounting system.

Electricity connections are provided by legally recognized construction design companies. The documentation required is:

Application form from the Ministry of Industry and Handicraft

Foreign investment license

Building permit

Tax license
After the Ministry of Industry and Handicraft approves the application, foreign investors must contact one of the approved construction design companies to survey the site and make a price quotation for an electricity connection. The price and the time required for connections vary from

location to location and also depend upon the size of the transformer and electricity phase (1, 2 or 3 phases).

The approximate time to get an electricity connection is 1-2 months for households and two to three months for plants.

Telephone Connections

Telephone connections are provided by Lao Telecom. Lao Telecom is a joint venture between a Thai investor and the Lao government. From major cities, international access via IDD is straightforward, fast and efficient. Sound produced over the lines is good and disconnects are rare. Rates for international calls, though still relatively expensive, have steadily lowered over the past few years.

Lao Telecom can usually provide a line within 2 weeks if lines adjacent to the property are in place. The connection fee is approximately $150 but can vary from location to location depending on the distance from the main switchboard in different areas.

The application process is straightforward. Foreign investors fill out an application form that includes the location where telephone hook-up is to be provided. After receiving the application, Lao Telecom will survey the location and prepare a quotation.

Forms of investment

Forms of Business Organization

Under the Business Law (1994), the Ministry of Trade and Tourism (MTT), Department of Enterprise Registration is responsible for registering all businesses in a Company Register. The Business Law makes no distinction between foreign and domestic companies. There are several types of business forms in Laos from which an investor may choose:

Representative office
Branch office
Sole Trader
Partnership
Limited Company
Public Company
Private-State Mixed Enterprise

The Business Law regulates the formation, conduct of affairs, and liquidation of all companies. (The Bankruptcy Law of 1994 also deals with liquidations.) In order for a company to be considered as a lawfully established juristic entity, it must be properly registered with the MTT and obtain an Enterprise Registration Certificate . If no errors or omissions are made in the application form or in the documentation submitted, the application will be processed within 10 to 30 days.

Most importantly, a foreign investor must first obtain a Foreign Investment License (FI License) before applying for a Business License. The Articles of Association of a foreign investor will already have been vetted and approved by the Department of Domestic and Foreign Investment (DDFI) as part of the approval process to obtain a FI License.

Representative and Branch Offices

The Business Law does not mention either representative offices or branch offices. Many branch and representative offices have been established in Laos. The FI Law permits the establishment of both representative offices and branch offices in Laos. The DDFI has standard descriptions for both these forms of business operations. Under the DDFI interpretation of a representative office, such an office cannot conduct business on its own, but must refer all business operations to units outside the country.

A foreign enterprise established in Lao PDR may be either a new company or a branch office of a foreign company. A branch office of a foreign company may have the Articles of Association of the parent company or separate Articles of Association providing they are consistent with the laws and regulations of the Lao PDR. The procedures for registering a branch office are the same as for any other type of company. A branch office is regarded as the same legal entity as its parent company. The parent company, therefore, can be held responsible for all liabilities of the branch in Laos.

Partnership

A partnership can be formed between two or more partners to carry out business. There is no capital requirement for a partnership. The partners each may contribute funds, capital equipment, land, patents and trademarks, and technological know-how based on a formula to which they have agreed. The partnership can be managed by either or all of the partners or by a designated manager. All partners are jointly and severally liable for the liabilities of the partnership.

Limited Liability Company

A limited liability company is comprised of from one to twenty shareholders. It must have a registered capital of at least kip 5,000,000 ($US470 as of April 2003) with at least half of the registered capital paid up upon registration of the company and the remaining capital paid up within two years of such registration. A limited liability company must establish reserve funds appropriated at 5 to 10% from its net profit. The shares of a limited liability company must all have the same value and are transferable only upon approval of two-thirds of the shareholders. A limited liability company must hold a general shareholder meeting at least once a year. One or more managers, chosen at a general shareholder meeting, may manage the company. The manager may bind the company and may be liable to the company and third parties for his or her wrongful acts.

A one-person limited liability company is a business unit created by a single person. It must have capital of at least 5,000,000 kip. This person is responsible for the company's liabilities only up to the extent of the company's registered capital.

A limited liability company is the most common structure for conducting business in Laos. By law, a company is regarded as a juristic person that has the right to own property and carry out business under its name. Its liabilities to others are separate from those of its shareholders.

Sole Trader Enterprise

A sole trader enterprise is a business entity with a minimum registered capital of 1,000,000 kip created by one person who is fully liable for the activities of the entity. The owner of such a business acts on behalf of the entity and may assign a manager to run the business.

Public Company

A public company can be created by a minimum of seven shareholders. All shares in the company must have equal value. Shareholders in public companies are liable up to the limit of their unpaid capital contribution. Shares in public companies may be paid in cash or in kind. The maximum value of each share is 10,000 kip. A public company's registered capital must be 50,000,000 kip or greater.

The management of a public company is conducted by the Executive Council, which includes 5 to 17 members, including one or two workers' representatives. A public company must hold an ordinary general meeting of shareholders at least once each year. Shareholders and proxies representing two-thirds of the shares can call an extraordinary general meeting upon first notification or half of the shareholders on second notification.

Shares of public companies may be sold to outsiders as well as inside shareholders. Shares in a public company are transferable. At present, however, there is no stock market in Laos. A public company is incorporated in a similar manner to a private company. A limited company

**For additional analytical, business and investment opportunities information,
please contact Global Investment & Business Center, USA
at (703) 370-8082. Fax: (703) 370-8083. E-mail: ibpusa3@gmail.com
Global Business and Investment Info Databank - www.ibpus.com**

may be transformed into a public company. Unlike a private company, a public company may issue debentures and shares to the public.

Mixed Enterprise

A Joint-Venture enterprise is a joint enterprise between the state on one side, and other forms of private business entities on the other side. In mixed enterprises, the state must hold at least 51% of the shares. Mixed enterprises are regulated by the same rules as public companies with the following exceptions:

The government has the decision over the transfer of shares owned by the state;

The private shares are managed as shares of public companies;
The share certificates are transferable;
The Chairman of the Board of Director is appointed by the Minister of Finance and the Vice-Chairman is selected by the private party and approved by the inister of Finance;
The President of the Board of Directors has a casting vote.

SELLING TO THE LAO PEOPLE'S DEMOCRATIC REPUBLIC

IMPORT POLICY, REGULATIONS AND PROCEDURES

A. General

The Ministry of Commerce has the role of managing the overall development of commerce throughout the country. One of the main tasks is to study and establish policy, laws and decrees concerning commerce development during each planning period, for submission to the Government and approval by the National Assembly.

The Customs Department under the Ministry of Finance is responsible for collecting import-export taxes in accordance with the law. Import and export activities are regulated by the Customs Law (1994).

The division of authority between the central Government and provincial authorities is regulated by decree No. 10 of the Council of Ministers, 12 March 1988, which describes the three administrative levels that are responsible for their own planning, implementation and distribution of benefits, namely, the central level, the local level provinces and districts, and the grass-roots level (companies, enterprises and state farms).

Any individual or legal entity that has been registered with a business licence (for further details on the registration process, please refer to Part 4, section II) is allowed to import goods according to the related laws and regulations.

On 10 June 2004, the Prime Minister issued Decree No. 12 in order to stop the excessive inspection and levying of fees on goods entering or leaving the country as well as the movement of goods within the country.

B. IMPORT APPROVAL

Any individual or firm seeking to import goods is required to make a six-month or one-year plan for each commodity, which is to be submitted to the Trade Section of the province, the Vientiane municipality, or the special region for acknowledgement and then to the Trade Section of the control unit in order to obtain the import approval.

As part of the import licence applications process, importers should submit a list of goods for import. The list may consist of one or many goods according to their capacity. Once approved, the list of goods is part of the import licence. The import operation should then be conducted in accordance with the list of goods as specified on the import licence, as well as the terms of the sell-buy contract.

C. LICENSING, QUOTAS AND PROHIBITIONS

Imports of goods controlled by the Government are subject to an import permit delivered by the Ministry of Commerce/provincial offices or related line Ministries as listed in table 3.

Table 3. Import authorization

Commodity	Permits issued by
All petroleum fuel products (27.10)	x x Foreign Trade Department, Ministry of Commerce x Department of Intellectual Property Standardization and Metrology, Science Technology and Environment Agency Trade Section of Provinces, Vientiane Municipality or Special Region.
Gas (27.11)	x x Foreign Trade Department, Ministry of Commerce Trade Section of Provinces, Vientiane Municipality or Special Region
All kinds of vehicles except bicycles and ploughs (87.02-11:87.16).	x x Foreign Trade Department, Ministry of Commerce Department of Transport, Ministry of Communications, Transport, Post and Construction
Parts of all kinds of vehicles except bicycles and ploughs (87.02-11:87.16)	x x Department of Industry - Handicraft, Ministry of Industry and x Handicrafts Foreign Trade Department, Ministry of Commerce Department of Transport, Ministry of Communications, Transport, Post and Construction
Valuable decorative objects (Diamond 721.02)	x Foreign Trade Department, Ministry of Commerce
All kinds of minerals (25.02-22;25.24-30;26.01-21)	x x Department of Geology - Mines, Ministry of Industry and Handicrafts Trade Section of Provinces, Vientiane Municipality or Special Region
Cement (25.23)	x x Department of Intellectual Property Standardization and Metrology, Science Technology and Environment Agency Trade Section of Provinces, Vientiane Municipality or Special Region
Iron and steel (72.01–29)	x x Department of Intellectual Property Standardization and Metrology, Science Technology and Environment Agency Trade Section of Provinces, Vientiane Municipality or Special Region
Edible meat or other parts of animals, fresh or frozen (02.01-10)	x Food and Drug Department, Ministry of Health
Fish, crab, shellfish, prawn, fresh or frozen (03.01-07)	x Food and Drug Department, Ministry of Health
Different kinds of dairy products (04.01-06)	x Food and Drug Department, Ministry of Health
All kinds of finished food products, including canned food	x Food and Drug Department, Ministry of Health

and fruit

Commodity		Permits issued by
All kinds of desserts	x	Food and Drug Department, Ministry of Health
Food colouring	x	Food and Drug Department, Ministry of Health
All kinds of preservative substances	x	Food and Drug Department, Ministry of Health
Sweetening substitutes	x	Food and Drug Department, Ministry of Health

Commodity		Permits issued by
All kinds of drinks (22.01-09)	x	Food and Drug Department, Ministry of Health
Ducks' eggs, hens' eggs (04.08-08)	x	Food and Drug Department, Ministry of Health
Food seasoning (fish sauce, soy sauce, monosodium glutamate and others)	x	Food and Drug Department, Ministry of Health
Medicine for humans	x	Food and Drug Department, Ministry of Health
Medical equipment	x	Curative and Therapy Department, Ministry of Health
Animal food	x	Department of Livestock and Fisheries, Ministry of Agriculture and Forestry
Animal medicine	x	Department of Livestock and Fisheries, Ministry of Agriculture and Forestry
Animals products	x	Department of Livestock and Fisheries, Ministry of Agriculture and Forestry
Animals and all kinds of animal breeds	x x	Department of Livestock and Fisheries, Ministry of Agriculture and Forestry Trade Section of Provinces, Vientiane Municipality or Special Region
Agricultural products	x x	Department of Agriculture, Ministry of Agriculture and Forestry Trade Section of Provinces, Vientiane Municipality or Special Region
Raw material and semi-finished products for use by factories	x	Department of Industry - Handicraft, Ministry of Industry and Handicrafts
All kinds of fertilizers	x x	Department of Forestry, Ministry of Agriculture and Forestry Trade Section of Provinces, Vientiane Municipality or Special Region
Insecticides	x	Department of Forestry, Ministry of Agriculture and Forestry
Video cassettes, tape cassettes, CDs, film, etc.	x	Mass Media Department, Ministry of Information and Culture
Luxury sets such as for games	x	Mass Media Department, Ministry of Information and Culture
Equipment for sculpture, drawing and carving	x	Mass Media Department, Ministry of Information and Culture
Printed matter, reference books, periodicals and so on	x	Publishing and Library Department, Ministry of Information and Culture
Sport guns and rifles	x x	Department of Sports, Ministry of Information and Culture Trade Section of Provinces, Vientiane Municipality or Special Region

Chemicals	x x Department of Intellectual Property Standardization and x x Metrology, Science Technology and Environment Agency (for chemicals that affect the environment only) Foreign Trade Department, Ministry of Commerce Department of Industry - Handicraft, Ministry of Industry and Handicrafts Trade Section of Provinces, Vientiane Municipality or Special Region
Valuable objects (gold bars, silver bars)	x International Department, Bank of Lao PDR
Telephone sets, fax machines and other communication equipment	x x Posts and Telecommunications Department, Ministry of Communications, Transport, Post and Construction Trade Section of Provinces, Vientiane Municipality or Special Region

Source: **Ministry of Commerce, Regulation No. 0285/MOC.FTD of 17 March 2004.**

Some quantitative restrictions are currently applied on the following products, which account for 45 per cent of imports:

x fuel and lubricants
x construction steel
x cement
x rice
x motor vehicles
x electricity
x tobacco
x timber products

The prohibition of imports applies to prohibited business activities, which are those involving private sector activities related to national security, poisons, poisonous chemicals, arms production and any professions or products monopolized by the State. According to Ministry of Commerce notification No. 0284/MOC.TFD of 17 March 2004, the list of goods prohibited for import effective 3 May 2004 is as follows:

1. **Any kind of explosive, weapons and war vehicles.**
2. **Different chemical substances that may be used to make explosives, weapons and war vehicles.**
3. **Any kind of drug products.**
4. **Any kind of products affecting the traditions of the country.**
5. **Industrial disposal and chemical products dangerous for public health and environment.**
6. **Antiques and sacred religious objects.**
7. **Food, medicine and medical equipment under strict control by a ministry concerned.**
8. **Wildlife, aquatic animals and their parts, which are forbidden by domestic law and under the international treaty signed by the Lao People's Democratic Republic.**
9. **All types of right-hand drive vehicles.**
10. **Toys affecting children's attitude, development and safety and peace of the country.**
11. **Literature, pornographic printed matter and other publications that go against the laws of the Lao People's Democratic Republic.**
12. **Second-hand goods that the Government has banned from import.**
13. **Bank notes printing equipment.**

14. Toxic insecticides, which are prohibited by the related sectors.
15. All types of log, sawed timber (processed timber), wood and forestry products that are banned according to internal regulations.

D. IMPORT REQUIREMENTS

Most import activities require the opening of a letter of credit through a foreign exchange bank. The same information as the notes on the import licence form must be used for the letter of credit. The amount of the letter of credit should not exceed the authorized amount and should be expressed in the same currency as the one specified in the import licence.

Lao sanitary and phytosanitary measures regulations and standards are based on the relevant international standards in order to control the risk to humans, animal and plant from pests and diseases, disease-causing organisms and pesticide contamination. In the case of imports of live animals, a certification that appropriate vaccinations have been undertaken is required. For imports of plants and foodstuffs, depending upon the origins, a phytosanitary certificate is required.

Goods imported through land border should be transported along routes determined by the authorities and declared to the nearest customs office or entry point. The use of other routes is not allowed and any violation will be considered as voluntary tax evasion.

Goods transported by air should be accompanied by air waybills certified by airline officers. At the landing to the point of entry airport, airline officers should present such air waybills to the airport customs for registration in the warehouse as detailed in the customs declarations.

Goods imported by boat on international rivers should be accompanied by shipping documents. Such documents should be certified by the ship's owner and contain all information as required in the forms. Crafts sailing on international rivers, whether transporting shipments or not, should only stop at ports where customs stations are established. The craft's owner should immediately declare the shipment to the customs officers after the craft's arrival or before its departure.

As for temporary transport, goods classified under the regime of temporary importation include: x Imported goods for any purpose and then re-exported in the original quantity and condition; x Imported goods for processing, assembly into finished products, improvement and repair, and then re-exported.

For the temporary importation of goods, importers should sign a contract in the temporary import declaration whereas such goods shall be re-exported or entered in the warehouse system or in the duty free zone pending their re-export and shall fully comply to the conditions provided by the law and regulations on temporary importation. In addition, the goods classified under the temporary import regime will be exempted from duty upon their importation and re-exportation according to outlined regulations and principles.

E. PACKING AND LABELLING REQUIREMENTS

There are no special packing requirements for import shipments. As a precaution against smuggling, imported goods should bear the importer's name on the label. Food distributed directly to consumers in the country must carry Lao language wording in a font and size that it is clearly visible. Foreign language wording is also permitted.

F. Inspections

Pre-shipment inspection is not used. Upon receipt of the shipments, the customs house inspector will verify that the contents of the shipments correspond with the description in the import licence.

REGISTRATION

If you are an importer wishing to import commercial goods into Laos you should, first of all, be a company registered with the *Ministry of Industry and Commerce Department of Enterprise Registration and Management,*

PROHIBITED GOODS

Before importing goods into Laos you should ensure that they do not fall into the category of prohibited goods. Prohibited goods cannot be imported, exported, transited, sold or circulated in Laos. Among prohibited goods are weapons, narcotics, psychotropic substances and hazardous chemical substances. You should refer to the specific laws and regulations that cover these prohibitions. The goods prohibited for imports are listed in *Notification No. 0973, Annex 1.*
If in doubt you should seek advice from the *Department of Customs* or from the *Department of Import and Export* (DIMEX) of the *Ministry of Industry and Commerce.*

This procedure applies to the following measure/s:

Name	Measure Type	Agency	Description	Comments	Legal Document	Validity To
Requirement to obtain automatic import license - Road Vehicles	Licensing Requirement	Ministry of Industry and Commerce	Road vehicle, except road vehicle with three wheels (87.04.31) Please check the relevant law for a list of the documents required to submit an import application.	For statistical purpose	Decision on the Management of Importation and Distribution of Vehicles in Lao PDR No. 0919/MOIC.DIMEX	31-12-9999
Requirement to obtain automatic import license - Petroleum and Gas	Licensing Requirement	Ministry of Industry and Commerce	Petroleum and Gas	For statistical purpose	Notification No. 0076/MoIC.DIMEX - Annex A List on Goods subject to Automatic and Non-automatic Import Licensing	31-12-9999
Requirement to obtain automatic import license - Logs, trunks, etc.	Licensing Requirement	Ministry of Industry and Commerce	Logs, trunks, barks and transformed timber	For statistical purpose	Notification No. 0076/MoIC.DIMEX - Annex A List on Goods subject to Automatic and Non-automatic Import Licensing	31-12-9999

Name	Measure Type	Agency	Description	Comments	Legal Document	Validity To
Requirement to obtain automatic import license - Unmilled rice, etc.	Licensing Requirement	Ministry of Industry and Commerce	Unmilled rice, low standard rice, premium rice, semi-milled or fully milled rice whether filtering or not. This license is obtained from the Provincial Office of MOIC.	For statistical purpose	Notification No. 0076/MoIC.DIMEX - Annex A List on Goods subject to Automatic and Non-automatic Import Licensing	31-12-9999
Requirement to obtain automatic import license - Steel bars and transformed steel	Licensing Requirement	Ministry of Industry and Commerce	Steel bars and transformed steel. This license is obtained from the Provincial Office of MOIC.	For statistical purpose	Notification No. 0076/MoIC.DIMEX - Annex A List on Goods subject to Automatic and Non-automatic Import Licensing	31-12-9999
Requirement to obtain automatic import license - Cement, mortar and concrete	Licensing Requirement	Ministry of Industry and Commerce	Cement, mortar, concrete. This license is obtained from the Provincial Office of MOIC.	For statistical purpose	Notification No. 0076/MoIC.DIMEX - Annex A List on Goods subject to Automatic and Non-automatic Import Licensing	31-12-9999
Requirement to obtain automatic import license - Printing products	Licensing Requirement	Ministry of Information, Culture and Tourism	Printing products	For statistical purpose	Notification No. 0076/MoIC.DIMEX - Annex A List on Goods subject to Automatic and Non-automatic Import Licensing	31-12-9999
Requirement to obtain automatic export license - Logs, trunks, timber, etc.	Licensing Requirement	Ministry of Industry and Commerce	Logs, trunk, bark, transformed timber and semi-finished timber from plantations	For monitoring the conformity of the implementation the Chain of Custody System (CoC)	Notification 0076/MoIC.DIMEX - Annex B List of Goods subject to Automatic and Non-automatic Export Licensing	31-12-9999
Requirement to obtain	Licensing Requirement	Ministry of Industry and	Unmilled rice, low	For statistical purpose	Notification 0076/MoIC.DIMEX	31-12-9999

Name	Measure Type	Agency	Description	Comments	Legal Document	Validity To
automatic export license - Unmilled rice, etc.		Commerce	standard rice, premium rice, semi-milled or fully milled rice whether filtering or not. This license is obtained from the Provincial Office of MOIC.		- Annex B List of Goods subject to Automatic and Non-automatic Export Licensing	
Requirement to obtain non-automatic export license - Logs, trunks, timber, etc.	Licensing Requirement	Ministry of Industry and Commerce	Logs, trunk, bark, transformed timber and semi-finished timber from natural forest	For monitoring the conformity of the implementation the Chain of Custody System (CoC)	Notification 0076/MoIC.DIMEX - Annex B List of Goods subject to Automatic and Non-automatic Export Licensing	

SANITARY AND PHYTOSANITARY REQUIREMENTS

If the goods trader intend to import are subject to sanitary and phytosanitary measures you will have to comply with the special regulations relating to those products.

Normally, trader may need to get a permit from the *Ministry of Agriculture and Forestry* either from the *Livestock Department* or from the *Plant Quarantine* department depending on what you are intending to import. A detailed description of the procedures and documentation required can be found on the *Procedures* page of this website.

Lao PDR has established an *SPS Enquiry Point* as required by the WTO *SPS Agreement*. Trader can contact the *SPS Enquiry Point* if you have any questions regarding sanitary and phytosanitary requirements.

TECHNICAL REQUIREMENTS

For certain types of products it may be necessary to obtain a permit that certifies that these products conform to certain technical standards. These technical regulations are administered by the *Ministry of Science and Technology*.

Trader can find out on this website which commodities are subject to these requirements by using the search facilities on the *Commodity Search* page. A detailed description of the procedures and documentation required can also be found on the *Procedures* page of this website.

Lao PDR has established a *TBT Enquiry Point* as required by the WTO *TBT Agreement*. Trader can contact the *TBT Enquiry Point* if you have any questions regarding technical standards.

IMPORT DECLARATION

All goods imported into Laos must be declared and duty is payable on them unless they are covered by an exemption or a suspension.

A declaration is made by submitting a duly completed and signed *ACDD Form* together with the following minimum supporting documents:

- A commercial invoice or contract of sale document from the supplier of the goods

- Transport documents such as Bill of Lading or Air Way Bill

- Packing List (if available)

- Certificate of Origin. This should have been supplied to you by the exporter.

- Any import licenses or permits obtained from other ministries depending on the type of goods you are importing

Declarations can be submitted at your regional Customs office. *Click here* to see a list of all the Customs offices where trader can submit a declaration and clear your goods.

A declaration must be submitted within 15 days from the date of lodgment with Customs of the transport documents (e.g. manifest) notifying Customs of the arrival of the cargo (see *Transport*).

Currently, at the Thanaleng border post only, all Customs declarations must be submitted via the Asycuda automated system. *Click here* to view the procedure for submitting declarations through Asycuda. In future, Asycuda will be rolled to all other border posts nation-wide. Until then, at these border posts, the normal procedure applies. *Click here* to view the normal procedure. Certain penalties may apply if you do not submit a declaration in time

ADVANCE DECLARATION

In order to facilitate the process of clearing imports trader can submit a pre-arrival Customs declaration. This can be done within 7 working days prior to the date of arrival of the goods following the same procedures as a normal declaration. Trader can pay the duties at the time of arrival of the goods.

CUSTOMS BROKER

Trader may engage a Customs Broker to carry out the import formalities on your behalf. For information pertaining to brokers *click here*. **Top**

CLASSIFICATION AND VALUE

Customs duty is payable on imported goods as a percentage of their declared value. The rate of duty payable on goods imported into Laos varies according to the commodity and the country of origin.

Commodities are classified using the 8-digit *Harmonized System (HS) Code* which is maintained and, from time to time, amended by the World Customs Organization (WCO). The Lao tariff classification conforms with ASEAN's AHTN standard (*ASEAN Harmonized Tariff Nomenclature*).

It is your responsibility to declare the correct classification, origin, value and quantity of the goods you are importing. If in doubt please seek advice from the Department of Customs.

The basis for the calculation of duties is the actual transaction value of the goods (as evidenced by the commercial invoice or other contract of sale document). If the value of the goods cannot established by this method Customs will attempt to establish the value of the goods using 5 more methods in line with *Article 7 of the General Agreement on Tariffs and Trade* (GATT 1947).

PAYMENT OF DUTIES

Once a declaration has been submitted and accepted by Customs, Customs will be required to pay the duties. At the major border posts you will be able to pay for duties at a bank nearby. Present the receipt to Customs in order to receive your clearance. At other border posts only cash is accepted and trader can pay for duties at the Customs cashier. *Top*

GOODS IMPORTED UNDER WAREHOUSE REGIME

Goods can be imported into Laos under the *Warehouse Regime* if you are not intending to release them for circulation into Laos immediately. Duty will be suspended for the period the goods are in the warehouse and will be payable when the goods are finally released into circulation.

You must submit an import declaration under the *Warehouse Regime* when you bring the goods into the warehouse and a normal Import declaration when you want to bring them into circulation. There are different types of warehouse. Please refer to *relevant article of the Customs Law*. Warehouses have to be approved by the Ministry of Finance.

TEMPORARY IMPORTS

Goods can be imported under the *Temporary Imports* regime under the following circumstances:

- Goods necessary for the manufacture, processing, assembly, transformation or repair of items which will subsequently be re-exported ("inward processing")

- Vehicles imported for the purpose of project supervision or for tourism or business visits as long as they are re-exported by the allotted time

- Materials required for project supervision purposes

- Exhibition, educational or scientific materials

For these types of import you must submit a declaration under *Temporary Imports* regime. No duties are payable on these imports.

In all the above cases certain documents or permits must be obtained from the relevant authority and presented to Customs. Before importing goods under this regime please contact Customs to obtain advice as to what documentation will be required for your specific circumstances.

To import a vehicle into the country for the purpose of a temporary visit you need to make a declaration under the Temporary Imports regime to Customs at the border crossing. You must present a valid registration certificate for that vehicle. Vehicles imported under this regime must be re-exported within the allotted timeframe or a penalty will be liable.

For goods imported for exhbition purposes a bond is payable to Customs which is refunded when the goods are re-exported. *Top*

EXEMPTIONS

Exemption from Customs duties and other obligations are available for diplomatic missions, for goods imported under a government investment promotion scheme or for certain economic zone and for other goods to be imported under certain circumstance. *Click here* to see a list of goods eligible for these exemptions.

Please contact Customs to find out what is required to take advantage of these exemptions.

Personal belongings of passengers arriving in Laos are also exempt from Customs duties. For specific limits concerning these goods please refer to section on *Passengers* on this website.

TARIFF SCHEDULE – CUSTOMS

A. GENERAL

As part of the Ministry of Finance, the Lao Customs Department is responsible for ensuring that all legislation governing the importation and exportation of goods into and out of the Lao People's Democratic Republic are fully complied with. The Lao Customs Department is also responsible for ensuring that all applicable duties and taxes have been paid.

B. CLASSIFICATION

The Lao People's Democratic Republic uses the Harmonized Commodity Description and Coding System, generally referred to as the Harmonized System, or HS, at an eight-digit level.

C. CUSTOMS DUTIES

Customs duties are calculated ad valorem on c.i.f. value of imports. The tariffs rate range from 0 to 40 per cent and the weighted average tariff is 14.7 per cent. The overall tariff structure is low tariffs on investment goods and inputs for industry and higher tariffs on non-essential goods. Imports, which are inputs into productive foreign investments, attract a special rate of 1 per cent.

The following products are exempted from import duty: certain types of food for travellers; certain family implements when changing residence; certain types of materials obtained from inheritance; belongings and presents of governmental delegations returning from abroad; certain types and quantity of personal belongings of Lao students, pupils, civil servants and diplomats imported after termination of studies, training or civil service abroad; fuel remaining in tanks of motor vehicles; fuel for international flights by Lao and foreign airplanes on the basis of agreement or mutual compensation; non-salable samples; present, assistance materials, loans or debt servicing by the Government; humanitarian assistance materials; specific defence and police equipment; certain types of necessary religious items based on the approval of the state agency concerned.

In 1997, the Lao People's Democratic Republic became a member of ASEAN[1] and committed to fully implement the ASEAN Free Trade Area (AFTA) in 2008. The backbone of AFTA is tariff reduction through the mechanism of the common effective preferential tariff (CEPT). Under CEPT, tariffs on goods traded within the ASEAN region will be reduced to 0-5 per cent by the year 2008 for the Lao People's Democratic Republic. By 2010-2015, the ASEAN countries have agreed to enact zero tariff rates on virtually all imports from the four newer ASEAN members, including Lao People's Democratic Republic.

ASEAN's newer members, namely Cambodia, the Lao People's Democratic Republic, Myanmar and Viet Nam, have already moved almost 80 per cent of their

[1] ASEAN member countries are Brunei Darussalam, Cambodia, Indonesia, the Lao People's Democratic Republic, Malaysia, Myanmar, the Philippines, Singapore, Thailand and Viet Nam.

products into their respective CEPT Inclusion Lists. Of these items, about 66 per cent already have tariffs within the 0-5 per cent tariff band.

Under CEPT, goods are classified in four categories, as follows:

1. Inclusion List: goods that will have a 0 or 5 per cent tariff rate by the deadline for each country. The Lao People's Democratic Republic has until 2008 to bring down the tariff of 98 per cent of the products in the Inclusion List to duty of no more than 5 per cent.
2. Temporary Exclusion List: sensitive goods that are temporarily excluded from the Inclusion List, and will be subject to 0 or 5 per cent tariff rates within the following seven years. For the Lao People's Democratic Republic, the deadline to transfer the items under the Temporary Exclusion List into the Inclusion List is 2005.
3. Sensitive List: goods that are given a longer time frame to transfer to the Inclusion List (2015 for the Lao People's Democratic Republic), including unprocessed agricultural products.
4. General Exceptions List: goods that are not subject to tariff reduction or elimination for reasons of national security, human, animal and plant life and health, including articles of artistic, historic and archaeological values.

The Inclusion List of the Lao People's Democratic Republic consists of 3,551 tariff lines (about 84 per cent of total tariff lines). The Inclusion List covers 2,967 tariff lines. Import duties on products in the Inclusion Lists of the Lao People's Democratic Republic will be eliminated not later than 1 January 2008. Flexibility, however, will be allowed for import duties on some sensitive products which will be eliminated not later than 1 January 2015. The full 2002 CEPT package for the Lao People's Democratic Republic is available at:

http://www.aseansec.org/economic/afta/2002_cept_package/LaoPDR2002.zip

The Lao People's Democratic Republic is a member of the Asia-Pacific Trade Agreement, but does not have a national schedule or concession for the five other countries, namely Bangladesh, China, India, the Republic of Korea and Sri Lanka.

D. TAXES AND SURCHARGES

The excise tax is calculated on the customs value plus import duty and other fees if these exist. According to the Tax Law, the rates of the excise tax are the following:

Alcohol or alcoholic drinks (above 15 degrees) 40 per cent

Beer, wine and other drinks (below 15 degrees) 30 per cent

Bottled soft drinks and other vitamin drinks 20 per cent

Packed and unpacked cigarettes, cigars 10 per cent

Perfumes and cosmetics 10 per cent

Most import duty rates are set at 5 or 10 per cent. Administrative fees are at a rate of 5 per cent ad valorem on equipment and materials.

FOREIGN EXCHANGE REGIME

A. GENERAL

Reform of the Lao economy began in 1986 when the Government adopted the New Economic Mechanism programme, with the main purpose of gradually transforming its centrally planned economy into a market-oriented economy. Elements of this programme that have been particularly important to private sector growth include legal reform, trade policy reform, banking reform and privatization of State-owned enterprises.

During the 1990s, the Lao People's Democratic Republic moved away from the mono-bank system by separating central banking from commercial banking and allowing joint venture and foreign banks to operate in the country.

The Bank of the Lao People's Democratic Republic, as central bank, has a mandate equivalent to ministry status. Its role is to assist the Government in maintaining the stability of the domestic currency and keep inflation low for the economy. Among other duties, the Bank is also responsible for supervision and participation in the Foreign Exchange Inter-bank Market to stabilize the activities of this market and according to the laws and conducts the exchange rate policy in a market-oriented manner by managing the spread between the bank and the parallel market rates at a rate of less than 1 per cent.

B. CURRENCY CONVERTIBILITY

The use of foreign exchange is largely for external payment. Domestic goods and service payments shall be made in kip except for duty free shops where payment in both foreign currency and kip is allowed. Other cases should be authorized by the Government based on the proposal of the Bank of the Lao People's Democratic Republic.

Purchase of foreign currency by the commercial banks or foreign shops amounting to or more than US$ 10,000 shall go along with source proof of the foreign exchange. Individuals or juristic persons can have deposit accounts in kip and in foreign currencies at the commercial banks.

C. FOREIGN EXCHANGE ALLOCATION

The commercial banks or authorized money changers shall sell foreign currency to the public according to their capacity, but the sale shall not be more than US$ 2,000 or its equivalent for one person for the purpose of health treatment and travelling and this shall go along with proof of the using purpose as indicated in Article 5 of the Instruction on Implementation of Decree Law on Management of Foreign Currency and Precious Metals NO 02/BOL.29/09/2003

Tourists and foreign visitors who want to change their money back to foreign currency must present the proof of having exchanged their foreign currency at a money changer or commercial bank in the Lao People's Democratic Republic within the period of their tour or visit.

Individuals or juristic persons who have invested in the Lao People's Democratic Republic who want to transfer the approved profit, dividend, capital and interest received from their business operation to their home country or a third country shall apply to the commercial bank with the following documents:

-Application for transfer;

-Evidence of bringing in the capital certified by the Bank of the Lao People's Democratic Republic;

-Account statement issued by the commercial bank.

-Tax payment certification;

-Decision of the board or shareholders on the dividend of the company

The commercial bank is responsible for considering the application and responding officially within no more than 5 working days from the date the fully completed application has been received. Approval can also be granted to send a large amount of capital back to a home country or to a third country in multiple transactions. The Bank of the Lao People's Democratic Republic shall cooperate with the related commercial bank to process the transfer in a timely manner.

D. MONEY AND FINANCE MEASURES

The methods of payment used in trade transactions are the standard international methods, namely, letter of credit, draft, wire transfer and direct payment order via post to the bank concerned.

E. BANKING

Currently, the banking system comprises four State-owned banks, three joint-venture banks, seven branches of foreign commercial banks and one representative office (see table 4). There are no domestic private banks.

Major commercial banks in the Lao People's Democratic Republic IV. DOCUMENTS

Bank	Ownership/ status

For additional analytical, business and investment opportunities information,
please contact Global Investment & Business Center, USA
at (703) 370-8082. Fax: (703) 370-8083. E-mail: ibpusa3@gmail.com
Global Business and Investment Info Databank - www.ibpus.com

Agricultural Promotion Bank Banque pour le Commerce Extérieur Lao Ltd. Lao May Bank Ltd. Lan Xang Bank Ltd. Lao-Viet Bank Vientiane Commercial Bank Joint Development Bank Bangkok Bank Public Company Ltd. Krung Thai Bank Public Company Ltd. Siam Commercial Bank Public Company Ltd. Thai Military Bank Public Company Ltd Thai Farmers Bank Public Company Ltd. Bank of Ayuddhya Public Company Ltd. Public Bank Berhard Public Company Ltd. Standard Chartered Bank	State-owned commercial bank State-owned commercial bank State-owned commercial bank State-owned commercial bank Joint-venture bank Joint-venture bank Joint-venture bank Branch of foreign commercial bank Branch of foreign commercial bank Branch of foreign commercial bank Branch of foreign commercial bank Branch of foreign commercial bank Branch of foreign commercial bank Branch of foreign commercial bank Representative office

IMPORTING FROM LAOS

The declaration form or single administrative document (SAD) is used for all customs transactions: import, export or transit. It must be duly completed to be accepted by Lao Customs authorities.

The Declaration of Goods Form must be accompanied by a bill of lading and a detailed customs declaration form. All types of import goods should be declared in detail and according to the tariff code, even if they are duty exempted. Detailed declarations should be handed over to the customs station within 10 days from the registration of warehouse entry exclusive of public holidays.

Regime/code description of types of transactions to be registered in the declaration form

10 Exportation of domestic goods

14 Exportation under a drawback regime

20 Temporary exportation

35 Re-exportation

40 Importation of goods for home consumption.

4A Importation of goods for diplomatic use, returning residents and humanitarian assistance; samples, educational materials and certain religious articles.

4B Goods ex-warehoused to duty free shops

4C Goods ex-warehoused for exportation out of the Lao People's Democratic

Republic

45 Home consumption of goods after temporary admission

47 Home consumption of goods entered under a warehousing regime

For additional analytical, business and investment opportunities information, please contact Global Investment & Business Center, USA at (703) 370-8082. Fax: (703) 370-8083. E-mail: ibpusa3@gmail.com Global Business and Investment Info Databank - www.ibpus.com

50 Temporary importation

62 Re-importation of goods exported temporarily

70 Warehousing of goods

80 Transits

Source: Lao Customs.

A pro-forma invoice is required for the establishment of a letter of credit. The following documentation is required to enable goods to be cleared through Lao Customs:

A. DOCUMENTS REQUIRED FOR IMPORTS

Document	Number of copies	Body concerned
Bill of lading/Air waybill Certificate of origin Form D, if required Commercial invoice Single administrative document Import permit Packing list Other permits, as required	3 2 2 3 sets 1 2	Shipping company/airline company Ministry of Commerce/ LNCCI Importer Customs department Line ministries (see table 3) Importer Ministries concerned

To qualify for ASEAN-CEPT treatment, products must be included in the CEPT products coverage list and comply with the ASEAN rules of origin (40 per cent local content). Once a product qualifies for CEPT, a proof of origin has to be issued for it to be recognized by the customs authorities in the country giving preference. This proof is the Certificate of Origin (Form D). The Rule of Origin Division under the Foreign Trade Department, the Ministry of Commerce is responsible for the issuance of the Certificate of Origin Form D.

Before applying for CEPT Form D, enterprises should inform the Ministry of Commerce of their capacity of production and export in each period, and their need for imported raw materials for the production of finished goods to be distributed either domestically or exported. They should also submit the application for registration with their business documents and tax registration documents.

Thereafter, the Ministry of Commerce together with the Committee of Inspection, consisting of representatives from the Ministry of Industry and Ministry of Finance (Customs Department), conduct a factory visit to assess whether the company in question has the capabilities, personnel and machinery. If it is approved, the enterprise must submit a cost statement for pre-exportation verification of the origin of products to the Rule of Origin division with the following documents:

(1)Commercial Invoice and Packing List of the products;
(2)Production cost declaration document;
(3)Certificate of Origin of imported material, Form D;
(4)Customs declaration document.

These documents must be submitted at least one week before the shipment of products. After receiving these documents, he Rule of Origin Division has to conduct a verification and before giving approval must ensure that these products are qualified for CEPT concession and have also complied with the rules of origin.

For further details on the issuance of Form D and the methods of ASEAN content calculation, please refer to the Ministry of Commerce website at: http://www.mot.gov.vn/Laowebsite/vbdetail.asp?id=7/23/1997

B. SPECIAL REQUIREMENTS

For most products there are no special requirements. If live animals are imported for sale and not for use as food, then a medical certificate from a veterinarian is required.

In addition to the import permit, certain types of products require authorization from other ministries, as follows:

x Ministry of Health: gives the authorization for drugs for local sale

x Ministry of Agriculture: gives the authorization for fertilizers and agricultural chemicals

x Ministry of Transport and Communications: responsible for checking standard techniques of the vehicles and gives the authorization for cars and other vehicles.

If claiming duty and tax exemptions apply, documents authorizing such exemptions must be presented with the declaration.

MARKETING AND DISTRIBUTION

A. MARKET REGULATIONS AND PRODUCT STANDARDS

The metric system is commonly used in the Lao People's Democratic Republic. Therefore all weights are expressed in kilograms and tons.

The Government is developing market regulations and product standards. The Standards and Quality Division of the Department of Intellectual Property, Standardization and Metrology is the government office in charge of product standards. The address is as follows:

Standards and Quality Division Department of Intellectual Property, Standardization and Metrology Nahaidio Rd, Vientiane - P.O. Box 2279 Lao People's Democratic Republic Tel.: +856-21 240784 Fax: +856-21 213472

Within the framework of the ASEAN Consultative Committee on Standards and Quality (ACCSQ), all member countries have accomplished the harmonization of standards for the 20 priority products and 81 standards for Safety and Electromagnetic Compatibility. In this context, the Lao People's Democratic Republic has approved the following standards: Portland cement P425 and P525, and nails.

Additionally, in 2004, the Lao People's Democratic Republic completed new national quality standards, which now cover a total of 11 products as follows:

1. **Green coffee**
2. **Mixed cement**
3. **Gasoline**
4. **Diesel**
5. **Deformed steel bars**

6. Round steel bars
7. Instant Lao coffee
8. Portland cement
9. Zinc
10. Nails
11. Brick
12. Construction steel.

B. PORT FACILITIES AND TRADING ROUTE

The Greater Mekong Subregion generally lacks adequate transportation infrastructure. The Lao People's Democratic Republic is a landlocked country and transportation costs as well as tariff and non-tariff barriers in the transit country might increase the final cost of imported goods.

The Lao People's Democratic Republic does not currently have a railway system, which hinders trade and the exploitation of minerals. Moreover, of the 32,624 kilometres of road in the country, around 4,000 kilometres are paved. In 1994 the Friendship Bridge was opened as a link across the Mekong River between the Lao People's Democratic Republic and Thailand.

Transit routes and border crossing in the Lao People's Democratic Republic are s follows:

(a)Route 3: Kunming-Yuxi-Yuanjiang-Mohei-Simao-Xiaomenyang-Mohan (China) - Boten-Houayxay (Lao People's Democratic Republic)-Chiang Khong-Chiang Rai-Tak-Bangkok (Thailand)
(i) Border crossing: Mohan (China) – Boten (Lao People's Democratic Republic)
(ii) Border crossing: Houayxay (Lao People's Democratic Republic) – Chiang Khong (Thailand)
(b)Route 9: Phitsanulok-Khon Kaen-Kalasin-Mukdahan (Thailand)-Savannakhet-Dansavanh (Lao People's Democratic Republic)-Lao Bao-Dong Ha-Hue-Da Nang (Viet Nam)

(i) Border crossing: Mukdahan (Thailand) – Savannakhet (Lao People's Democratic Republic)

(ii) Border crossing: Dansavanh (Lao) – Lao Bao (Viet Nam)

Thailand, the State enterprise Express Transport Organization has the monopoly in transporting goods to the border of the Lao People's Democratic Republic. In addition, the Government of Thailand lists certain items for which transit is not permitted. The number of those items has been reduced from 61 to 29.

GOVERNMENT PROCUREMENT AND STATE-OWNED ENTERPRISES

A. GOVERNMENT PROCUREMENT

The Government of the Lao People's Democratic Republic has regulated its procurement activities with Decree No. 31/ PM of 9 January 2004on Government Procurement of Goods, Construction, Maintenance and Services and Decree No. 0063/ MOF of 12 March 2004 on Implementing Rules and Regulation.

Decree No. 31/PM applies to government entities at the central, provincial and local levels; to State-owned enterprises, and joint ventures in which the Sate holds a share.

The following is a reference list of suppliers and contractors:

(1)

Each year, the Ministry of Finance, in cooperation with the component authorities, shall maintain the list of firms, enterprises, joint ventures, individuals and foreign contractors and suppliers participating in public procurement that have experience, qualifications and financial stabilities.

(2)

The reference list of contactors and suppliers will demonstrate their stability and qualifications according to the Public Procurement Degree. Registration of contractors and suppliers on the reference list is not a prerequisite for bidding. Other interested bidders shall be given an equal opportunity of submitting bids. Post-qualification of successful bidders shall be undertaken prior to awarding the contract.

As a reference for the assessment of bidders' qualifications, the Ministry of Finance is entrusted to issue each year a list of enterprises with their capacity, experience and financial situation, as well as to publicize the criteria for inclusion in such a list.

Procurement methods used in the Lao People's Democratic Republic are:

- Public bidding

- Limited bidding

- Direct contracting

- Price comparison.

The selection of consultant services is carried out under the following procedure:

1. The main procedure is Quality and Cost-based Selection Method. This method uses a competitive process among short-listed firms that takes into account the quality of the proposal of the cost of services in the selection of a successful firm. The short list of up to six (6) firms and not less than three (3) is compiled from different sources of information.
2. Quality-Based Selection is appropriate for complex or highly specialized assignments for which it is difficult to define precise items of reference and the required input from the consultants that have a high downstream impact and in which the objective is to have high-quality expertise.
3. Fixed budget, least-cost selection based on consultants' qualifications and single-source selection may be used as specified in the Implementing Rules and Regulation.

In the case of large-scale, technically complex and high-value projects, the suitability of bidders is evaluated prior to carrying out the bidding.

Threshold values of each form of bidding are set by the Ministry of Finance periodically as appropriate and in accordance with the socio-economic context.

In any form of bidding, except for direct contracting and price comparison, bidders are required to provide bid securities, which must be effective for 30 days longer than the validity of the bid. Bids are effective for at least 30 days since the day of opening.

Bid validity. Bidders are required to submit bids valid for a period specified in the tender documents, which shall be sufficient to enable the comparison and evaluation of bids and obtain the necessary approval so that the contract can be awarded within that period.

B. STATE-OWNED ENTERPRISES

State-owned enterprises (SOEs) have been a central feature of the Lao People's Democratic Republic economy. However, during the 1990s, the Lao People's Democratic Republic made significant progress in reforming SOEs by closing down, leasing, merging and selling a large number of them. Although the number of SOEs has been reduced, they still play an important role in the economy.

Decree No. 17 of the Council of Ministers of 16 March 1990 called for the privatization of SOEs. The Government has classified 31 SOEs (7 central and 24 provincial) for sale and liquidation in addition to the 9 SOEs that are currently undergoing restructuring (see table 5). Prime Minister Notice No. 058/ CPMO and No. 059/CPMO of 15 January 2004 adopted the key elements for the SOEs restructuring plans.

Table 5. SOEs undergoing restructuring

Large SOEs	Other SOEs
Agriculture Industry Development Import-Export State Owned Enterprise (DAI) Bolisat Phatthana Khet Phoudoi (BPKP) Development of Agricultural-Forestry and Industry (DAFI) Lao Airlines Lao State Fuel Enterprise Nam Papa Laos	Agro-industrial Development Company (DAI) Bridge-Road Construction No. 13 Company Lao Import-Export Trading Company Pharmaceutical Factory 3

Source: **Ministry of Finance. Currently, the situation of the large SOEs is as follows:**

x Lao Airlines: The Government has decided to propose conversion of Lao

Airlines into a joint-venture entity and is currently seeking a partner.

Discussions are under way with a regional airline.

x Bolisat Phatthana Khet Phoudoi: Most of the non-core business activities

have been proposed for sale or liquidation. Wood processing and

construction activities continue to operate although independent audits are

expected to draw a clear picture. The tourism centre is reported to have been separated and it is being run as a State-owned entity.

x Nam Papa Laos: The asset revaluation has been completed and the

company has started implementing its restructuring plan.

x Pharmaceutical Factory 3: The revaluation of assets and the accounting

audit have been completed.

Most of the infrastructure services in the Lao People's Democratic Republic (electricity, water, telecommunications and aviation) are provided by SOEs although there are more and more private sector firms providing these services.

PRINCIPAL IMPORT ITEMS

Table 6. Direction of imports (Millions of United States dollars)

1998		1999	2000	2001	2002	2010
Thailand	411.3	452.0	419.1	451.7	444.0	501.8
Viet Nam	80.7	181.8	77.7	70.8	76.8	87.6
China	19.6	24.4	33.9	59.9	59.7	108.1
Singapore	22.1	37.0	32.9	28.9	29.1	22.4
Japan	21.0	24.9	23.6	13.0	19.6	16.7
France	6.2	7.6	27.5	8.5	8.9	11.8
Hong Kong, China	8.7	11.0	7.9	10.1	6.1	8.2
Australia	2.3	2.5	4.2	8.3	12.6	9.5
Republic of Korea	5.3	11.9	4.9	6.9	5.0	5.6
Germany	15.4	9.5	3.6	7.4	4.1	5.9
World Total	644.6	808.9	685.9	719.4	730.9	844.9

BUYING FROM THE LAO PEOPLE'S DEMOCRATIC REPUBLIC

I. EXPORT POLICY, REGULATIONS AND PROCEDURES

A. General

The export of goods from the Lao People's Democratic Republic requires a series of procedures including the conclusion of an export contract, the issuance of export approval and customs clearance and shipment. Most Lao export transactions are made under a Letter of Credit.

The Prime Minister's Order No. 24/PM of 22 September 2004 on facilitating import and export procedures and domestic movements of goods mandates relevant ministries and local administration to review and streamline import-export procedures and to facilitate the movements of goods across the country. It has a mandate to avoid burdensome and lengthy technical certification by relevant authorities. The Order reinforces the implementation of single-window service at border checkpoints, which is composed of customs, commerce and other technical regulation authorities.

The Ministry of Commerce issues annual regulations to implement the Prime Minister's Decree 24/PM of 22 September 2004 and Notification No. 1691/PMO of 7 October 2004. The current regulation is the Order on import and export No. 0962/MOC.FTD of 13 October 2004. It reinforces the single-window service by coordinating with line agencies. It also has a mandate to streamline and facilitate import and export procedures particularly for trading businesses located along the borders.

The export procedure is rather simple. The exporters can go directly to the Customs checkpoint to undergo clearance, except gold and copper which require an export licence.

B. Export approval

Some commodities are subject to an export authorization delivered by the Ministry of Commerce/provincial offices or/and related line ministries as listed in table 7.

The relevant agencies produce their list of exports, subject to control for the purpose of technical regulations, health, information and culture, agriculture and forestry, industry and handicraft.

In some cases the Government conducts inspections of designated export items prior to shipment. Export inspection is not required for all commodities but is required for the export of precious stones such as cut diamonds.

Procedures of inspection can be classified under four categories: quality of packaging, condition of material, design and manufacturing method.

Table 7. Export authorization

Commodity	Permits issued by
Valuable objects (Diamond 721-02)	x Foreign Trade Department, Ministry of Commerce
All kinds of minerals (25.02-22;25.24-30; 26.01-21)	x x Department of Geology - Mines, Ministry of Industry and Handicrafts Trade Section of Provinces, Vientiane Municipality or Special Region
Plant seeds	x Department of Agriculture, Ministry of Agriculture and Forestry
Domestic animals and animal products	x Department of Livestock and Fisheries, Ministry of Agriculture and Forestry
Wood products	x Department of Forestry, Ministry of Agriculture and Forestry
Wild forestry products	x Department of Forestry, Ministry of Agriculture and Forestry

Source: Ministry of Commerce, Regulation No. 0285/MOC.FTD of 17 March 2004.

C. Licensing, quotas and prohibitions

An enterprise can export all kinds of commodities as long as they are not on the list of goods prohibited or restricted through quotas. According to Ministry of Commerce notification No. 0284/MOC.TFD of 17 March 2004, the list of goods prohibited for export effective 3 May 2004 is as follows:

PROHIBITED GOODS FOR EXPORT

1. Any kind of explosives, weapons and war vehicles.
2. Any kind of chemical substances that may be used to produce explosives, weapons and war vehicles.
3. Any kind of addictive drugs.
4. Any kind of cultural antiques or products related to the tradition of the nation.
5. Wildlife, aquatic animals and their parts which are forbidden by domestic law and any international convention signed by the Lao People's Democratic Republic.
6. All type of logs, sawn wood, rattan and unprocessed Ketsana wood.
7. Wild forestry products such as orchids, Bialai, Chandai and others prohibited according to internal law.
8. Sulphur (bat manure).
9. Equipment for printing of bank notes.

D. Other requirements

The Committee for Food and Drug Control is responsible for quality control of goods. Quality control is required for food, drinks and medicines. A veterinary certificate is required for the export of live animals.

E. Documentary evidence under trade agreements and preferential schemes

As a least developed country, the Lao People's Democratic Republic receives tariff preferences from different countries. However, Lao exporters still face difficulties in making use of the preferences due to a number of constraints such as certification of products/ origin, quality, transport costs, customs clearance and local capacity.

The Lao National Chamber of Commerce and Industry (LNCCI), provides access to the documents and forms required to export under the non-different preferential schemes. See annex 1 for samples of the following:

-certificate of origin for exports of wood and agricultural products;

-certificate of origin for exports of textiles outside the EU;

-certificate of origin and export license for exports of textiles to the EU.

ASEAN INTEGRATION SYSTEM OF PREFERENCES

Beginning on 1 January 2002, ASEAN adopted the ASEAN Integration System of Preferences (AISP) scheme whereby preferential tariffs are offered to the newer members by the older members on a voluntary and bilateral basis.

AISP is implemented based on products proposed by Cambodia, the Lao People's Democratic Republic, Myanmar and Viet Nam (CLMV countries). About 1,117 tariff lines from these CLMV countries are eligible for tariff preferences in Brunei Darussalam, Indonesia, Malaysia and Thailand. Thus far, Malaysia, the Philippines and Thailand have issued their legal enactments to implement the AISP.

Under the AISP, Malaysia has offered the Lao People's Democratic Republic preferential treatment on 12 products, which include agriculture, wood, plastics, ceramics, articles of iron and electrical products. This year, at the request of the Lao People's Democratic Republic, Malaysia will add 73 products to the list, including vegetable, wooden furniture, textiles and garments. Companies from the Lao People's Democratic Republic should make use of the AISP privileges to increase their share of Malaysia's growing imports

The Philippines has granted preferential tariffs on 12 products for the Lao People's Democratic Republic and 62 products for all CLMV countries, as per Presidential Executive Order No. 448 dated 22 July 2005 (see http://www.tariffcommission.gov.ph/EO%20448.htm).

2. Australia

As of 1 July 2003, Australia has allowed the entry of goods manufactured or produced in least developed countries free of import duty. Two categories of goods, namely, raw products and manufactured goods, will be considered for the purposes of duty-free entry.

Goods are the manufacture of a least developed country if:

(a)
　　The last process in the manufacture of the goods was performed in a least developed country;
(b)
　　The allowable factory cost of the goods is not less than 50 per cent of the total factory cost of the goods.

Before claiming duty free entry, importers need to obtain sufficient evidence that the goods meet the rules of origin for least developed countries. For example, importers could obtain a declaration from the producer or manufacturer of the goods.

However, a declaration from a supplier that is not the producer or manufacturer of the goods is not sufficient evidence that the goods meet the rules of origin for least developed countries.

3. Bangkok Agreement

As a least developed country member of the Asia-Pacific Trade Agreement, the Lao People's Democratic Republic enjoys preferential access to certain member countries, such as India, the Republic of Korea and Sri Lanka. Further details are available at http://www.unescap.org/tid/apta.asp.

4. Canada

In January 2003, the Government of Canada launched its initiative to eliminate all duties and quotas on most imports from the 48 least developed countries. Implementation of the initiative involved a number of new measures for imports of textiles and apparel products, as well as the enactment on February 2004 of Bill C-21 extending the General Preferential Tariff (GPT) scheme and the Least Developed Country Tariff (LDCT) legislation for a further 10 years until June 2014.

Currently, most products from the least developed countries can be imported duty free and quota free under Canada's LDCT. This initiative also allows products that are not currently covered by the LDCT to be imported without duty or quota, provided they meet the rules of origin.

In order to benefit from this initiative, the Government of the Lao People's Democratic Republic signed a Memorandum of Understanding on market access with the Government of Canada in March 2003.

Canada Customs has created a new certificate to reflect the rules of origin. Importers must have the proof of origin at the time a product is imported if preferential treatment under the LDCT is to be claimed. The exporter in the country where the goods were finished should issue Form A, Certificate of Origin, (http://www.cbsa-asfc.gc.ca/E/pub/cm/d11-4-4/d11-4-4-e.html#P415_57022) or the Exporter's Statement of Origin (http://www.cbsa-asfc.gc.ca/E/pub/cm/d11-44-e.html#P452_61587). Either document may be used to support a claim for preferential treatment for goods imported under the GPT and, with the exception of textile and apparel goods, under the LDCT.

Textile and apparel products exported from least developed countries are eligible for duty free treatment provided they have been manufactured or formed from inputs from any of the 48 eligible least developed countries, or they have been formed from inputs from the GPT beneficiary countries, provided the value added in the exporting least developed country is at least 25 per cent. For more information on the specific rules of origin, please consult the appropriate official publication in the *Canada Gazette*, Part II of 1 January 2003. at:

http://canadagazette.gc.ca/partII/2003/20030101/pdf/g2-13701.pdf.

The Certificate of Origin for textile and apparel goods originating in a least developed country, importers in Canada must use the Form B255, Certificate of Origin - Textile and Apparel Goods Originating in a Least Developed Country (http://www.cbsa-asfc.gc.ca/E/pbg/cf/b255/README.html), when claiming the LDCT for textile and apparel goods classified within Chapters 50-63 (textile and apparel goods) of the Harmonized System of Tariff Classification.

5. European Union

As a least developed country, the Lao People's Democratic Republic benefits from preferential access to the EU market under different schemes and agreements, such as the GSP, the EU-Lao People's Democratic Republic agreement on trade in textile products, the regional accumulation advantage and the Everything but Arms initiative.

A. GSP scheme

Under the EU GSP scheme, certificates of origin Form A (http://europa.eu.int/comm/taxation_customs/resources/documents/guide-annex_4-en.pdf) are issued by the EU-recognized competent governmental authorities of the exporting country (usually ministerial bodies) if they determine that the exports meet the requirements of the rules of origin. In the Lao People's Democratic Republic, the competent authority is the Foreign Trade Department.

Under certain conditions, an invoice declaration may be submitted instead of a certificate of origin Form A. Such an invoice declaration may be made by an approved exporter or by any other exporter for any consignment of a total value up to 6,000 euros. The declaration may be made on an invoice, a delivery note or any other commercial document that describes the products concerned in sufficient detail to be identified.

B. EU-Lao People's Democratic Republic agreement on trade in textiles

The access of Lao textile exports to the EU single market was given a further boost when the EU-Laos Agreement on Trade in Textile Products became effective in December 1998.

Under this agreement, certain products are allowed to enter the EU free of quantitative limits (see Annex I of the agreement). Quantitative restrictions could be established if the EU determines that the level of imports in a given category exceeds certain rates in relation to the level of imports in the preceding year.

Products covered by the agreement require a specific certificate of origin, which must always be certified by the Lao competent authorities and must conform to the model set out in the Protocol to the agreement. This certificate of origin is not required if the textile products are already covered by the GSP scheme, in which case they only require certificate of origin Form A, as mentioned above.

Similarly to products under the GSP scheme, goods included in Groups III, IV and V in Annex I of the agreement may be introduced into the EU on the production of a declaration by the exporter on the invoice or other commercial document stating that the products originate in the Lao People's Democratic Republic.

The EU-Lao People's Democratic Republic Agreement on Trade in Textile Products establishes a double-checking system for certain categories of textiles (see Annex II of the agreement), some of which are subject to quantitative restrictions or quotas.

Since January 2005, the double-checking system of an export license has been abolished.

C. Regional cumulation advantage

A further and permanent relaxation of the Preferential Rules of Origin was introduced in January 1999 when the EU granted the Regional Cumulation advantage (http://europa.eu.int/comm/trade/issues/global/gsp/eba/ug.htm).

This advantage - reserved for members of regional groupings such as ASEAN

- allows the Lao People's Democratic Republic to consider intermediary inputs, such as fabric imported from another ASEAN country, as having been produced in the Lao People's Democratic Republic.

D. Everything but Arms

The Lao People's Democratic Republic also benefits from the EU Everything but Arms (http://europa.eu.int/comm/trade/issues/global/gsp/eba/index_en.htm) initiative introduced in March 2000. This scheme allows the duty and quota free export to the EU of all products from least developed countries with the exception of arms and munitions.

6. Japan

The Japan GSP scheme is used by the Lao People's Democratic Republic to export handicrafts, natural mushrooms, textiles and wood products.

7. United States of America

The Government of the United States launched the GSP in 1976 and it now offers duty-free treatment for more than 4,650 products from 144 designated countries and territories throughout the world. The GSP scheme has been renewed periodically since, most recently in 2002 when the Government enacted the necessary legislation to extend the GSP program until 2006.

Until December 2004, the United Stated did not have normal trade relations with the Lao People's Democratic Republic. On 4 February 2005, the Government of the United States granted permanent normal trade relation status to the Lao People's Democratic Republic and enacted legislation to normalize trade relations. The Lao People's Democratic Republic-United States of America Bilateral Trade Agreement (http://www.bilaterals.org/IMG/pdf/US-LA_FTA.pdf) was concluded in 1997 and signed on 18 September 2003.

The agreement is intended to promote trade cooperation between the two countries and help to remove all obstacles and non tariff on a reciprocal basis, The main concept of normal trade relations and bilateral trade agreements focuses on market access, transparency and national treatment making it easier for the Lao People's Democratic Republic to export to the American market at a favourable tariff rate. It is also hoped that it will encourage both nationals and foreign investors to invest in the Lao People's Democratic Republic.

EXPORT CHARGES

Export taxes are assessed based on the quantity, volume, weight, price and other factors multiplied by a fixed rate or a percentage. Export valuation is based on the f.o.b. price at the Lao People's Democratic Republic border. No export duties are levied.

SETTLEMENTS OF BILLS, LETTER OF CREDIT

Any of the standard international methods of payment may be used in the Lao People's Democratic Republic (draft, wire transfer or payment order) but most export transactions are made under letter of credit.

DOCUMENTS

Document	Number of copies	Body concerned
Application for export permit Bill of lading/air waybill Commercial invoice Single Administrative Document Export licence, if required Export permit GSP Form A Other permits, as required Packing list	5 2 1 1 1 1 1 1	Exporter Shipping company/airline company Exporter Customs department Ministry of Commerce, Provincial trade officer Ministry of Commerce, Provincial authorities Ministry of Commerce, Foreign Trade Department Ministries concerned Exporter

Source: LNCCI/ MOC.

STATE MONOPOLY FOR EXPORT ITEMS

The state monopoly for the export of strategic items has been abolished, although a number of products perceived as strategic remain under government price control.

Group	Product	Items
Group 1	Energy	1 item: fuel and gas
Group 2	Construction materials	4 items: steel bars, cement, roof tiles and galvanized sheets
Group 3	Agricultural	2 items: fertilizer and animal food
Group 4	Foods	6 items: rice, sugar, beef, pork and eggs

Source: World Bank Economic Monitor, May 2004 and Ministry of Commerce.

VI. PRINCIPAL EXPORT ITEMS

Over the past decade, the structure of exports from the Lao People's Democratic Republic has changed from commodity-based to more process-based exports (see table 8).

Table 8. Composition of exports, by principal commodities

(Millions of United States dollars)

1998		1999	2000	2001	2002	2003
Wood products	115	55	73	79	71	61
Electricity	67	91	112	106	104	92
Coffee	48	15	12	15	9	10
Garments	70	66	92	99	100	93

Source: Based on data from ADB.

Exports from the Lao People's Democratic Republic depend heavily on two neighbouring countries, Viet Nam and Thailand, which represents around 40 per cent of the country's total exports. Exports to the European Union account for about 25 per cent of the total.

Table 9. Direction of exports

(Millions of United States dollars)

1998		1999	2000	2001	2002	2003
Viet Nam	119.5	179.4	96.1	61.9	67.1	76.6
Thailand	28.8	51.6	68.9	81.0	85.0	94.4
France	23.3	18.2	27.1	33.7	33.8	33.5
Germany	21.4	27.0	20.8	25.5	22.0	25.2
Belgium	12.8	13.5	13.6	10.4	13.6	17.6
United Kingdom	7.7	12.5	7.2	9.3	13.4	14.1
Netherlands	5.4	8.9	10.0	9.7	10.6	10.2
Italy	9.5	5.9	9.2	10.9	10.1	10.3
Japan	17.8	12.3	10.9	6.3	6.1	7.3
China	7.2	8.7	4.9	6.8	8.8	10.2

Total, world	370.8	462.5	389.7	375.4	396.0	441.6

Source: **Based on data from ADB.**

References for part three: buying from the Lao People's Democratic Republic

Australia Customs http://www.customs.gov.au/webdata/resources/notices/ACN_03412.pdf Canada Border Service Agency http://www.cbsa-asfc.gc.ca/import/accountingintroe.html#P305_26310 Canada Department of Foreign Affairs and International Trade http://www.dfaitmaeci.gc.ca/tna-nac/ldc_back-en.asp , http://www.dfait-maeci.gc.ca/tna-nac/socialen.asp#development

Department of Foreign Trade: 'What and how to do business in the Lao People's Democratic Republic' (1998) EU bilateral relations with Lao People's Democratic Republic

http://europa.eu.int/comm/external_relations/lao/intro/

EU Delegation to Lao People's Democratic Republic

http://www.dellao.cec.eu.int/en/eu_laos_sea/laos_trade.htm EU textiles sector http://trade-info.cec.eu.int/textiles/legis_texts.cfm EU trade and development http://europa.eu.int/comm/trade/miti/devel/index_en.htm EU User's guide to the EU GSPs, Special Arrangements for Least Developed Countries

http://europa.eu.int/comm/trade/issues/global/gsp/eba/ug.htm EU-Laos Agreement on Trade in Textile Products http://tradeinfo.cec.eu.int/doclib/html/111335.htm http://www.customs.gov.au/site/page.cfm?u=5337 http://www.customs.gov.au/webdata/resources/notices/ACN_03412.pdf Lao-U.S. Trade Agreement http://www.bilaterals.org/IMG/pdf/US-LA_FTA.pdf LNCCI http://www.lncci.laotel.com/Lao%20Import%20&%20Export.htm MOC Lao People's Democratic Republic

http://www.mot.gov.vn/Laowebsite/vbdetail.asp?id=0203/MOC.TFD

U.S.Department of State http://www.state.gov/r/pa/ei/bgn/2770.htm
U.S.Embassy in Lao People's Democratic Republic http://usembassy.state.gov/laos/
U.S.Federal Register, 11 February 2005
http://a257.g.akamaitech.net/7/257/2422/01jan20051800/edocket.access.gpo.gov/2005/pdf/0
5 -2723.pdf
U.S.Trade Representative

http://www.ustr.gov/Trade_Development/Preference_Programs/GSP/Section_Index.html

World Bank Economic Monitor, May 2004

http://siteresources.worldbank.org/INTLAOPRD/Resources/2935821096519010070/lao_eco
n_monitor_may2004.pdf

INVESTING IN THE LAO PEOPLE'S DEMOCRATIC REPUBLIC

I. FOREIGN INVESTMENT POLICY AND REGULATIONS

Since the adoption of the New Economic Mechanism (NEM) in 1986 and the Constitution in 1991, the Lao People's Democratic Republic has promulgated a number of laws and regulations which promote foreign investment and form the legal basis for the development of the private sector.

The policy framework for foreign investment in the Lao People's Democratic Republic is based on the new Law on the Promotion of Foreign Investment (2004) effective 14 January 2005 (which replaced the Law on the Promotion and Management of Foreign Investment of 1994), the Business Law (1994), the Customs Law (1994), and the Tax Law (1995).

The Law on the Promotion of Foreign Investment states the forms of acceptable foreign investment as well as the rights, benefits and obligations that come with each type of investment. It also explains the responsibilities of the Committee for Promotion and Management of Investment (CPMI) at the central and provincial levels. The law excludes indirect investment, such as loans, aid and general buying and selling of commodities.

The Government's role is that of a facilitator to help create an enabling environment for expanding private investment, both domestic and foreign. The CPMI is acting as a one-stop service on investment issues and the coordinating body with sectoral organizations at the central level and provincial levels.

Foreign investment is welcome in all production, businesses, sectors and zones of the country except in business activities which are (a) detrimental to national security, (b) cause a negative impact on the environment in the present or long term and (c) detrimental to health or national customs and traditions.

The Lao People's Democratic Republic has concluded bilateral investment agreements with the following 20 countries:

Bilateral Investment Agreements

Australia	Germany	Singapore
China	India	Sweden
Cuba	Indonesia	Switzerland
Democratic People's	Malaysia	Thailand
Republic of Korea	Mongolia	United Kingdom
Denmark	Republic of Korea	United States of America
France	Russian Federation	Viet Nam

A separate bilateral agreement for the avoidance of double taxation has been signed with Thailand.

Foreign direct investment (FDI) in the Lao People's Democratic Republic has shown substantive growth in recent years. In 2003-2004,[2] actual investment increased almost 20 per cent with

For additional analytical, business and investment opportunities information, please contact Global Investment & Business Center, USA at (703) 370-8082. Fax: (703) 370-8083. E-mail: ibpusa3@gmail.com
Global Business and Investment Info Databank - www.ibpus.com

regard to the period 2002-2003, from US$ 150 million to US$ 180 million. Approved investment grew by 8 per cent during the same period.

Investment has flowed into the following sectors: garments, wood processing, tourism, hydropower generation and mining. Of these, the industrial sector (mining, handicrafts and wood processing) has been the main recipient of FDI over the past years, accounting for almost 70 per cent of the total FDI approvals. Agriculture and services sectors made up for 25 per cent of total FDI approvals each.

During the period 2003-2004, the main foreign investors in the Lao People's Democratic Republic were Australia (US$ 293 million), Viet Nam (US$ 63 million), Thailand (US$ 51 million), Switzerland (US$ 30 million) and China (US$ 28 million). Other investors are France, Malaysia, Netherlands, the Republic of Korea, Singapore and the United States of America.

As the role of the public private sector dialogue was recognized as one of the most effective ways to promote better understanding between the Government and the business community, in March 2005 the Government signed a Memorandum of Understanding with the International Finance Cooperation (World Bank Group) and Mekong Private Sector Development Facility (MPDF) to launch the Lao Business Forum to be organized twice a year. The first meeting took place on 9 March 2005.

II. INVESTMENT PROCEDURES

A foreign investor has the following choices when investing in the Lao

People's Democratic Republic:

x Business cooperation by contract;

x Joint ventures between foreign and domestic investors, where foreign equity should not be less than 30 per cent of the registered capital;

x One hundred per cent foreign-owned enterprises.

A. Foreign investment licence

Foreign companies or investors who wish to invest in the Lao People's Democratic Republic should fill out an application form available at the one-stop service of CPMI at the central or provincial levels. Application forms are free of charge.

The competed application must be submitted to CPMI with the following

attachments:

x Copy of the passport

x Resume of the foreign investor

x Feasibility study or business plan

x Statement certifying the legal and financial status of the legal entity

x In the case of a joint venture, a copy of the joint venture agreement.

[2] World Bank, Economic Monitor, November 2004.

Upon receipt of an application with the above-listed attachments, CPMI would coordinate with relevant sector and local authorities, when necessary, to consider and respond in writing to the foreign investor pursuant to the following time frame:

x Project falling in the lit of promoted activities: 15 working days

x Project falling in the lit of open activities with conditions: 25 working days

x Project involving the grant of a concession: 45 working days

Foreign investors who qualify shall obtain a foreign investment licence as well as an enterprise registration certificate and a tax registration certificate from CPMI. The activity must start within 90 days from the date of receipt of the investment licence, otherwise the licence shall be terminated.

Since August 2004,[3] the Department of Domestic and Foreign Investment (DDFI) operating under the Prime Minister's Office, acts as a one-stop service to foreign investors by providing information and assistance during the investment process. DDFI is a central government agency under the supervision of CPMI. The DDFI web page offers information on how to conduct business in the Lao People's Democratic Republic, laws and regulations, start-up procedures, as well as access to investment application forms required.

At the central level, CPMI is designing and planning the foreign investment policies while at the provincial level it is responsible of implementing the policies within its jurisdiction.

B. Business registration

Under the Business Law (1994), Domestic Trade Department Business Registration Division of the Ministry of Commerce (MOC) is responsible for registering all businesses in a company register. The Business Law makes no distinction between foreign and domestic companies.

A Guiding Order has established a provision of two days for the registration of local businesses in the trade sector at one of the following three levels: central (MOC), provincial and district. The application must include:

x an application form

x personal biography

x a statement of criminal records No. 3

x a copy of ID card and three 3x4 photographs

x financial statement

x charter by-law approved by trade agency (for entity as company only).

There is a division of tasks for business registration approval between different levels of government agencies as follows:

x MOC registers foreign companies (with registered capital of

US$ 200,000 or more), enterprises dealing with imports of vehicles and

fuel and exports of wood and wood products, State enterprises and joint ventures established at the central level.

[3] See PM Decision No. 43/PM of 27 August 2004 on the new procedure for registration and approvals of FDI.

x Provincial trade authorities provide registration to foreign investors (with registered capital below US$ 200,000), enterprises in the agricultural, industrial and services sectors, trading firms, state enterprises and joint ventures established by local governments.

x District offices can register and manage retail stores, shops, small supermarkets and other small services.

For further information concerning investment policy, regulations of the Lao People's Democratic Republic and to obtain an application form, trader may contact:

Investment Promotion Division Luang Prabang Road Vientiane 01001 Tel.: (856-21) 222 690, (856-21) 215 491 E-mail: fimc@laotel.com URL: http://invest.laopdr.org

III. INVESTMENT INCENTIVES AND SPECIAL PROMOTION ZONES

The Government of the Lao People's Democratic Republic offers incentives to foreign investors according to specific activities and zones. According to the Law on the Promotion of Foreign Investment, the promoted activities are the following:

1. Production for export;
2. Activities relating to agriculture or forestry, and agricultural, forestry and handicraft processing activities;
3. Activities relating to industrial processing, industrial activities using modern techniques and technology, research and development, and activities relating to the protection of the environment and biodiversity;
4. Human resource development, skills development and public health;
5. Construction of infrastructure;
6. Production of raw materials and equipment to be supplied to key industrial activities;
7. Development of the tourism industry and transit services.

The three promoted zones identified by the law, based on geographical location and socio-economic conditions in the zones, are:

Zone 1: Mountainous, plain and plateau zones with no economic infrastructure to facilitate investment.

Zone 2: Mountainous, plain and plateau zones with a moderate level of economic infrastructure suitable to accommodate investment to some extent.

Zone 3: Mountainous, plain and plateau zones with good infrastructure to support investment.

A. Duties and tax incentives

According to the Law on the Promotion of Foreign Investment (2004), the foreign investment enterprises investing within the promoted activities and zones as listed above are entitled to the following duty and tax incentives:

Zone 1: Profit tax exemption for 7 years and a concessional 10 per cent profit tax rate after the exemption period.

Zone 2: Profit tax exemption for 5 years followed by a reduced profit tax rate of 7.5 per cent for 3 years and after a concessional 15 per cent profit tax rate.

Zone 3: Profit tax exemption for 2 years followed by a reduced profit tax rate of 10 per cent for 2 years and after a concessional 20 per cent profit tax rate after the exemption period.

The starting date for the profit tax exemption is the date the foreign investment enterprise carries out operations, while for tree plantation activities it is the date the enterprise starts to make a profit.

In addition, foreign investors investing in the listed promoted activities are entitled to the following incentives: x During the tax exemption and reduced tax periods, the enterprise is exempted from the minimum tax; x The profit used for the expansion of licensed business activities are exempted from profit tax during the accounting year;

x Exemption from import duties and taxes on: + Equipment, spare parts and vehicles directly used for production; + Raw materials not available domestically or that exist but are insufficient in number and semi-finished products imported for manufacture or processing for re-export; and x Exemption from export duty on exported products.

Additionally, raw materials and semi-finished products imported for manufacture assembly or processing for import substitution will be exempted or allowed a reduced rate of import duties and taxes.

B. Non-tax incentives

The Government provides the following non-tax incentives to all foreign investors: x Right to employ foreign technicians, experts and managers but should not

exceeding 10 per cent of the enterprise's labour force x Investment term is up to 75 years x Personal income tax at a flat rate of 10 per cent x Foreign investors are also allowed to expatriate their earnings back home

or to a third country.

The Government also offers guarantees against nationalization, expropriation or requisition without compensation.

For further details on investment incentives, please refer to the DDFI website at http://invest.laopdr.org/.

C. Special economic zone

Approximately 500 km south of Vientiane, the province of Savannakhet is located along the East-West Economic Corridor (EWEC) linking Myanmar, Thailand, Lao People's Democratic Republic and Viet Nam (Road No. 9). EWEC crosses the Indo-China peninsula and forms a land bridge between the South China Sea and the Andaman Sea. The reconstruction of Road No.9 in Savannakhet province was completed in mid-2004. A free traffic system and operation of a single custom inspection point of the corridor among the countries concerned should be implemented soon.

According to Prime Minister Decree No. 148/PM on the establishment of the Savan-Seno Special Economic Zone (SSEZ) located in Savannakhet province dated 29 September 2003, the zone composes the following:

x Site A (305 ha), located immediately upstream of Savannakhet capital city

   in Khanthabouly district, next to the new Mekong River Bridge,

x Site B (20 ha) in Seno town located 28 km East from site A, at the junction

   between the National Road No. 13 and National Road No. 9.

The main objectives of SSEZ are:

x To attract and promote investment

x To create jobs and upgrade labour skills

x To develop and modernize the country industrialization

x To become a trade and service hub on EWEC The categories of business activities to be developed in SSEZ are the following:

x Export Processing Zone

x Free Trade Zone

x Free Service and Logistic Centre (which should include tourism, banking and other activities)

According to Prime Minister Decree No. 177/PM on the management regulations and incentive policies regarding SSEZ dated 13 November 2003, the SSEZ governance is the responsibility of

SSEZ Authority. The primary function of the Authority is to ensure prompt and transparent authorization of licensing of investment in the zone and to provide investors and developers with all the necessary facilities and assistance, including processing of their investment requests through a One-Stop Station Service. SSEZ has an autonomous budget and full responsibility in the management, design and construction of the Zone.

Interested investors should submit the investment application form directly to SSEZ. The approval or rejection of the application and granting of the licence would be done within 5 working days.

For further details on investment possibilities in SSEZ please contact: Savan-Sena Special Economic Zone Authority

P.O. Box 200 Phetsalad Road, Khanthabouli District Savannakhet

Tel./Fax: (856 41) 251487 E-mail: sonphet@laotel.com Website: www.invest.laopdr.org

IV. TAXATION

All persons or legal entities consuming goods or services, conducting business, performing independent professions and generating income in the Lao People's Democratic Republic are subject to pay taxes.

According to the Tax Law of 1995, the tax system of the Lao People's Democratic Republic consists of direct and indirect taxes as follows:

Indirect taxes	Direct taxes	Other taxes
Excise tax	Income tax	Fees/charges
Turnover tax	Profit tax	Minimum tax
	Social security tax	

Enterprises operating in the country must pay one of the following two taxes, whichever produces the higher tax return, the minimum tax, at a flat rate of 1 per cent of gross profit or the profit tax, based on net profit.

The latest legislations relevant to taxation are the Prime Minister Decree No. 241 dated 25 December 1998 and the Ministry of Finance Decree No.1 dated 4 January 1999.

A. Excise tax

Excise tax is an indirect tax collected on certain types of goods. As specified in article 23 of the Tax Law, 1995, goods subject to excise tax include fuel (2-23 per cent), alcohol (30-40 per cent), tobacco products (30 per cent) and cosmetics (10 per cent).

B. Turnover tax

Turnover tax is collected on imports and the sale of general imported or locally produced goods. In addition, general services, constituting the supply of labour to others against a service fee as compensation, are also subject to turnover tax. Rates of turnover tax are 5 or 10 per cent.

Payment is made to the relevant tax authorities on a monthly basis, before the tenth day of the following month. Deductions are made from these monthly turnover taxes if the importer has already paid at the port of entry. Paid taxes are carried forward to the next month if necessary. Goods, whether imported or locally produced, constructions or services that are used by the operator are also subject to turnover tax.

Importers of goods for re-export to third countries, export-oriented producers or providers of services which have been subjected to turnover taxes at the port of entry are entitled to deduct these payments from the taxes payable at the next import of goods, raw materials, etc.

Imports on equipment, means of production, spare parts and other materials used in the operation of foreign investors' projects or in their productive enterprises are taxed at a uniform flat rate of 1 per cent of the imported value. Raw materials and intermediate components, imported for the purpose of processing and then exported, are exempt from such import duties.

C. Income tax

This is a direct tax collected from income generated in the Lao People's Democratic Republic. Taxable income includes: x Income from salaries such as wages, bonuses, position bonuses and other material benefits, including benefits-in-kind

x Income from movable assets, such as dividends or other benefits for shareholders of a company, loan interest and guarantee fees or other liens

x Income from the lease of assets

x Income from patents or other rights, including lease of rights, production formulae, trademarks and copyrights.

Certain types of income are exempt from tax. These include social insurance and salaries of foreign experts involved in projects in the Lao People's Democratic Republic.

A salary tax on earnings of foreign personnel is levied at a flat rate of 10 per cent on gross income, including most benefits-in-kind. It is paid on a monthly basis through withholding at payment. Foreign personnel receiving salaries abroad are liable to pay income tax in the Lao People's Democratic Republic when they reside in the country for over 180 days in a given tax year.

Salary tax is levied at a progressive rate of up to 45 per cent on gross income of local personnel. Salary and wage earners are entitled to deduct 200,000 kip from their monthly salary in the computation of tax payable. This deduction is an allowance for "expenses for living costs".

D. Profit tax

Taxes on profits are set at 35 per cent on net profits for all Lao business enterprises and for foreign business enterprises, please see details in chapter III of this part. Taxable profit includes:

x Profit from business generated from agro-forestry, industrial and handicraft production, the exploitation of natural resources, import/export, wholesale or retail trade and general services

x Profit from independent professionals

x Certain expenses can be deducted when determining annual profit. These include:

- **General expenses in business activities, including utility costs, travel and entertainment, advertising, salaries, lease costs and insurance**
- **Expenses on travel and entertainment - these are only deductible up to a limit of 0.2 per cent of turnover**
- **Expenses on gifts, allowances, presents and prizes - these are only deductible up to a limit of 0.15 per cent of turnover**

x Depreciation, which can be claimed on a straight line or cost reduction method. In the year of acquisition or disposal, depreciation can be claimed for the portion of the year the asset was owned

x Reserves for unexpected expenses and risks relating to items such as valuation of inventory or receivables.

Profit taxes, income taxes on salaries, salaries paid to partners in partnerships, luxury expenses and interest payments to shareholders are examples of non-deductible expenses. Individuals receiving income from business profits are entitled to an annual deduction of 1,200,000 kip.

The profit tax is remitted on a quarterly basis, based on estimated profit or the prior year's profit. Tax returns are made to the tax authorities prior to the fifteenth day of the month following the end of each quarter. The balance of the Profit or Minimum Tax due should be remitted before 15 April of the following year. If the quarterly profit tax is overpaid, the amount is not refunded in cash but can be deducted from future profit tax calculations. Tax can also be payable on a lump-sum basis.

E. Value added tax

Following recommendations by the IMF, the Government has pledged to introduce a value added tax regime, which will replace the turnover tax. This is partly designed to offset the anticipated loss of customs revenue as tariffs are lowered in line with the commitments of the Lao People's Democratic Republic with ASEAN-AFTA. The value added tax would be introduced in 2007.

The Tax Law sets out a simple system of tax payment which associates turnover tax and profit tax into one payment. The simple system of tax payment requires an agreement between the tax authority and the taxpayer. The agreement becomes effective within one year of the signature of the contract. In order to cancel the agreement, the taxpayer should inform the tax authority 60 days before expiration of the contract. The tax authority may cancel the agreement at any time if it is discovered that the taxpayer has violated the limits of business operations stated in the contract.

Rates for the simple system of tax payment

Rates for each type of activities			
Estimated annual income	(percentage)		
(kip)	Production, construction and	Trade restaurants	Services and

		transport	
Less than 2,000,000 Kip	1	2	3
2,000,001 - 4,000,000	2	3	4
4,000,001 - 8,000,000	3	4	5
8,000,001 - 12,000,000	4	5	6
12,000,001 - 16,000,000	5	6	7
16,000,001 - 20,000,000	6	7	8
20,000,001 - 24,000,000	7	8	9

Source: **Tax Law 1994, p. 29**

V. FOREIGN EXCHANGE

The policy framework for foreign exchange is based on the following laws and regulations: Law on the Bank of the Lao People's Democratic Republic, No. 05/LNA, dated 14 October 1995 and the amended version No. 05/LNA, dated 14 October 1999 as well as the Presidential Decree No. 01/OP dated 9 August 2002 on governing the management of foreign exchange and precious metals.

The national currency is the kip. Official currency exchange facilities are provided by a range of Lao banks, including the *Banque du Commerce Extérieur* or at a foreign exchange bureau licensed by the Bank of the Lao People's Democratic Republic.

All foreign enterprises are considered to be Lao residents for the purpose of foreign exchange. They must deposit all foreign exchange earnings into accounts with banks in the Lao People's Democratic Republic and cannot open accounts abroad except where deemed necessary.

In conformity with the law and regulations governing the management of foreign exchange and precious metals, foreign investors may repatriate earnings and capital from their foreign investments to their own home countries or third countries. They may do this through a Lao bank or a foreign bank established in the Lao People's Democratic Republic, using the exchange rate prevailing on the date of repatriation, as quoted by the Bank of Lao People's Democratic Republic.

Foreign personnel with foreign investments may also repatriate their earnings, after paying Lao personal income taxes and all other taxes due. After paying the annual profit tax, foreign investors have to devote 5 per cent of their profit each year to various reserve funds designed to ensure that enterprises continuously improve their efficiency, in accordance with the enterprise's policy and Articles of Association.

VI. LABOUR ISSUES

A central piece of legislation covering labour and employment in the Lao People's Democratic Republic is the Labour Law, 1994. The law covers the rights and obligations of employees and employers.

A. Main provisions under the Labour Law, 1994

Working hours	Prohibition of work in excess of 8 hours per day, 6 days per week or 48 hours per week; for workers in jobs in hazardous or unpleasant -abnormally hot or cold, or underground - environments, a maximum of 6 hours per day or 36 hours per week applies. Shift workers are entitled to a 45-minute meal break. Production workers are entitled to rest for at least 5-10 minutes every two hours.
Overtime	Maximum overtime of 30 hours per month, with a maximum of 3hours in each period. Overtime rates are 150 per cent of the standard rate if worked by day and 200 per cent if worked by night. If overtime is worked on Saturdays, Sundays or public holidays these rates are 250 per cent by day and 300 per cent by night (unless workers' contracts already require them to work on those days).
Minimum age	The minimum age of employment is 15 years. Between the ages of 15 and 18 the maximum work week is 6 hours per day or 36 hours per week; workers under 18 may not perform hazardous or arduous work.
Wages	Fixed salaries or wages must be paid at least monthly; hourly wages must be paid at least every 16 days.
Holidays	Workers are entitled to 15 days' holiday per year, or 18 days per year if performing arduous or hazardous work; these are in addition to official holidays or weekly rest days.
Sick leave	Workers are entitled to a maximum of 30 days sick leave per year upon presentation of a medical certificate.
Maternity	Women may take 90 days paid maternity leave. The law also prohibits work involving heavy lifting or long periods of continuous standing during pregnancy and for the 6 months after a pregnancy.
Retirement	The law provides for company pensions for long service and retiring employees and bonuses for elderly employees. The retirement age is 60 years for men and 55 years for women. Workers who have reached retirement age, have completed 25 years of service and have paid social security contributions for 25 years are entitled to a pension upon retirement. The ages and time periods are reduced by 5 years each for those in hazardous or arduous occupations.
	For injuries sustained while performing occupational duties at the workplace, the employer or the social security fund shall bear the costs of treatment and hospitalization. Where a worker dies through occupational injury, the employer shall pay at least 6 months' salary to cover funeral expenses and pay a lump-sum benefit to the beneficiaries of the deceased. Workers who sustain an occupational injury are also entitled to full salary for up to 6 months and 50 per cent of their salary for a further 18 months. After 18 months, benefits are granted under the social security system.

Source: DDFI website at http://invest.laopdr.org/labour%20law.htm.

B. Labour contract

The Labour Law requires a written contract between an employer and an employee. In limited circumstances, a verbal contract is possible, for example for temporary or daily work or employment involving only a small amount of work. The contracts can be for a fixed term or indefinite period.

A probationary period is allowed to determine workers' ability to perform their duties. The period lasts a maximum of 30 days for work requiring no experience or specialized skills and a maximum of 60 days in other cases. The probationary period can be extended by a maximum of 30 days. Probation can be terminated at any time, but 3 days (or 6 days for skilled workers) notice must be given.

As for the termination of the contract, if workers are employed on an indefinite contract, 45 days notice must be given to skilled workers and 15 days to other workers. Workers may be dismissed in the case of inadequate skills or if there is a need to reduce the total number of workers.

In the case of dismissal to reduce staff numbers, dismissed workers are entitled to compensation according on their length of service. In the case of dismissal because of wrongdoing by the worker (e.g. dishonesty, deliberate damage to employer's property, or unexplained absences of four consecutive days), the employer has the right to terminate the contract with 3 days notice. However, the employer must also notify the trade union or worker's representative in the labour unit and the local labour administration.

C. Social security

The Social Security Decree came into force in June 2001 and is being introduced gradually. It applies to:

x Employees of State-owned enterprises, private enterprises and joint enterprises

x Enterprises that employ 10 or more employees

x An enterprise that has less than 10 employees, but is a branch of a larger enterprise If an enterprise is subject to the Social Security Decree, but later reduces its number of employees to less than the minimum requirement, it must still maintain its application of the Social Security Decree. However, the Government has set a ceiling where the deductions will cease to apply. Salaries above 1 million kip per month will be ignored for Social Security. As a result, the maximum charge will be 50,000 kip per month from employers and 45,000 kip per month from employees.

The employer is responsible for ensuring that the payments are made, by withholding the employee's contribution from wages.

VII. DISPUTE SETTLEMENT

As a member of ASEAN, the Lao People's Democratic Republic adheres to the ASEAN Protocol on Enhanced Dispute Settlement Mechanism signed in Vientiane on 29 November 2004, which provides rules and procedures on dispute settlements for all member States.

The Labour Law makes a distinction between (a) disputes over rights: disputes concerning the provisions of the Labour Law, labour regulations, employment contracts, labour unit regulations, etc; (b) disputes over interests: claims on the employer for new benefits or rights.

In the case of dispute over rights, the parties are encouraged to resolve the claim between themselves. If this is not possible then the worker is entitled to submit the claim to the labour administration for conciliation. If the dispute still cannot be resolved, the claim can be submitted to the People's Court.

The above also applies in respect of disputes over interests. If the labour administration fails to resolve the dispute, then the case goes to the Labour Dispute Arbitration Committee for a final decision.

For additional analytical, business and investment opportunities information, please contact Global Investment & Business Center, USA at (703) 370-8082. Fax: (703) 370-8083. E-mail: ibpusa3@gmail.com Global Business and Investment Info Databank - www.ibpus.com

In practice, Lao courts appear to do all they can to resolve disputes by arbitration. It is therefore rare for any case going to a Lao court to be resolved quickly and according to the strict letter of a contract.

VIII. PROTECTION OF PROPERTY RIGHTS

The Government is engaged in the modernization of its industrial property administration and in the early stages of developing its legal and procedural system for the protection of intellectual property.

Trademarks, patents, industrial design and copyrights are governed by the following legislative framework: x Decree of the Prime Minister on Trademark Registration, No. 06/PM, 18 January 1995 x Regulation on Registration of Trademarks, No. 466/STEA-PMO, 7 March 2002 x Decree of the Prime Minister on Patents, Industrial Designs and Utility Models, January 2002 x Regulation on the Implementation of the Decree on Patents, Industrial Designs and Utility Models, 2 July 2002 x A new Decree on Industrial Property Matters has been drafted and submitted to the Prime Minister's Office for approval.

Since 1999, the Science, Technology and Environment Agency (STEA), attached to the Prime Minister's Office, is responsible for the protection of intellectual property rights in the Lao People's Democratic Republic as well as for the improvement of the country's ability to adhere to conventions and international protocols.

Within the STEA, the Department of Intellectual Property, Standardization and Metrology (DISM) gives guidance on trademark registration and is also responsible for drafting Industrial Property laws. DISM also registers trademarks for use within the Lao People's Democratic Republic. The Intellectual Property division within this Department is responsible for the protection of patents, petty patents, industrial designs and trademarks.

Lao People's Democratic Republic signed the World Intellectual Property Organization (WIPO) Convention in January 1995 and the Paris Convention (Industrial Property) in October 1998. WIPO's contribution is playing a vital role in the establishment of an intellectual property system in the country. The Lao People's Democratic Republic plans to join the ASEAN Trademark and Patent Common Filing System and is actively participating in the ASEAN Cooperation on Intellectual Property.

A. Trademarks

Trademark indicates a sign used to mark goods or services to designate the goods and services as belonging to the owner of the created trademark.

Enforcement measures consist of administrative measures or claims and disputes that can be resolved by mediation through the DISM or the Economic Arbitration Committee; or/and judicial procedures for intellectual property protection, which can involve both the Civil Code and the Penal Code.

There are designated government offices which act as enforcement agencies for intellectual property rights in the country. For further details on enforcement and designated agencies, please refer to the STEA website at: http://www.stea.la.wipo.net/enforcement/index.html

The application for the registration of a trademark should contain:

x An application for the registration of trademark

x Some specimens of the trademark

x A power of attorney if application is made through an authorized representative

x A list of the goods or services with the description of characteristics and quality that are to bear the mark and other necessary relevant documents

x The rules governing the use of the mark (in case of a collective mark)

x The receipt of the prescribed charges for trademark registration and other services

An individual or legal entity who has been assigned the right to use the trademark should request to register trademark in the Lao People's Democratic Republic. An application may contain permission of the owner of the trademark, defining the characteristics and quality of goods and services bearing the mark. In the case of partial assignments, the agreement shall provide for the right of the owner of trademark to verify the quality of goods or services.

The request to register a trademark should be forwarded to STEA, which reviews the application, undertakes the substantial examination, issues the certificate of registration, records the mark on the Trademark Registry and publishes the registered mark on the Official Trademark Gazette. The certificate of registration of the trademark will be for a period of 10 years starting from the filing date of the application for registration and may be renewed every 10 years.

The fees for trademark registration, as set out in the Guidance on Registration of Trademark in the Lao People's Democratic Republic, are as follows:

Type of services for trademark registration or renewal	Fee (in US dollars)
Trademark registration or trademark renewal Consultation Verification Application Search of Trademark Modification of items on application Licensing Cancellation Duplication of a registration certificate Issuance of certified document relating to the trademark registration or renewal Publication of the result of trademark registration or renewal	80 per mark 5 per mark 5 per mark 2 per mark 10 per mark 10 per mark 40 per mark 20 per mark 10 per mark 5 per one copy 20 per one copy

Source: STEA website at http://www.stea.la.wipo.net/trademark/fees.html.

For a list of trademark agents, go to http://www.stea.la.wipo.net/trademark/list.html.

B. Patents, petty patents and industrial designs

The owner of a patent, petty patent or an industrial design, before allowing another person to use such patent, petty patent or industrial designs in the Lao People's Democratic Republic, should notify STEA by written declaration.

1. Patents and petty patents

As defined in Decree No. 01/PM January 2002, a "patent" indicates the title granted to protect an invention whereas an "invention" indicates an idea of an inventor which permits in practice the solution to a specific problem in the field of technology. A "petty patent" indicates the title granted to protect device whereas a "device" indicates a technical creation utilizing rules of nature.

The application for a patent or a petty patent should be filed with STEA and should contain the following:

x A request, which should include a petition to the effect that a patent be granted, the name of and other prescribed data concerning the applicant, the inventor and the agent, if any, and the title of the invention
x A description
x One or more claims
x One or more drawings, if required
x An abstract.

At the request of the registry, the applicant will furnish the date and number of any application for a patent or petty patent filed in a foreign country, particularly relating to the same inventions as that claimed in the application filed in the Lao People's Democratic Republic.

The documents to be submitted regarding the foreign applications are as follows:

x A copy of certified results of any search or examination carried out in respect of the foreign application

x A copy of the patent granted on the basis of the foreign application

x A copy of any final decision refusing the grant of patent requested in the foreign application

After examination, if the application fulfils all conditions established in the regulations, the Registry Unit will notify the applicant to pay the prescribed fee, it will publish it to the public and issue a certificate of the grant of the patent.

A patent will expire 20 years after the filing date of the application. A petty patent will expire 7 years after the filing date of the application. In order to maintain the patent and/or petty patent, an annual fee should be paid in advance by the owner of the patent. For details on fees derived from registration and maintenance of patents (petty patens and industrial designs), please refer to the table below.

2. Industrial designs

An "industrial design" indicates any composition of lines or colours or any three-dimensional form, whether or not associated with line or colours, which can serve as a pattern for a product of industry or handicraft or give a special appearance to such a product, and appeals to and is judged by the eye.

The application for registration of an industrial design should contain: x A request x Drawings, photographs or other adequate graphic representations and an indication of the kind of products for which the industrial design is to be used x A specimen of the article embodying the industrial design, where the industrial design is two-dimensional x A statement justifying the applicant's right to the registration of the industrial design, where the applicant is not the creator

An industrial design will expire 5 years after the filing date of the application and may be renewed for 2 continuous periods. Each period takes 5 years, where the application for renewal will apply for 90 days before expiry.

Table 10: Registration and maintenance fees for patent, petty patent and industrial design

	Registration fees (in US dollars)		
Types of services	Patent	Petty patent	Industrial design
Official fee for granting Application form for registration of Consultation Request against registration Amendment of application Licensing Duplicate Publication	30 per one item 20 per one item 10 per one item 20 per one item 10 per one item 40 per one item 10 per one copy 40 per one item	30 per one item 10 per one item 10 per one item 10 per one item 10 per one item 40 per one item 10 per one copy 30 per one item	20 per one item 10 per one item 10 per one item 10 per one item 10 per one item 40 per one item 10 per one copy 30 per one item

Maintenance fees (in US dollars)			
	Patent	Petty patent	Industrial design
Starting the	5th year	2nd year	2nd year
Official fee Services fee	30 per one item 20 per one item	15 per one item 10 per one item	10 per one item 5 per one item

For the following years, please refer to regulation No. 322/STEA-PMO, July 2002

An individual or a legal entity who is the owner of a patent, petty patent or industrial design can apply for settlement of dispute relating to the infringement of his or her registered invention, device and industrial design with STEA. An individual or a legal entity who is the owner of a patent, petty patent or industrial design has the right to propose the method of settlement of dispute and claim for damages from another person who infringes on the rights of the invention.

References for part four: investing in the Lao People's Democratic Republic

Austrade, Lao People's Democratic Republic country profile

http://www.austrade.gov.au/australia/layout/0,,0_S2-1_-2_-3_PWB192923-4_-5_-6_7_,00.html Customs Law, 1994 http://invest.laopdr.org/customs%20law.htm DDFI, Business Guide http://invest.laopdr.org/business%20guide.htm DDFI, FI law, http://invest.laopdr.org/investment%20law.htm DDFI, SEZs http://invest.laopdr.org/specialper cent20zone.htm STEA http://www.stea.la.wipo.net/aboutdism/index.html Tax Law, 1995 http://invest.laopdr.org/tax%20law.htm Trademark Decree, 1995 http://www.stea.la.wipo.net/download/decree.zip http://invest.laopdr.org/trademark%20decree.htm

UNCTAD, Country Fact Sheet on FDI, November 2004 WIPO Guide to Intellectual Property Worldwide, Country Profiles (Last updated May 2004)

http://www.wipo.int/about-ip/en/ipworldwide/pdf/la.pdf World Bank – Doing Business Database http://rru.worldbank.org/DoingBusiness/ World Bank, Lao People's Democratic Republic Economic Monitor, May 2004

http://siteresources.worldbank.org/INTLAOPRD/Resources/2935821096519010070/lao_econ_monitor_may2004.pdf

World Bank, Lao People's Democratic Republic Economic Monitor, November 2004

http://siteresources.worldbank.org/INTLAOPRD/Resources/2935821096519010070/lao_econ_monitor_nov2004.pdf

INVESTMENT CLIMATE

LAOS INVESTMENT AND BUSINESS CLIMATE - STRATEGIC INFORMATION AND CONTACTACT FOR STARTING BUSINESS IN LAOS

Contact Point
Matt Younger
Economic and Commercial Officer
American Embassy Vientiane, Rue Bartholonie, That Dam, Lao PDR
856-21-26-7156
youngermb@state.gov

After a decade-long experiment with a pure Marxist economy following the founding of the Lao People's Democratic Republic, the Lao PDR launched the "New Economic Mechanism" in 1986. Since that time, the country has gradually implemented the reforms and built the institutions necessary to a market economy. Over the last thirty years, the trend has been slow but steady progress, culminating in accession to the World Trade Organization in February, 2013. Since 2009, annual GPD growth has averaged approximately eight percent.

In order to meet the requirements for entry to the WTO, Laos engaged in major reforms of its economic and trade laws and regulations. The Lao government is now working to implement the commitments embodied in those laws, and to meet the 2015 goal for creation of the ASEAN Economic Community (AEC), which will further liberalize the trading environment and economy. Additionally, WTO and AEC requirements reinforce fuller implementation of the conditions of the 2005 U.S.-Laos Bilateral Trade Agreement.

Economic progress and trade expansion in Laos remain hampered by a low level of human resource development, weak education and health care systems, and a poor, although improving, transportation infrastructure. Institutions, especially in the justice sector, are a work in progress, and regulatory capacity is low. Additionally, increasing corruption has recently become a major concern, and the country has suffered through fiscal and monetary crises in the past year. The Lao economy is highly dependent on exploitation of natural resources, particularly in copper mining and hydropower. Although the services and industrial sectors have grown in recent years, the economy is in need of further diversification, and the majority of the Lao population is still employed in agriculture.

According to the 7th National Socio-Economic Development Plan (NSEDP) 2011-2015, Laos seeks to continue an annual economic growth rate in the neighborhood of 8%. To accomplish this, the government of Laos estimates that it needs approximately US$15 billion of total investment in the next five years, US$7 to US$8 billion of which it plans to source from foreign and domestic private investment. The plan directs the government to formulate "policies that would attract investments in addition to attracting Overseas Development Assistance; begin to implement public investment and investment promotion laws; and increase cooperation with friendly countries and international organizations."

1. OPENNESS TO, AND RESTRICTIONS UPON, FOREIGN INVESTMENT

The government of Lao PDR (GOL) officially welcomes both domestic and foreign investment as it seeks to graduate from Least Developed Country status by the year 2020. The pace of foreign investment has increased over the last several years. Mining and hydropower compose eighty percent of Foreign Direct Investment (FDI). China, Vietnam, Thailand Korea, and Japan are the largest sources of foreign investment.

The 2010 Law on Investment Promotion introduced uniform business registration requirements and tax incentives that apply equally to foreign and domestic investors. Foreigners may invest in any sector or business except those that the government deems to be detrimental to national security, health or national traditions, or to have a negative impact on the natural environment. There are no statutory limits on foreign ownership or control of commercial enterprises, but in practice, many companies seek a local partner. Companies involved in large FDI projects, especially in mining and hydropower, often either find it advantageous or are required to give the government partial ownership, frequently with money borrowed from the investor or multilateral institutions.

Foreign investors seeking to establish operations in Laos are typically required go through several steps prior to commencing operations. In addition to an investment license, foreign investors are required to obtain other permits, including; an annual business registration from the Ministry of Industry and Commerce; a tax registration from the Ministry of Finance; a business logo registration from the Ministry of Public Security; permits from each line ministry related to the investment (i.e., Ministry of Industry and Commerce for manufacturing; Ministry of Energy and Mines for power sector development); appropriate permits from local authorities; and an import-export license, if applicable. Obtaining the necessary permits can pose a challenge, especially in areas outside the capital. In 2013, the Lao government began allowing businesses to apply for tax registration at the time of incorporation, slightly simplifying the business registration process.

The Lao government has attempted to streamline business registration through the use of a "one-stop shop" model. For general business activities, this service is located in the Ministry of Industry and Commerce. For activities requiring a government concession, the service is located in the Ministry of Planning and Investment. For Special Economic Zones (SEZ), one-stop registration is run through the Secretariat to the Lao National Committee on Special Economic Zones (SNCSEZ) in the Office of the Prime Minister. According to PM Decree 177, the Savan-Seno SEZ authority is required to establish one-stop service to facilitate the issuing of investment licenses and improve the efficiency of business operations. In practice, it appears as though SEZ applications involve several different permissions and vary widely across SEZs. For clarification of one-stop shop procedures it is recommended that investors contact the SNCSEZ directly at: **sez@sncsez.gov.la**

Foreign partners in a joint venture must contribute at least thirty percent (30%) of the venture's registered capital. Capital contributed in foreign currency must be converted into kip based on the exchange rate of the Bank of the Lao People's Democratic Republic on the day of the capital contribution. Wholly foreign-owned companies may be either a new company or a branch of an existing foreign enterprise. Throughout the period of operation of a foreign investment enterprise, the assets of the enterprise must not be less than its registered capital.

For additional analytical, business and investment opportunities information, please contact Global Investment & Business Center, USA at (703) 370-8082. Fax: (703) 370-8083. E-mail: ibpusa3@gmail.com Global Business and Investment Info Databank - www.ibpus.com

Individual companies in the petrochemical industry are required to file an annual import plan. The government controls the retail price and profit margins of gasoline and diesel. Government documents articulating the restrictions and explaining the policy are difficult to obtain. Goods prohibited for import and export range from explosives and weapons, to literature that presents a negative view of the Lao government, to certain forestry products and wildlife. Agriculture production and most manufacturing production are private. State-owned enterprises (SOEs) currently account for only one percent of total employment. Over 90% of manufacturers have fewer than 10 employees. Equity in medium and large-sized SOEs can be obtained through a joint venture with the Lao government.

Although accurate statistics are difficult to obtain, there is no question that foreign investment has trended dramatically upward over the last several years, going from $1.2 billion in 2014 to $1.8 billion in 2013. There are also small but growing signs of growth in higher-quality FDI, focused on manufacturing, largely through one Special Economic Zone in the southern part of the country.

Measure	Year	Rank or value	Website Address
TI Corruption Perceptions index	2013	(140 of 177)	http://cpi.transparency.org/cpi2013/results/
Heritage Foundation's Economic Freedom index	2013	(144 of 178)	http://www.heritage.org/index/ranking
World Bank's Doing Business Report "Ease of Doing Business"	2013	(159 of 189)	http//doingbusiness.org/rankings
World Bank GNI per capita	2014	USD 1270	http://data.worldbank.org/indicator/NY.GNP.PCAP.CD

TABLE 1B – 2014 Lao PDR Millennium Challenge Scorecard:

MCC Scorecard Categories	Year	Percentage Score	Raw Score
MCC Government Effectiveness	FY 2014	56%	.04
MCC Rule of Law	FY 2014	60%	.07
MCC Control of Corruption	FY 2014	40%	-.13
MCC Fiscal Policy	FY 2014	49%	-3.1
MCC Trade Policy	FY 2014	12%	58.6
MCC Regulatory Quality	FY 2014	44%	-0.09
MCC Business Start-Up	FY 2014	23%	0.771
MCC Land Rights and Access	FY 2014	66%	0.68
MCC Natural Resource Protection	FY 2014	81%	93.9
MCC Access to Credit	FY 2014	36%	22
MCC Inflation	FY 2014	72%	4.3

The Millennium Challenge Corporation, a U.S. Government entity charged with delivering development grants to countries that have demonstrated a commitment to reform, produced scorecards for countries with a 2014 per capita gross national income (GNI) or $4,085 or less. A list of countries/economies with MCC scorecards and links to those scorecards is available here: **http://www.mcc.gov/pages/selection/scorecards**. Details on each of the MCC's indicators and a guide to reading the scorecards are available here: **http://www.mcc.gov/documents/reports/reference-2013001142401-fy14-guide-to-the-indicators.pdf**

2. CONVERSION AND TRANSFER POLICIES

In 2013, Laos suffered fiscal and monetary difficulties which resulted in low levels of foreign reserves. In response, the Bank of the Lao PDR (BOL) imposed daily limits on converting funds from Lao Kip into U.S. Dollars and Thai Baht, leading to difficulties in obtaining foreign exchange in Laos. The BOL also imposed restrictions on loans made in USD and Baht, limiting them to businesses which generated foreign currency. There were no reports of restrictions on, or difficulties in, repatriating or transferring funds associated with an investment.

In order to facilitate business transactions, foreign investors generally open commercial bank accounts in both local and foreign convertible currency at domestic and foreign banks in Laos. The Enterprise Accounting Law places no limitations on foreign investors transferring after-tax profits, income from technology transfer, initial capital, interest, wages and salaries, or other remittances to the company's home country or third countries provided that they request approval from the Lao government. Foreign enterprises must report on their performance annually and submit annual financial statements to the Ministry of Planning and Investment (MPI).

The Bank of Lao PDR manages the Lao currency, the kip, under a managed floating exchange rate in which it seeks to maintain its value in a band of plus or minus five percent around the nominal exchange rate with the U.S. dollar and Thai baht. Lao PDR is listed as a high-risk jurisdiction for money laundering/combating the financing of terrorism by the Financial Action Task Force (FATF) and has strategic deficiencies in its AML/CFT regime. In 2013, the Bank of Lao PDR agreed with the Asia Pacific Group, a regional FATF-body, to implement an action plan to address AML/CFT deficiencies.

3. EXPROPRIATION AND COMPENSATION

Foreign assets and investments in Laos are protected by laws and regulations against seizure, confiscation, or nationalization except when deemed necessary for a public purpose, in which case foreign investors are supposed to be compensated. Revocation of an investment license cannot be appealed to an independent body, and companies whose licenses are revoked must then quickly liquidate their assets.

Since 2014, Sanum Investments, a subsidiary of Lao Holdings, Inc., a company incorporated in Aruba and owned by American citizens, has been involved in a business dispute with its Lao partner. Thus far, court decisions in the case have been uniformly in favor of the Lao partner and could be construed as implicitly forcing local ownership. In addition, the company was subjected to audits and tax enforcement decisions that Sanum has alleged amount to expropriation. Sanum filed a case against the Lao PDR at the World Bank's International Center for the Settlement of Investment Disputes in 2014.

4. DISPUTE SETTLEMENT

The Lao judicial system is not independent and faces challenges in meeting the needs of a modern market economy. Contract law in Laos is lacking in many areas important to trade and commerce. While it does provide for sanctity of contracts, in practice contracts are subject to political interference and patronage. A contract can be voided if it is disadvantageous to one party, or if it conflicts with state or public interests. Foreign businessmen have described contracts in Laos as being considered "a framework for negotiation" rather than a binding agreement. Although a commercial court system exists, in practice most judges adjudicating commercial disputes have little training in commercial law. Those considering doing business in Laos are strongly urged to contact a reputable law firm for additional advice on contracts.

According to the Law on Investment Promotion, investors should resolve disputes in the following order: mediation; administrative dispute resolution; dispute resolution by the Committee for Economic Dispute Resolution; and finally, litigation. However, due to the poor state of the Lao legal system and low capacity of most Lao legal administrators, foreign investors are generally advised to seek arbitration outside the country.

Laos is not a member of the International Center for the Settlement of Investment Disputes. It became a party to the New York Convention of 1958 on the Recognition and Enforcement of Foreign Arbitral Awards on September 15, 1998, but Laos has never been asked to enforce a foreign arbitral award. Laos is a member of the United Nations Convention on International Trade Law.

In disputes involving the Ministry of Planning and Investment, decisions can only be appealed back to the Ministry itself. There is no separate independent body. Thus a company which feels it is receiving unfair treatment from the government has no independent recourse. Lao laws often contradict each other and lack implementing regulations. Some laws have been officially translated into English, including the business, tax, bankruptcy, customs, and secured transaction laws. The reliability of unofficial translations varies considerably. Application of Lao law remains inconsistent and knowledge of the laws themselves is often limited (especially outside the capital). The existence of a large number of government decrees, sometimes unpublished, further complicates the situation.

A commercial court does exist in Laos. Laos has no anti-trust statutes. The bankruptcy law permits either the business or creditor the right to petition the court for a bankruptcy judgment, and allows businesses the right to request mediation. There is no record of foreign-owned enterprises, whether as debtors or as creditors, petitioning the courts for a bankruptcy judgment.

5. PERFORMANCE REQUIREMENTS AND INVESTMENT INCENTIVES

Laos does not impose performance requirements and its regulations appear to be broadly consistent with WTO Trade Related Investment Measures (TRIMs), although it has notified the WTO that it will avail itself of transition periods for least-developed countries in completely phasing out local content and export performance requirements. Foreign investors are encouraged to give priority to Lao citizens in recruiting and hiring. Foreign personnel can be hired, although they may not normally exceed 10% of the enterprise's total labor force, with exceptions for skilled labor or politically important projects. Before bringing in foreign labor, foreign enterprises must apply for work permits from the Ministry of Labor and Social Welfare. A list of foreign personnel must also be submitted to MPI.

Laos grants incentives for foreign investment depending on industry sectors and activities promoted by the government, and the level of infrastructure and socio-economic development in specific geographic zones. Under Articles 49, 50 and 51 of the Law on Investment Promotion, the government defines agriculture, industry, handicraft and services as promoted activities.

Investment promotion is divided into 3 levels: Level 1 - high, Level 2 - medium and Level 3- low. Additionally, the country is divided into three promotion zones. Zone 1 is defined as areas lacking in socio-economic infrastructure – primarily mountainous and remote areas – and is assigned a high level of investment promotion. Zone 2 applies to areas with socio-economic infrastructure that is partially able to facilitate investments and is given medium priority. Zone 3 has infrastructure available to support investments and is assigned a low level of investment promotion.

In Zone 1, Level 1 investments receive profit tax exemptions for 10 years, Level 2 investments for 6 years and Level 3 investments for 4 years.

In Zone 2, Level 1 investments receive profit tax exemptions for 6 years, Level 2 investments for 4 years and Level 3 investments for 2 years.

In Zone 3, Level 1 investments receive profit tax exemptions for 4 years, Level 2 investments for two years and Level 3 investments for 1 year. Profit tax exemptions in all zones start from the date the enterprise commences operations.

Incentives related to customs duties, access to finance, and other taxes are described in Articles 52, 53 and 54 of the Law on Investment Promotion. As of 2011, foreign investors and workers must pay an income tax of 24% to the Lao Government, unless they are citizens of a country with which the Lao Government has signed a double-taxation agreement. Previously, this rate was 10%.

The United States does not have a double-taxation agreement with Laos. Article 67 of the Law on Investment Promotion stipulates that foreign investors and their families, including foreign professionals and foreign employees of an enterprise, may obtain multiple entry visas with a maximum term of five years. The government routinely approves long-term residence in the Lao PDR for foreign investors.

The government began replacing the turnover tax with a Value Added Tax (VAT) in 2010. Foreign investors are not required to pay import duty on equipment, spare parts and other materials used in the operation of their enterprises. Raw materials and intermediate goods imported for the purpose of processing and re-export are also exempt from import duties. Raw materials and intermediate goods imported for the purpose of import substitution are eligible for import duty reductions on a case-by-case basis.

Foreign enterprises are also eligible for profit tax and import duty reductions or exemptions on an individual basis, if the investment is determined by the GOL to benefit to Laos' socio-economic development. To date the Lao Government appears to have honored its incentives. Annual business license renewal is contingent upon certification that corporate income taxes have been paid. Investors report difficulties in obtaining tax certifications in a timely manner.

6. RIGHT TO PRIVATE OWNERSHIP AND ESTABLISHMENT

The GOL recognizes the right of private ownership, and foreigners may transfer shares of a foreign-invested company without prior government approval. However, the business law requires that all shareholders be listed in the articles of association, and changes in the articles of association of a foreign-invested company must be approved by Ministry of Planning and Investment. Thus, transferring shares in a foreign-invested company registered in Laos does require the indirect approval of the government.

7. PROTECTION OF PROPERTY RIGHTS

Foreign investors are not permitted to own land in fee-simple. However, Article 58 of the Law on Investment Promotion stipulates that foreign investors with registered investment capital of US$500,000 or above are entitled to purchase land use rights of less than 800 square meters in

For additional analytical, business and investment opportunities information, please contact Global Investment & Business Center, USA at (703) 370-8082. Fax: (703) 370-8083. E-mail: ibpusa3@gmail.com Global Business and Investment Info Databank - www.ibpus.com

order to build housing or office buildings. The GOL grants long-term leases, and allows the ownership of leases and the right to transfer and improve leasehold interests. Government approval is not required to transfer property interests, but the transfer must be registered and a registration fee paid.

A creditor may enforce security rights against a debtor and the concept of a mortgage does exist. Although the GOL is engaged in a land parceling and titling project through the Ministry of Natural Resources and Environment, it remains difficult to determine if a piece of property is encumbered in Laos. Enforcement of mortgages is complicated by the legal protection given mortgagees against forfeiture of their sole place of residence.

Laos provides for secured interest in moveable and non-moveable property under the 2005 Law on Secured Transactions and a 2011 implementing decree from the Prime Minister. In 2013, the State Assets Management Authority at the Ministry of Finance launched a new Secured Transaction Registry (STR), intended to expand access to credit for individuals and smaller firms. The STR allows for registration of movable assets such as vehicles and equipment so that they may be easily verified by financial institutions and used as collateral for loans.

Intellectual Property: A government reorganization in 2011 created the Ministry of Science and Technology, which controls the issuance of patents, copyrights and trademarks. Laos is a member of the ASEAN Common Filing System on patents but lacks qualified patent examiners. Since Thailand and Laos have a bilateral Intellectual Property Rights (IPR) agreement, in principle a patent issued in Thailand would also be recognized in Laos.

Copyright protection in Laos is weak. There is no system to issue copyrights in Laos, only a certification of copyright information. Laos is a member of the World Intellectual Property Organization (WIPO) Convention and the Paris Convention on the Protection of Industrial Property but has not yet joined the Bern Convention on Copyrights.

In 2011 the National Assembly passed a comprehensive revision of the Law on Intellectual Property which brings it into compliance with WIPO and Trade-Related Aspects of Intellectual Property standards (TRIPS). The consolidation of responsibility for IPR under the Ministry of Science and Technology is a positive development, but it lacks enforcement capacity.

For additional information about treaty obligations and points of contact at local IP offices, please see WIPO's country profiles at **http://www.wipo.int/directory/en/**.

Embassy point of contact: Matt Younger **youngermb@state.gov**

8. TRANSPARENCY OF THE REGULATORY SYSTEM

Principal laws, regulations, decrees and guidelines governing international trade and investment are available to the public, although not all have been officially translated into English. Laws and their schedules for implementation are customarily published in Lao daily newspapers, and relevant line ministries are beginning to put laws and regulations on websites.

The National Assembly includes a step for public consultations in the legislative process prior to sending laws to the Prime Minister for consideration. However, a highly centralized decision-making process, combined with difficulties in obtaining information, can make the regulatory system appear arbitrary and inscrutable. The government purports to seek the advice given of the business community through the Lao Business Forum.

In 2014, the National Assembly passed the Law on Making Legislation, which requires 60-day periods for public comment and regulatory impact assessment notes of all new draft legislation. In 2013, the Lao Official Gazette opened online, a landmark achievement in legal transparency for the country. The gazette will facilitate the 60-day comment period, and the Ministry of Justice has committed to publishing all current Lao laws on the site. The gazette can be accessed here: **http://laoofficialgazette.gov.la/index.php?r=site/index**

9. EFFICIENT CAPITAL MARKETS AND PORTFOLIO INVESTMENT

Laos does not have a well-developed capital market, although government policies increasingly support the formation of capital and free flow of financial resources. Due to a monetary and fiscal crisis in 2013, there have been liquidity concerns, particularly related to foreign currency. The soundness of the banking system also appears to have suffered in the past year due to lending to off-budget infrastructure projects, and there are reports of some companies in the construction sector facing asset seizures by commercial banks.

The largest denomination of currency is 100,000 kip (about $12.50). Credit is generally not available on the local market for large capital investments, although letters of credit for export can sometimes be obtained locally. In January 2014, Laos issued a second round of government bonds denominated in Thai Baht, raising approximately $90 million. Its first foreign currency denominated bond sale, also in Thai Baht, raised $49 million in 2013.

The banking system is under the supervision of the Bank of Lao PDR, and includes 32 banks with assets of approximately US$6.8 billion. Private foreign banks can establish branches in all provinces of Laos. Domestic credit growth has been very high in the last decade and remained so at 31% year-over-year through September 2013. The BOL reports an increase in ATMs from 442 in 2014 to 622 through the middle of FY 2013. Technical assistance to Laos' financial sector has led to some reforms but overall capacity within the governance structure remains poor.

The Lao Securities Exchange (LSX) began operations in 2011 with two stocks listed, both of them state-owned – the Banque Pour l'Commerce Exterieur (BCEL), and electrical utility Electricity du Laos (EDL). In 2013, the LSX listed a third company that runs exhibitions and convention centers and appears to be largely privately-held. In 2014, the GOL increased the proportion of shares that foreigners can hold on the LSX from 10 to 20 percent.

10. COMPETITION FROM STATE-OWNED ENTERPRISES

The GOL maintains ownership stakes in key sectors of the economy such as telecommunications, energy, finance, and mining. Where state interests conflict with private ownership, the state is in a position of advantage.

In 2011, under the auspices of the Ministry of Post and Telecommunications, four large telecoms with high state ownership stakes cut service to a foreign-owned telecom in retaliation for alleged marketing violations. In 2014, private carrier Lao Central Airlines opened service on international and domestic routes, challenging the monopoly previously enjoyed by state-owned Lao Airlines.

There are reportedly 139 State-Owned Enterprises in Laos with $2.4 billion in assets. The government appears to be considering methods to increase private ownership in some SOE such as Lao Airlines, potentially through listing on the LSX.

11. CORPORATE SOCIAL RESPONSIBILITY

Corporate Social Responsibility is not yet well understood and recognized by Lao producers and consumers, but protection of the environment and mitigation of social impacts are stressed by some foreign companies, particularly in the natural resources and energy sectors.

12. POLITICAL VIOLENCE

Laos is a peaceful and politically stable country. The risk of political violence directed at foreign enterprises or businesspersons is low.

13. CORRUPTION

Corruption is a serious problem in Laos and appears to be growing alongside the economy. The GOL has developed several anti-corruption laws but enforcement remains weak, with no high-profile cases ever having been brought to trial. According to the State Inspection Authority, the Lao Government has prosecuted some individuals for corruption but it cannot publicize the information. In September 2009, Laos ratified the United Nations Convention Against Corruption.

The State Inspection Authority, located in the Prime Minister's Office, is charged with analyzing corruption at the national level and serves as a central office for gathering details and evidence of suspected corruption. Additionally, the State Inspection Department in each Ministry is responsible for combat internal ministry corruption. Laos is not a signatory to the OECD Convention on Combating Bribery. Both giving and accepting bribes are criminal acts punishable by fine and/or imprisonment. Foreign businesses frequently cite corruption as an obstacle to operating in Laos. Officials commonly accept bribes for the purpose of approving or expediting applications.

In 2014 an asset declaration regime entered into force for government officials requiring them to declare income, assets and debts for themselves and their family members. Assets over $2500 are required to be disclosed, including land, structures, vehicles and equipment, as well as cash, gold, and financial instruments. However, the effectiveness of this program has yet to be determined.

14. BILATERAL INVESTMENT AGREEMENTS

Laos has bilateral investment agreements with Australia, Burma, Cambodia, China, Cuba, Denmark, France, Germany, India, Indonesia, Japan, Kuwait, Malaysia, Mongolia, Netherlands, North Korea, Pakistan, Philippines, Russia, South Korea, Singapore, Sweden, Switzerland, Thailand, the United Kingdom, and Vietnam. On February 1, 2005 a Bilateral Trade Agreement (BTA) came into force between the U.S. and the Government of Laos. Laos and the United States do not have a bilateral taxation treaty.

15. OPIC AND OTHER INVESTMENT INSURANCE PROGRAMS

The United States and Laos signed an Overseas Private Investment Cooperation (OPIC) agreement in March 1996. OPIC does not have any projects ongoing in Laos but the potential exists in the Lao economy for OPIC involvement. In 1998 Laos signed an agreement with the Multilateral Investment Guarantee Agency (MIGA). The Lao kip is not an internationally traded currency and fluctuated in a narrow range against the U.S. dollar in 2014.

16. LABOR

70% of Laos' work force is engaged in subsistence agriculture. There are shortages in skilled labor across virtually the entire economy. The lack of a skilled workforce is consistently cited by foreign and domestic companies as the main constraint to growth. The estimated migration of Lao labor to Thailand numbers in the hundreds of thousands. At the same time, Laos has in recent years received a large influx of labor from China and Vietnam who largely come to work with Chinese and Vietnamese companies. Generally, the current extremely tight labor market places labor-management relations on a somewhat equal footing; if employees are not satisfied at their current job, they simply leave.

The 1994 labor law provides for the formation of trade unions; specifies working hours and compensation standards; allows for maternity leave and benefits; workers' compensation and retirement benefits; and establishes procedures for labor dispute resolution. There are, however, no unions independent of the Lao Federation of Trade Unions, a Communist Party organization. In January 2014, the Lao government raised the minimum wage for unskilled workers to US$78 per month based on a six-day, eight hour per day work week. Reforms to the labor law passed in 2014 contained the first mention in Lao law of collective bargaining, but the country still lacks freedom of association for labor, independent unions, or a detailed framework for independent collective bargaining. There is virtually no avenue for, or risk of, labor strikes in Laos currently. In 2014, Laos approved a national plan of action to combat the worst forms of child labor and the Ministry of Labor and Social Welfare is working to improve its capacity for labor inspections.

Laos has human resource deficiencies in virtually all sectors. English is not widely spoken. In 2014, about 16 percent of the population age 15 and above remained illiterate. The shortage of skilled labor is particularly acute in high-tech sectors. The country has a few technical colleges, one scientific research facility-- the National Institute of Hygiene and Epidemiology--and almost no effective post-graduate degree programs.

The Lao Government has dedicated few of its own resources to improve the country's education system and tends to rely heavily on international donors for support; there are a few state training programs and some foreign funded programs. Potential investors should note the need to dedicate substantial resources, both human and capital, to train employees. It is not unusual for foreign investors to bring in Thai managers due to a lack of skilled local personnel.

17. FOREIGN TRADE ZONES/FREE PORTS

The Foreign Investment Law allows for the establishment of Special Economic Zones (SEZ) and Specific Economic Zones as an investment incentive. Prime Ministerial Decree 443 on Special Economic Zones and Specific Economic Zones was issued in 2010 and provides guidance on the establishment of the zones.

Special Economic Zones are intended to support development of new infrastructure and commercial facilities and include incentives for investment. Specific Economic Zones are meant to develop existing infrastructure and facilities and provide a lower level of incentives and support than Special Economic Zones. Laos plans to construct 25 special and specific zones in the next ten years via foreign direct investment of US$3 billion.

There are currently 10 different economic zones across the country, including: Savan-Seno Special Economic Zone, Golden Triangle Special Economic Zone, Boten Beautiful Land Specific Economic Zone, Vientiane Industrial and Trade Zone, Saysettha Development Zone, Phoukyou Specific Economic Zone, Thatluang Lake Specific Economic Zone, Longthanh – Vientiane Specific Economic Zone, Dongphosy Specific Economic Zone and Thakhek Specific Economic Zone.

For additional analytical, business and investment opportunities information, please contact Global Investment & Business Center, USA at (703) 370-8082. Fax: (703) 370-8083. E-mail: ibpusa3@gmail.com
Global Business and Investment Info Databank - www.ibpus.com

The Savan-Seno Special Economic Zone in Savannakhet province is legitimately developing as a production, supply, and distribution center with increasingly sophisticated manufacturing businesses and advanced infrastructure. Other SEZ's in the northern part of the country have experienced problems associated with casino gambling, prostitution and drug trafficking.

Lao laws pertaining to trade are supposedly applied uniformly across the entire customs territory of Laos, including all sub-central authorities, special economic zones, specific economic zones and border trade regions. In reality, however, customs practices vary widely at ports of entry in the provinces. Centralization of customs collection by the central government has led to more uniform practices and increased the flow of customs revenue to the central government. In order to comply with National Single Window requirements under the ASEAN Single Window, in 2014 Laos began operating the Automated System for Customs Data (ASYCUDA) at the busiest point of cross-border trade, the Lao-Thai Friendship Bridge linking Vientiane with Thailand and has slowly expanded the use of ASYCUDA at other border crossings as well.

18. FOREIGN DIRECT INVESTMENT AND FOREIGN PORTFOLIO INVESTMENT STATISTICS

Key Macroeconomic data, U.S. FDI in host country/economy

	Bank of the Lao PDR Annual Report		USG or international statistical source		USG or international Source of data (Source of Data: BEA; IMF; Eurostat; UNCTAD, Other)
Economic Data	Year	Amount	Year	Amount	
Host Country Gross Domestic Product (GDP) (Millions U.S. Dollars)	2014	9100	2014	9400	http://www.worldbank.org/en/country
Foreign Direct Investment	Ministry of Planning and Investment		USG or international statistical source		USG or international Source of data: BEA; IMF; Eurostat; UNCTAD, Other
U.S. FDI in partner country (Millions U.S. Dollars, stock positions)	3.513	NA	Insert 2014	Amount 0	(BEA) click selections to reach. Bureau of Economic Analysis Balance of Payments and Direct Investment Position Data U.S. Direct Investment Position Abroad on a Historical-Cost Basis By Country only (all countries) (Millions of Dollars)
Host country's FDI in the United States (Millions U.S. Dollars, stock positions)	NA	NA	NA	NA	(BEA) click selections to reach Balance of Payments and Direct Investment Position Data Foreign Direct Investment Position in the United States on a Historical-Cost Basis By Country only (all countries) (Millions of Dollars)
Total inbound	Insert	Amount	Insert	Amount	

stock of FDI as % host GDP (calculate)	2014	20.3%	(Year)		

LAWYERS IN LAOS - IMPORTANT CONTACTS

There are a limited number of independent lawyers in Laos. A lawyer seeking to represent a foreign citizen in a criminal matter may need to obtain prior permission from the Ministry of Justice.

The U.S. Embassy in Vientiane, Laos assumes no responsibility or liability for the professional ability or reputation of, or the quality of services provided by, the following persons or firms. Inclusion on this list is in no way an endorsement by the Department of State or the U.S. Embassy. Names are listed alphabetically, and the order in which they appear has no other significance. The information in the list on professional credentials, areas of expertise and language ability are provided directly by the lawyers; the Embassy is not in a position to vouch for such information. You may receive additional information about the individuals on the list by contacting the local bar association or the local licensing authorities.

1.   Mr. William GREENLEE, Jr.
Tel: 856-21-242-068
  856-21-242-069
856-21-242-070
DFDL Mekong Law Group   Fax: 856-21-218-422
PO Box 2920
Vientiane, Lao PDR   Website:www.dfdl.com
        Email: Laos@dfdl.com
        William.Greenlee@dfdlmekong.com
Languages: English, Mandarin, Thai, Bahasa Indonesian
Areas of Expertise: Banking/Financial, Commercial/Business, Foreign Investments, Marketing, Patents/Trademarks/Copyrights, Damages, Collections, Contracts, Transportation, Corporations, Foreign Claims, Estates, Taxes, Government Relations, Labor

2. Mr. Brennan COLEMAN
Tel: 856-21-242-068
856-21-242-069
856-21-242-070
DFDL Mekong Law Group   Fax: 856-21-218-422
PO Box 2920   Cell: 856-20-7878-7699
Vientiane, Lao PDR   Website: www.dfdl.com
                                         Email: Brennan.Coleman@dfdl.com

Languages: English
Areas of Expertise: Banking/Financial, Commercial/Business, Foreign Investments, Marketing, Patents/Trademarks/Copyrights, Damages, Collections, Contracts, Transportation, Corporations, Foreign Claims, Taxes, Government Relations, Labor

3. Mr. Somphou KEOMOUNMANY   Tel: 856-21-454-300
Ban Naxay, Xaysettha District   Cell: 856-20-5562-6676
Vientiane, Lao PDR   Email:bearsomphou@yahoo.com
Languages (in addition to Lao): English
Areas of Expertise: Child Custody, Child Protection, Marriage/Divorce, Patents/Trademarks/Copyrights, Contracts, Labor

4. Mr. Viengsavanh PHANTHALY
Ban Phonpapao, Sisattanak District
Vientiane, Lao PDR

Tel: 856-21-330470
Cell: 856-20-5422-3377
Email: vlaw@live.com
v.phanthaly@vlaw.la
www.vlaw.la

Languages (in addition to Lao): English, Vietnamese, Thai, Japanese
Areas of Expertise: Family, Adoptions, Marriage/Divorce, Insurance, Banking/Financial,
Commercial/Business, Foreign Investments, Marketing, Patents/Trademarks/Copyrights, Civil,
Criminal, Damages, Contracts, Transportation, Corporations, Foreign Claims, Estates, Taxes,
Government Relations, Labor, Immigration, Accidents

5. Mr. Sabh PHOMMARATH
Ban Anou, Chanthabury District
Vientiane, Lao PDR

Cell: 856-20-2220-2297
Email:sabhpr123@gmail.com

Languages (in addition to Lao): English, French, Thai
Areas of Expertise: Family, Marriage/Divorce, Foreign Investments, Marketing, Civil, Criminal,
Contracts

6. Mr. Veng SAYSANA
Ban Naxay, Xaysettha District
Vientiane, Lao PDR

Cell: 856-20-5561-2883
Email:vengsaysana@yahoo.com

Languages (in addition to Lao): English, French
Areas of Expertise: Family, Adoption, Child Custody, Parental/Child Abduction, Child Protection,
Marriage/Divorce, Banking/Financial, Commercial/Business, Foreign Investments, Marketing,
Patents/Trademarks/Copyrights, Civil, Criminal, Damages, Narcotics, Collections, Contracts,
Corporations, Aeronautical/Maritime, Estates, Government Relations, Labor

7. Mr. Vannloh SISOPHA
128 Saigon Rd.
        Email:vannloh@gmail.com
Ban Anou, Chanthabury District
Vientiane, Lao PDR

Tel: 856-21-218-426
Cell: 856-20-5582-8178

Languages (in addition to Lao): English, French
Areas of Expertise: Family, Commercial/Business, Civil, Criminal

8. Mr. Douangsim SOUPHANTHONG
Lao Bar Association, Ban Anou
Vientiane, Lao PDR

Cell: 856-20-5561-8379

Languages (in addition to Lao): French, limited English
Areas of Expertise: Family, Adoption, Child Protection, Marriage/Divorce, Foreign Investment,
Civil, Criminal, Damages, Contracts, Government Relations, Labor, Immigration, Accidents

9. Mr. Mixay THEPMANY
Ban Savang, Chanthabury District
Vientiane, Lao PDR

Cell: 856-20-5567-6383
Fax: 856-21-219051
Email: mthepmany@yahoo.com

Languages (in addition to Lao): English, French, Thai
Areas of Expertise: Family, Adoption, Child Custody, Child Protection, Marriage/Divorce,
Commercial/Business, Foreign Investments, Civil, Criminal, Contracts, Labor

10. Mr. Sysavong VITHASAY
Ban Phayawath, Sisattanak District
Vientiane, Lao PDR

Fax: 856-21-353953
Cell: 856-20-5551-4259

Languages (in addition to Lao): French, Thai, limited English

For additional analytical, business and investment opportunities information,
please contact Global Investment & Business Center, USA
at (703) 370-8082. Fax: (703) 370-8083. E-mail: ibpusa3@gmail.com
Global Business and Investment Info Databank - www.ibpus.com

Areas of Expertise: Family, Marriage/Divorce, Commercial/Business, Foreign Investments, Marketing, Civil, Criminal, Damages, Narcotics, Contracts, Labor

11. Mr. Manolin THEPKHAMVONG
Ban Sapanthong-kang, Sisattanak District
Vientiane, Lao PDR   Email: m.thepkhamvong@vlaw.la
Languages (in addition to Lao): English, Thai
Areas of Expertise: Family, Civil, Criminal, Damages, Public Interest, land, environment protection, water and water recourses, narcotic, woman and children protection.

MARKET OVERVIEW

• The Lao market economy has grown at a steady pace for the last two decades and

is heading into a new phase of regional and global integration. Laos acceded to the World Trade Organization in 2013, and trade surpluses from exports of electricity and raw materials are likely in the near future.

• Laos is one of five remaining communist countries in the world and this legacy

continues to weigh on both governance and the economy. The Lao economic

model bears some relation to its Chinese and Vietnamese counterparts, in that it

has implemented market-based economic practices while maintaining a very high

degree of political control. Laos is politically stable.

• Laos and the United States signed a bilateral trade agreement in 2005, although the

terms of the agreement are still being implemented in Laos, with U.S. assistance.

Since 2005 trade has increased from $14 million to $58 million per year in 2014. Vietnam, China and Thailand have dominant trade and investment roles in the Lao economy, with participation in certain sectors by Korea, France, Japan, Australia, Malaysia and Singapore. Bilateral trade between Laos and Thailand, its largest trading

partner by far, totaled $3.91 billion in 2014.

• Laos' GDP was $9.4 billion in 2014, up 8 percent from the prior year. Laos has

had consistently high economic growth rates over the last decade, averaging above

7 percent per year. Inflation moderated somewhat last year, at 5.5 percent in 2014.

• The Lao economy is based primarily on agriculture and natural resource extraction,

with services and manufacturing making moderate yearly gains. In 2014, natural

resources accounted for approximately 16 percent of GDP, services 39.2 percent, agriculture 26.7 percent, and manufacturing 28 percent. Most Lao manufacturing is

small scale, with over 97 percent of manufacturers employing 10 or fewer workers.

• The Lao population was estimated at 6.5 million in 2014. 70 percent of the

workforce is employed in agriculture, mostly in small scale farming. The Lao

population is young, with more than half of the population under 20 years of age.

• Gross National Income per capita continued to rise in 2014, edging up to $1,355. However, income distribution is unevenly spread, and the country has a small middle class.

• Laos ran a trade deficit in 2014 of approximately $1.3 billion. According to World

Bank statistics, total imports were $4.1 billion while total exports were $2.8 billion. Laos imported $26.1 million from the United States and exported $58.9 million to

the United States in 2011. Top U.S exports to Laos in the past include precious

stones, machinery, metals and vehicles. Top U.S. imports from Laos have been

garments, chemicals, plastics and precious stones.

> • The Lao Trade Portal, established in 2014, has extensive information for exporters and importers: http://www.laotradeportal.gov.la/index.php?r=site/index

Useful Web links:

Lao Chapter of The American Chamber of Commerce: http://www.amchamthailand.com/acct/asp/cmtedetails.asp?MenuCatID=8&CmteID=129&Menulte mID=3&SponsorID=888%20

Lao Trade Portal: http://www.laotradeportal.gov.la/index.php?r=site/index

U.S. Embassy in Vientiane, Laos: http://vientiane.usembassy.gov/

U.S. Census Trade data: http://www.census.gov/foreign-trade/statistics/country/

CIA World Factbook: https://www.cia.gov/library/publications/the-world-factbook/geos/la.html

MARKET CHALLENGES

• Commercial law and the commercial court system in Laos are developing slowly and

are not transparent. Business disputes are rarely adjudicated in favor of the foreign

investor. Sanctity of contract is not well understood in Laos and concessions or property rights granted by the government are liable to overlap or conflict with other

claims.

• Customs procedures are improving but remain opaque.. Customs clearance speed has improved markedly in recent years with the introduction of automated customs procedures, dropping from an average 18 hours in 2010 to 11 hours in 2014. The cost and average number of days required to import and export has fallen but remains high at 26 days and approximately $2,100 for a standard shipping container. These remain significantly higher than regional averages.

• Despite government efforts to establish "one stop service" for business registration

and licensing, procedures for investment are cumbersome and approvals often do

not occur within stated times or rules.

• Human resources are not well developed in Laos, and employers frequently have a

difficult time finding and retaining qualified employees. For skilled employees, the

labor market offers frequent incentives to change employers.

• Laws and procedures are subject to change at short notice and without prior

consultation with, or notification of, the private sector. This includes taxation law.

Tax administration is consistently cited as one of the largest barriers to commerce in Laos in surveys of small and medium enterprises.

• The World Bank's "Doing Business" project compares Laos with 185 other

economies at: http://www.doingbusiness.org/ExploreEconomies/?economyid=107

• Corruption is a major problem for U.S. and other western businesses and seriously

hampers the efficient operation of the Lao economy and society. Competitors from

countries without the legal or moral sanctions against corrupt practices have a major

advantage in securing government approvals and concessions. Frequent bribes and

payoffs are an accepted part of Lao business culture. http://cpi.transparency.org/cpi2014/results/

MARKET OPPORTUNITIES

• Increases in disposable income and a slowly expanding middle class mean that the

consumer and services sectors are likely to experience continued growth in the future.

- 169 -

• The power sector is open to foreign investment, with many international firms

represented. Hydropower, coal, and transmission infrastructure will be the focus of

increasing investment by the GOL as it develops its power industry.

• Laos has a very poorly developed infrastructure with virtually no rail, few decent

roadways, and underdeveloped medical, water and sewage systems. The GOL is

likely to make investments in these areas in coming years in keeping with its ambitious

goal of graduating from Least Developed Country status by 2020.

• The minerals and mining sector is a major driver of growth in Laos. Commodities

prices in recent years have favored Lao gold and copper producers. Other mineral

resources include bauxite and potash.

• The Lao government has targeted tourism, especially ecotourism, as a major area of

future growth, and in 2014 it became the second highest income sector after mining, earning
$514 million.

MARKET ENTRY STRATEGY

• American companies considering investments in Laos are advised to visit the country several
times, as personal relationships are key to locating suitable Lao business partners and avoiding
misunderstandings. Many foreign businesses take on a Lao partner or agent.

• The American Chamber of Commerce (AMCHAM) in Laos was established in 2014. Foreign
businesses can also apply for membership in the Lao National Chamber of Commerce and
Industry. http://www.lncci.laotel.com/

• In addition to AMCHAM, there are business chambers or associations from China, France,
Australia-New Zealand, Japan, Vietnam, Taiwan, India, Korea, and the European Chamber of
Commerce and Industry.

SELLING U.S. PRODUCTS AND SERVICES

USING AN AGENT OR DISTRIBUTOR

Employing a Lao agent or finding a Lao business partner is an efficient method for

developing contacts with Lao businesses, customers and government officials. There

are also a number of expatriate Lao who are either American citizens or legal permanent

residents, and who may be able to assist in arranging government meetings.

**For additional analytical, business and investment opportunities information,
please contact Global Investment & Business Center, USA
at (703) 370-8082. Fax: (703) 370-8083. E-mail: ibpusa3@gmail.com
Global Business and Investment Info Databank - www.ibpus.com**

Numerous import-export companies are based in Vientiane and in the cities located at or

near border crossings in the provinces of Luang Namtha, Bokeo, Bolikhamxay, Khammouane, Savannakhet and Champasack.

Most import-export companies are ill-equipped to handle large-scale distribution. U.S. firms looking for a distributor or an agent in a particular province should contact the provincial branch of the Lao National Chamber of Commerce (LNCC) at http://www.laocci.com/ and the Trade and Investment Department of the respective province for assistance in identifying potential business partners.

ESTABLISHING AN OFFICE

Foreign investors seeking to establish operations in Laos are required to obtain a foreign

Investment and Businesses license, an enterprise registration certificate, and a tax registration certificate.

Depending on the size of the investment, investors first submit project proposals to the "One Stop Shop" Unit in the Department of Investment Promotion (DIP) in the Ministry of

Planning and Investment (MPI), or to the Investment Promotion in General Business Department at the Ministry of Industry and Commerce.

http://www.moic.gov.la/contact.asp

DIP screens projects for financial and technical feasibility before forwarding them to

relevant line ministries for review. Depending on the size of the investment, they are

then sent to the Prime Minister's Office (PM) or Government Office for adjudication.

In addition to the investment license, foreign investors are required to obtain other

permits, including; an annual business registration from the Ministry of Industry and

Commerce; a tax registration from the Ministry of Finance; a business logo registration

from the Ministry of Public Security; permits from each line ministry related to the

investment (e.g., Ministry of Industry and Commerce for manufacturing; Ministry of

Energy and Mines for power sector development); appropriate permits from local

authorities; and an import-export license, if applicable. Obtaining the necessary permits

can pose a challenge, especially in areas outside the capital.

The GOL is supposed to respond to proposed new business investment within 15–45

For additional analytical, business and investment opportunities information,
please contact Global Investment & Business Center, USA
at (703) 370-8082. Fax: (703) 370-8083. E-mail: ibpusa3@gmail.com
Global Business and Investment Info Databank - www.ibpus.com

working days. Foreign enterprises must begin business activities within 90 days from the date of receipt of an investment license, or the license is subject to termination

FRANCHISING

Franchising is a relatively untested business model in Laos and the country has no specific law regulating franchises. In 2014, a team of American, Thai, and Lao investors added a second location to the first fast food franchise in Laos, originally opened in 2010.

DIRECT MARKETING

Direct marketing in Laos has improved as the density of telecommunications coverage has increased to an estimated 76 in 100 households. Although the road network is improving, there is limited postal coverage. The literacy rate is officially estimated to be 80% for those older than 15 years.

JOINT VENTURES/LICENSING

Care in selection of suitable business partners for joint ventures is crucial in Laos. As in other countries in the region, joint venture partners can contribute local knowledge of language and culture, local contacts and access to human resources. There can also be challenges in a joint venture arrangement, including different management styles, different cultural expectations and difficulty in exiting business arrangements with a local partner.

Lao foreign investment law recognizes joint ventures, but requires the foreign partner to contribute at least thirty percent of registered capital. Capital contributed in foreign currency must be converted into Kip based on the exchange rate of the Bank of the Lao People's Democratic Republic on the day of the capital contribution.

Foreign partners' equity may be foreign currency, plant and equipment, capital goods, technology, and/or skills and management. Lao partners (including the Lao government) may contribute money, land, water rights, natural resources, and/or capital goods. The value of the inputs and assets of each side are assessed at international market rates

and converted into local currency at the prevailing exchange rate on the date of equity

payment.

Licensing arrangements also require a trustworthy Lao partner and opportunities should

be thoroughly researched with, among others, the Lao government and the Lao National

Chamber of Commerce.

SELLING TO THE GOVERNMENT

The Lao Government is a leading consumer of goods and services, but procurement

procedures are opaque. The national budget is heavily financed by Official Development
Assistance (ODA), and donors commonly encourage government purchases from their home
industries as part of aid deals. Laos is not a party or an observer to the WTO Agreement on
Government Procurement.

Most business opportunities involving Lao Government entities are associated with

donors and their development projects. Contracts in support of these projects are often

advertised for bid in the newspapers (Vientiane Times and KPL).

http://www.vientianetimes.org.la/ and http://www.kplnet.net/

These bidding events have not been verified as open and fair, as no American

company has reported success through this channel. However, niche opportunities are

known to exist for direct private sales to government entities with past examples in such

areas as telecommunications and aviation.

DISTRIBUTION AND SALES CHANNELS

Generally, import-export wholesale companies import goods into Laos and sell goods to

retailers. Goods may enter Laos by air, road, or (less formally) by river. There is just one active
railroad in Laos, a short spur line from Nong Khai, just across the river in Thailand, that began
operations in 2009.

The lack of a well-developed road system and basic infrastructure in many areas makes

distribution outside of the main urban areas in Vientiane, Luang Prabang, Savannakhet,

and Pakse difficult, time-consuming, and costly. Road improvements are ongoing, with

For additional analytical, business and investment opportunities information,
please contact Global Investment & Business Center, USA
at (703) 370-8082. Fax: (703) 370-8083. E-mail: ibpusa3@gmail.com
Global Business and Investment Info Databank - www.ibpus.com

several decent roads in the northern provinces and along the southern corridor

connecting Thailand, Laos and Vietnam. However, Laos is still operating a mid-

twentieth century distribution and logistics network, with large inventories on hand. Use

of modern logistics techniques such as just-in time supply would likely be difficult given the
current state of the Lao infrastructure.

SELLING FACTORS/TECHNIQUES

American products generally enjoy a good reputation for technological sophistication and

high quality in Laos. The consumer products of Laos' regional neighbors are far better

known, however, and the Lao market can be difficult for American products due to their

relatively high prices.

To compete successfully, some US firms have combined routine advertising with

workshops, training programs, trade shows, and product launching events for

wholesalers and distributors, as well as customers. The Thai and Lao languages are not

identical but are very similar. Thai products with Thai language packaging are ubiquitous in Laos
and most educated Lao can read Thai, so Thai language packaging often suffices. American
products that include Lao-language packaging and/or promotional materials are likely to be
positively received.

ELECTRONIC COMMERCE

Electronic commerce is not widely used in Laos, due to underdevelopment of the

telecommunications infrastructure and the low rate of formal banking and credit card

use. Broadband internet access is widely available in Vientiane. The Lao government passed a
law on electronic transactions in 2014, paving the way for future growth in electronic commerce.

TRADE PROMOTION AND ADVERTISING

Advertising and trade promotion are important marketing tools for American products.

Since nearly all Lao who own televisions watch Thai advertisements, a good reputation

and strong advertising campaign in Thailand will likely have a positive effect on Lao

consumers as well.

Many companies advertise in two Lao local newspapers, Vientiane Mai, a Lao language

For additional analytical, business and investment opportunities information,
please contact Global Investment & Business Center, USA
at (703) 370-8082. Fax: (703) 370-8083. E-mail: ibpusa3@gmail.com
Global Business and Investment Info Databank - www.ibpus.com

newspaper, and the Vientiane Times, an English language newspaper. A brief listing of major newspapers, business journals, radio, television stations and business advertising companies follows. All newspapers and television stations are state owned, and all communications are state controlled:

Major Newspapers:

Vientiane Times (English Language) http://www.vientianetimes.org.la/

Lao News Agency, KPL (English Language) http://www.kplnet.net/

Pasaxon (Lao Language) http://www.pasaxon.org.la

Vientiane Mai (Lao Language) http://www.vientianemai.net

Vientiane Thurakit Sangkhom (Lao Language)

Target Business Magazine

Lao National Radio c/o Ministry of Information and Culture: nationalradio@hotmail.com

Lao National Television 1 and 3 http://www.lntv.gov.la/

Lao Star Television http://www.laostartv.com/

Lao International Trade, Exhibition, and Conference Center (ITECC) http://www.lao-itecc.la/

PRICING

Lao consumers are sensitive to price due to low levels of disposable income. The Lao government continues to control the retail price of gas and diesel, as well as a number of other "sensitive" goods. As a new member of the World Trade Organization in 2013, price controls as well as unwieldy import restrictions in Laos should decline in the future. Although the Government often discusses the need to control food prices, in practice markets set the price. A value added tax (VAT) came into force in January 2010 although the state of implementation is uneven.

SALES SERVICE/CUSTOMER SUPPORT

Customer support and service tend to be the province of large multinationals such as automobile manufacturers, which offer excellent in-country support. In general, attitudes towards customer service, especially at the retail level, are still in the developing stages.

Availability of spare parts is limited and replacement/replenishment is slow.

INTELLECTUAL PROPERTY

Protecting Your Intellectual Property in Laos

Several general principles are important for effective management of intellectual property ("IP") rights in Laos. First, it is important to have an overall strategy to protect your IP. Second, IP is protected differently in Laos than in the U.S. Third, rights must be registered and enforced in Laos, under local laws. Your U.S. trademark and patent registrations will not protect you in Laos. There is no such thing as an "international copyright" that will automatically protect an author's writings throughout the entire world. Protection against unauthorized use in a particular country depends, basically, on the national laws of that country. However, most countries do offer copyright protection to foreign works under certain conditions, and these conditions have been greatly simplified by international copyright treaties and conventions.

Registration of patents and trademarks is on a first-in-time, first-in-right basis, so you should consider applying for trademark and patent protection even before selling your products or services in the Lao market. It is vital that companies understand that intellectual property is primarily a private right and that the US government generally cannot enforce rights for private individuals in Lao PDR. It is the responsibility of the rights' holders to register, protect, and enforce their rights where relevant, retaining their own counsel and advisors. Companies may wish to seek advice from local attorneys or IP consultants who are experts in Lao law. The U.S. Commercial Service can provide a list of local lawyers upon request: http://laos.usembassy.gov/legal_assistance.html

While the U.S. Government stands ready to assist, there is little we can do if the rights holders have not taken these fundamental steps necessary to securing and enforcing their IP in a timely fashion. Moreover, in many countries, rights holders who delay

enforcing their rights on a mistaken belief that the USG can provide a political resolution to a legal problem may find that their rights have been eroded or abrogated due to legal doctrines such as statutes of limitations, laches, estoppel, or unreasonable delay in prosecuting a law suit. In no instance should U.S. Government advice be seen as a substitute for the obligation of a rights holder to promptly pursue its case.

It is always advisable to conduct due diligence on potential partners. Negotiate from the position of your partner and give your partner clear incentives to honor the contract. A good partner is an important ally in protecting IP rights. Consider carefully, however, whether to permit your partner to register your IP rights on your behalf. Doing so may create a risk that your partner will list itself as the IP owner and fail to transfer the rights should the partnership end. Keep an eye on your cost structure and reduce the margins (and the incentive) of would-be bad actors. Projects and sales in Laos require constant attention. Work with legal counsel familiar with Lao laws to create a solid contract that includes non-compete clauses, and confidentiality/non-disclosure provisions.

It is also recommended that small and medium-size companies understand the importance of working together with trade associations and organizations to support efforts to protect IP and stop counterfeiting. There are a number of these organizations, both Lao and U.S.-based. These include:

• The U.S. Chamber and local American Chambers of Commerce

- National Association of Manufacturers (NAM)

- International Intellectual Property Alliance (IIPA)

- International Trademark Association (INTA)

- The Coalition Against Counterfeiting and Piracy

- International Anti-Counterfeiting Coalition (IACC)

- Pharmaceutical Research and Manufacturers of America (PhRMA)

- Biotechnology Industry Organization (BIO)

IP Resources

A wealth of information on protecting IP is freely available to U.S. rights holders. Some excellent resources for companies regarding intellectual property include the following:

- For information about patent, trademark, or copyright issues -- including enforcement issues in the US and other countries -- call the STOP! Hotline: 1-866-999-HALT or register at www.StopFakes.gov .

- For more information about registering trademarks and patents (both in the U.S. as well as in foreign countries), contact the US Patent and Trademark Office (USPTO) at: 1-800-786-9199.

- For more information about registering for copyright protection in the US, contact the US Copyright Office at: 1-202-707-5959.

- For more information about how to evaluate, protect, and enforce intellectual property rights and how these rights may be important for businesses, a free online training program is available at www.stopfakes.gov .

- For US small and medium-size companies, the Department of Commerce offers a "SME IP Advisory Program" available through the American Bar Association that provides one hour of free IP legal advice for companies with concerns in Brazil, China, Egypt, India, Russia, and . For details and to register, visit: http://www.abanet.org/intlaw/intlproj/iprprogram_consultation.html

- For information on obtaining and enforcing intellectual property rights and market-specific IP Toolkits visit: www.StopFakes.gov This site is linked to the USPTO website for registering trademarks and patents (both in the U.S. as well as in foreign countries), the U.S. Customs & Border Protection website to record registered trademarks and copyrighted works (to assist customs in blocking imports of IP-infringing products) and allows you to register for Webinars on protecting IP.

- The U.S. Commerce Department has positioned IP attachés in key markets around the world. Trader can get contact information the IP attaché who covers Laos at: peter.fowler@trade.gov

DUE DILIGENCE

Due diligence is key in the Lao market. Companies are advised to make numerous trips to Laos prior to investing in order to meet both with potential partners and with relevant government officials. Working with a local lawyer (see below) is recommended.

LOCAL PROFESSIONAL SERVICES

The legal community is small in Laos and it is wise to ask for recommendations. Please see the following website for information on local professional services:

http://laos.usembassy.gov/attorneys.html

WEB RESOURCES

Lao National Chamber of Commerce and Industry (LNCCI): http://www.lncci.laotel.com/

The Ministry of Science and Technology:

http://www.laopdr.gov.la/ePortal/nbocompany/listdivisions.action?contentType=4&contentGroupId=11565&organizationContentId=18065&subType=100&request_locale=en_US

Lao Bar Association: http://www.laobar.org/welcome.php

Lao Ministry of Industry and Commerce: http://www.moic.gov.la/contact.asp

LEADING SECTORS FOR U.S. EXPORT AND INVESTMENT

TOURISM INFRASTRUCTURE AND RESORTS

Unit: USD thousands

	2011	2014
Total Market Size	406,000	514,000

The tourism industry in Laos is developing rapidly, with particular emphasis on eco- tourism. The major tourist destination is the world heritage site and ancient capital of Luang Prabang. Eco-tourism featuring the undeveloped Lao countryside is gaining in popularity.

WEB RESOURCES

Information on Luang Prabang: http://whc.unesco.org/en/list/479

Lao Ministry of Information, Culture and Tourism:
http://www.ecotourismlaos.com/worldheritagesites.htm

For additional analytical, business and investment opportunities information,
please contact Global Investment & Business Center, USA
at (703) 370-8082. Fax: (703) 370-8083. E-mail: ibpusa3@gmail.com
Global Business and Investment Info Databank - www.ibpus.com

ARCHITECTURE, CONSTRUCTION AND ENGINEERING SERVICES

Laos has an underdeveloped infrastructure, including its road networks, and its public water and electricity systems. Transportation projects will be high demand as the country modernizes. There are also several large construction projects ongoing in the capital of Vientiane, including office buildings and shopping malls.

Chinese, Vietnamese and Thai companies are the most active participants in infrastructure development in Laos. The Lao government makes use of donor funding, development banks and other financing methods to pay for infrastructure projects. Laos is undergoing development of its airport and aviation system, including provincial airports.

Laos is seeking to modernize and integrate its electrical grid in the next decade as it seeks to meet its goal of supplying Thailand and Vietnam with electricity exports, while at the same time providing electricity to 90 percent of the population by 2020. To do this it will need to invest in modern power distribution and power management equipment and expertise.

WEB RESOURCES

World Bank:
http://web.worldbank.org/WBSITE/EXTERNAL/COUNTRIES/EASTASIAPACIFICEXT/LAOPRDE
XTN/0,,menuPK:293689~pagePK:141159~piPK:141110~theSitePK:293684,00.html

Asian Development Bank: http://beta.adb.org/countries/lao-pdr/main

PHARMACEUTICALS, MEDICAL SUPPLIES AND MEDICAL EQUIPMENT

The health care system in Laos is very basic but developing. Maternal and child health is an important priority for the GOL as it seeks to graduate from Least Developed Country status by 2020. The Ministry of Health controls the import of medical equipment, supplies and pharmaceuticals. Refurbished medical equipment and low-cost pharmaceuticals are market possibilities.

TRADE REGULATIONS, CUSTOMS AND STANDARDS

IMPORT TARIFFS

The Lao import tax system aims to promote importation of inputs for investment and production while protecting domestic production and limiting luxury imports. Foreign investors do not pay import duty on imports of capital machinery and equipment for production, or on spare parts.

Raw materials and intermediate goods needed for export production are also exempt.

Raw materials and intermediate goods imported for import substituting industries can be accorded special treatment based on an incentive agreement.

There are standard ASEAN import tariff rates varying from zero, to40 percent, excluding non-ASEAN countries and according to the Tariff Nomenclature of Lao PDR based on ASEAN Harmonized Tariff Nomenclature (AHTN 2007/1). These published rates are levied by the Customs Department.

For additional analytical, business and investment opportunities information,
please contact Global Investment & Business Center, USA
at (703) 370-8082. Fax: (703) 370-8083. E-mail: ibpusa3@gmail.com
Global Business and Investment Info Databank - www.ibpus.com

Importers may face turnover as well as excise taxes. Excise ranges from 5-90% on many goods. The Lao government began to introduce a Value Added Tax (VAT) to replace turnover taxes in January 2010, with business turnover tax set at 10%. Additional tariff, excise tax, and turnover tax information can be found at the Tax Department, Ministry of Finance

TRADE BARRIERS

The Lao Government has simplified its tariff structure and is gradually amending non-tariff barriers. There are reports that Lao customs officials continue to charge arbitrary tariffs on some imported goods. The Bilateral Trade Agreement with the United States lowers tariffs on a range of American products and offers importers the ability to appeal tariff decisions they feel are improper.

IMPORT REQUIREMENTS AND DOCUMENTATION

Application for an import license must be made to the provincial trade authority where the importing enterprise is located. An import/export license is valid for the life of the business, but investors must periodically notify the authorities that they intend to continue operating their businesses. The Lao Government offers quotas for importing duty-free vehicles to qualifying individuals and companies.

For general goods, importers are required to have the following documentation for each shipment: 1) invoice; 2) packing list; 3) transport documents; 4) bill of lading; and 5) a customs clearance report. Importers of raw materials for re-export are required to have the same documents as other importers, except for a contract and import license.

The Lao military controls and profits from an unpublicized quota system in which automobile quotas are sold to private sector entrepreneurs who pass those costs on to consumers. Automobile importers, individuals or companies, unless they have obtained duty free status, must pay an import tax, turnover tax, excise tax, and additional tax for luxury goods to the government based on the tariff rates.

Exporters should have the following documents when applying for an export declaration:

1) an application for export declaration; 2) an import/export license (only for goods under control of the ministry or government, e.g. rough or polished diamonds); 3) an invoice of goods; 4) a packing list; 5) a certificate of country of origin and generalized system of preferences certificate of origin if applicable; 6) phyto-sanitary certificate for food exports; and 7) industrial products certification for industrial products.

To import or export pharmaceuticals, food, or chemical products, in addition to the aforementioned documents, the importer must obtain a license from the Food and Drug Control Import Division of the Food and Drug Department of the Ministry of Public Health. Pre-shipment inspection is required for exported goods in accordance with the requirements of the destination country. Laos has no special labeling or marking requirements.

U.S. EXPORT CONTROLS

Several United States export controls apply to Laos. For the most part, these export controls fall under the categories of National Security licensing requirements and the Chemical Weapons Convention. For detailed information regarding U.S. export controls please contact the Bureau of Industry and Security within the U.S. Department of Commerce at http://www.bis.doc.gov

TEMPORARY ENTRY

Products imported for the purposes of processing, assembly into finished products, or for exhibition and subsequent re-export, are exempt from duty. Trans-shipment of goods through Laos requires the same documents normally needed for import and export. Goods traveling through Laos are not subject to import or export taxes.

LABELING AND MARKING REQUIREMENTS

Laos has no laws governing product labeling and marking.

PROHIBITED AND RESTRICTED IMPORTS

In February 2010, the Lao government launched the Decree on Import and Export Licensing procedures of Controlled Goods, No. 180 PMO, in a bid to comply with the World Trade Organization (WTO) and World Customs Organization (WCO) rules. Laos also began implementing the Notification for Goods Subject to Non-Automatic Import and Export Licensing and Goods Subject to Automatic Import and Export Licensing, No 2151/MOIC.

For more information, please contact the Department of Import and Export Management: http://www.moc.gov.la/default.asp

CUSTOMS REGULATIONS AND CONTACT INFORMATION

Please see: http://laocustoms.laopdr.net/laws_and_regulations.htm

The Lao Trade Portal, established in 2014, has extensive information for exporters and importers: http://www.laotradeportal.gov.la/index.php?r=site/index

STANDARDS

Laos has no specific law on standards for imported or exported goods. Imported goods are allowed to enter based on the certification of the country of export.

STANDARDS ORGANIZATIONS

Laos currently has no independent standards organizations. In 2011, the Department of Standards and Metrology in the Ministry of Science and Technology was established as an independent department alongside the Department of Intellectual Property. http://www.laotradeportal.gov.la/index.php?r=site/displayb&id=220

NIST Notify U.S. Service

Member countries of the World Trade Organization (WTO) are required under the Agreement on Technical Barriers to Trade (TBT Agreement) to report to the WTO all proposed technical regulations that could affect trade with other Member countries. Notify U.S. is a free, web-based e-mail subscription service that offers an opportunity to review and comment on proposed foreign technical regulations that can affect your access to international markets. Register online at Internet URL: http://www.nist.gov/notifyus/

CONFORMITY ASSESSMENT

Laos currently has no conformity assessment.

PRODUCT CERTIFICATION

Laos currently has no product certification.

ACCREDITATION

Laos currently has no accreditation bodies.

PUBLICATION OF TECHNICAL REGULATIONS

Laos currently does not publish technical regulations, although the Official Gazette, designed to publish all proposed and enacted legislation, is currently under development.

LABELING AND MARKING

According to regulation 027/CFDC, all foodstuffs imported into Laos for consumer use

must be labeled in accordance with Food and Drug Control Department requirements.

In practice, this requirement does not appear to be enforced.

CONTACTS

Department of Standards and Metrology: Department of Intellectual Property.
http://www.laotradeportal.gov.la/index.php?r=site/displayb&id=220

U.S. Embassy Vientiane Economic and Commercial Officer: youngermb@state.gov

TRADE AGREEMENTS

Laos acceded to the World Trade Organization (WTO) in 2013, and is working towards meeting the requirements of the ASEAN Economic Community by 2015.

The following countries have granted Generalized System of Preference (GSP) status to Laos: Canada, Japan; Australia (no import tax); European Union; South Korea; Norway and Switzerland. Lao PDR is under review in 2013 for eligibility for U.S. GSP status,

which would remove import tariffs for over 5000 products exported to the United States from Laos. A final decision on granting GSP to Laos is expected in 2013.

Laos has also signed trade agreements with 15 countries, including: Vietnam; China; Cambodia; Burma; Thailand; North Korea; Mongolia; Malaysia; Russia; India; Belarus; Argentina; the United States; Kuwait and Turkey.

WEB RESOURCES

http://www.nist.gov/notifyus/

http://laocustoms.laopdr.net/laws_and_regulations.htm

http://www.moc.gov.la/default.asp

http://www.laotradeportal.gov.la/index.php?r=site/displayb&id=220

EXPORT DOCUMENTS AND PROCEDURES

PART I : DOCUMENTATION

- Cargo Control Document
- Invoice
- Declaration Form
- Certificate of Origin

You will be able to obtain release of your goods upon presentation of a fully completed declaration package consisting of the following:

1. 3 copies of the cargo control document
2. 2 copies of the invoice
3. 2 carrier advice notes
4. 2 copies of any permit issued by a relevant Ministry or Department
5. 2 certificates of origin showing origin of goods
6. 3 sets of the declaration form

CARGO CONTROL DOCUMENT

A cargo control document in the form of an airway bill for goods arriving by air or a manifest for goods arriving by highway or river will be sent to you together with an advice note issued by the carrier to inform you that a shipment has arrived and is awaiting customs clearance.

You will need the cargo control number from the airway bill or manifest to complete the appropriate field on the declaration form.

Three copies of the cargo control document and two copies of the advice note must accompany the declaration form.

INVOICE

For all shipments entering or leaving Lao PDR, a commercial invoice which indicates the buyer and seller of the goods, the price paid or price payable, and an adequate description of the goods including quantity of the goods contained in the shipment, should be produced to support the declaration. The invoice must be prepared by the exporter. Locally produced invoices are not acceptable. Click here to download an invoice sample

Declaration Form

For additional analytical, business and investment opportunities information,
please contact Global Investment & Business Center, USA
at (703) 370-8082. Fax: (703) 370-8083. E-mail: ibpusa3@gmail.com
Global Business and Investment Info Databank - www.ibpus.com

Certificate of origin

<h1 style="text-align:center">PART II :CLASSIFICATION OF GOODS</h1>

- Harmonized System

General Information on the Harmonized Commodity Description and Coding (HS) Based Tariff

The H.S. based tariff is logically structured and divided into twenty-one sections. For the most part, commodities are arranged in these sections according to the decree of manufacture or processing.

Within the twenty-one sections there are 99 chapters. Chapter 77 is reserved for possible future expansion. The last chapter, 99 is set aside for special use by individual countries.

Chapters are arranged according to levels of processing, with primary commodities classified in the earlier chapters and technically more complex products treated later on.

Each chapter begins with a title page. Section and chapter legal notes precede certain chapters and sections. However, these notes only define the scope and limits of the chapter and sections they precede. Following the chapter notes, you will find the classification numbers of all products covered by the chapter.

STRUCTURE OF THE CLASSIFICATION NUMBER

Classification in the HS is a systematic process. To use this process, it is essential to understand the structure of the classification number.

With the entry of Lao PDR in ASEAN, the classification number consists of eight digits. This eight-digit number is sub-divided at various levels to provide greater details and definitions for a product than the previous level at the six digits.

Each level is identified as follows:

01.01 HEADING
01.01.20 1st SUB-HEADING
01.01.20.00 2sd Sub-Heading

International Lao and ASEAN
Requirement Requirement

The first six digits represent the international portion of the classification number and are the numbers that will be used by all countries acceding to the Harmonized System. The last two digits reflect the Lao and ASEAN requirements for tariff and statistical purposes.

The structure of the classification number, i.e., the breakdown of the number by heading, and sub-headings is the basis for classifying your product in the H.S. Once a product has been located in a heading, an appropriate eight-digit number of sub-headings within the selected heading must be determined.

PART III : VALUE FOR DUTY

- Transaction Value Method
- Other Methods of Valuing Imports
- Importer's Responsibility
- Importer's Rights

The Lao PDR system of valuing imported goods is known as the transaction value system. It is based on an internationally approved set of rules, under the General Agreement on Tariffs and Trade. The system is now used by most trading nations and provides for a fair and uniform means of valuing goods for customs duty.

The transaction value system stipulates that the transaction value method must be used whenever possible. This value method bases the customs value on the price paid by the importer to the exporter for the imported goods. If the transaction value method cannot be used, one of the other five methods must be used, in the sequence presented. These other methods are known as

- Transaction value of identical goods
- Transaction value of similar goods
- Deductive value
- Computed value
- Flexible value

TRANSACTION VALUE METHOD

1. The transaction value method will be used for valuation of most imported goods, except in situations where there is a relationship between the importer and exporter that may influence the value, or where the imported goods are rented or leased, or are sent on consignment, or where the exporter imposes certain conditions such as restricting the trading level or the area of resale, or barter trade.

2. When using the transaction value method, the following costs must be included in the customs value:
- Transportation costs to Lao PDR
- Insurance costs
- Packing, packaging and special handling costs
- Fees paid to the exporters for royalties, licenses, etc.
- Storage charges in the country of export that are paid by the importer
- All escalation costs charged after the goods are ordered
- All selling costs such as commissions, etc that are charged to the importer
- Assists are goods or services supplied by the importer to the exporter free or at a reduced cost that were used in the production of the goods.

3. Costs which may be deducted from the customs value are:
- Discounts for volume purchases, payment for the goods in advance or within an agreed period (such discount must be shown on the invoice and granted before importation)
- If goods were sold by the exporter on a duty and tax paid basis, deduct the amount paid for duties and taxes

- Amount paid to the exporter for work that will be performed in Lao PDR, such as construction, erection, assembly, maintenance or technical assistance related to the imported goods (such costs must be shown separately on the invoice or in a contract)

OTHER METHODS OF VALUING IMPORTS

The five other methods of valuation are more complex and the necessary information may not be readily available. The following is therefore only for the importer's information and, if it is necessary to apply these methods the importer may wish to consult with a customs officer to determine the value for duty.

IDENTICAL OR SIMILAR GOODS METHOD

Under these methods the value for duty is based on the customs value of other identical or similar goods which have been previously exported to Lao PDR, at or about the same time as the goods being imported. The customs value can be adjusted to allow for differences in the trade level of purchases and in the cost of transportation. It is unlikely that the importer will be able to use these methods, as it requires information on values declared to customs for imports of identical or similar goods. Values for duty under these methods is therefore usually calculated in conjunction with the assistance of a customs officer.

DEDUCTIVE VALUE METHOD

Under the deductive value method, the value for duty is based on the most common selling price of goods imported into Lao PDR. From this resale price is deducted an amount which represents the average profit and general expenses involved in selling the goods in the Lao PDR. Included in the general expenses involved in the expenses will be items such as Lao PDR duties and taxes, all transportation, warehousing, selling and distribution costs, also any packaging or further processing costs in Lao PDR, should also be deducted in calculating the value for duty.

The purpose behind this method is to determine what the cost of the goods would have been had they been purchased, in the same condition as when imported, from an unrelated exporter. This method would only be used in situations such as goods being imported on consignment or barter trade.

COMPUTED VALUE METHOD

The computed value method is the cost of production of the imported goods, plus an amount for normal profit and general expenses experienced by the exporter, when selling the same type of goods to importers in Lao PDR.

As most exporters are reluctant to release this information, the use of this valuation method will generally be limited to those importers who are related to the exporter and where the exporter is the manufacturer of the goods being appraised.

FLEXIBLE METHOD

If the other methods of valuation can not be used, the flexible method must be applied. This method does not provide specific rules, but stipulates that the rules of one of the other five methods is applied in a flexible manner and that the information used is available in the Lao PDR.

IMPORTER'S RESPONSIBILITY

The importer of commercial goods into Lao PDR is responsible for the self-assessment of the duty and tax liabilities on all goods imported. This means that the importer or his authorized agent must prepare all necessary documents for presentation to customs.

CUSTOMS' RESPONSIBILITY

Customs is responsible to ensure that all legislation governing the importation and exportation of goods into and out of the Lao PDR have been fully complied with. Customs is also responsible to insure that all applicable duties and taxes have been paid. Customs will also review customs declarations after release of the goods and may issue notices for payment of additional, duties and tax as a result of the review, or reassessment of value or redetermination of tariff.

IMPORTER'S RIGHTS

An importer has the right to request customs to reconsider any reassessment of value and any redetermination of tariff classification. Further, the importer has the right to appeal the customs reassessment notice to higher authorities.

PART IV : CODING INSTRUCTIONS

Annex
I List of Customs Offices and Codes
II List of Country and Currency Codes
III List of Regional Customs Offices and Addresses

THE DECLARATION FORM

The declaration form or single administrative document is used for all customs transactions; import, export or transit. It must be complete to be acceptable in customs.

Click here to view a sample form

THE DECLARATION FORM HAS THREE SEGMENTS.

1. In the first section(Boxes No.1-23) enter general information on importer, exporter and declarant as well as transport and transaction details.

2. In the second section (Boxes No.24-42) enter details on the item declared, including amount of duties and taxes payable or exempted.

3. Summary of Payment and Responsibility of Declaration Section.

It is presented in the form of (i.) a header sheet, which is used to declare importation, exportation or in transit information for each commodity item (ii.) continuation sheets to declare other commodity items and (iii.) section sheet for official use.

Note. Declaration forms are on sale at all Regional Customs offices.
Instructions to fill each box of the form.

Box No.1 Declaration Regime

Inscribe one of the following codes to identify the type of transaction the declaration is for:

Regime Code Description
10 Exportation of domestic Goods
14 Exportation under a drawback regime
20 Temporary Exportation
35 Re-Exportation
40 Importation of goods for Home consumption.
4A Importation of goods for diplomatic use, returning residents, and humanitarian assistance; samples, educational materials and certain religious articles.
4B Goods ex-warehoused to duty free shops
4C Goods ex-warehoused for exportation out of Lao PDR
45 Home Consumption of Goods after temporary admission
47 Home Consumption of Goods entered under a warehousing regime
50 Temporary Importation
62 Re-Importation of Goods Exported temporarily
70 Warehousing of Goods
80 Transit

Office Codes.

Enter the code of the office where the declaration is presented. See Annex I for a list of all customs offices and their codes.

Manifest /Airway bill number.

Enter the cargo control number from the air waybill if the goods arrive or leave by air or from the manifest if goods arrive or leave by any other mode of transport.
Declaration Number and Date.

Customs will assign the declaration number and the date when the declaration is presented and registered with customs.

Box No.2 Exporter and Address

If you enter goods for exportation, indicate your name and address as well as the taxpayer identification number (TIN) issued by the Tax Department. If you have not yet been issued a TIN please obtain a number from the nearest tax office and use it on all subsequent customs declarations. Also include your office telephone number. For diplomatic and personal exportations, leave the number field blank.

Box No.3 Gross Mass Kg.

Indicate the gross weight in kilograms of the entire consignment of goods as declared on the manifest or air waybill.

BOX NO.4 ITEMS

Indicate the total number of items as shown on the invoice.

BOX NO.5 TOTAL PACKAGES.

Indicate the total number of packages as declared on the manifest or airway bill. In case of bulk cargo, indicate BULK only.

BOX NO. 6 IMPORTER AND ADDRESS

If you enter goods for importation, indicate your name and address as well as the taxpayer identification number (TIN) issued by the Tax Department. If you have not been issued a TIN please obtain a number from the nearest tax office and use it on all subsequent customs declarations. Also include your office telephone number. For diplomatic and personal importations, leave the number field blank.

BOX NO.7 CONSIGNEE.

If you are importing goods on behalf of another person, or the other party holds title to the good at time of importation indicate the name and address of the consignee as well as the TIN issued by the Tax Department. Please contact the nearest tax office for a number and use on all subsequent declarations, or obtain the TIN number from the consignee if one has been issued to the consignee by the tax department. For diplomatic importations, leave the number field blank.

BOX NO.8 DECLARANT.

If you are a licensed agent authorized to transact business in customs, enter the TIN issued by the Tax Department. If you do not have a TIN, contact the nearest tax office.

BOX NO.9 COUNTRY OF CONSIGNMENT/DESTINATION.

For importation, indicate the country and the code from where the goods have been consigned. For exportation, indicate the country and the code to where the goods are exported or re-exported.

See Annex II: List of Country and Currency Codes.

Box No.10 Type of License.

Indicate the type of trade or industry license held by you.

Box. No.11 Delivery Terms.

Indicate the terms of delivery of goods either CIF for importation, or FOB for exportation.

Box No.12 Total Invoice in Foreign Currency.

For importation, indicate the total amount of the invoice in foreign currency. See list of Country and Currency Codes in Annex II.

Box No.13 Total Invoice in Local Currency.

Enter here the total value of the invoice in Kip by converting the value declared in box No. 12 with the rate of exchange indicated in box No.16. If there is only one item, this value should correspond to the value declared in box no.38. If there are many items, the total value should correspond to the total of values declared in all the boxes no.38 on the Continuation sheets.

Box No.14 Total FOB (Exports)

Indicate the FOB value of the goods in foreign currency.
(if known)

Box No. 14 Total FOB (Imports)

Enter the FOB value in foreign currency. (if known)

Box No.15 Total FOB Ncy (Import/Export)

For import, leave blank.
For export, indicate the FOB value of the goods in Kip.

Box No.16 Rate of Exchange.

Indicate the rate of exchange of the foreign currency to the Kip and the code of the foreign currency. (The exchange rate shall be that which is in force at time of importation, unless otherwise advised).

Box No.17 Mode of Transport.

Indicate the mode of transport, the voyage number. Also the country code of the nationality of the aircraft, truck or ship.
(if known)

The codes for mode of transport are:

SEA 1
RAIL 2
ROAD 3
AIR 4

Box No.18 Port of Loading/Unloading.

For imports indicate the name and the code of the foreign country where goods are loaded,
For exports, indicate the name and the code of the foreign country where goods are destined.

See Annex II for a list of Country Codes.

Box No.19 Place of Shipping/ Landing.

For additional analytical, business and investment opportunities information,
please contact Global Investment & Business Center, USA
at (703) 370-8082. Fax: (703) 370-8083. E-mail: ibpusa3@gmail.com
Global Business and Investment Info Databank - www.ibpus.com

For imports, indicate the place in Lao PDR where goods have arrived. At export, or re-export, indicate the place in Lao PDR from where the goods are exported or re-exported.

Box No.20 Entry/Exit Office.

Indicate the code of the Lao customs office where the declaration is presented for clearance.

In a transit operation, indicate the code of the customs office where the transit operation commences. Also indicate the code of the exit customs office where the transit operations is to be terminated.

Box No.21 Identification Warehouse (Leave blank until bonded warehouses are established)

Indicate the code of the bonded warehouse where goods are to be warehoused or ex-warehoused.

Box No.22 Financial and Banking Data.

Indicate the terms of payment of the transaction, as well as the name of the bank and the branch where payment for the commercial transaction is made.

Box No.23 Attached Documents.

Indicate the codes of attached documents, which support your declaration. (Documents must be originals or certified as true copies).

1234567891011 InvoiceManifestAirway billPacking ListCertificate of Origin (If required)Phytosanitary Certificate (If required)Import Permit from Ministry of Trade (If required)Import permit from Ministry of Agriculture (If required)Import Permit from Ministry of Heath (If required) Authorization from Department of Transport (If required)If claiming duty and tax exemptions, documents authorizing such exemptions must be presented with the declaration.

Box No.24 Marks, Numbers and Description of Goods

Indicate the marks and numbers of the packages as shown on the manifest or airway bill.

If goods arrive or leave by containers, indicate the container number as shown on the manifest.

The total number of packages should correspond to the total number of packages indicated in box No.5.

Give a detailed description of the goods. Avoid, as far as possible, trade names. Except in the case of vehicles and electronic devices, provide make and model.

Box No.25 No. of Items.

Indicate the number of items on the invoice.

Box No.26 Tariff Code

Indicate the classification code of the commodity imported. This classification code in based on the AHTN and must be eight digits.

Box No.27 Customs Procedure Codes.
(Leave blank at this time)

Box No.28 Country of Origin/Destination

For imports, indicate the code of the country of origin of the goods imported, if the country of origin of the goods is different from the country where the goods have been consigned.

Box No.29 Zone.
It the goods originate from ASEAN member countries and are supported by a certificate of origin enter ASEAN. For other countries enter GEN. At export enter XPT.

Box No.30 Valuation Code

Indicate the code of the valuation method used to determine the customs value for duty.

There are six valuation methods and coded as follows:

Valuation Method Code
Transaction Method 1
Identical Goods Method 2
Similar Goods Method 3
Deductive Method 4
Computed Method 5
Flexible Method 6

Note: The transaction valuation method must be used as the primary method for valuation if possible.

Box No.31 Gross Mass.

Enter the gross weight in kilograms for the item on the first page only. The total weight of all items on the continuation sheets in the declaration should be equal to the weight declared in box no.3 of the general segment.

Box No.32 Net Mass.

Enter the net weight of the goods in kilograms for each item declared. If a continuation sheet is used a net mass must be inscribed for each item.

Box No.33 FOB Foreign Currency.

Enter the FOB value of the item in foreign currency (if known).

Box No.34 FOB Local Currency, only if transport and insurance are not prepaid by exporter. If prepaid, enter the value that includes transportation and insurance.

Enter the FOB value of the item in Kips, only if transport and insurance are not prepaid by exporter. If prepaid, enter the value that includes transportation and insurance.

Box No. 35 Freight.

Enter the amount of freight paid or payable for the item in Kip. For a shipment of various items, the freight charges are apportioned according to freight paid or payable and by weight. If freight is prepaid by exporter and included in the value, mark the box "Prepaid".

Box No.36 Insurance.

Enter the amount of insurance in Kip for the item.

For a shipment of various items, the insurance paid or payable is to be apportioned.

If the insurance is prepaid by the exporter and included in the value, mark the box "prepaid"

Box No.37 Other Costs.
Enter other costs and expenses incurred for the import of goods and paid to the exporter for the imported goods.

Box No.38 Customs Value in Local Currency.

Enter the customs value for the item, which is the total of values of boxes 33, 34, 35 and 36.

Box No. 39 Supplementary Unit/Quantity.

Some of the most common international units of quantity are as follows:

Unit Code
Cubic Metre MTQ
Gigawatt-hour GWH
Hundred CEN
Kilogram KGM
Litre LTR
Metre MTR
Number NMB
Number of packs NMP
Square Metre MTK
Ten TEN
Ten Pairs TPR
Thousand MIL
Tonne TNE

Enter any of the code, which describes the unit quantity of goods imported/exported. If the units of imports or exports are not included in this list, consult a customs officer for more detailed lists.

Box No.40 Duty Payable.

Enter the amount of duties and taxes payable for the item declared per category of duty, tax and excise.

Enter also the taxable base for each category of duty, tax and excise. Duty rate is calculated on the Customs value. The tax is calculated on the customs value plus the duty payable. The excise tax is calculated on the customs value plus duty payable plus tax payable.

For other items of the declaration, on the continuation sheets enter the duty, tax and excise payable.

Box No.41 Permit Numbers.

Enter permit number and date of issue for the shipment, if required.

Box No.42 Previous Declaration.

If the declaration refers to a previous declaration, the registration number and date of the previous declaration is entered here.

Present a copy of the previous declaration with the declaration you have just prepared.

Responsibility of Declaration

You must enter your full name, indicate the capacity in which you are acting. And sign the declaration.

You must also indicate the mode of payment by which duty and taxes are to be paid.

After you have completed your declaration, trader can now lodge it at the designated customs office where your goods are held.

After customs review and approval of the declaration, please make the payment of all applicable duties and taxes, and present a copy of the payment receipt to the customs office where the declaration was presented.

On receipt of the customs release note, present the release note to the warehouse keeper for delivery of the imported goods and sign for receipt of the goods or have the carrier sign for receipt.

FOREIGN INVESTMENT OPPORTUNITIES IN LAOS

FOREIGN INVESTMENT LICENSED IN LAOS

Rank	Countries	Number of Projects	Investment in US $ x 1000	Percentage
1.	Thailand	233	$2,278,289	44.78%
2.	USA	39	1,482,717	29.14
3.	R. Korea	17	394,785	7.76
4.	France	68	312,806	6.15

5.	Malaysia	11	188,731	3.71
6.	Australia	41	134,026	2.63
7.	Taiwan	31	64,764	1.27
8.	Norway	1	56000	1.10
9.	China	61	38,921	0.76
10.	UK.	13	28,685	0.56
11.	Hong Kong	23	28,266	0.56
12.	Canada	13	17,914	0.35
13.	Russian	12	17,564	0.35
14.	Singapore	16	12,217	024
15.	Japan	17	7,913	0.16
16.	Indonesia	2	5,140	0.10
17.	DPK Korea	1	3300	0.06
18.	Germany	7	3,019	0.06
19.	Vietnam	10	2,724	0.05
20.	Macao	2	2,560	0.05
21.	Sweden	7	2,203	0.04
22.	Italy	6	1,973	0.04
23.	Holland	3	770	0.02
24.	New Zealand	5	734	0.01
25.	India	2	645	0.01
26.	Belgium	2	500	0.01
27.	Denmark	6	406	0.01
28.	Switzerland	2	240	0.00
29.	Ukraine	1	200	0.00
30.	Austria	3	172	0.00
31.	Myanmar	3	65	0.00
	Laos' Shares		1,158,400	
	TOTAL:	658 projects	US$6,246,649,000	100%

SELECTED BUSINESS AND INVESTMENT OPPORTUNITIES

AGRO-FORESTRY SECTOR

Agriculture : The economic growth of the Lao PDR **Depends to a large extend,** upon the, performance of the Agricultural sector which contributed in 1993 for 56% of the GDP and employed about 0% of the labor force.

Coffee is by far the most promising **product for export.** In 1992, export of coffee accounted for around 80% of the export value in the agricultural sector and contributed for 7.4% of the total export value of the country. Export also includes several annual and perennial corps of limited quantities.

The Lao PDR has the **highest potential land/person** in the Greater Mekong Subregion large and unexploited fertile land and favorable climatic conditions, particularly in the **boloven basaltic plateau.** This could offer promising **opportunities** for low-intensive investment in the **agro-processing industry** for export based on annual and perennial crops.

The on-going improvement of main National Roads linking major provinces, together with the high rate of urbanization have created **favorable conditions** for investment in the **import-substitution** agro-processing industries.

Forestry : It has been estimated that the Lao PDR has **the highest ratio** of forest to total area in ASIA. Wood products including lumber are one of the main **export earning** of Lao PDR. In 1993, it accounted for **22% of the total export value.** In view of the long term sustainable development and the preservation of the environment, the Government has been implementing the policy of striking **a balance** between exploitation and conservation and shifting from exports of logs and lumbers towards the **promotion of wood** processing. Due to **shortage** of capital and the technical know-how in the country, the development of wood processing subsector also needs the investment and the introduction of new technology of the **foreign investors.**

ENERGY SECTOR

Electricity requirements in the region-. are increasing rapidly it has been predicted that 23,958 MW of new generation will be needed between now and year 2000. Lao PDR. is rich in energy resources: **Hydropower, coal, oil and gas. The uneven distribution** of the energy resources among the countries, particularly the hydropower resources : Countries with higher power demand have limited resources while those with limited requirements are well endowed with the hydropower resources.

Lao PDR has a hydropower potential of about **15,000 MW** within its territory. Up to now, slightly over 1% of the total potential has been developed with 70 to 75% of the production exported to Thailand.

With the huge resources located close to the biggest power demand country in the subregion **(Thailand)** and the low domestic demand, the hydropower sector will continue to be **one of the main foreign exchange earning of Lao PDR.**

Without other financial sources than **The public investment funds and the external soft loan** the hydropower development would provably continue with the similar **slow rate** as experienced in the eighties. This would lead to a loss of opportunity for foreign exchange earning badly needed for development of other sectors.

For additional analytical, business and investment opportunities information, please contact Global Investment & Business Center, USA at (703) 370-8082. Fax: (703) 370-8083. E-mail: ibpusa3@gmail.com Global Business and Investment Info Databank - www.ibpus.com

On the basis of the above and in line with the new economic policy, the Government has begun, since the beginning of the nineties, **to seek participation of foreign investors** for projects beyond the financial capacity of the public and soft loan investment.

Within the short timeframe, experiences have proven that such policy is correct and several projects with the aggregate generation capacity about **10 times higher than the existing capacity** are being implemented in 1994 and expected to be completed by **the 2000** as shown 'm the attached figure.

The funds for these projects are from both the private sector **(BOT schemes)** for large schemes and soft loan for small/medium schemes. Agreements between the Government and the developers have been signed for most of the BOT schemes of the 1994-2000 peroid.

All the a above-mentioned BOT schemes have a provision for **equity sharing by the government** ranging from 25% to 60%.

Information given in following tables and figures are aimed to show the potential and the relative advantages of the hydropower resources in Lao PDR. It also indicates the, long-term forecast of power and electric energy demands of the countries in the Greater Mekong Subregion.

MINING SECTOR

Foreign investment is particularly sought in the Mining Sector because of its capital-intensive investment combined with scarce domestic financial resources and its high potential for export.

In 1991, the foreign investment in this sector was ranked second in terms of aggregate value (about 25% of the total).

Fiscal regulations such royalty rate, income taxes and incentives in the Mining Sector are widely recognized as **competitive** by international standard. This indicates the firm commitment and strong support of the Government to **pave the way** for foreign investment in the sector.

The following location maps of various minerals and fossil fuels such as coal lignite, oil and natural gas show that the country possess huge mineral resources.

Market for fossil fuel in **Thailand** is tremendous as the country has to import about **60% of its requirements.** This would be an area of **high prospects** for foreign investors. Recently, an agreement was signed with private investors to implement a **lignite power plant** project in Hongsa (Northwest of Lao PDR) for exporting the electricity to Thailand.

In the **short-term,** other minerals having high prospects for export would be gemstones which require simple extraction equipment and could be easily transported.

Some **medium-and long-term** investment opportunities offered by the Ming Sector would be :

    a). **The potash production** in the **Vientiane** province, the largest known deposits in the subregion with the estimated reserves exceeding by far those in Thailand;

    b). The significant **iron ore** deposits in the province of **Xiengkhouang,** the occurrences of **base metals** (components needed for steel) and the planned hydropower development on the Nam Ngum river, both in the northeast of Vientiane and in

Xiengkhoang Province, suggest the region could provide opportunities for both iron ore and steel export;

c). The **boloven** basaltic plateau in the southern Laos well endowed with both the competitive **hydropower** potential and **bauxite** might also offer opportunities for aluminum melting plants.

Having been fully aware that the absence of railways and inadequacy -of the road network are the major constraints for the development of the Mining Sector, the Government is now seeking all financial means to develop the transport sector including the **concession arrangement** with private investors Mining and transport development could be tied together in a **Single package** for concession arrangement.

ROADS

The Second and Third conferences in Subregion Economic Cooperation have identified the following priority projects in the road subsector :

a). Upgrading of the **Ho Chi Minh City- Phnom Penh- Bangkok road connection,** including possible extension to Vung Tau in Vietnam;

b). Construction of a **Thai- Lao PDR- Vietnam east-west Corridor;**

c). Development of a good quality road linking **Chiang Rai-Kunming via Myanmar;**

d). Development of a good quality road linking **Chiang Rai-Kunming via Lao PDR;** and

UPGRADING KUNMING -LAOSHIO ROAD SYSTEM.

RAILWAY, WATER AND TRANSPORT SUB-SECTOR

The Subregion Transport Sector Study by ADB considers 3 projects in railway subsector, 2 in the water transport subsector and 2 in the air transport subsector which are directly concerned Lao PDR.

a). **Projects in railway subsector** :

- Yunnan Province- Thailand Railway Project with two out of three optimal via Lao PDR.

- Extension Thailand Railway to Lao PDR (150 km) through the firstinternational Mekong bridge.

- Construction of new railway line from Lao PDR's Xiengkhouang Province to a Cualo port in Vietnam mainly for export of iron ore.

b). **Water Transport Subsector** :

- Upper Mekong River Navigation Improvement Project.

- Southem Lao PDR- Cambodia River Navigation Improvement Project.

c). **Air Transport Subsector** :

- Project to upgrade the airport in Lao PDR

- Project to Establish New Subregional Air Routes involving Luang Prabang.

TOURISM AND HOTEL SECTOR

Within the Subregion, links and networks in the tourism sector **already exist :** Government-to-government and the commercial sector.

The commun interest among all six countries is to promote nature and culture types of tourism. The major problem is the **gaps** in most countries in the **basicinfrastructure** and **support services** necessary for maximizing tourism potential.

The subregional cooperation will primarily focus on :

1. **Promoting the Subregion as a tourism destination.**
2. **Establishing Subregional Tourism Forum.**
3. **Training the trainers in the basic craft skills of tourism.**
4. **Training the Resource Management in Conservation and Tourism.**
5. **mekong River Tourism Promoting Study.**

TRANSPORT

In most countries, transportation infrastructures are inadequate and are considered as a **major impediment** to trade , cooperation and the exploitation of rich mineral resources, particularly those located in the hinterlands.

Further major commitments are required before minimum standards can be satisfies and most of the shortcomings could only be addressed by **cooperation efforts**.

Through several meetings and consultations, the six countries have agrees that :

a). **Priority** should be on to the improvement and rehabilitation of existing facilities and Subregional projects on which there is already agreement among the countries directly concerned;

b). **The formulation of projects** should consider trade generation impacts, especially considering the economic transformation taking place in the Subregion;

c). Transport projects should be **implemented in sections or stretches** in order to facilitate project(s) implementation and provide immediate benefits;

d). Given financial constraints, **criteria** for project(s) selection will need to be established, including consideration of the subregional versus national character of the project and financial resources available.

TRADE AND SERVICES SECTOR

Most of the countries trade more often with countries outside the subregion than within.

However, trade and investment **within the subregion** are being **development steadily** owing to the growing openness and revitalization of the economies, and the favorable legal and regulatory framework for local and foreign investors.

The countries in the subregion have many **commun problems** (such as severe infrastructure shortage) and also commun goals (such as outward-oriented economy and promotion of the participation of private sector). All countries recognize that the attraction of foreign investor **depend to a great extend** on the trade and investment environment.

The cooperation aiming at improving the Trade and Investment Climate in the Subregion would enable investors to consider their own strategies in the **subregional context** which is more attractive than the national context. Projects and initiatives emerged from the Third Conference on the Economic Cooperation in the Greater Mekong Subregion includes :

(a) Two Projects aiming at Facilitating and Enhancing Trade Flows
(b) Three Projects aiming at Improving Investment Climates
(c) Two Projects on Building a Strong Science and Technology Base
(d) One Project aiming at Increasing the Role of Private Sector

IMPORTANT BUSINESS AND INVESTMENT OPPORTUNITIES

20 MILLION ENVIRONMENT & SOCIAL PROGRAM

1. The proposed USD20 million loan project for Lao's Environment and Social program project is expected to be approved by the Asian Development Bank's (ADB) Board on **December 6, 2001**. This cable is intended to:

-- Alert Embassies and AID missions to ADB-financed projects, and

-- Provide U.S. businesses with as much lead time as possible concerning procurement and consulting opportunities.

-- For more information on this project or ADB lending opportunities, firms should contact Ms. Chantale Wong, Alternate U.S. Executive Director, Asian Development Bank at phone no. (63-2) 632-6051, and fax no. (63-2) 632-4003 or Mr. Stewart Ballard, The U.S. Commercial Liaison Office for the ADB at telephone nos.: (63-2) 887-1345 to 46 and fax no. (63-2) 887-1164. For in-country inquiry, please contact Mr. Scott Rolston, Commercial Officer, American Embassy, Vientiane; Tel.: (856-21) 212-581; Fax: 212-584.

2. For post, USADB requests AmEmbassy and AID mission views on the Project before **December 06, 2001** based on currently available information.

A. PROJECT RATIONALE:
- Lao People's Democratic Republic (Lao PDR) is a small landlocked country, characterized by its mountainous terrain, low population density, limited skilled human resources, and a wealth of natural resources and environmental assets. As natural resources underpin economic development and poverty reduction prospects) the Government attaches priority to conserving the environment and ensuring the environmental and social sustainability of all development activities.

- Improving environmental management and social safeguards performance has been the subject of considerable policy dialogue and technical assistance. Enactment of the

Environment Protection Law (EPL) in 1999 was a breakthrough. Together with environmental provisions in laws on electricity, roads, land, water resources, and forests, the EPL provides a framework for implementing safeguards. However, effective enforcement requires the adoption of enabling regulations, compliance mechanisms, and measures to enhance Government capacity and financial sustainability. Without this, the integration of environmental management and social safeguard issues across sectors will remain elusive.

- The Government aims to go beyond case-by-case remedial action on environment and social impacts towards a pro-active approach that integrates these concerns within national, sectoral, and area-based planning. The Government has sought Asian Development Bank (ADB) assistance to develop and implement a program aimed at shifting the country onto a more sustainable development trajectory, focusing initially on the energy and transport sectors. This will require five closely related sets of constraints to be addressed: (i) incomplete policy and regulatory framework; (ii) lack of implementation capacity at sectoral and provincial levels; (iii) inadequate compliance and enforcement mechanisms; (iv) absence of integrated area-based planning frameworks to guide investments in energy and transport; and (v) insufficient attention to sustainable finance for environment management.

B. PROJECT OBJECTIVES:
- The objective is to support the Government's policy reform agenda for improved environmental management and social safeguards in the energy and transport sectors. The scope covers five closely linked priority areas for policy action: (i) strengthening national policy and regulatory framework for environment management and social safeguards; (ii) enhancing policy implementation measures and capacity at sectoral and provincial levels; (iii) improving compliance and enforcement; (iv) promoting river basin management as a multi-sectoral and integrated planning framework for energy and transport development; and (v) establishing sustainable financing mechanisms, including an environment fund.

C. PROJECT DESCRIPTION:
- The Environment and Social Program (the Program) will assist the Lao PDR implement a targeted policy reform agenda for environmental management and social safeguards in the energy and transport sectors, focusing on hydropower and roads, with a proposed program loan of USD20.0 million.

D. EXECUTING AGENCY:
- The Science, Technology and Environment Agency (STEA) will be the Executing Agency for the Program, in close coordination with the Committee for Planning and Cooperation (CPC), Ministry of Finance (MOF), Ministry of Communication, Transport, Post and Construction (MCTPC), Ministry of Industry and Handicrafts (MIH), and Ministry of Agriculture and Forestry (MAF). STEA will have overall responsibility for ensuring effective implementation of the Program. MOF will monitor the use of loan proceeds and counterpart funds.

E. TOTAL PROJECT COST: USD20.0 million

F. PROGRAM PERIOD AND TRANCHING:
- The Program period will be 36 months (FY2002- FY2004). The proposed loan is to be disbursed in three tranches. The first tranche of USD5.0 million will be made available upon loan effectiveness, while the second tranche of USD10.0 million will be disbursed within 14 months after the first tranche, subject to the Government's compliance with the conditions set for the release of that tranche. A third tranche of USD5.0 million will be

made available when the Government establishes a proposed environment fund during the 36 months of loan utilization.

G. PROCUREMENT:
- The proceeds of the loan will finance the full foreign exchange costs, excluding local duties and taxes, of imports procured in and from ADB's member countries, other than those specified in the list of ineligible items and those financed by other multilateral and bilateral official sources. Procurement of eligible items under ADB's loan will be based on normal commercial practices for procurement by the private sector or standard Government procurement procedures acceptable to ADB for procurement by the public sector. In the case of goods commonly traded on international commodity markets, procurement will be done in accordance with procedures appropriate to the trade and acceptable to ADB.

H. COUNTERPART FUNDS:
- The Government will use counterpart funds generated by the loan to (i) finance additional public investment costs in transport and power projects to ensure strengthened social and environment safeguards; (ii) build institutional capacity to plan, design, and enforce environment and social safeguards; (iii) provide local counterpart resources for development projects aimed at river basin planning and management; (iv) address mitigation costs of existing infrastructure where social and environment costs were not adequately addressed; and (v) establish an environment fund.

I. CONSULTING SERVICES:
- No consulting services are required under the Program.

J. PROJECT BENEFITS:
- Program benefits include: (i) reducing the environmental and social costs of projects developed with inappropriate safeguards; (ii) increasing equity and resource use efficiency by internalizing social and environmental considerations in sector development; (iii) reducing the costs associated with "fixing" environmental and social problems resulting from inadequate regulatory framework and weak enforcement of safeguards; (iv) attracting increased commercial investment in infrastructure development; and (v) ensuring more sustainable and less risky project designs that better reflect local concerns, needs, and opportunities.

- The Program will also contribute to the country's poverty reduction goals. Improved environmental management will help maintain and enhance the livelihood base of the rural poor. Land use planning and watershed management will improve prospects for sustainable use of natural resources. Road transport developed, conceived within an area based planning framework, will directly benefit isolated communities through improved market linkages and access to services. Over the medium term, it is expected that revenues from hydropower projects will also allow the government to increase the share of public expenditure allocated to health, education and social development. Introduction of social safeguards in infrastructure development will ensure that vulnerable groups are not impoverished or marginalized by adverse impacts.

PREPARATORY TECH ASSISTANCE PROJECTS

This report alerts U.S. firms to US$3.6 million in new, potential national procurement of consulting services under the Asian Development Bank's (ADB) technical assistance (TA) grant programs. Opportunities are reported for Azerbaijan, India, Laos, Maldives, and Pakistan. In 2000, U.S. firms, including many small consulting firms, succeeded in winning USD 57 million ADB-funded national technical assistance contracts out of a total ADB-financed consulting budget of USD 348 million.

The ADB selects a consultant for a TA grant based on its prior Expression of Interest (EOI). An EOI can be transmitted on-line through the ADB's website (www.adb.org); afterward it will be acknowledged automatically. Firms may opt to send a hardcopy follow-up EOI addressed to Mr. S. Thuraisingham, Manager, Consulting Services Division, with a copy to the ADB Project Officer. The EOI should relate a firm's experience and expertise to the ADB project. It is important for a U.S. firm to emphasize its similar project experience in the country or in a similar geographic area rather than presenting a general profile of its consulting activities. A separate EOI should be submitted for each project. The project name indicated in the EOI should exactly match that listed in the ADB Business Opportunities publication to avoid confusion.

To be considered for employment, consultants must register on the ADB's DACON (Data on Consulting Firms) and DICON (Data on Individual Consultants)
Systems, otherwise, their EOIs will not be accepted. DACON and DICON registration can now be done on-line at www.adb.org/consulting.

Firms may also send a notification copy of their EOIs to the U.S. mailing address for the U.S. Commercial Liaison Office for the ADB, Attention: Stewart Ballard, Senior Commercial Officer, PSC 500 Box 33, FPO AP 96515-1000, or to the same office at its international mailing address: 25th Floor Ayala Life-FGU Center, 6811 Ayala Avenue, Makati City, Metro Manila, Philippines 1226; Phone: (63-2) 887-1345; Fax: (63-2) 887-1164; E-mail: manila.adb.office.box@mail.doc.gov. This office works closely with the Office of the U.S. Executive Director to the ADB to increase American awareness of, and participation in, the ADB's activities.

The projects listed in this cable are now being actively processed by the ADB. For more information on these projects, the name of the ADB project officer is indicated in the project brief. The U.S Commercial Liaison Office is ready to provide assistance to U.S. firms upon request. (Please see paragraph 4.)

The following TA projects will be listed for the first time in the January 2002 issue of the Asian Development Bank's (ADB) Business Opportunities (ADBBO). (Note: The ADBBO is also available on the ADB's website <http://www.adb.org>.

NAME OF PROJECT: GMS: Northern Economic Corridor
Project No.: LAO34231-01
Executing Agency: Ministry of Communication, Transport, Post and Construction, Lanexang Avenue, Vientiane, Lao PDR
Fax: 856-21-414132
Tel. No.: 856-21-412741
TA Amount: US$600.0 Thousand
Sector/Subsector: Transport and Communications/Roads and Road Transport

Objectives and Scope: The Project will help to improve access and potential market linkages of a remote area of the Lao PDR to two large and growing economies in the region. Two main objectives of this TA are (i) to assist the Government to update all project parameters of the pre-feasibility study for the existing road in the Lao PDR from Houei Sai to Boten, and (ii) to prepare a pre-investment study to determine feasibility of developing a viable economic corridor. The TA will adopt a holistic approach to plan integrated development of the region. It will undertake surveys and hold stakeholder consultations with potential business leaders and private investors to identify projects and investment opportunities. The pre-investment study will also identify policy, institutional and human resource constraints and suggest an action plan to develop this region into a vibrant economic corridor.

Consulting Services: The TA is expected to commence in January 2002 and completed by December 2002 and will have duration of 12 months.

The TA will involve a total of 66 person-months of consulting services, divided between international (about 18 person-months) and domestic (about 48 person-months) consultants. The TA will be implemented with a multidisciplinary team of international and domestic consultants, headed by an economist as team leader with the main output related to update the cost estimates and providing overall supervision of the TA. Other expertise and skills required for the TA include engineers, environmental, social and resettlement experts, transport economist, business economist, and financial analyst. Familiarity with transport and communication sectors and region's economies, especially of the private sector operations will be essential.

Recruitment of Consultants: No action has yet been taken to recruit consultants.
Environmental Analysis: Required
Project Processing Stage:
SRC Completed: 3 Dec 2001
Project Officer: Rita Nangia (632-6801)
Transport and Communications Division West
In-country Commercial Officer: Scott Rolston, Commercial Officer, U.S. Embassy, Vientiane; E-mail: RolstoSL@state.gov.

NAME OF PROJECT: Northern and Central Water Supply and Sanitation Sector
Project No.: LAO34197-01
Executing Agency: Ministry of Communication, Transport, Post and Construction, Lane Xang Avenue, Vientiane
TA Amount: USD700.0 Thousand

Sector/Subsector: Social Infrastructure/Water Supply and Sanitation
Objectives and Scope: The ensuing Project will address the Government's highest priorities in the water supply sector and will help in its long-term vision of providing safe and convenient water supplies and sanitation facilities to 80 percent of all urban communities as contained in the Government's Sector Investment Plan. The Project will identify the demand for expanded urban water supply and sanitation services in the selected small urban communities, develop selection criteria for the participation of urban communities, develop strategies to strengthen the regulatory framework and build institutional capacity, and prepare new investment project covering a number of small urban communities in the Northern and Central regions.

Consulting Services: Consulting services yet to be determined.
Recruitment of Consultants: Requirements for consulting services to be completed during Fact-finding Mission.
Environmental Analysis: Not Required

Project Processing Stage:
Beginning of Fact-finding Mission: Jan 2002.
Project Officer: Keiichi Tamaki (632-6843)
Water Supply, Urban Development and Housing Division West
In-country Commercial Officer: Scott Rolston, Commercial Officer, U.S. Embassy, Vientiane; E-mail: RolstoSL@state.gov.

U.S.$37 MILLION VIENTIANE URBAN INFRASTRUCTURE & SRV PROJ

. The proposed USD 37 million loan project for Laos' Vientiane Urban Infrastructure and Services project is expected to be approved by the Asian Development Bank's (ADB) Board on August 23, 2001. This report is intended to:

-- Alert Embassies and AID missions to ADB-financed projects, and

-- Provide U.S. businesses with as much lead time as possible concerning procurement and consulting opportunities.

-- For more information on this project or ADB lending opportunities, firms should contact Ms. Cinnamon Dornsife, U.S. Executive Director, Asian Development Bank at phone no. (63-2) 632-6051 and fax no. (63-2) 632-4003 or Mr. Stewart Ballard, The U.S. Commercial Liaison Office for the ADB at telephone nos.: (63-2) 887-1345 to 46 and fax no. (63-2) 887-1164. For in-country inquiry, please contact Ms. Patricia Mahoney, American Embassy, Vientiane; Tel.: (856) 21-212581; Fax: 856) 21-212584; e-mail: mahoneypa@vientiwpoa.us-state.gov.

2. For post, USADB requests AmEmbassy and AID mission views on the Project before August 23, 2001 based on currently available information.

A. BACKGROUND
- Current deficiencies in urban infrastructure and services in Vientiane impede economic growth and undermine the quality of life of the urban residents. especially the poor. Despite the recent investments in primary road and drainage networks, the poor condition of secondary and tertiary infrastructure constrains the full potential of and benefits from recent improvements to primary infrastructure and services. The inadequate infrastructure and services at community level has a particularly adverse impact on the lives of the poor, the majority of whom live in low-lying land, flooded for most of the year. Sustained growth and the quality of life of the residents are further constrained by the present urban institutional framework and nascent urban management that are still evolving in the process of ongoing reforms for decentralization. While considerable progress has been made toward a decentralized form of urban governance and development of Vientiane Urban Development Administration Authority (VUDAA) as a new entity responsible for urban management in Vientiane, the extent of further reforms yet needed to fully achieve decentralized urban governance requires extensive and long-term support. There is a need at this stage to shift the focus of efforts to secondary and tertiary infrastructure and services to ensure that environmental improvements are felt by all, especially the poor. Equally important is the further progress in the decentralization process and development of VUDAA with adequate management systems and skills and financial resources.

B. PROJECT OBJECTIVES
- The Project aims to improve the quality of life of the urban residents and especially the poor and enhance urban productivity and economic growth in Vientiane urban area. To this end, the Project has two specific objectives. One is to support decentralization and urban governance reforms and the process toward an autonomous, well-functioning, and self-sufficient urban local government that is capable of planning, managing, and financing urban development and providing services in a sustainable manner. The second is to target investments in infrastructure and services to maximize the utility of existing infrastructure by completing the remaining gaps and focussing on secondary and tertiary level infrastructure and services. The Project represents AD6's second investment in the Vientiane urban area, and builds on lessons learned from the experience of the first intervention, Vientiane Integrated Urban Development Project.

The scope of the Project includes (i) Part A: citywide urban infrastructure and services, comprising critical missing links of primary and secondary roads and drainage, efficiency improvements in solid waste management, traffic management and safety , and institutional infrastructure and maintenance improvements; {ii) Part B: village area improvements (VAI), adopting a demand-led and participatory approach, seeking as a prerequisite the willingness of villages to participate in and contribute to a portion of the cost of the improvements, and combining community infrastructure and services with community-level capacity building and awareness raising in environmental health, participatory local planning and community-based infrastructure development and service delivery; and (iii) Part C: a comprehensive capacity building program to support the accomplishment of the urban policy and institutional reform agenda, and enhance planning, operation and maintenance, revenue mobilization and financial management capabilities of VUDAA.

C. PROJECT DESCRIPTION

- The Project is designed to improve the urban environment in Vientiane and reinforce the Government's reforms for effective and responsive urban management. It combines physical infrastructure and service improvements with interventions for decentralized urban governance and extensive capacity building of VUDAA. Physical investments consist of improvements to drainage, roads, traffic management and safety, solid waste management, and sanitation. The Project incorporates a social strategy to ensure active participation of the urban communities in the implementation of the Project and effective targeting of the poor and vulnerable. The Project area covers a hundred urban villages with a population of about 162,000 residents within Vientiane that falls under the jurisdiction of VUDAA.

D. EXECUTING AGENCY
- Vientiane Prefecture (the Provincial Government of
- Vientiane City)
- Contact: Mr. Thongmy Phomvisay, President
- Fax: 856-21-212104

E. TOTAL PROJECT COST: USD 37.0 MILLION

- Foreign Exchange : USD 20.0 million
- Local Currency: USD 17.0 million

F. MEANS OF FINANCING
- Bank Loan: USD 25.0 million
- Government and Community: USD 7.6 million
- AFD Cofinancing: USD 4.4 million

G. PROCUREMENT
- Procurement will be carried out by VUDAA. All procurement will follow the ADB's Guidelines for Procurement. International competitive bidding (ICB) procedures will be used for major civil works contracts estimated to cost over USD 1.0 million and for supply contracts estimated to cost over USD 500.000. For civil works, with a value up to USD 1.0 million, local competitive bidding (LCB) procedures will be used. The package of work per village under VAI component is relatively small ranging from USD 30,000 to USD 100,000. The works are labor-intensive and do not require sophisticated technologies. Therefore, for the works, estimated to cost less than USD 50,000 and where the capacity of the community to undertake the works is adequate, community participation in procurement will be applied.

H. CONSULTING SERVICES
- The selection and engagement of consultants under the loan will be in accordance with ADB's Guidelines on the Use of Consultants and other arrangements satisfactory to ADS for engaging domestic consultants. A team of consultants with a total input of 270 person-months (76 international and 194 domestic) is required to assist PIMU in overall Project implementation management, detailed engineering design, construction supervision, demand-led village area improvements, and development of legal and financial reforms for decentralized governance. Additionally, services of domestic consultants are required to assist in community preparation and awareness program and construction supervision. A further 191 person-months of consultancy inputs, including 173 person-months (65 international and 108 local) for capacity building and 18

person-months (5 international and 13 local) for traffic management and safety components will also be provided under a parallel financing arrangement funded by AFD.

I. PROJECT BENEFITS

- The Project will benefit about 162,000 Vientiane urban residents, 18 percent of whom belong to low-income groups. The overall population will benefit from the Project directly or indirectly through upgrading of roads, improved traffic and safety conditions, and enhanced urban management capacities within VUDAA, leading to sustainable delivery of urban services. The Project will directly improve the living conditions of 81,000 residents of Vientiane through improved community infrastructure and services under VAI, a partially coincident 60,000 people through drainage improvements, and 50,000 people through improved solid waste collection and disposal. The Project will promote good governance through supporting decentralized urban governance and empowerment of village communities in local planning, project implementation, and operation and maintenance of urban infrastructure and services.

3. For U.S. businesses and consultants: The shorlisted consultants will receive a request for proposals, selection of and contract negotiation with the firm submitting the best technical proposal will be completed, and preparation of bid specifications and contract documents will begin.

- Potential equipment suppliers and contractors should maintain regular contact with the executing agency and its consultants so that they may act quickly when tenders or prequalification notices are issued. Procurement notices and prequalification announcements are also released by the U.S. Commercial Liaison Office for the ADB and the Commerce Business Daily. These are also published on http://www.adb.org.

NEW ADB LOAN PROJECTS

. This report alerts U.S. firms to USD 101.2 million in new, potential national procurement of goods and services in Cambodia, Laos, and Nepal. These opportunities are an example of the many procurements financed by Asian Development Bank (ADB) loans to 33 ADB member developing countries. In 2000, U.S. contractors and equipment suppliers succeeded in winning USD 196 million in such national procurements as well as another USD 153 million in national consulting services financed by ADB loans.

This report notifies prospective U.S. exporters early on the current formal consideration of development projects by the ADB Board of Directors. Generally tender documents are issued 12-24 months later. Interested prospective U.S. contractors and equipment suppliers should contact the persons listed below to position themselves for future opportunities. U.S. consultants should contact the persons listed below and submit an Expression of Interest (EOI) to the national executing agency to market their firms' expertise and experience on similar past projects.

3. U.S. Consultants must also register with the ADB DACON (Data on Consulting Firms) system. DACON registration may now be completed on-line at <http://www.adb.org/consulting/dacon>. For loan projects, primary responsibility for hiring consultants rests with the executing agency in the borrowing country. A good way to facilitate contact with the executing agency is by working with the appropriate U.S. Commercial Service officer listed below.

4. Firms may also send a notification copy of their EOIs to U.S. Commercial Liaison Office for the ADB, Attention: Stewart Ballard, Senior Commercial Officer, PSC 500 Box 33, FPO AP 96515-1000, or to the same office at its international mailing address: 25th Floor Ayala Life-FGU Center, 6811 Ayala Avenue, Makati City, Metro Manila, Philippines 1226; Phone: (63-2) 887-1345; Fax: (63-2) 887-1164; E-mail: manila.adb.office.box @mail.doc.gov. This office works closely with the

Office of the U.S. Executive Director to the ADB to increase American awareness of, and participation in, the ADB's activities.

5. The projects listed in this cable are now being actively processed by the ADB. For more information on these projects, the name of the ADB project officer is indicated in the project brief. The U.S Commercial Liaison Office is ready to provide assistance to U.S. firms upon request. (Please see paragraph 4.)

6. The following loan projects will be listed for the first time in the August 2001 issue of the Asian Development Bank's (ADB) Business Opportunities (ADBBO). (Note: The ADBBO is also available on the ADB's website <http://www.adb.org>.

7. LOAN PROJECTS FOR CAMBODIA, LAOS, AND NEPAL

A. CAMBODIA
NAME OF PROJECT: Rural Development
Project No.: CAM34207-01
Executing Agency: Ministry of Rural Development
Contact: His Excellency Ngy Chanphal, Undersecretary
Fax: 855-23366-790
Loan Amount: USD 25.0 Million
Sector/Subsector: Agriculture and Natural Resources/ Irrigation and Rural Development

Objectives and Scope: The project will target poor, rural populations in selected rural areas where significant number of soldiers will be demobilized and will settle in host communities. Activities in support of area development would include rural infrastructure (rural roads, water supply, village-level social infrastructure), facilitating provision of social services (rural finance, skill training, microenterprise development) through existing provider programs, institutional strengthening and capacity building.

Procurement:
Goods: To be determined.
Services: To be determined.

Environmental Category: B

Project Processing Stage:
Fact-Finding in Field: 2 Jul 2001
Project Officer: Alain Goffeau (632-6955)
Agriculture and Rural Development Division West
In-country Commercial Officer: Bruce Levine, Economic and Commercial Officer, American Embassy Phnom Penh

LAOS
NAME OF PROJECT: Second Education Quality Improvement Project
Project No.: LAO31345-01
Executing Agency: Ministry of Education
Department of Planning and Cooperation
Vientianne
Contact: Dr. Sikhamtath Mitaray, Director
Fax: 856-21-216006
Tel. No.: 856-21-217927

Loan Amount: USD 20.0 Million

Sector/Subsector: Social Infrastructure/Education
Objectives and Scope: The Project will: (i) improve the relevance, quality and efficiency of primary and secondary education, by providing teacher training programs, and by introducing measures to improve the professional status and development of teachers; (ii) expand access to and improve retention in primary schools in the poor, underserved areas, by constructing new complete and/or multigrade schools, and renovating existing schools; and (iii) strengthen the institutional capacity to manage education at the MOE, PES, DEB, village/community, and school levels.

Procurement:
Goods: None.
Services: To be determined.
Environmental Category: C
Project Processing Stage:
Appraisal Completed: 15 Jun 2001
Project Officer: Yasushi Hirosato (632-6949)
Education, Health and Population Division West
In-country Commercial Officer: Patricia Mahoney, Commercial Officer, American Embassy Vientiane

USD 1.55 MILLION ADB BUSINESS OPPORTUNITIES

1. This report alerts U.S. firms to USD 1.55 million new, potential national procurement of consulting services under the Asian Development Bank's (ADB) technical assistance (TA) grant programs. Opportunities are reported for Cook Islands, Laos, and Nepal. In 2000, U.S. firms, including many small consulting firms, succeeded in winning USD 57 million ADB-funded national technical assistance contracts out of a total ADB-financed consulting budget of USD 348 million.

2. The ADB selects a consultant for a TA grant based on its prior Expression of Interest (EOI). An EOI can be transmitted on-line through the ADB's website (www.adb.org); afterward it will be acknowledged automatically. Firms may opt to send a hardcopy follow-up EOI addressed to Mr. S. Thuraisingham, Manager, Consulting Services Division, with a copy to the ADB Project Officer. The EOI should relate a firm's experience and expertise to the ADB project. It is important for a U.S. firm to emphasize its similar project experience in the country or in a similar geographic area rather than presenting a general profile of its consulting activities. A separate EOI should be submitted for each project. The project name indicated in the EOI should exactly match that listed in the ADB Business Opportunities publication to avoid confusion.

3. Although not required for employment, consultants should register on the ADB's DACON (Data on Consulting Firms) and DICON (Data on Individual Consultants) Systems, otherwise, their EOIs will not be accepted. DACON and DICON registration can now be done on-line at www.adb.org/consulting.

4. Firms may also send a notification copy of their EOIs to the U.S. mailing address for the U.S. Commercial Liaison Office for the ADB, Attention: Stewart Ballard, Senior Commercial Officer, PSC 500 Box 33, FPO AP 96515-1000, or to the same office at its international mailing address: 25th Floor Ayala Life-FGU Center, 6811 Ayala Avenue, Makati City, Metro Manila, Philippines 1226; Phone: (63-2) 887-1345; Fax: (63-2) 887-1164; E-mail: manila.adb.office.box @mail.doc.gov. This office works closely with the Office of the U.S. Executive Director to the ADB to increase American awareness of, and participation in, the ADB's activities.

For additional analytical, business and investment opportunities information,
please contact Global Investment & Business Center, USA
at (703) 370-8082. Fax: (703) 370-8083. E-mail: ibpusa3@gmail.com
Global Business and Investment Info Databank - www.ibpus.com

5. The projects listed in this cable are now being actively processed by the ADB. For more information on these projects, the name of the ADB project officer is indicated in the project brief. The U.S Commercial Liaison Office is ready to provide assistance to U.S. firms upon request. (Please see paragraph 4.)

6. The following TA projects will be listed for the first time in the July 2001 issue of the Asian Development Bank's (ADB) Business Opportunities (ADBBO).
(Note: The ADBBO is also available on the ADB's website http://www.adb.org.

7. PROJECT PREPARATION TECHNICAL ASSISTANCE
FOR COOK ISLANDS, LAOS, AND NEPAL

COOK ISLANDS
NAME OF PROJECT: Outer Islands Development
Project No.: COO29645-01
Executing Agency: Ministry of Finance and Economic
Management
TA Amount: USD 250.0 Thousand
Sector: Others
Objectives and Scope: To prepare a project to help accelerate outer islands development.
Procurement: About 10 person-months of international consultants and 10 person-months of domestic consultants.
Status of Consulting Services: No action has yet been taken to recruit consultants.
Environmental Analysis: Not Required
Project Processing Stage: Beginning of Fact-finding Mission: Sep 2001.
Project Officer: Michel D. Latendresse (632-6129)
Pacific Operations Division
In-country Commercial Officer: c/o AmConsul Auckland

LAOS
NAME OF PROJECT: Northern Community-Managed Irrigation Sector Project
Project No.: LAO34188-01
Executing Agency: Department of Irrigation
Vientiane, Lao PDR
Contact: Mr. Phuovieng Latdavong,
Permanent Secretary
TA Amount: USD 700.0 Thousand

Sector/Subsector: Agriculture and Natural Resources/ Irrigation and Rural Development
Objectives and Scope: The objective of the TA is to prepare a follow-on sector investment project which will address the poverty reduction, environmental protection and gender issues through the development of community-managed irrigation (CMI) schemes in selected northern provinces. CMI development demonstrated the effectiveness to increase the yields of rice and other value crops and to reduce the shifting cultivation under the ongoing Project (ADB's Community-Managed Irrigation Sector Project: Loan No. 1488-LAO). The TA will comprise the following major activities: (i) review relevant water sector policies; (ii) review the lessons learnt from ongoing Projects; (iii) undertake institutional capacity analyses of organizations; (iv) determine the northern provinces to be included in the proposed project by taking into consideration the stakeholders' demand, Government's strategy, implementation capacity, etc.; (v) review and upgrade the completed appraisal studies on sample subprojects; (vi) conduct a social and environmental assessment of sample subprojects with particular emphasis on poverty reduction and environmental protection; (vii) analyze the cost effectiveness and financial sustainability; and

(viii) develop a sector investment package and necessary supporting mechanism for sustainable and affordable CMI considering all above. The investment package may have sustainability of CMI schemes in the following components: (i) community mobilization and training; (ii) development of community-managed irrigation schemes; and (iii) institutional support for CMI development.

Procurement: The TA work will be carried out by a team of experts from an international consulting firm in association with domestic consultants.
Other details of consulting services to be required will be determined during the fact-finding mission. Procurement of one service vehicle will be proposed to facilitate the work of the consultants.
Status of Consulting Services: No action has been taken to recruit consultants.
Environmental Analysis: Required
Project Processing Stage:
Fact-Finding in Field: 11 Jun 2001
Project Officer: Toshio Kondo (632-6779)
Forestry and Natural Resources Division West
In-country Commercial Officer: Patricia Mahoney, Commercial Officer, AmEmbassy Vientiane

NEPAL
NAME OF PROJECT: Third Irrigation Sector
Project No.: NEP33209-01
Executing Agency: Department of Irrigation, Kathmandu
Jawalakjel, Lalitpur
Fax: 977-1-537169
E-mail: doi@jwlk.mos.com.np
TA Amount: USD 600.0 Thousand

Sector/Subsector: Agriculture and Natural Resources/ Irrigation and Rural Development
Objectives and Scope: Farmer-managed irrigation schemes are a major focus of the Government's irrigation strategy. This PPTA will prepare a sector project to cover about 300 small farmer-managed irrigation schemes covering about 40,000 ha for as many households.

Main components of the project will include water users' associations mobilization and training, construction and rehabilitation of irrigation schemes, provision of vehicles and equipment to the executing agency, staff training and capacity building for both the Department of Irrigation and Agriculture. The TA will develop specific intervention package including measures for improving sector policy, plan, and institutions through (i) water sector policy and institutions/review; (ii) assessment of ongoing Second Irrigation Sector Project; and (iii) feasibility study of sample subprojects.

Procurement: A total of about 45 person-months (pms) of consulting services' inputs : (i) 15 pms of international consultants including water resource institutional specialist (Team Leader); water resource engineer; resource economist; agronomist; environmental and social specialists; and (ii) 30 pms of water resource planner (Deputy Team Leader); water resource institutional specialist; agronomist; agricultural economist; environmental, social and poverty specialists.

Status of Consulting Services: No action has yet been taken to recruit consultants.

Environmental Analysis: Required
Project Processing Stage:
Beginning of Fact-finding Mission: Jul 2001.
Project Officer: Kenichi Yokoyama (632-6937)

For additional analytical, business and investment opportunities information,
please contact Global Investment & Business Center, USA
at (703) 370-8082. Fax: (703) 370-8083. E-mail: ibpusa3@gmail.com
Global Business and Investment Info Databank - www.ibpus.com

Forestry and Natural Resources Division West
In-country Commercial Officer: John Dyson, Political/Economic Officer, AmEmbassy Kathmandu

PRIMARY HEALTH CARE EXPANSION PROJECT

The proposed loan grant application for Lao for the Primary Health Care Expansion Project is expected to come to the ADB Board in about five weeks. This cable is intended to:
Alert Embassies and AID missions to upcoming ADB-financed projects, and
Provide U.S. businesses with as much lead-time as possible concerning procurement and consulting opportunities. For more information on this project of ADB lending opportunities, firms should contact Ms. Cinnamon Dornsife, U.S. Executive Director, Asian Development Bank at phone no. (63 2) 632 6051 and fax no. (63 2) 632 4003 or Mr. Alex Severens, The U.S. Commercial Liaison Office to the ADB. For in-country inquiry, please contact Ms. Trish Mulhoney of AmEmbassy Vientiane at telephone nos.: (856 21) 212581, 212582, 212585 and fax no.: 212584.

2. For Post: USADB requests AmEmbassy and AID Mission views on the said Project on or before August 20 based on currently available information.

Background: With a per capita income of $283 and half of the population living in poverty, Lao PDR is one of the poorest countries in the Asia and Pacific Region. The rural poor, in particular women and children, ethnic minorities and other vulnerable groups living in the inaccessible northern hills suffer from extremely poor health. Life expectancy of only 51 years is the lowest in the region. Most sickness and deaths are from common communicable diseases such as malaria, acute respiratory infections, diarrhea and measles, most of which are preventable or easily curable. Maternal and infant mortality and fertility are among the highest in the region, yet maternal and child health and family planning services are not readily available. The existing network of health facilities has inadequate coverage and mainly provides a limited range of curative services of often sub-standard quality. Much as half of the rural population does not have access to preventive and promotive services and first referral care, in particular in the northern hills.

The Government, as a cornerstone of its social policy, accords high priority to the improvement of the health status of the population. Primary health care (PHC) has been identified as the most cost-effective approach to provide basic health services. The Government recently approved a PHC policy that aims to make a basic package of health care available to the entire population, and restructured Ministry of Health (MOH) in support of PHC. The Government has requested Asian Development Bank (ADB) to support expansion and improvement of PHC delivery, strengthen PHC planning and management, and develop an effective financial mechanisms. The Project is specially designed to improve the health status of women and children, ethnic minorities and the rural poor.

Project Objectives: The Project will contribute to the Government's goals of improving the health status and reduce poverty of the population of Lao PDR. The Project will improve PHC for the rural poor by (i) expanding and improving the quality of PHC in the northern region, and (ii) strengthening the institutional capacity of PHC.

The Project will target women and children, ethnic minorities and the rural poor by (i) increasing their physical, social and financial access to essential services, (ii) focusing on interventions and diseases that affect them disproportionally, and (ii)improving the quality of services for these groups. The Project will give priority to cost-effective interventions benefiting women and children including health promotion, reproductive health care, prevention and treatment of common infections and micronutrient deficiencies, and first referral services.

Component 1 will develop PHC in the northern provinces by (i) increasing access to PHC at health center and village levels; (ii) improving the quality of PHC including training of ethnic minority staff, (iii) strengthening maternal and child health and family planning services, and (iv) supporting village health care and promotion.

Component 2 will strengthen the institutional capacity for PHC nationwide by (i) strengthening PHC coordination; (ii) standardizing management systems; (iii) supporting staff development and training for PHC management; and (iv) testing innovating financing approaches.

Project Description: The Project will develop primary health care (PHC) in the eight northern provinces of Bokeo, Louang-Namtha, Phongsali, Houaphan, Louangphrabang, Xiangkhoang, Oudamxai, and Xaignabouri. It will improve access to and quality of essential preventive, promotive and curative health services at village, health center and district levels in 34 underdeveloped districts with a total population of 0.9 million, and improve referral services for 1.7 million people. It will also strengthen the institutional capacity of the MOH and all Provincial Health Offices to plan, manage, monitor and finance PHC.

Executing Agency:

Ministry of Health
PHC Extension Project
Contact: Dr. Prasongsidh Boupha, Project Director
Fax No.: (856 21) 223146
Tel.No.: (856 20) 518422

Total Project Cost: $25.0 million (Foreign Exchange: $8.4 million; Local Currency: $16.6 million)

Procurement: All ADB-financed procurement for the Project will be in accordance with ADB's Guidelines for Procurement. Related equipment and material will be combined into packages to simplify procurement. Supply contracts costing more than $500,000 equivalent or less will follow international shopping procedures, except for some equipment and supplies like hostel beds and furniture that are locally manufactured and unlikely to attract foreign suppliers. These will be procured through local competitive bidding in accordance with Government procedures acceptable to ADB. Packages of less than $100,000 may be procured on a direct purchase basis. Equipment and materials required at provincial level and costing less than $10,000 may be procured by the PIO according to Government procedures acceptable to ADB.

The Project includes construction of 41 health centers and seven hospitals and renovation or upgrading of six health centers and 17 hospitals. The health facilities are located in remote and scattered locations and are unlikely to attract international bidders. Civil works contracts will be awarded according to local competitive bidding procedures acceptable to ADB. However, if any package is estimated to cost $1.0 million or more, international competitive bidding procedures will be followed.

g.) All consultants financed under the loan will be selected and engaged in accordance with ADB Guidelines on the Use of Consultants and other procedures acceptable to ADB on the recruitment of domestic consultants. Six international and six domestic individual consultants and one domestic firms will be provided. The international consultants will include chief technical adviser (36 person-months), education and training specialist (6 person-months), management specialist (12 person-months), health sector financing specialist (6 person-months), procurement specialist (6 person-months), and architect (6 person-months). Domestic consultants will include education and training specialist (72 person-months), management specialist (72person-months), health sector financing specialist (72 person-months), accountant (72 person-months), procurement specialist (72 person-months), and architectural monitoring and evaluation specialist (72 person-months). A domestic firms will be contracted for five years for building design and construction supervision.

For US Businesses and Consultants: The loan is now at a point where, shortly after ADB Board approval, shortlisted consultants will receive a request for proposals, selection of and contract negotiation with the firm submitting the best technical proposal will be completed, and preparation of bid specifications and contract documents will begin.

Potential equipment supplies and contractors should maintain a regular contact with the executing agency and its consultant so that they may act quickly when tenders or prequalification notices are issued. Procurement notices and prequalification announcement are also released by the U.S. Commercial ADB Liaison Office and made available on the National Trade Data Bank (NTDB) and the Commerce Business Daily. These are also published on the Asian Development Bank's homepage, http//www.adb.org.

IMPORTANT LAWS AND REGULATIONS AFFECTING BUSINESS

LAW ON THE PROMOTION AND MANAGEMENT OF FOREIGN INVESTMENT IN LAO PDR[3]

SECTION ONE: GENERAL PROVISIONS

Article 1 : The Government of the Lao People's Democratic Republic encourages foreign persons, either individuals or legal entities, to invest capital in the Lao People's Democratic Republic (hereinafter "the Lao PDR") on the basis of mutual benefit and observance of the laws and regulations of the Lao PDR. Such persons hereinafter shall be referred to as "foreign investors ".

Article 2 : Foreign investors may invest in and operate enterprises in all fields of lawful economic activity such as agriculture and forestry, manufacturing, energy,, mineral extraction, handicrafts, communications and transport. construction, tourism trade, services and others.

Foreign investors may not invest in or operate enterprises which are detrimental to national security, the natural environment, public health or the national culture, or which violate the laws and regulations of the Lao PDR.

Article 3 : The property, and investments in the Lao PDR of foreign investors shall be fully-protected by the laws and regulations of the Lao PDR. Such property and the investment may not be requisitioned. confiscated or nationalized except for a public purpose and upon payment of prompt, adequate and effective compensation.

SECTION TWO: FORMS OF FOREIGN INVESTMENT

Article 4 : Foreign investors may invest in the Lao PDR in either of two forms:

(1) A Joint Venture with one or more domestic Lao investors-; or
(2) A Wholly Foreign-Owned Enterprise.

Article 5 : A Joint Venture is a foreign investment established and registered under the laws and regulations of the Lao PDR which is jointly owned and operated by one or more foreign investors and by one or more domestic Lao investors.

The organization, management and activities of the Joint Venture and the relationship between its parties shall be governed by the contract between its parties and the Joint Venture's Articles of Association, in accordance with the laws and regulations of the Lao PDR.

Article 6 : Foreign investors Who invest in a Joint Venture must contribute a minimum portion of thirty percent (30%) of the total equity investment in that Venture. The contribution of the Venture's foreign party or parties shall be converted in accordance with the laws and regulations of the Lao PDR into Lao currency at the exchange rate then prevailing on the date of the equity payment(s), as quoted by the Bank of the Lao PDR.

[3] National Assembly No. 01/94

For additional analytical, business and investment opportunities information, please contact Global Investment & Business Center, USA at (703) 370-8082. Fax: (703) 370-8083. E-mail: ibpusa3@gmail.com Global Business and Investment Info Databank - www.ibpus.com

Article 7 : A wholly Foreign-Owned Enterprise is a foreign investment registered under the laws and regulations of the Lao PDR by one or more foreign investors without the participation of domestic Lao investors. The Enterprise established in the LAO PDR may be either a new company or a branch or representative office of a foreign company.

Article 8 : A foreign investment which is a Lao branch or representative office of a foreign company shall have Articles of Association which shall be consistent with the laws and regulations of the Lao PDR and subject to the approval of the Foreign Investment Management Committee of the Lao PDR.

u The incorporation and registration of a foreign investment shall be in conformity with the Enterprise Decree of the Lao PDR.

SECTION THREE: BENEFITS, RIGHTS AND OBLIGATIONS OF FOREIGN INVESTORS

Article 10 : The Government of the Lao PDR shall protect foreign investments and the property of foreign investors in accordance with the laws and regulations of the Lao PDR. Foreign investors may lease land within the Lao PDR and transfer their leasehold interests; and they may own improvements on land and other moveable property and transfer those ownership interests.

Foreign investors shall be free to operate their enterprises within the limits of the laws and regulations of the Lao PDR. The Government shall not interfere in the business management of those enterprises.

Article 11 : Foreign investors shall give priority to Lao citizens in recruiting and hiring their employees. However, such enterprises have the right to employ skilled and expert foreign personnel when necessary and with the approval of the competent authority of the Government of the Lao PDR.

Foreign investors have an obligation to upgrade the skills of their Lao employees , through such techniques as training within the Lao PDR or abroad.

u The Government of the Lao PDR shall facilitate the entry into, travel within, stay within, and exit from Lao territory of foreign investors, their foreign personnel, and the immediate family members of those investors and those personnel. All such persons are subject to and must obey the laws and regulations of the Lao PDR while they are on Lao territory.

Foreign investors and their foreign personnel working within the Lao PDR shall pay to the Lao government personal income tax at a flat rate of ten percent (10 %) of their income earned in the Lao PDR.

Article 13 : Foreign investors shall open accounts both in Lao currency and in foreign convertible currency with a Lao bank or foreign bank established in the Lao PDR.

Article 14 : In the management of their enterprises, foreign investors shall utilize the national system of financial accounting of the Lao PDR. Their accounts shall be subject to periodic audit by the Government's financial authorities in conformity with the applicable Lao accounting regulations.

Article 15 : In conformity with the law and regulations governing the management of foreign exchange and precious metals, foreign investors may repatriate earnings and capital from their

For additional analytical, business and investment opportunities information,
please contact Global Investment & Business Center, USA
at (703) 370-8082. Fax: (703) 370-8083. E-mail: ibpusa3@gmail.com
Global Business and Investment Info Databank - www.ibpus.com

foreign investments to their own home countries or to third countries through a Lao bank or foreign bank established in the Lao PDR at the exchange rate prevailing on the date of repatriation. as quoted by the Bank of the Lao PDR.

Foreign personnel of foreign investments may also repatriate their earnings, after payment of Lao personal income taxes and all other taxes due.

Article 16 : Foreign investments subject to this law shall pay a Lao PDR'. annual profit tax at a uniform flat rate of twenty percent (20%), calculated in accordance with the provisions of the applicable laws and regulations of the Lao PDR.

Other Lao taxes, duties and fees shall be payable in accordance with the applicable laws and regulations of the Lao PDR.

For foreign investments involving natural resources exploitation and energy generation, sector-specific taxes and royalties shall be prescribed in project agreements entered into between the investors and the Lao Government.

Article 17 : Foreign investments shall pay a Lao PDR import duty on equipment, means of production, spare parts and other materials used in the operation of their investment projects or in their productive enterprises at a uniform flat rate of one percent (1%) of their imported value. Raw materials and intermediate components imported for the purpose of processing and then re-exported shall be exempt from such import duties. All exported finished products shall also be exempted from export duties.

Raw materials and intermediate components imported for the purpose of achieving import substitution shall be eligible for special duty reductions in accordance with the Government's applicable incentive policies.

Article 18 : In highly exceptional cases and by specific decision of the Government of the Lao PDR, foreign investors may be granted special privileges and benefits which may possibly include a reduction in or exemption from the profit-tax rate prescribed by Article 16 and/or a reduction in or exemption from the import-duty rate prescribed by Article 17, because of the large size of their investments and the significant positive impact which those investments are expected to have upon the socioeconomic development of the Lao PDR.

In the event of the establishment of one or more Free Zones or Investment Promotion Zones. the Government shall issue area-specific or general regulations or resolutions.

Article 19 : After payment of its annual profit tax, a foreign investor shall devote a portion of its profit each year to various reserve funds necessary for the operation and development of the enterprise in order to continuously improve the enterprise's efficiency, in accordance with the policy and the Articles of Association of the enterprise.

Article 20 : Foreign investments approved under this law shall at all times be operated in accordance with the laws and regulations of the Lao PDR . In particular, foreign investors shall take all measures necessary and appropriate to ensure that their investments' facilities, factories and activities protect the natural environment and the health and safety of the workers and the public at large, and that their investments contribute to the social insurance and welfare programs for their workers in conformity with the policy and the laws and regulations of the Lao PDR.

For additional analytical, business and investment opportunities information,
please contact Global Investment & Business Center, USA
at (703) 370-8082. Fax: (703) 370-8083. E-mail: ibpusa3@gmail.com
Global Business and Investment Info Databank - www.ibpus.com

Article 21 : In the event of disputes between foreign parties within a foreign investment, or between foreign investors and Lao parties , the disputants should first seek to settle their differences through consultation or mediation.

In the event that they fail to resolve the matter , they shall then submit their dispute to the economic arbitration authority of the Lao PDR or to any other mechanism for dispute resolution of the Lao PDR, a foreign country or an appropriate international organization which the disputants can agree upon.

SECTION FOUR: THE ORGANIZATION OF FOREIGN INVESTMENT MANAGEMENT

Article 22 : The Government of the Lao PDR has established a State organization to promote and to manage foreign investment within the Lao PDR titled the Foreign Investment Management Committee (hereinafter called "the FIMC").

The FIMC is responsible for administration of this law and for the protection and promotion of foreign investment within the Lao PDR.

Article 23 : All foreign investments established within the Lao PDR shall be assisted, licensed and monitored through the "1-stop-service " of the FIMC, acting as the central focal point for all Government interactions with the investors, with the collaboration of the concerned ministries and the relevant provincial authorities.

Article 24 : A foreign investment shall be considered to be legally established within the Lao PDR only upon the investment's receipt of a written foreign investment license granted by the FIMC.

Article 25 : A foreign investor which seeks a license for a foreign investment shall submit to the FIMC an application and such supporting documentation as the FIMC may prescribe by regulation.

The FIMC may grant preliminary approval-in-principle for investment projects being specially promoted by the Government.

Article 26 : Upon receipt of a completed application and supporting documentation, the FIMC shall screen them, take a foreign-investment licensing. decision and notify the applicant of that decision within 60 days of the application's submission date.

Within this same overall 60-day period, concerned ministries and provincial authorities consulted by the FIMC for their views shall have a maximum of 20 days in which to reply.

Article 27 : Within 90 days of receiving its foreign investment license from the FIMC. a foreign investor shall register that license and commerce operation of its investment in conformity with the implementation schedule contained in the investment's feasibility study and with the terms and conditions of the license granted by FIMC, and in accordance with the laws and regulations of the Lao PDR.

Article 28 : The FIMC has responsibility to coordinate with other concerned ministries and provincial authorities in monitoring and enforcing the implementation of a foreign investment in conformity with the investment's feasibility study and with the terms and conditions of the investment license, and in accordance with the laws and regulations of the Lao PDR.

The concerned ministries and provincial authorities have the responsibility to perform their respective monitoring and enforcement obligations.

Article 29 : If a foreign investor violates the agreement and the terms and conditions of its foreign investment license or the laws and regulations of the Lao PDR, the investor shall be notified of the detected violation and shall be instructed to promptly desist. In the event the investor fails to desist or in case of a serious violation, the investor's foreign investment license may be suspended or revoked and the investor may additionally be subject to other sanctions under the applicable laws and regulations of the Lao PDR.

SECTION FIVE: FINAL PROVISIONS

Article 30 : This law shall come into force 60 days after its ratification.

Upon the entry into force of the present law, the foreign investment law of the Lao people's Democratic Republic No. 07/PSA dated 19 April 1988 shall cease to have effect, without prejudice to the rights and privileges granted to, and the obligations imposed upon, foreign investments under the law.No. 07/PSA.

Notwithstanding this provision, a foreign investor which received its license tender the prior law may elect to petition the FIMC in writing, within 120 days of the coming into force of this law, to become subject to the terms of this law. The FIMC may grant such petitions at its discretion. For a foreign investor whose petition is granted, the rights and benefits previously granted. and the obligations previously imposed under the law No. 07/PSA shall thereafter prospectively cease to have effect .

Article 31 : The Government of the Lao PDR shall, by decree, issue detailed regulations for the implementation of this law.

LAW ON THE PROMOTION AND MANAGEMENT OF FOREIGN INVESTMENT IN THE LAO PEOPLE'S DEMOCRATIC REPUBLIC

SECTION: GENERAL PROVISIONS

Article 1: The Government of the Lao people's Democratic Republic encourages foreign persons, either individuals or legal entities, to invest capital in the Lao People's Democratic Republic (hereinafter "the Lao PDR") on the basis of mutual benefit and observance of the laws and regulations of the Lao PDR. Such persons hereinafter shall be referred to as "foreign investors".

Article 2: Foreign investors may invest in and operate enterprises in all fields of lawful economic activity such as agriculture and forestry, manufacturing, energy, mineral extraction, handicrafts, communications and transport, construction, tourism, trade, services and others.

Foreign investors may not invest in or operate enterprises which are detrimental to national security, the natural environment, public health or the national culture, or which violate the laws and regulations of the Lao PDR.

Article 3: The property and investments in the Lao. PDR of Foreign investors shall be fully protected by the laws and regulations of the Lao PDR. Such property and investments may not be requisitioned, confiscated or nationalized except for a public purpose and upon payment of prompt, adequate and effective compensation.

SECTION TWO: FORMS OF FOREIGN INVESTMENT

Article 4: Foreign investors may invest in the Lao PDR in either of two forms:

1. A Joint Venture with one or more domestic Lao investors or (2) A Wholly Foreign-Owned Enterprise.
2. A Wholly Foreign-Owned Enterprise.

Article 5: A Joint Venture is a foreign investment established and registered under the laws and regulations of the Lao PDR which is jointly owned and operated by one or more foreign investors and by one or more domestic Lao investors.

The organization management and activities of the Joint Venture and the relationship between its parties shall be governed by the contract between its parties and the Joint Venture's Articles of Association, in accordance with the laws and regulations of the Lao PDR.

Article 6: Foreign investors who invest in a Joint Venture must contribute a minimum portion of thirty percent (30%) of the tota1 equity investment in that Venture. The contribution of the Venture's foreign party or parties shall be converted in accordance with the laws and regulation of the Lao PDR into Lao currency at the exchange rate then prevailing on the date of the equity payment(s), as quoted by the Bank of the Lao PDR

Article 7: A wholly Foreign-Owned Enterprise is a foreign investment registered under the laws and regulations of the Lao PDR by one or more foreign investors without the participation of domestic Lao investors. The Enterprise established in the Lao PDR may be either a new company or a branch or representative of5ce of a foreign company.

Article 8: A foreign investment which is a Lao branch or representative office of a foreign company sha11 have Articles of Association which shall be consistent with the laws and regulations of the Lao PDR and subject to the approval of the Foreign investment Management Committee of the Lao PDR.

Article 9: The incorporation and registration of a foreign investment sha11 be in conformity with the Enterprise Decree of the Lao PDR.

SECTION THREE: BENEFITS, RIGHTS AND OBLIGATIONS OF FOREIGN INVESTORS

Article 10: The Government of the Lao PDR shall protect foreign investments and the property of foreign investors in accordance with the laws and regulations of the Lao PDR. Foreign investors may lease land within the Lao PDR and transfer their leasehold interests; and they may own improvements on land and other moveable property and transfer those ownership interests.

Foreign investors shall be free to operate their enterprises within the limits of the laws and regulations of the Lao PDR. The Government shall not interfere in the business management of those enterprises.

Article 11: Foreign investors sha11 give priority to Lao citizens in recruiting and hiring their employees. However, such enterprises have the right to employ skilled and expert foreign personnel when necessary and with the approval of the competent authority of the Government of the Lao PDR.

Foreign investors have an obligation to upgrade the skills of their Lao employees, through such techniques as training within the Lao PDR or abroad.

Article 12: The Government of the Lao PDR shall facilitate the entry into, travel within, stay within, and exit from Lao territory of foreign investors, their foreign personnel, and the immediate family members of those investors an those personnel. All such persons are subject to and must obey the laws and regulations of the Lao PDR while they are on Lao territory.

Foreign investors and their foreign personnel working within the Lao PDR shall pay to the Lao government personal income tax at a flat rate of ten percent (10%) of their income earned in the Lao PDR.

Article 13: Foreign investors shall open accounts both in Lao currency and in foreign convertible currency with a Lao bank or foreign bank established in the Lao PDR.

Article 14: In the management of their enterprises, foreign investors shall utilize the nationa1 system of financia1 accounting of the Lao PDR. Their accounts shall be subject to periodic audit by the Government's financial authorities in conformity with the applicable Lao accounting regulations.

Article 15: In conformity with the law and regulations governing the management of foreign exchange and precious metals, foreign investors may repatriate earnings and capital from their foreign investments to their own home countries or to third countries through a Lao bank or foreign bank established in the Lao PDR at the exchange rate prevailing on the date of repatriation, as quoted by the Bank of the Lao PDR.

Foreign personnel of foreign investments may also repatriate their earnings, after payment of Lao personal income taxes and all other taxes due.

Article 16: Foreign investments subject to this law shall pay a Lao PDR annual profit tax at e uniform flat rate of twenty percent (20%), calculated in accordance with the provisions of the applicable laws and regulations of the Lao PDR.

Other Lao taxes, duties and fees shall be payable in accordance with the applicable laws and regulations of the Lao PDR.

For foreign investments involving natural resources exploitation and energy generation, sector-specific taxes and royalties shall be prescribed in project agreements entered into between the investors and Lao Government.

Article 17: Foreign investments shall pay a Lao PDR import duty on equipment, means of production, spare parts and other materials used in the operation of their investment projects or in their productive enterprises as a uniform flat rate of one percent (1%) of their imported value. Raw materials and intermediate components imported for the purpose of processing and then re-exported shall be exempt from such import duties. All exported finished products shall also be exempted from export duties.

Raw materials and intermediate components imported for the purpose of achieving import substitution shall be eligible for special duty reductions in accordance with the Government's incentive policies.

Article 18: In highly exceptional cases and by specific decision of the Government of the Lao PDR, foreign investors may be granted special privileges and benefits which may possibly include a reduction in or exemption from the profit-tax rate prescribed by Article 16 and/or a reduction in or exemption from the import-duty rate prescribed by Article 17, because of the large size of their investments and the significant positive impact which those investments are expected to have upon the socio-economic development of the Lao PDR.

In the event of the establishment of one or more Free Zones or Investment Promotion Zones, the Government shall issue area-specific or general regulations or resolutions.

Article 19: After payment of its annual profit tax, a foreign investor shall devote a portion of its profit each year to various reserve funds necessary for the operation and development of the enterprise in order to continuously improve the enterprise's efficiency, in accordance with the policy and the Articles of Association of the enterprise.

Article 20: Foreign investments approved under this law sha11 at all times be operated in accordance with the laws and regulations of the Lao PDR. In particular, foreign investors sha11 take al1 measures necessary and appropriate to ensure that their investments facilities, factories and activities protect the natura1 environment and the health and safety of the workers and the public at large, and that their investments contribute to the socia1 insurance and welfare programs for their workers in conformity with the policy and the laws and regulations of the Lao PDR.

Article 21: In the event of disputes between foreign parties within a foreign investment, or between foreign investors and Lao parties, the disputants should first seek to settle their differences through consultation or mediation.

In the event that they fail to resolve the matter, they shall then submit their dispute to the economic arbitration authority of the Lao PDR or to any other mechanism for dispute resolution of the Lao PDR, a foreign country or an appropriate international organization which the disputants can agree upon.

SECTION FOUR: THE ORGANIZATION OF FOREIGN INVESTMENT MANAGEMENT

Article 22: The Government of the Lao PDR has established a State organization to promote and to manage foreign investment within the Lao PDR titled the Foreign Investment Management Committee (hereinafter called "the FIMC").

The FIMC is responsible for administration of this law and for the protection and promotion of foreign investment within the Lao PDR.

Article 23: All foreign investments established within the Lao PDR shall be assisted, licensed and monitored through the "1-stop-service" of the FIMC, acting as the central focal point for all

Government interactions with the investors, with the collaboration of the concerned ministries and the relevant provincial authorities.

Article 24: A foreign investment shall be considered to be legally established within the Lao PDR only upon the investment's receipt of a written foreign investment license granted by the FMC.

Article 25: A foreign investor which seeks a license for a foreign investment shall submit to the FMC an application and such supporting documentation as the FMC may prescribe by regulation.

The FMC may grant preliminary approval-in- principle for investment projects being specially promoted by the Government.

Article 26: Upon receipt of a completed application and supporting documentation, the FIMC shall screen them, take a foreign-investment licensing decision and notify the applicant of the decision within 60 days of the application's submission date.

Within the same overall 60-day period, concerned ministries and provincial authorities consulted by the FIMC for their views shall have a maximum of 20 days in which to reply.

Article 27: Within 90 days of receiving its foreign investment license from the FIMC, a foreign investors shall register that license and commence operation of its investment in conformity with the implementation schedule contained in the investment's feasibility study and with the terms and conditions of the license granted by the FIMC, and in accordance with the laws and regulations of the Lao PDR.

Article 28: The FIMC has responsibility to coordinate with other concerned ministries and provincial authorities in monitoring and enforcing the implementation of a foreign investment in conformity with the investment's feasibility study and with the terms and conditions of the investment license, and in accordance with the laws and regulations of the Lao PDR. he concerned ministries and provincial authorities have the responsibility to perform their respective monitoring and enforcement obligations.

Article 29: If a foreign investor violates the agreement and the terms and conditions of its foreign investment license or the laws and regulations of the Lao PDR, the investor shall be notified of the detected violation and shall be instructed to promptly desist. In the event the investor fails to desist or in case of a serious violation, the investor's foreign investment license may be suspended or revoked and the investor may additionally be subject to other sanctions under the applicable laws and regulations of the Lao PDR.

SECTION FIVE: FINAL PROVISIONS

Article 30: This law shall come into force 60 days after its ratification.

Upon the entry into force of the present law, the foreign investment law of the Lao People's Democratic Republic No. 07/PSA dated 19 April 1988 shall cease to have effect, without prejudice to the rights and privileges granted to, and the obligations imposed upon, foreign investments under the law No. 07/PSA

Notwithstanding this provision, a foreign investor which received its license under the prior law may elect to petition the FIMC in writing, within 120 days of the coming into force of this law, to become subject to the terms of this law. The FIMC may grant such petitions at its discretion. For a foreign investor whose petition is granted, the right and benefits previously granted, and the obligations previously imposed under the law No. 07/PSA shall thereafter prospectively cease to have effect.

Article 31: The Government of the Lao PDR shall, by decree, issue detailed regulations for the implementation of this law.

NOTIFICATION ON PROCEDURE FOR BUSINESS REGISTRATION IN LAO P D R.

- According to additional announcement No.0530/MOC,dated 10/May/2002 & No.0538/MOC,dated 13/May/2002.
 Ministry of Commerce, Domestic Trade Department (Business Registration Division) hereby notify the procedures for Business Registration and documents required for Enterprises.
* Business Registration takes place at 3 Levels

I. MINISTRY (CENTER) LEVEL.

The following are required registered at the Ministry :
1. Foreign investment whose registered capital is more than $ 200.000.
2. Enterprises engaged in import of Vehicles, Gas and export of wood products .
3 . State enterprises and state-owned joint venture enterprises who obtained
    licenses from the Ministry.

II. PROVINCES, CAPITAL AND SPECIAL ZONE LEVEL.

1. Foreign investors whose registered capital is less than $199,999.
2. Enterprises regulated by or have dealings with other main sectors such as:
-    Agriculture, Industry and Services .
3. Commercial :Enterprises engaged in export--import trade out side administered by the Ministry will be transferred to provinces.
4. All enterprises who have license from provincial governments.

III. DISTRICTS LEVEL.

Small business enterprises who opera out side from the Ministry and Provincial jurisdiction should register with the district office these are:
1. Branches .
2. Small shops.
3. Others

DOCUMENTS TO BE COMPLETED BY FOREIGN INVESTORS

- License from Foreign Investment Management Committee (FIMC)
- Registration form .
- Copy of passport.
- 3 photos of size 3x4 inches .
- Letter of authority from the manager of company .

DOCUMENTS TO BE COMPLETED BY DOMESTIC INVESTORS AND ENTERPRISES OTHER THAN COMMERCE.

- License from the concerned sector.
- Registration form .
- Curriculum Vitae (CV)

- Certificate of Assets
- Criminal noted No 3, copy of ID card,3 photos of size 3x4 inches

DOCUMENTS TO BE COMPLETED BY DOMESTIC INVESTORS AND CONTROLLED BY COMMERCE SECTORS:

- Registration form from commerce
- Curriculum Vitae (CV)
- Certificate of finance
- Criminal noted No 3 , copy ID card, 3 photos of size 3x4 inches .
- Regulation confirmed by commerce sector.
- Economic evaluation.

Fees. See Minister of Finance additional announcement No. 0341/MF,dated   21/02/2002 .
Notes 1: If all documents are complete as required , registration will be completed in 24 hours.
Notes 2: This notification translated from additional announcement No.0530/MOC,dated 10/May/2002 & No.0538/MOC,dated 13/May/2002.

NOTIFICATION ON LIST OF GOODS SUBJECT TO IMPORT-EXPORT CONTROL AND PROHIBITION

- According to the Decree on the import-export management, No 205/PMO of 11 October 2006 .
- According to the Regulation on the Import-Export Licensing of Controlled goods, No 106/MOC.FTD dated 25/1/2002.
- According to Prime Minister Order on import-export facilitation and distribution of goods throughout country No. 24/PMO,dated 24/09/2004..
- According to the list of goods needed approval from related government agencies.

The Minister of Industry and Commerce issues the notification on the list of goods subject to import-export control and prohibition, as follows:

I. GOODS SUBJECT TO IMPORT-EXPORT PROHIBITION

Goods subject to import – export prohibition are dangerous and have a severe effect on national security, peace and public safety in order to protect the social/public order; the standard of living; national cultures and traditions; human, animal and plant life or health; national treasures of artistic, historic or archaeological value; architectural value; and national resource preservation; to comply with the United Nations treaties and national laws and regulations. The list of goods subject to import-export prohibition includes:

A. There are five categories of goods subject to import prohibition
1. Guns, bullets, all kinds of explosives, war weapons and war vehicles
2. Opium seeds, opium flowers, cannabis
3. Dangerous pesticide
4. Game Machines that lead to bad attitudes
5. Pornography and literatures that affect on cultures and national security

B. There are nine categories of goods subject to export prohibition
1. Guns, bullets, explosives, war weapons and war vehicles
2. Opium seeds, opium flowers, cannabis
3. Animals and animal products which are prohibited to export according to the law
4. Log, timber and Akar wood from the forest
5. All kinds of orchids from the forest and Dracaena Loureiri
6. All kinds of rattan

7. Bat manure
8. Antique objects; national treasures of historic or archaeological and cultural value and naturally national historic objects.
9. Old/antique Buddha and angel images; and religiously respectful objects

II. GOODS SUBJECT TO IMPORT-EXPORT APPROVAL OR CERTIFICATE

Goods subject to import-export approval or certificate means that those need to get approval or certification from related government agencies prior to the import – export in order to comply with the national laws and international treaties that Lao PDR is a party member; to ensure the safety of use; to inspect the quality and standards; and to prevent epidemic disease. The List of goods subject to import – export approval is:

A. There are 25 categories of goods subject to import approval or certificate

1. Live animal, fish and aquatic animals
2. Animal meat and other parts for human consumption; and products from animals and processed products from animal meat.
3. Milk products
4. Rice in the husk (paddy); rice
5. Cereals, products from vegetables, other processing for human consumption
6. Beverage, alcohol and orange juice
7. Food for animals
8. Cements, mortars and concretes
9. Fuel
10. Gas
11. Chemicals that are reacted to Ozone and products contained such chemical substances
12. Bio-chemical products
13. Pharmaceutical products, medicine for human and animal as well as medical equipment
14. Chemical fertilizer
15. Some types of cosmetic
16. Pesticide and toxic products for mouse and germs /microbes / bacteria
17. Sawn wood processed by sawmill company
18. Log and seedling
19. Textbooks and books
20. Rough diamonds
21. Silver and gold
22. Steel (long and round piece of steel and other shapes)
23. All kinds of vehicles and parts (except bicycles and tractors)
24. Game machine
25. Explosive substances

B. There are seven categories of goods subject to export approval or certificate
1. Live animal, fish and aquatic animals
2. Rice in the husk (paddy); rice
3. Resin and forestry products
4. Mining
5. Wood and wooden products
6. Rough diamond
7. Gold and silver

Ministry of Industry and Commerce will regularly improve the notification on the list of goods subject to import – export control and prohibition, where it is appropriate, in order to facilitate the business and to comply with the international treaties that Lao PDR is a party member.

This Notification replaces the notification on List of goods subject to import-export prohibition N. 0284/MOC.FTD date 17/6/2004 and the notification on List of goods subject to import-export approval from trade and other related government agencies.

NOTIFICATION LIST OF PROHIBITED GOODS FOR IMPORT AND EXPORT

- According to decree on export and import management no. 205/PMO, dated 11 October 2001;
- According to decree on export and import licensing with trade sectors for control goods, no. 106/MOC.FTD, dated 25 January 2002;
- According to notification on list of goods from related sectors.

Minister of Commerce issues the list of prohibited goods for import-export to notify the trade units, concerned organization and implementing as follow:

A.   Prohibited goods for importation:
1.   Any kind of explosive, weapons and armament
2.   Any kind of drug addict
3.   Any kind of products affecting tradition of the nation
4.   Industrial disposal and chemical product that dangerous for health and environment
5.   Antiques
6.   Food, medicine and prohibited doctor equipments from related sectors
7.   Wild life, aquatic animals and their parts which are forbidden by domestic law and international subcontract that Lao PDR had signed.
8.   All type of right hand side driving vehicles
9.   Toys affecting children attitude, growth, safety and peace of the society
10.   Literature work, nude publication and other that against Lao PDR
11.   Second hand goods that government banned from import
12.   Equipment for printing of bank note
13.   Dangerous insecticides which prohibited by related sectors
14.   All type of log, sawed timber (processed timber), wood and forestry product that banned according to internal regulation

B.   List of export prohibition goods
1.   Any kind of explosive, weapons and armament
2.   Any kind of drug addict
3.   Any kind of products affecting tradition of the nation
4.   Wild life, aquatic animals and their parts which are forbidden by domestic law and international subcontract that Lao PDR had signed
5.   All type of log, sawed timber (processed timber), all type of rattan and unprocessed eaglewood
6.   Forestry product such as: Orchids, Ã€Â®Ã‰Â¨-Ã¬Â¾Â¨, Ã•-Â´Ã±-Â¨Â¾Â¤, Â¥Ã±-ÃƒÂ© and etc that prohibited according to internal law
7.   Sulfur (bat manure)
8.   Equipment for printing of bank note

List of prohibited goods for import and export is goods that badly damaged and dangerous to economic and social situation, politic, peace, safety and traditional of the country. All type of goods mentioned above are prohibited to import and export with an exception to Article 8 of decree numbers 205/PMO, dated 10/11/01 on export and import management. The detail of procedures and regulations are requested to follow the regulation numbers 106/MOC.FTD, dated 25/01/2002 on export and import licensing with trade sectors for control goods.

So this notification is prepared to notify organizations, related business units and be strictly implemented.

REGULATION ON THE IMPORT AND EXPORT LICENSING PROCEDURES OF CONTROLLED GOODS FROM TRADE AUTHORITIES

- Pursuant to the Decree on the establishment and operation of the Ministry of Commerce and Tourism No. 24/PM, dated 24 March 1999
- Based on the Decree on import and export No. 205/PM, dated 11 October 2001

The Minister of Commerce sets out

CHAPTER I GENERAL PRINCIPLES

Article 1. Licensing

An import or export licensing is a measure to administer import and export of goods in the Lao PDR, with an aim:
- To control the implementation conditions, criteria of the applicants for import or export activities;
- To monitor the conditions and criteria of import or export applicants, and to collect statistics of controlled-good imports or exports;
- To avoid a severe adverse impact on domestic production or national balance of payments;
- To control the import or export of prohibited goods which are occasionally needed for import or export.

Article 2. Applicant

An applicant comprises of importer, exporter as specified in Article 9 and Article 10 of the Decree on Import and Export No. 205/PM, dated 11 October 2001.

Article 3. Goods subject to licensing

The goods subject to an import or export license are controlled goods by which the Minister of Commerce has specified the criteria for import or export. The importer or exporter must strictly follow every procedure and regulation in this Regulation and in the laws and regulations of relevant sectors.
The detail of goods items subject to import or export licensing will be announced later.

CHAPTER II LICENSING PROCEDURES

Article 4. Licensing authority

Importer or exporter who wishes to import or export goods subject to control is required to submit an application with trade authorities as follows:
- Prohibited goods: approval from the Ministry of Commerce with a permission from the Prime Minister;
- Some controlled goods: approval from the Ministry of Commerce;
- Other controlled goods: approval from trade services in provinces, Vientiane municipality, and special zones.

Article 5. Licensing procedures

A license needs to be acquired prior to the import or export where accompanying documents include:
- Business registration and tax certification;
- Application form;
- Buying or selling contract;
- Technical certification from relevant authorities.

Article 6. Licensing consideration
The consideration of licensing application shall be in time, simple, and transparent for importer or exporter who supplies all required documentation as specified in this regulation.
The delay of licensing process without justification or unjustified reasons is considered in breach of this regulation and penalties shall be applied case by case.

Article 7. Time validity of a license
How long a license is valid depends on types of imports or exports. Related authorities specified in Article 4 of this regulation shall determine the time validity of licensing.

CHAPTER III PENALTIES

Article 8. Breach of licensing regulation
An importer or export who does not adhere to this regulation shall not have the right to import or export.

Article 9. Fraud, claim and other breaches
Any act related to fraud, claim, and other breaches to acquire a licensing shall be penalized according to seriousness or is subject civil penalty.

CHAPTER IV FINAL PROVISIONS

The Foreign Trade Department acts as a focal point to coordinate with related authorities, including trade services in the provinces, Vientiane Municipality and special zones, to implement in detail and for effectiveness of this regulation. The list of additional or reducing imports or exports subject to licensing shall also be provided to the Ministry of Commerce in subsequent notification.

Article 11. Enforcement
This regulation shall be into force from its date of signatory. Any other provisions and regulations inconsistent with this regulation shall be nullified.

DECREE ON IMPORT AND EXPORT MANAGEMENT

- Based on the Law on the Government of the Lao PDR No. 01/95 dated 8 March 1995,
- Based on the Business Law No. 03/94/NA dated 18 July 1994,
- Based on the Decree on the Customs Law No. 04/94 dated 18 July 1994,
- Based on the proposal of the Minister of Trade No. 1165/MCT dated 9 October 2001,
- Based on the Decision of the Government Meeting in November 2001,

The Prime Minister of the Lao PDR has decreed:

SECTION I: GENERAL PROVISIONS

ARTICLE 1:   FUNCTION OF THE DECREE

This decree has the function of stipulating management regulations on exports and imports in accordance with the laws, focused on production and export promotion, reasonable import control, promotion of international trade, improving living standards of people and active contribution to the national socio-economy.

ARTICLE 2:   DEFINITION

"Export" means exports of goods from the Lao PDR to other country.
"Import" means imports of goods from other country to the Lao PDR.

ARTICLE 3:   BASIC PRINCIPLE OF ORGANIZATION AND OPERATION

Any organization and operation of import and export within the Lao PDR shall be conducted strictly in accordance with this decree and other related laws and regulations.

SECTION II: GOODS CONTROL, CONTROLLED GOODS ON IMPORT AND EXPORT
Article 4:   Goods Control

The government of the Lao PDR encourages export and import of all goods except those goods which are under state control specified in this decree or other related laws or regulations.

According to this decree, control on import or export of a certain goods means the implementation of measures on these goods as necessary to maintain the economic and social stability, to preserve the national culture and tradition, and to protect other benefits of the state and society.

Application of import control is to protect the domestic production and consumer, to prevent price speculation in the country, and to maintain equilibrium of imports and exports.

Application of export control is needed to prevent the shortage of goods and to accumulate stocks within the country to ensure the export of some goods according to the international agreements that the Lao PDR is a party.

Article 5:   Measures of control

Import and export control may be conducted through the following measures:

- Prohibit import or export;
- Require import or export application;
- Demand documentation such as bill of origin and quality certificate of the imported or exported goods based on the agreement or traditional procedure of the international trade.
- Forbid or restrict import or export of some goods;
- Issue specific conditions for the business license;
- Charge import or export fees;
- Stipulate certain quality including amount, packing, type, kind, size, weight, price, trade name or brand, country of origin and export or import country,
- Apply other necessary measures on import and export such as equilibrium plan, customs and tax policy, organize related group or association.

The measures of control specified in this article, which may be in conflict with the laws and regulations of the international trade systems that the Lao PDR is committed to or is member of, will be cancelled.

Article 6:   Controlled Goods

Controlled Goods are those one which the measures are applied on import â€" export control as indicated in the article of this decree.

The list of controlled goods may be changed as necessary.

The Ministry of Commerce shall stipulate, cancel and apply the list and measures on controlled goods periodically, except those goods controlled by other sectors or being covered by other measures.

ARTICLE 7:   CONTROLLED GOODS UNDER OTHER SECTORS

Goods under control of other sectors are those under the direct management of the related sectors. Importer and exporter of those goods shall conduct business according to measures issued by the related sectors.

The goods mentioned in paragraph 1 above and controlled measures on them shall be stipulated and issued as necessary by the related sectors. Then the list of these goods shall be reported officially to the Ministry of Commerce to add to the list of goods under the state control.

The Ministry of Commerce shall announce this list to business entity and related sectors.

Article 8:   Permission Needed Goods

Goods that need to be permitted before import or export comprise forbidden goods and some controlled goods.

The Ministry of Commerce shall issue approval and lay down regulations on application procedures. The Ministry of Commerce has to coordinate with the related sectors and each approval shall be agreed by the Prime Minister.

SECTION III: IMPORTER AND EXPORTER

ARTICLE 9:   IMPORTER

Importer includes individual or juristic entity who has registered as a business according to this decree. Imported goods of these business entities are for sale within the Lao PDR.

Individual or juristic entity who has been registered with a business license may import some goods according to the related laws and regulation to serve their specific purpose as indicated in article 18 of this decree.

ARTICLE 10:   EXPORTER

Individual or juristic entity who hold a business license may operate the export business.

Article 11:   Importer or Exporter of Goods (for Self Consumption)

Importers or exporters of goods (for self consumption) are individual or organizations who have been authorized temporarily to bring in or out some goods for noncommercial purposes.

SECTION III: ESTABLISHMENT AND OPERATION OF THE EXPORT AND IMPORT BUSINESS

ARTICLE 12: ESTABLISHMENT OF THE IMPORT COMPANY

Individual or juridic entities who want to set up a import company as indicated in the first paragraph of Article 9 above shall apply to the Commercial Section for establishment and business registration and to the Financial Section for tax registration.

ARTICLE 13: ESTABLISHMENT OF THE EXPORT COMPANY

All business entities registered with a business license as indicated in Article 10 above can operate an export business.

Those who do not have a business license as specified in the first paragraph above, but want to operate an export business, shall apply for establishment as indicated in Article 12.

ARTICLE 14: BUSINESS ORGANIZATION

The organization of the import or export company may be set up in accordance with the type and form as indicated in the Business Law.

ARTICLE 15: REGISTERED CAPITAL

Registered Capital to set up an export or import business shall be undertaken as indicated in the Business Law, except for export or import of some commodities, for which the laws and regulations specify for a higher Registered Capital.

ARTICLE 16: APPROVED GOODS ON THE LICENSE

Individual or juridic entity shall submit the goods list along with the application for a import business license. The applied list may consist of one or many goods according to its capacity.

Individual or juridic entity received the import license according to the first paragraph above may trade in export of any kind of goods, except those goods controlled by the state which require the export license, those forbidden by the state and others specified in the laws.

The list of approved goods shall be shown on the import license of importer who is dealing with specific goods, as specified in the second paragraph of Article 9.

The Ministry of Commerce shall indicate goods that require an export license.

ARTICLE 17: CONSEQUENCE FROM NON-OPERATION

A business license of the import or export business entity, which is not operative for one year after approval, will be cancelled , except when a reasonable reason has been reported to the Commercial Section before the end of the one year limit.

SECTION V: IMPORTATION

ARTICLE 18:   IMPORT BY THE IMPORT COMPANY

Import by the import company shall be conducted in accordance with the following:

- import according to the goods list specified on the import license;
- holding of a sell-buy contract

ARTICLE 19:   SPECIFIC PURPOSE IMPORT

Specific purpose importer has the rights to import equipment, machinery and raw materials which will be used directly in production or business based on plan adopted by the related sectors.

Article 20:   Import Procedure

Import company or specific purpose importer who has complied with the conditions specified in this decree can submit the import document directly to the related office at the border station to bring in the goods.

Article 21:   Import of goods (for self consumption)

Authorized import (for self consumption) shall be conducted in accordance with the list, limit, type and amount of goods indicated in the customs law.

SECTION VI: EXPORTATION

ARTICLE 22:   EXPORT BY THE EXPORT COMPANY

Export by the export company shall be accompanied by the sell-buy contract with the foreign counterpart. For export of controlled goods, the company shall abide by the specific regulations on each controlled goods.

Article 23:   Export Procedure

Exporters as indicated in Article 10 of this decree can submit export documents directly to the related office at the border station to bring out the goods.

Article 24:   Export for self consumption

Authorized export for self consumption shall be conducted in accordance with the Customs Law.

SECTION VII: SANCTIONS

Article 25: Individual or juristic entity who breach the regulations on controlled goods, in addition to the withdrawal the license, shall be fined and be subject to legal proceedings.

For additional analytical, business and investment opportunities information,
please contact Global Investment & Business Center, USA
at (703) 370-8082. Fax: (703) 370-8083. E-mail: ibpusa3@gmail.com
Global Business and Investment Info Databank - www.ibpus.com

ARTICLE 26:   OTHER VIOLATIONS

Any violation of the importer, exporter and government officer such as falsifying documents or misuse of the position shall be punish according to the law.

SECTION VIII: FINAL PROVISION

ARTICLE 27:   IMPLEMENTATION

The Prime Minister Office, the Ministry of Commerce, the Ministry of Finance, Ministries, comparable organizations, provinces, municipality and special zone shall implement this decree throughout the country.

ARTICLE 28:   EFFECTIVENESS

This decree takes effect from its signature date. All promulgated decrees and regulations in conflict with this decree are herewith abrogated.

DECREE ON GOODS TRADING BUSINESS

- Based on the law on the Government of the Lao PDR No. 01/95 dated 8 March 1995,
- Based on the Business Law No. 03/94/NA dated 18 July 1994,
- Based on the Tax Law No. 04/95/NA dated 14 October 1995,
- Based on the proposal of the Minister of Trade No. 1165/MTT dated 9 October 2001,
- Based on the decision of the Government Meeting dated 25 December 2000.

The Prime Minister of the Lao PDR has decreed:

SECTION I: GENERAL PROVISIONS

ARTICLE 1: FUNCTION OF THE DECREE
This decree has the function of setting up management regulations on domestic goods trading business in accordance with the law, focused on sufficient goods circulation, promotion of goods production, price and exchange rate stabilization, improving living standard of people and active contribution to the national socio-economic development.

ARTICLE 2: GOODS TRADING BUSINESS
Goods Trading Business means business on goods traffic within the country which covers the first sale of local produced goods or imported goods through the last sale to the consumer of both whole and retail sale.

The first sale is the first ownership transfer of goods from the domestic producer or the importer to a person or entity against money or other benefit.

Article 3: Basic Principle of Organization and Operation
Any organization and operation of Goods Trading Business shall be conducted strictly in accordance with this decree and other related laws.

Section II: Management of Conditional Goods

Article 4: Management on Distribution of Conditional Goods

For additional analytical, business and investment opportunities information, please contact Global Investment & Business Center, USA at (703) 370-8082. Fax: (703) 370-8083. E-mail: ibpusa3@gmail.com Global Business and Investment Info Databank - www.ibpus.com

The Government of the Lao PDR promotes the circulation of any commodity liberally in accordance with the law, except commodities, that the government stipulates conditions on distribution in this decree and other laws and regulations related.

Management on distribution of Conditional Goods is the stipulation for the trading business of a certain commodity according to its nature, specific, important, affect, risk or danger.

Article 5: Control Measures of Conditional Goods
Conditional Goods may be controlled by one of the following measures:
- Forbid or restrict business on trading of some goods as necessary;
- Stipulate Registered Capital higher than indicated in the Business Law;
- Require certain qualification of the director, manager, owner or staff;
- Set up standard, quality of goods, trading mark, accounting and other;
- Indicate part which will be permitted for business;
- Set up the price limits and the margins of stocks accumulation periodically.

The measure indicated for a certain conditional goods should not hinder the mentioned business, which can have a negative effect on supply, price, money and competition at reasonable level.

ARTICLE 6: CONDITIONAL GOODS

Conditional Goods are those controlled by the measures in the above Article 5. The list of Conditional Goods may be change as necessary.

Designate the Ministry of Commerce to set up or cancel the list of Conditional Goods and to issue detail management measures for each type of commodity periodically, except those commodities managed by other sector or being covered by other measures.

Article 7: Conditional Goods under other sectors
Conditional Goods under other sectors are those under the direct management of the related sectors. Traders of those goods shall conduct business according to measures issued by the related sectors.

The related sectors shall set up and issue the type and detailed management measures of Conditional Goods mentioned in paragraph 1 above as necessary, then report its list of Conditional Goods officially to the Ministry of Commerce to compile into the list of Conditional Goods of the state.

Assign the Ministry of Commerce to announce this list of business entity and related sectors.

Article 8: Forbidden Goods Trading
Trading of Forbidden Goods shall be permitted by the Ministry of Commerce based on the agreement of the Prime Minister.

In case the Forbidden Goods are under direct management of the related sectors, the Ministry of Commerce shall coordinate with the related sectors before making proposal to the Prime Minister.

SECTION III: FOUNDATION AND OPERATION OF GOODS TRADING BUSINESS

ARTICLE 9: FOUNDATION

Individual or juristic entities who want to set up a Goods Trading Business shall apply to the Commercial Section for foundation and business registration and to the Financial Section for tax registration.

ARTICLE 10: REGISTERED CAPITAL

Registered Capital to set up a Goods Trading Business shall be undertaken as indicated in the Business Law, except for trading of some commodities which the laws and regulations specify for a higher Register Capital.

Article 11: Approved goods on the license

Individual or juristic entity who want to set up a Goods Trading Business may apply for trading of one or many kinds of commodities.

Article 12: Business Organization

The organization of Goods Trading Business may be set up in accordance with the type and form as indicated in the Business Law.

Article 13: Business Activity

Individual or juristic entities who have been licensed for Goods Trading Business may chose the form of trading according to capacity, but have to conduct business in accordance with the related regulations of the selected form of trading.

Article 14: Consequence from Non-operation

A business License of the Goods Trading Business entity, which is not operative for one year after approval, will be cancelled, except in case a reasonable reason has been reported to the Commercial Section before the end of the one year limit.

SECTION IV: SANCTION

ARTICLE 15: VIOLATION OF THE REGULATIONS ON CONDITIONAL GOODS

Individual or juristic entities who breach the regulations on Conditional Goods, in addition to the withdrawal the license, shall be fined and be subject to legal proceedings.

ARTICLE 16: OTHER VIOLATIONS

Any violation of trader and government officer such as false documentation and misuse of position shall be punished according to the law.

SECTION V: FINAL PROVISION

Article 17: Implementation

The Prime Minister's Office, the Ministry of Commerce, the Ministry of Finance, Ministries comparable organizations, provinces, municipality and special zone shall implement this decree throughout the country.

Article 18: Effectiveness

This decree takes effect from its signature date. All promulgated decrees and regulations in conflict with this decree are herewith abrogated.

DECREE ON TRADE COMPETITION

Based upon the Law regarding the Government No. 02/NA, dated 8 May 2003; Based upon the Business Law No. 03194/NA, dated 18 July 1994;

Based upon the proposal of the Minister of Commerce, No. 0713 /MOC.ERIT, dated 18 July 2003,

The Prime Minister issues
Decree:

CHAPTER I GENERAL PROVISIONS

ARTICLE 1   OBJECTIVES

This Decree is issued to define rules, measures and enforcement to regulate monopolization and unfair competition in trade of all forms, aiming to promote fair trade competition, protect the rights and legal interests of consumers and to encourage business activities in the Lao PDR to function efficiently in the market economy mechanism as determined by the Government of the Lao PDR.

ARTICLE 2   DEFINITIONS

In this Decree:
- "acquisition" means the power in business management of one business entity by purchasing the property or buy all or part of the shares of another business entity;
- "business person" means a person who sells goods, buys goods for further processing and sale or buys goods for resale or is a service provider;
- "Commission" refers to the Trade Competition Commission;
- "consumer" means any buyer and/or user of goods and services purchased from a seller;
- "goods" refers to products designed for durable and non-durable consumption, including document certifying the ownership of these goods; "trade" means trade in goods and services;
- "market dominance" means sales volume or market share of any goods or services of one or more business entities is above that prescribed by the Trade Competition Commission;
- "merger" means two or more business entities coming together and forming into one business entity with the result the individual business entity will cease to exist;
- "monopoly" means the dominance of the market individually or in collusion with other businesses;
- "price" means price charged in the sale of goods and services;
- "service" means accepting to perform or performing services, giving for use or interest in goods or any activity for payment in return or other consideration, except wages;

Article 3   Fundamental principle in competition

Business activities of all sectors are equal under the law, they cooperate and compete with each other in a fair manner by in compliance with this Decree and concerned Laws and regulations.

ARTICLE 4   SCOPE OF APPLICATION

This Decree applies to the sale of goods and services in business activities.

CHAPTER 2 THE TRADE COMPETITION COMMISSION

ARTICLE 5   THE TRADE COMPETITION COMMISSION

The Trade Competition Commission shall consist of concerned parties of the trade sector and a number of relevantly experienced people.

The Minister of Trade, by virtue of his position, is the Chairman and appoints members of this Commission.

The Trade Competition Commission shall have its office and its permanent secretariat within the Ministry of Commerce.

ARTICLES 6   RIGHTS AND DUTIES OF THE COMMISSION

The Fair Trading Commission has the rights and duties as follows:
- Determine rules on activities, rights and duties of the secretariat, and supervise the functioning of the secretariat;
- Formulate and stipulate further regulations in enforcing this Decree;
- Establish a sub-commission to implement a specific duty when necessary;
- Consider submissions and give approval for any business person as stipulated in Article 13   of this Decree;
- Determine and publish a list of parties and type of businesses as stipulated in Article 13 of this Decree;
- Call on concerned persons for consultations, advice or clarification on any matter;
- Monitor and control business activities and order any business entity to solve, change, suspend or stop its behavior that is unfair;
- Determine market share, and the total volume amount of a business which is found to be dominating the market;
- Determine market share or assets that are considered to dominate business management of another business entity;
- Consider complaints from business persons and consumers;
- Submit to the concerned organizations to take measures for those who breach;
- Coordinate with the media and concerned business entities to publicise various activities   and issues on matter relating to competition;
- Implement any other duties and responsibilities as may assigned by the Government.

CHAPTER 3 COMPETITION IN TRADE

ARTICLE 7   PROMOTING A FAIR TRADE COMPETITION

The Government of the Lao PDR encourages business entities of all economic sectors to undertake businesses under competitive conditions with equality, fairness, and cooperation.

ARTICLE 8   ANTI-MONOPOLY

It is prohibited for a business person to perform any act stipulated in Articles 9, 10, 11 and 12 of this Decree so as to monopolize any market of goods and services.

ARTICLE 9   MERGER AND ACQUISITION

It is prohibited for a business person to monopolize the market in the form of a merger or acquisition that destroys competitors or substantially reduces or limits competition.

ARTICLE 10   ELIMINATION OF OTHER BUSINESS ENTITIES

It is prohibited for a business entity to act or behave so as to cause losses directly or indirectly, by such conduct as dumping, limiting or intervening with intent to eliminate other business entities.

ARTICLE 11   COLLUSION AND ARRANGEMENTS

It is prohibited for a business entity to collude or make arrangements to engage in unfair trade practices in any form, such as:
- Price fixing, and fixing the sale and purchase price of goods and services;
- Stocking goods, limiting, reducing the quantity or limiting the production, purchase, sale, distribution or import of goods and services;
- Colluding in tenders for purchase, sale and supply of goods and services;
- Fixing conditions that, directly or indirectly, force their customers to reduce production, purchase or sale of goods or the supply of services;
- Limiting the customer's choice to purchase, sell goods and receive services;
- Prohibiting their suppliers or retailers from purchasing or selling goods to other business entities;
- Entering into allocation arrangements of markets, customers or suppliers restricting competition;
- Appoint, or give authority to an individual the for sole right to sell goods or supply services in one market;
- Arrangements to fix conditions or the manner of purchase and sale of goods or services to restrict other business entities;
- Other acts that are contrary to the trade competition regulations prescribed by the Trade Competition Commission.

Article 12   Cartel with foreign business persons

It is prohibited for any business entity to establish and operate a business in the Lao PDR that has business relations with a foreign business entity either by contract, share holding or other form to act to limit the opportunity of local businesses to choose to purchase from or sell goods or provide services directly to, a foreign business entity.

ARTICLE 13   EXEMPTION

Any act stipulated in Article 8, 9,10, 11 and 12 of this Decree may be exempted for some specific sector or business for socio-economic or security reasons.

The Trade Competition Commission is assigned to consider and provide exemptions from time to time.

CHAPTER 4 MEASURES AGAINST OFFENDERS

ARTICLE 14   MEASURES AGAINST BUSINESS ENTITIES WHO COMMIT OFFENCES

A business entity that commits offences under this Decree shall be dealt with as follows;
- Notice to change and rectify its behavior;
- Temporary suspension of activity until the behavior is rectified and changed;
- Close down indefinitely the activity and may be punished according to the law;
- Compensate a business entity that has incurred losses as a result of the offences.

Article 15   Other offences

All civil servants and authorities that commit offences under this Decree will be dealt according to the law.

CHAPTER 5 FINAL PROVISIONS

ARTICLE 16   IMPLEMENTATION

The Ministry of Commerce and the Trade Competition Commission are assigned to implement this Decree.

ARTICLE 17   ENFORCEMENT

This Decree is effective from August 1st, 2004.

All rules and regulations, which are contrary to this Decree, are superseded.

For additional analytical, business and investment opportunities information, please contact Global Investment & Business Center, USA at (703) 370-8082. Fax: (703) 370-8083. E-mail: ibpusa3@gmail.com Global Business and Investment Info Databank - www.ibpus.com

TRAVELING TO LAOS

US STATE DEPARTMENT SUGGESTIONS

COUNTRY DESCRIPTION: Laos is a developing country with a socialist government that is pursuing economic reform. Outside of Vientiane, the capital, and Luang Prabang, tourist services and facilities are relatively undeveloped.

ENTRY REQUIREMENTS: A passport and visa are required. Visas are issued upon arrival in Laos to foreign tourists and business persons, subject to certain conditions, at the following points of entry: Wattay Airport, Vientiane; Luang Prabang Airport; Friendship Bridge, Vientiane; Ban Huay Xai, Bokeo Province; and Vantao, Champasak Province. In the United States, U.S citizens may apply for visas and obtain further information about entry requirements directly from the Embassy of the Lao People's Democratic Republic, 2222 S St. N.W., Washington, D.C. 20008, tel. 202-332-6416, fax 202-332-4923, Internet home page: http://www.laoembassy.com. U.S. citizens should not attempt to enter Laos without valid travel documents or outside official ports of entry. Unscrupulous travel agents have sold U.S.-citizen travelers false Lao visas, which have resulted in those travelers being denied entry into Laos.

SAFETY AND SECURITY: The security situation in Laos can change quickly. Please refer to any Department of State Public Announcements for Laos for additional information.

Since the Spring of 2000, a number of bombings have occurred in public places frequented by foreign travelers in Vientiane, and there have been credible reports of other explosive devices found in Savannakhet and Pakse cities. While there is no evidence that this violence is directed against American citizens or institutions, American citizens should be aware that more such incidents could occur in the future. American citizens traveling to or residing anywhere in Laos are advised to exercise caution and to be alert to their surroundings.

Persons traveling overland in some areas, particularly Route 13 north between Kasi and Luang Prabang; Saisombun Special Zone; Xieng Khouang Province, including the Plain of Jars; and Route 7 east from the Route 13 junction, run the risk of ambush by insurgents or bandits. There have been violent incidents in these areas in the past year. Some groups have warned of impending insurgent attacks in these areas. Americans considering travel outside urban centers by road or river are advised to contact relevant Lao government offices and the U.S. Embassy for the most current security information.

American citizens should also avoid traveling on or across the Mekong River at night along the Thai border. In some areas, Lao militia forces have been known to shoot at boats on the river after dark.

INFORMATION ON CRIME: While Laos generally has a low rate of crime, visitors should exercise appropriate security precautions and remain aware of their surroundings. Street crime has been on the increase, particularly motorcycle drive-by theft of handbags and backpacks. The loss or theft abroad of a U.S. passport should be reported immediately to the local police and the U.S. Embassy. Useful information on safeguarding valuables and protecting personal security while traveling abroad is provided in the Department of State pamphlet, *A Safe Trip Abroad*, available from the Superintendent of Documents, U.S. Government Printing Office, Washington, D.C. 20402, via the Internet at http://www.access.gpo.gov/su_docs, on the Bureau of Consular Affairs home page at http://travel.state.gov and autofax service at 202-647-3000, or at the U.S. Embassy in Vientiane.

MEDICAL FACILITIES: Medical facilities and services are severely limited and do not meet Western standards. The blood supply is not screened for HIV or AIDS.

MEDICAL INSURANCE: U.S. medical insurance is not always valid outside the United States. U.S. Medicare and Medicaid programs do not provide payment for medical services outside the United States. Doctors and hospitals often expect immediate cash payment for health services. Uninsured travelers who require medical care overseas may face extreme difficulties.

Please check with your own insurance company to confirm whether your policy applies overseas, including provision for medical evacuation, and for adequacy of coverage. Serious medical problems requiring hospitalization and/or medical evacuation to the United States can cost tens of thousands of dollars. Please ascertain whether payment will be made to the overseas hospital or doctor or whether you will be reimbursed later for expenses that you incur. Some insurance policies also include coverage for psychiatric treatment and for disposition of remains in the event of death.

Useful information on medical emergencies abroad, including overseas insurance programs, is provided in the Department of State, Bureau of Consular Affairs brochure, *Medical Information for Americans Traveling Abroad*, available via the Bureau of Consular Affairs home page at http://travel.state.gov and autofax service at 202-647-3000.

OTHER HEALTH INFORMATION: Vaccination recommendations and prevention information for traveling abroad may be obtained through the Centers for Disease Control and Prevention's international travelers hotline from the United States at 1-877-FYI-TRIP (1-877-394-8747), via its toll-free autofax service at 1-888-CDC-FAXX (1-888-232-3299), or via their Internet site at http://www.cdc.gov.

ROAD SAFETY: While in a foreign country, U.S. citizens may encounter road conditions that differ significantly from those in the United States. The information below concerning Laos is provided for general reference only, and may not be totally accurate in a particular location or circumstance:
Safety of Public Transportation: Poor
Urban Road Conditions/Maintenance: Poor
Rural Road Conditions/Maintenance: Poor
Availability of Roadside Assistance: Poor

Roads are mostly unpaved, pot-holed and poorly maintained in most parts of the country, although there has been a successful effort to improve roads and drainage in the capital in recent years. There are no railroads. Public transportation in Vientiane is generally poor and unreliable, and it is very limited after sunset. Taxis are available. Drivers speak little or no English. Most taxis are old and poorly maintained. Traffic is increasing, and local drivers remain undisciplined. Pedestrians and drivers should exercise great caution at all times. Theoretically, traffic moves on the right, but most cars, like pedestrians and bicycles, use all parts of the street. Cyclists pay little or no heed to cars on the road, and bicycles are rarely equipped with functioning lights or reflectors. This makes driving especially dangerous at dusk and at night. Defensive driving is necessary. The U.S. Embassy in Vientiane advises its personnel to wear helmets, gloves, and sturdy shoes while operating motorcycles.

AVIATION OVERSIGHT: Serious concerns about the operation of Lao Aviation, particularly regarding its safety standards and maintenance regime, have caused the U.S. Embassy to advise its personnel to limit domestic travel on Lao Aviation to essential travel only. Americans who are required to travel by air within Laos may wish to defer their travel or consider alternate means of transportation.

Also, since there is no direct commercial air service at present, nor economic authority to operate such service between the U.S. and Laos, the U.S. Federal Aviation Administration (FAA) has not assessed Laos' Civil Aviation Authority for compliance with international aviation safety standards for oversight of Laos' air carrier operations. For further information, travelers may contact the Department of Transportation within the U.S. at tel. 1-800-322-7873, or visit the FAA Internet home page at http://www.faa.gov/avr/iasa/iasa.pdf. The U.S. Department of Defense (DOD) separately assesses some foreign air carriers for suitability as official providers of air services. For information regarding the DOD policy on specific carriers, travelers may contact the DOD at tel. 1-618-229-4801.

RELIGIOUS WORKERS: Religious proselytizing or distributing religious material is strictly prohibited. Foreigners caught distributing religious material may be arrested or deported. The Government of Laos restricts the import of religious texts and artifacts. While Lao law allows freedom of religion, the government registers and controls all associations, including religious groups. Meetings, even in private homes, must be registered, and those held outside established locations may be broken up and the participants arrested.

MARRIAGE TO A LAO CITIZEN: The Lao Government imposes requirements on foreigners intending to marry Lao citizens. U.S. citizens may obtain information about these requirements at the U.S. Embassy in Vientiane. A marriage certificate is not issued by the Lao Government unless the correct procedures are followed. Any attempt to circumvent Lao law governing the marriage of Lao citizens to foreigners may result in deportation of the foreigner and denial of permission to re-enter Laos. Similar restrictions exist prohibiting the cohabitation of Lao nationals with nationals of other countries.

PHOTOGRAPHY AND OTHER RESTRICTIONS: Police and military may arrest persons taking photographs of military installations or vehicles, bridges, airfields and government buildings, and confiscate their cameras. Confiscated cameras are seldom returned to the owners. The photographers may be arrested. Export of antiques, such as Buddha images and other old cultural artifacts, is restricted by Laotian law.

CRIMINAL PENALTIES: While in a foreign country, a U.S. citizen is subject to that country's laws and regulations, which sometimes differ significantly from those in the United States and do not afford the protections available to the individual under U.S. law. Penalties for breaking the law can be more severe than in the United States for similar offenses. Persons violating the law, even unknowingly, may be expelled, arrested or imprisoned. Penalties for possession, use or trafficking in illegal drugs in Laos are strict, and convicted offenders can expect jail sentences and fines. Local police and immigration authorities sometimes confiscate passports when outstanding business disputes and visa matters remain unsettled.

CONSULAR ACCESS: The United States and Laos are parties to the Vienna Convention on Consular Relations (VCCR). Article 36 of the VCCR provides that if an arrestee requests it, foreign authorities shall, without delay, inform the U.S. Embassy. U.S. consular officers have the right to be notified of a U.S. citizen's detention and to visit the arrestee. Lao authorities do not always notify the U.S. Embassy or grant U.S. consular officers access to incarcerated U.S. citizens in a timely manner. Nevertheless, American citizens who are arrested or detained in Laos should always request contact with the U.S. Embassy.

CUSTOMS REGULATIONS: Lao customs authorities may enforce strict regulations concerning temporary importation into or export from Laos of items such as religious materials and artifacts, and antiquities. It is advisable to contact the Embassy of the Lao People's Democratic Republic in Washington for specific information regarding customs requirements. (Please see sections on "Religious Workers" and "Photography and Other Restrictions" above.)

CHILDREN'S ISSUES: For information on international adoption of children and international parental child abduction, please refer to our Internet site at http://travel.state.gov/children's_issues.html or telephone (202) 736-7000.

REGISTRATION/EMBASSY LOCATION: U.S. citizens living in or visiting Laos are encouraged to register at the U.S. Embassy where they may obtain updated information on travel and security within the country. The U.S. Embassy is located at Rue Bartholonie (near Tat Dam), B.P. 114, in Vientiane; mail can be addressed to American Embassy Vientiane, Box V, APO AP 96546; telephone (856-21) 212-581, 212-582, 212-585; duty officer's emergency cellular telephone (856-020) 511-740; Embassy-wide fax number (856-020) 518-597; Embassy-wide fax number (856-21) 212-584; Internet home page: http://usembassy.state.gov/laos/.

PRACTIVCAL INFORMATION FOR TRAVELERS

The Lao People's Democratic Republic, strategically located at the hub of Indochina-sharing borders with China, Vietnam, Cambodia, Thailand and Myanma □ is emerging as the region's newest fledgling economy.

After a lengthy period of political instability, the Lao People's Democratic Republic was established in 1975. As a result of the government's New Economic Mechanism launched in 1986, and with Lao PDR's imminent entry into ASEAN, the past decade has been marked by unprecedented growth. Signs of new prosperity are especially visible in the capital of Vientiane, where advancements in infrastructure and services have been occurring rapidly.

Parallel to this recent economic development is the opening of Lao PDR as a tourist destination. With its rich culture, traditional lifestyle, expanding economy and unspoil natural beauty, the Lao PDR welcomes adventurers and business visitors alike.

Step in and experience the great diversity of cultural sights and attractions, restaurants, leisure activities and shopping areas. The Lao PDR is yours to discover.

CULTURAL FESTIVALS

Colorful religious and cultural festivals involve the whole community □ come and celebrate in distinctive Lao style. Some of the major festivals are featured on these two pages. If you are fortunate enough to be here for one of our holidays, we hope you will join in the festivities with us.

Pi Mai □ **Mid-April**

From the washing of religious icons to the drenching of friends and strangers, water is central to *Pi Mai* or Lao New Year celebrations. Wander through temple compounds as worshippers pour perfumed water over Buddha images □ and each other. Even if you miss the significance of cleansing and renewal, you won't escape the traditional water throwing. Expect to be ambushed by celebrants with buckets of water. No one stays dry - or really wants to - during *Pi Mai*.

Three days in mid-April are official public holidays. Exact dates are announced by the government.

Boun Bang Fai - May

On the verge of planting season, the Rocket Festival or *Boun Bang Fai* is held to coax rain and fertility back to the earth. Bamboo rockets adorned with brightly colored decorations are carried to the launch in rowdy procession. Some celebrants paint their faces or wear wild masks and outlandish costumes. All come to enjoy Lao music, dance, and drama □ especially the bawdy *maw lam* □ at its most playful.

Join Boun Bang Fai celebrations on weekends in May at varying locations.

Boun Khao Phansa □ July to October

Boun Khao Phansa is the first day of the Buddhist Lent, which is held from full moon in July to full moon in October. During this time of austerity, monks fast and people make offerings to gain merit. Traditionally, no weddings or celebrations are scheduled during these three months.

Early in the morning on the first day of Lent, people flock to temples carrying silver bowls full of gifts to offer the monks. For a breathtaking sight, go to one of the larger temples, like *That Luang*, where hundreds of worshippers □ mostly women in vividly-colored silks□ kneel row upon row.

Boun Ok Phansa □ October/November

Boun Ok Phansa □ the final and most important day of Lent □ also features an early morning temple ceremony. After dusk, candlelit processions grace temple grounds and buildings glow with candles burning in honor of Buddha.

Also after dusk is *Lai Heua Fai*, a river ceremony during which small hand-made boats is floated down-river by people praying and making vows. The candlelit rafts hob away into darkness, symbolically dismissing bad luck, disease, and sin. This festival is similar to Thailand's *Loy Krathong* festival, which is held in December.

Boun Souang Heua□ October

Held the day after *Ok Phansa*, *Boun Souang Heua* or the Boat race Festival draws crowds of excited spectators to the Mekong River. Fifty-member teams in wooden longboats row to the rhythm of drums as they compete for the coveted trophy. The races are held close to Vientiane. A carnival provides additional entertainment along the riverbank.

Boun That Luang□ November

Held during the time of the full moon in November, the *That Luang* Festival is celebrated in honor of Lao PDR's national shrine. The festival begins with a Morning Prayer and alms giving ceremony on the first day of the three-day festival.

Masses of faithful worshippers come to pay homage to the hundreds of monks gathered at *That Luang*. This ceremony, like *Khao Phansa*, is solemn yet colorful.

For additional analytical, business and investment opportunities information, please contact Global Investment & Business Center, USA at (703) 370-8082. Fax: (703) 370-8083. E-mail: ibpusa3@gmail.com Global Business and Investment Info Databank - www.ibpus.com

A carnival held during these three days offers food and handicraft stalls, bumper cars, a shooting gallery, curiosity booths, pinball, games of chance, and musical entertainment. For sports fans, the highlight of *Boun That Luang* is *tee khee*, or field hockey.

In 1995, two weeks before the actual festival, an international trade fair was held for the first time. Many large local and international companies were present at this important event.

Lao National Day December 2

On this important public holiday, parades and speeches commemorate the 1975 Lao People's Revolutionary Victory over the monarchy.

Vietnamese & Chinese New Year January/February

Firecrackers explode all through this holiday, and mouth-watering sweetmeats and other delicacies are made especially for the occasion. Celebrations are held in January or February, with many business and market stalls closing for three days.

OFFICIAL HOLIDAYS

The following official public holidays for 1996 have been announced by the Prime Minister's Office:

1-3 January International New Year's Day

20 January Military Day (Military only)

8 March Lao Women's Day (Women only)

13-15 April Lao New Year

1 May Labor Day

7 October Teacher's Day (Teachers only)

2 December Lao National Day

VIENTIANE

Vientiane's small size allows easy travel around the city. Most tourist attractions and shopping areas are within walking distance of major hotels. If preferred, most tour operators can organize a one-day tour to these attractions. For day excursions outside Vientiane, it is best to consult a travel agent.

That Luang

The national shrine of the country, *That Luang*, or Great Sacred Stupa, stands 45 meters tall and is believed to contain a relic of the Lord Buddha. The original structure was built by King Setthathirath in 1566, and the present structure was restored in 1953. The gold-colored central structure of this stupa echoes the curving lines of an elongated lotus bud, and the gold is a symbol of the country's wealth. This shrine is the center of the *That Luang* festival held in November.

Revolutionary Monument

Located close to That Luang, this monument stands as a memorial to those who died in the Revolutionary War.

Patuxai

Built in 1962, *Patuxai*, or the Victory Monument, is a memorial to those who died in wars before the Revolution. Known to some as *Anousavali*, or "the monument," the arch and the surrounding park area attract those who wish to relax with friends and watch Vientiane's traffic speed by. For 200 kip, energetic visitors can climb to the top of the monument for a view of the city. The *Patuxai* itself is open from 08:00 to 17:00, but people continue to enjoy the park into the evening.

That Dam

An old legend tells of a seven-headed dragon that protected the people of Vientiane from Siamese invaders during the 1828 war. This dragon is said to be hidden under *That Dam*, or the Black Stupa, and continues to protect the city to this day.

Revolutionary Museum

This impressive example of French colonial architecture houses a collection of artifacts weapons paintings and photographs depicting the history of the Lao People's Revolution. Most captions are written in Lao and English.

Wat Sisaket

Wat Sisaket is the oldest temple in Vientiane-only one to survive the Siamese invasion in 1828. All other temples have since undergone extensive restoration.

The *wat* features a library, which was ransacked during the invasion, as well as unique frescoes and a grand total of 6,840 Buddha images, hundreds of which are framed in small wall niches.

Wat Phra Keo

Once the royal temple of the Lao monarchy, *Wat Phra Keo* was built in 1566. After being destroyed by the Siamese invaders in 1828 it was rebuilt between 1936 and 1942, and has been used as a museum since the 1970s. The main building-which originally housed the *Phra Keo*, or Emerald Buddha-now contains fine examples of Buddhist sculpture and artifacts including antique drums and palm leaf manuscripts. A short description of each exhibit is given in French.

Wat Simuang

Wat Simuang was built when King Setthathirath established Vientiane as the nation's capital in 1563. This temple enshrines the foundation pillar of Vientiane, and is home to the city's guardian spirit.

Local folklore surrounding the temple's construction tells of a pregnant girl who, for the good of the city, sacrificed herself to the spirit by jumping into the hole before the foundation pillar was lowered.

This temple is one of Vientiane's most popular centers of worship, largely because it houses a Buddha image believed to answer the questions of worshippers who lift it three times, repeating

For additional analytical, business and investment opportunities information, please contact Global Investment & Business Center, USA at (703) 370-8082. Fax: (703) 370-8083. E-mail: ibpusa3@gmail.com Global Business and Investment Info Databank - www.ibpus.com

the same question each time. The oddly shaped image is always surrounded by fruit and flowers- offerings of thanks from those who have received its answers.

Wat Ong Teu

Wat Ong Teu, or the Temple of the Heavy Buddha, is the residence of the Deputy Patriarch of the Lao monastic order. The Deputy Patriarch directs Vientiane's Buddhist Institute where monks from all over Laos come to study. The temple also houses a 16th century Buddha weighing several tones.

Suan Vathanatham

Located near the Lao-Thai Friendship Bridge, *Suan Vathanatham* (National Ethnic Cultural Park) offers the visitor a taste of Lao PDR's cultural and natural heritage. Shady paths wind past traditional Lao architecture, an small zoo (featuring alligators, bears, monkey, snakes, hawks, civets, and jungle cats), textile and handicraft shops, food and drink stands, towering dinosaurs, and sculptures of Lao literacy characters including *Sinxai* and the Four Eared Elephant.

Wat Xieng Khouan (Buddha Park)

Situated by the Mekong River about 21 kilometers out of Vientiane municipality, *Wat Xieng Khouan*, despite its name, is not a temple but a sculpture park. Created in 1958, the park captivates visitors with unusual and somewhat disturbing Buddhist and Hindu imagery. For a bizarre experience, climb into the three level model of hell. *Wat Xieng Khouan* offers food and drinks stalls, and is a popular spot for picnics and recreation.

SPORT AND LEISURE ACTIVITIES

Golf

Santisouk Lane Xang Golf and Resort

Located on Thadeua Road, out toward the Friendship Bridge, this gold course claims an international standard. Along with a nine-hole course, the Santisouk Lane Xang offers a driving range, gold shoes and club rental, shower room, and restaurant.

Vientiane Golf Course

The first golf course in Lao PDR, the nine-hole Vientiane golf course is located at Km 6 on Route 13 South.

Night Life

Vientiane offers a wide range of nightclubs and bars with an unique blend of Eastern and Western music. The city's dance floors cater to different tastes from the traditional Lao lamvong to rap. Many establishments offer entertaining light and sound shows and feature popular local bands.

Dokmaideng Fun Park

The Dokmaideng Fun Park is Vientiane's choice destination for children of all ages for an afternoon or evening of bumper cars, swing rides, miniature trains, and video games. Plans are underway to expand the park, adding a waterslide and more.

Thoulakhom Zoo

Another place that is worth visiting is Vientiane province's Thoulakhom Zoo. Located fifty kilometers north of Vientiane municipality, this zoo features many exotic and rare animals from Lao PDR's jungles, from magnificent tigers to mouse deer, elephants, monkeys, parrots, and the newly arrived kangaroos.

SHOPPER'S HEAVEN

Lao PDR is treasure trove of exquisite handicrafts and antiques. Silk and cotton textiles, hand-woven baskets, fine silver-work, detailed woodcarvings, traditional musical instruments and pottery are the pride of the Lao artisan tradition. Art galleries in town feature a wide selection of drawings, watercolors, and oil paintings by local artists.

Many small jewelry and handicraft shops dot the city, and the main shopping center, the *Talat Sao*, houses a head-spinning array of woven textiles, antiques, silver items, and gold jewelry.

Talat Sao

The *Talat Sao* (Morning Market) is comprised of three large pavilions, each with its own Lao style green-tiled roof. The *Talat Sao* offers the shopper everything from silk and fine jewelry to toiletries, electronic equipment and hardware.

The second level of this market is crammed with silver and gold smiths, and there is a good selection of handicrafts and antiques both upstairs and downstairs. The Morning Market also has conveniently-located licensed moneychangers.

Credit Cards

Credit cards are becoming more widely used in Laos, with the most common being VisaCard, MasterCard and American Express. Most major hotels, restaurants and some shops will accept credit cards, but many of the smaller shops, even in the Morning Market, only accept cash.

Nongbouathong Village Weavers

Traditional Lao textile weaving is proudly upheld in this village, and the exquisite results are displayed at the local Pheng Mai Gallery. Nongbouathong village is just a ten-minute drive out of town, and lovers of weaving should not miss this opportunity to watch the weavers at their looms.

The Art of Silk

This silk museum is run by the Lao Women's Union and features a variety of traditional silk pieces created by skillful weavers from different provinces. The items on display are also for sale.

Culinary Treats

Visitors are pleasantly surprised by the many excellent eating establishments in Vientiane. From fabulous Lao, French, Italian, Chinese, Indian, Japanese, and Thai restaurants to mouth-watering chicken roasted over open grills in street stalls, even the most choosy eater will find something to satisfy the plate.

Noodle Houses and Street Stalls

Vientiane abounds with noodle houses-just ask a local to point out the most popular places in town. Different restaurants specialize in different types of noodle dishes, so be adventurous and savour the variety.

Street stalls add undeniable character to the city, and most of them start bustling at sunset. For a Lao food extravaganza, visit Khounboulom Road in the heart of town and try sweet sticky rice with coconut, rich Lao cakes, and loti, the egg pastry roll-ups drizzled with sweetened condensed milk... The list goes on and on and you will not be disappointed.

TRAVELLING OUTSIDE VIENTIANE

Major provincial capitals are serviced by regular Lao Aviation domestic flights. Although internal travel permits are no longer required by foreigners travelling to these areas, it is advisable that travel outside Vientiane is organized through one of the major travel agencies listed in the Gold Pages.

Luang Prabang

This lovely town nestled in the mountains was once capital of Laos. A short forty-minute flight from Vientiane, Luang Prabang is a step back to a time when tradition, culture and religion motivated most activities in Lao society.

Visit the Royal Palace Museum for a fascinating glimpse into the past. Personal artifacts of the Royal Family and gifts from foreign governments are especially interesting. Take a boat trip to *Tham Ting* Caves to see the hundreds of Buddha images enshrined there years ago to protect them from invaders.

Xieng Khouang & Plain of Jars

Xieng Khouang province is home to the Plain of Jars. Scattered across a grassy slope 12 kilometers outside of the provincial capital, are more than 300 ancient stone jars weighing up to six tonnes each. Xieng Khouang was one of Lao PDR's most heavily bombed provinces between 1964 and 1973.

Tham Piu care is a sobering historical sight. *Tham Piu* was used as a bomb shelter by Lao villagers until 1969 when a single rocket fired into the cave killed about 400 people - mostly women and children. Rock debris and human bones from the explosion still litter the cave.

Travelling through the Region

Vientiane is a convenient point from which to travel to other parts of Indochina. The capital is serviced by the national flag carrier, Lao Aviation, and a growing number of foreign airlines, including Air Cambodia, Air Vietnam, Southern China Airlines, Silk Air and Thai International Airways.

For additional analytical, business and investment opportunities information, please contact Global Investment & Business Center, USA at (703) 370-8082. Fax: (703) 370-8083. E-mail: ibpusa3@gmail.com Global Business and Investment Info Databank - www.ibpus.com

Travel from Vientiane to Thailand is convenient with the recent opening of the Australian-built Friendship Bridge, the first bridge across the Mekong River. From the border town of *Nongkhai*, the nearest Thai airport is 60 kilometers away in *Udon Thani*.

BUSINESS INFORMATION

Hotels in Vientiane

There are several excellent hotels and guest-houses in Vientiane offering clean, air-conditioned comfort and genuine Lao hospitality. Most hotels have restaurants, and some of the larger ones have business facilities with facsimile and word processing services. A wide range of prices and features serves the needs of every traveler.

Transport within Vientiane

Vientiane is a small city and easy to move around in. Travelling by jumbo or tuk-tuk is inexpensive and convenient. These vehicles can be hailed from the side of a street or found waiting for customers near markets, restaurants, and hotels. It is wise to know the Lao name of your destination. For most destinations in the city, you should pay no more than 500 kip per passenger. Negotiate the fare before starting on your journey. Taxis are available for hire. Most taxis congregate around the Morning Market and the newer ones have meters. Bicycles and motorcyles can also be hired for a nominal fee.

Clothing and Climate

The climate is tropical, with the monsoons from June until October and the dry season from November to May. The winter months, December to February, can be quite cool and light jackets and sweaters are recommended. If you travel in the provinces during winter months warmer clothing is required as it gets very cold in the mountain areas.

In Vientiane, keep your clothing light, simple and modest. Natural fibers such as silk and cotton are recommended.

Water

Tap water is unsafe for drinking, but purified bottled water is available everywhere. It is not advisable to ear food that has just been rinsed under the tap. Avoid unpeeled fruit and uncooked vegetables.

Electricity

The Lao PDR uses 220 volt power at 50 HZ. Power pints will accept a plug with two flat pins or two round pins. Various adaptors can be purchased at the Morning Market.

SUPPLEMENTS

IMPORTANT WEBSITES

Name	Internet address
ACCSQ	http://www.aseansec.org/4951.htm
ADB	www.adb.org
AFTA	http://www.aseansec.org/economic/afta/afta.htm
ASEAN	www.aseansec.org
ASEAN Protocol on Enhanced Dispute Settlement Mechanism	http://www.aseansec.org/16754.htm
Bangkok Agreement	http://www.unescap.org/tid/Bkkagr.asp
Business Law (1994)	http://www.bkklaoembassy.com/Lao laws/Business Laws.pdf
Constitution	http://www.kplnet.net/English/constitution.htm
Customs Law (1994)	http://laocustoms.laopdr.net/laws_and_regulations.htm
Decree of the Prime Minister on Trademark Registration	http://www.stea.la.wipo.net/download/decree.zip
Department of Domestic and Foreign Investment	http://invest.laopdr.org/
EU-Laos Agreement on Trade in Textile Products	http://trade-info.cec.eu.int/doclib/html/111335.htm
FAO	www.fao.org
IBRD	www.worldbank.org
ICAO	http://www.icao.org/
IDA	www.worldbank.org
IFAD	www.ifad.org
ILO	www.ilo.org
IMF	www.imf.org
ITU	www.itu.int
Labour Law (1994)	http://invest.laopdr.org/labour law.htm
Lao Customs Department	http://laocustoms.laopdr.net/index.htm
Law on the Promotion of Foreign Investment (2004)	http://invest.laopdr.org/investlaw04.pdf
MIGA	www.miga.org
MRC	http://www.mrcmekong.org/
Science, Technology and Environment Agency	http://www.stea.la.wipo.net/aboutdism/index.html
Tax Law (1995)	http://invest.laopdr.org/tax law.htm
UNCTAD	www.unctad.org
UNDP	www.undp.org
UNDP Lao	www.undplao.org
UNDP Human Development index	http://hdr.undp.org/reports/global/2004/pdf/hdr04_HDI.pdf
UNESCO	www.unescao.org
UNIDO	www.unido.org
UPU	www.upu.int
WHO	www.who.org
WIPO	www.wipo.org

| WMO | www.wmo.ch |
| WTO | www.wto.org |

CUSTOMS OFFICE CODES

VIENTIANE	10
1. Banvang	10.1
2. Salakham	10.2
PHONGSALY	02
3. Mouangkhoa	02.1
4. Pakha	02.2
LUANGNAMTHA	03
5. Nateuay	03.1
6. Botenh	03.2
OUDOMXAY	04
BOKEO	05
7. Houaysai	05.1
8. Muongmone	05.2
LUANGPRABANG	06
HOUAPHANH	07
9. Nameo	07.1
10. Pahang	07.2
11. Xiengkheuang	07.3
SAYABOURY	08
12. Kenethao	08.1
XIENGKHOUANG	09
13. Namkan	09.1
VIENTIANE MUNICIPALITY	01
14. Thanaleng	01.1
15. Wattay Airport	01.2
16. Post	01.3
17. Fuel	01.4
18. Thadeua	01.5
19. Friendship Bridge	01.6
BOLIKHAMXAY	11
20. Khamkeuth	11.1
21. Paksan	11.2
22. Namkading	11.3
KHAMMOUANE	12
23. Thakhek	12.1
24. Paksebangfai	12.2
25. Hineboune	12.3
26. Chilo	12.4

SAVANNAKHET	13
27. Denesavanh	13.1
28. Khanthaboury	13.2
29. Thapasoom	13.3
30. Kengkabao	13.4
SALAVANE	14
31. Paktaphane	14.1
SEKONG	15
CHAMPASACK	16
32. Vangtao	16.1
33. Vennekhame	16.2
ATTAPEU	17
34. Phouyang	17.1
Special Zone	18
Headquarters	99

EMBASSIES AND CONSULATES

There are a total of 20 embassies in the Lao People's Democratic Republic:

Australia Nehru Street Vat Phonsay area. Vientiane Tel.: 41-3610, 41-3805, 41-3602

http://www.laos.embassy.gov.au/laos

Brunei Darussalam

No. 333 Unit 25 Ban Phonxay Xaysettha District Lanexang Avenue Vientiane Tel.: 856 2141 6114 Fax: 856 2141 6115 E-mail: kbnbd@laonet.net

Bulgaria

Sisangvone Area Vientiane Tel.: 41-110

Cambodia

Thadeua Road; KM2 Vientiane B.P. 34 Tel.: 31-4950/52 Fax: 31-4951 E-mail: recamlao@laotel.com

China

Vat Nak Street Sisattanak Area Vientiane Tel.: (021) 315100 Fax: (021) 315104 E-mail: embassyprc@laonet.net

Cuba

Saphathong Nua Area Vientiane Tel.: 31-4902

France

Setthathirath Road Vientiane Tel.: 21-5258, 21-5259 Fax: 21-5255

http://www.ambafrance-laos.org

Germany

26 Sokpaluang Road Vientiane Tel.: 31-2111, 31-2110 E-mail: germemb@laotel.com

India

That Luang Road Vat Phonsay Area Vientiane Tel.: 41-3802 E-mail: indemblaos@laonet.net
http://www.indianembassylao.com/laopdr.html

Indonesia

Phon Kheng Road Vientiane Tel.: 41-3910, 41-3909, 41-3907, 41-3914

Japan

Sisangvone Road Vientiane Tel.: 21-2623, 41-4400-2, 41-4406 Fax: 41-4403

Malaysia

That Luang Street, Vat Phonsay Area Vientiane Tel.: 856-21-414205/06 Fax: 856-21-414201
E-mail: mwvntian@laonet.net

Myanmar

Sokpaluang Street, Sisattanak Area Vientiane Tel.: 31-2439, 31-4910

People's Democratic Republic of Korea

Vat Nak Street, Sisattanak Vientiane Tel: 31-5261, 31-5260

Poland

Thadeua Road, Km 3 Vientiane Tel.: 31-2219, 31-2085

Russian Federation

Vientiane Tel.: 31-2219, 31-222

For additional analytical, business and investment opportunities information,
please contact Global Investment & Business Center, USA
at (703) 370-8082. Fax: (703) 370-8083. E-mail: ibpusa3@gmail.com
Global Business and Investment Info Databank - www.ibpus.com

Sweden

Sokpaluang Street, Vat Nak Vientiane Tel.: 31-5018, 31-5000, 31-3772 Fax: 31-5003

Thailand

Phonkheng Road Vientiane Tel.: 21-4582-3, 21-4585

United States of America Viet Nam

That Dam That Luang Road Vientiane Vientiane Tel.: 21-2580-2, 31-2609 Tel.: 41-3400, 41-3409, 41-3403 Fax: 21-2584

http://usembassy.state.gov/laos/wwwhmain.ht ml

The Lao People's Democratic Republic has embassies and consulates general in the following countries:

Australia	Germany
1 Dalmain Crescent O'Malley Canberra ACT 2606 Tel.: (+61 6) 286-4595, 286-6933 Fax: (+61 6) 290-1910 E-mail: lao.embassy@ interact.net.au	Bismarckallee 2A 14193 Berlin Tel.: Tel: +49(0)30 890 606 47 Fax: +49(0)30 890 606 48 http://www.laosbotschaft.de E-mail: hong@laos-botschaft.de
Belgium Av. De La Brabanconne 19-21 1000 Brussels Tel.: (+32 2) 02.7400950 Fax : (+32 2) 02.7341666 http://home.tiscali.be/rambalaobx/	India E53 Panchsheel Park New Delphi-17 Tel.: (+91 11) 642-7447 Fax: (+91 11) 642-8588
Cambodia 15-17 Thanon Keomani PO BOX 19 Phnom Penh Tel.: (+855 23) 26-441, 24-781 Fax: (+855 23) 27-454	Indonesia Jalan Kintamani Raya C-15 No 33 Kuningam Timur Jakarta 12950 Tel.: (+62 21) 520-2670, 522-9602 Fax: (+91 11) 522-9601 E-mail: laoembjktof@hotmail.com
China 11 Sanlitun Dongsie Jie Beijing 100600 Tel.: (+86 1) 532-1224 Fax: (+86 1) 532-6748.	Japan 3-3-22 Nishi-Azabu Minato-Ku Tokyo 106 Tel.: (+81 3) 5411-2291, 5411-2292 Fax: (+81 3) 5411-2293.
Consulate General of the Lao People's Democratic Republic	

Room 3226 Camellia Hotel
154 East Dong Feng Road
Kunming 650041
Tel.: (+86 871) 317-6623, 317-6624
Fax: (+86 871) 317-8556
Cuba
7 Ave Calle 36 A
505 Miramar
Havana
Tel.: (+53 7) 33-1056, 33-1057, 33-1058.

France
74 Ave Raymond Poincaré
75116 Paris
Tel.: (+33 1) 4553-0298, 4554-7047
Fax: (+33 1) 4727-5789
http://www.laoparis.com

Malaysia
108 Jalan Damai
Kuala Lumpur 55000
Tel.: (+60 3) 248-3895
Fax: (+60 3) 242-0344
Mongolia
Ikh Toiruu
P.O. Box 1030
Ulaanbaatar
Tel.: (+976 1) 326-440, 329-898
E-mail: laoemb@ mongol.net

Myanmar
NA1 Diplomatic Quarters
Franser Road
Yangon
Tel.: (+95 1) 22-482, 27-445
Fax: (+95 1) 27-446

Poland
UL Rejtana 15/26
02-516 Warsaw
Tel.: (+48 22) 484-786, 488-949
Fax: (+48 22) 497-122
E-mail: embaslao@warman.com.pl

Russian Federation
Moscow 121069
Ul Katchalov 18
Tel.: (+7 095) 203-1454, 291-8966
Fax: (+7 095) 290-4226

Singapore
101 Thomson Road, #05-03A, United Square
Singapore 307591
Tel.: 2506044, 2506741
Fax: 2506014
E-mail: laoembsg@singnet.com.sg

Sweden
Hornsgatan 82-B1 TR 11721
Stockholm
Tel.: (+46 8) 668-5122
Fax: (+46 8) 669-2176

Thailand
520.502/1-3 Soi Ramkhamhaeng 39

United States of America
2222 S. Street NW
Washington, DC 20008
Tel.: (+1 202) 332-6416, 332-6417
Fax: (+1 202) 332-4923
http://www.laoembassy.com
E-mail: laoemb@erols.com

Viet Nam
22 Rue Tran Bing Trong
Hanoi
Tel.: (+84 4) 25-4576, 29-6746
Fax: (+84 4) 22-8414.

Consulate General of the
Lao People's Democratic Republic
181 Haiba Trung
Ho Chi Minh City
Tel.: (+84 8) 29-7667, 29-9275
Fax: (+84 8) 29-9272.

Consulate General of the
Lao People's Democratic Republic
12 Tran Quy-Cap
Danang
Tel.: (+84 51) 21-208, 24-101
Fax: (+84 51) 22-628

For additional analytical, business and investment opportunities information,
please contact Global Investment & Business Center, USA
at (703) 370-8082. Fax: (703) 370-8083. E-mail: ibpusa3@gmail.com
Global Business and Investment Info Databank - www.ibpus.com

Bangkapi
Bangkok 10300
Tel.: (+66 2) 538-3696, 538-3735
Fax: (+66 2) 539-6678
http://www.bkklaoembassy.com
E-mail: banethok@loxinfo.co.th

Permanent Mission of Lao People's
Democratic Republic to the
United Nations
317 East 51st Street
New York, NY 10022
Tel.: (+1 212) 832-2734
Fax: (+1 212) 332-4923
http://www.un.int/lao

Sources: http://www.laoembassy.com/news/embassyabroad.htm
http://www.mofa.gov.la/Addresses/AddressOfLaoDiplomatic.htm

COUNTRY AND CURRENCY CODES

Country Name	Country Code	Currency Code
AFGHANISTAN	AF	AFA
ALBANIA	AL	ALL
ALGERIA	DZ	DZD
AMERICAN SAMOA	AS	USD
ANDORRA	AD	ESP/FRF
ANGOLA	AO	AOK
ANGUILLA	AI	XCD
ANTIGUA AND BARBUDA	AG	XCD
ARGENTINA	AR	ARP
ARMENIA	AM	RUR
ARUBA	AW	AWG
AUSTRALIA	AU	AUD
AUSTRIA	AT	ATS
AZERBAIJAN	AZ	RUR
BAHAMAS	BS	BSD
BAHRAIN	BH	BHD
BANGLADESH	BD	BDT
BARBADOS	BB	BBD

For additional analytical, business and investment opportunities information,
please contact Global Investment & Business Center, USA
at (703) 370-8082. Fax: (703) 370-8083. E-mail: ibpusa3@gmail.com
Global Business and Investment Info Databank - www.ibpus.com

BELARUS	BY	RUR
BELGUIM	BE	BEF
BELIZE	BZ	BZD
BENIN	BJ	XOF
BERMUDA	BM	BMD
BHUTAN	BT	INR/BTN
BOLIVIA	BO	BOB
BOSNIA-HERZEGOVINA	BA	
BOTSWANA	BW	BWP
BOUVET ISLAND	BV	NOK
BRAZIL	BR	BRC
BRITISH INDIAN OCEAN TERRITORY	IO	USD
BRITISH VIRGINIS	VG	USD
BRUNEI DARUSSALAM	BN	BND
BULGARIA	BG	BGL
BURKINA FASO	BF	XOF
BURUNDI	BI	BIF
Entity Name		
CAMEROON	CM	XAF
CANADA	CA	CAD
CAPE VERDE	CV	CVE
CAYMAN IS	KY	KYD
CENTRAL AFRICAN REPUBLIC	CF	XAF
CHAD	TD	XAF
CHILE	CL	CLP
CHINA	CN	CNY
CHRISTMAS IS	CX	AUD
COCOS (KEELING) ISLANDS	CC	AUD
COLOMBIA	CO	COP
COMOROS IS	KM	KMF
CONGO	CG	XAF
COOK IS	CK	NZD
COSTA RICA	CR	CRC
COTE D'IVOIRE	CI	XOF

For additional analytical, business and investment opportunities information, please contact Global Investment & Business Center, USA at (703) 370-8082. Fax: (703) 370-8083. E-mail: ibpusa3@gmail.com Global Business and Investment Info Databank - www.ibpus.com

CROATIA	HR	
CUBA	CU	CUP
CYPRUS	CY	CYP
CZECH REPUBLIC	CZ	CZK
DENMARK	DK	DKK
DJIBOUTI	DJ	DJF
DOMINICA	DM	XCD
DOMINICAN REPUBLIC	DO	DOP
EAST TIMOR	TP	TPE
ECUADOR	EC	ECS
EGYPT ARAB REP OF	EG	EGP
EL SALVADOR	SV	SVC
EQUATORIAL GUINEA	GQ	GOE
ESTONIA	EE	
ETHIOPIA	ET	ETB
FAEROE IS	FO	DKK
FALKLAND ISLANDS (MALVINAS)	FK	FKP
FIJI	FJ	FJD
FINLAND	FI	FIM
FRANCE	FR	FRF
FRENCH GUIANA	GF	FRF
Entity Name		
FRENCH POLYNESIA	PF	XPF
FRENCH SOUTHERN TERRITORIES	TF	FRF
GABON	GA	XAF
GAMBIA	GM	GMD
GEORGIA	GG	RUR
GERMANY, FEDERAL REPUBLIC OF	DE	DEM
GHANA	GH	GHC
GIBRALTAR	GI	GIP

GREECE	GR	GRD
GREENLAND	GL	DKK
GRENADA	GD	XCD
GUADELOUPE	GP	FRF
GUAM	GU	USD
GUATEMALA	GT	GTQ
GUINEA	GN	GNS
GUINEA-BISSAU	GW	GWP
GUYANA	GY	GYD
HAITI	HT	HTG
HEARD AND MCDONALD ISLANDS	HM	USD
HONDURAS	HN	HNL
HONGKONG	HK	HKD
HUNGARY	HU	HUF
ICELAND	IS	ISK
INDIA	IN	INR
INDONASIA REP OF	ID	IDR
IRAN, ISLAMIC REPUBLIC OF	IR	IRR
IRAQ	IQ	IQD
IRELAND	IE	IEP
ISRAEL	IL	ILS
ITALY	IT	ITL
JAMAICA	JM	JMD
JAPAN	JP	JPY
JORDAN	JO	JOD
KAMPUCHEA, DEMOCRATIC	KH	KHR
KAZAKHSTAN	KK	RUR
Entity Name		
KENYA	KE	KES
KIRIBATI	KI	AUD

For additional analytical, business and investment opportunities information, please contact Global Investment & Business Center, USA at (703) 370-8082. Fax: (703) 370-8083. E-mail: ibpusa3@gmail.com Global Business and Investment Info Databank - www.ibpus.com

KOREA, DEM PEOPLE'S REPUBLIC OF	KP	KPW
KOREA, REPUBLIC OF	KR	KRW
KUWAIT	KW	KWD
KYRGYZSTAN	KG	RUR
LAOS PEOPLE DEMOCRATIC REPUBLIC	LA	LAK
LATVIA		
LEBANON	LV	
LESOTHO	LB	LBP
LIBERIA	LS	ZAR/LS
LIBYA	LR	LRD
LIECHSTENSTEIN	LY	LYD
LITHUANIA	LI	CHF
LUXEMBOURG	LT	
	LU	LUF
MACAU	MO	MOP
MALAGASY REPUBLIC	MG	MGF
MALAWI	MW	MWK
MALAYSIA	MY	MYR
MALDIVES REP OF	MV	MVR
MALI	ML	MLF
MALTA	MT	MTL
MARSHALL IS	MH	USD
MARTINIQUE	MQ	FRF
MAURITANIA	MR	MRO
MAURITIUS	MU	MUR
MEXICO	MX	MXP
MICRONESIA	FM	USD
MOLDOVA	MD	RUR
MONACO	MC	FRF
MONGOLIAN PEO REP	MN	MNT
MONTSERRAT	MS	XCD
MOROCCO	MA	MAD
MOZAMBIQUE	MZ	MZM

MYANMAR	BU	BUK
Entity Name		
NAMIBIA	NA	ZAR
NAURU	NR	AUD
NEPAL	NP	NPR
NETHERLANDS	NL	NLG
NETHERLANDS ANTILLES	AN	ANG
NEW ZEALAND	NZ	NZD
NEW CALEDONIA	NC	XPF
NICARAGUA	NI	NIC
NIGER	NE	XOF
NIGERIA	NG	NGN
NIUE	NU	NZD
NORFOLK ISLAND	NF	AUD
NORTHERN MARIANA IS	MP	USD
NORWAY	NO	NOK
OMAN	OM	OMR
PAKISTAN	PK	PKR
PALAU	PW	USD
PANAMA	PA	PAB/USD
PAPUA NEW GUINEA	PG	PGK
PARAGUAY	PY	PYG
PERU	PE	PES
PHILIPPINES	PH	PHP
PITCAIRN	PN	NZD
POLAND	PL	PLZ
PORTUGAL	PT	PTE
PUERTO RICO	PR	USD
QATAR	QA	QAR
REUNION	RE	FRF
ROMANIA	RO	ROL

For additional analytical, business and investment opportunities information,
please contact Global Investment & Business Center, USA
at (703) 370-8082. Fax: (703) 370-8083. E-mail: ibpusa3@gmail.com
Global Business and Investment Info Databank - www.ibpus.com

RUSSIA	RU	RUR
RWANDA	RW	RWF
SAINT KITTS-NEVIS	KN	XCD
SAINT LUCIA	LC	XCD
SAINT VINCENT AND THE GRENADINES		
	VC	XCD
Entity Name		
SAN MARINO	SM	ITL
SAO TOME AND PRINCIPE	ST	STD
SAUDI ARABIA	SA	SAR
SENEGAL	SN	XOP
SEYCHELLES	SC	SCR
SIERRA LEONE	SL	SLL
SINGAPORE	SG	SGD
SLOVAK REPUBLIC	SK	SKK
SLOVENIA	SI	
SOLOMAN IS	SB	SBD
SOMALI	SO	SOS
SOUTH AFRICA	ZA	ZAR
SPAIN	ES	ESP
SRI LANKA	LK	LKR
ST HELENA	SH	SHP
ST PIERRE ET MIQUELON	PM	FRF
SUDAN	SD	SDP
SURINAM	SR	SRG
SVALBARD AND JAN MAYEN IS	SJ	NOK
SWAZILAND	SZ	SZL
SWEDEN	SE	SEK
SWITZERLAND	CH	CHP
SYRIAN ARAB REPUBLIC	SY	SYP
TAIWAN	TW	TWD
TAJIKISTAN	TJ	RUR
TANZANIA	TZ	TZS

THAILAND	TH	THB
TOGOLESE	TG	XOF
TOKELAU	TK	NZD
TONGA	TO	TOP
TRAINIDAD AND TOBAGO	TT	TTD
TUNISIA	TN	TND
TURKEY	TR	TRL
TURKMENISTAN	TM	RUR
TURKS AND CAICOS IS	TC	USD
TUVALU	TV	AUD
Entity Name		
UGANDA	UG	UGS
UKRAINE	UA	RUR
UNITED ARAB EMIRATES	AE	AED
UNITED KINGDOM	GB	GBP
UNITED STATES	US	USD
UNITED SATES MINOR OUTLYING ISLANDS	UM	USD
URUGUAY	UY	UYP
UZBEKISTAN	UZ	RUR
VANUATU	VU	VUV
VATICAN CITY STATE	VA	ITL
VENEZUELA	VE	VEB
VIETNAM SOC REP OF	VN	VND
VIRGIN ISLANDS (US)	VI	USD
WALLIS AND FUTUNA	WF	XPF
WESTERN SAHARA	EH	ESP/MAD
WESTERN SAMOA	WS	WST
YEMEN ARAB REPUBLIC OF	YE	YER
YEMEN PEOPLE'S DEMOCRATIC REPUBLIC	YD	YDD

YUGOSLAVIA	YU	YUD
ZAIRE	ZR	ZRZ
ZAMBIA	ZM	ZMK
ZIMBABWE	ZW	ZWD

THE DECLARATION FORM

The declaration form or single administrative document is used for all customs transactions; import, export or transit. It must be complete to be acceptable in customs.

The declaration form has three segments.

1. In the first section(Boxes No.1-23) enter general information on importer, exporter and declarant as well as transport and transaction details.

2. In the second section (Boxes No.24-42) enter details on the item declared, including amount of duties and taxes payable or exempted.

3. Summary of Payment and Responsibility of Declaration Section.

It is presented in the form of (i.) a header sheet, which is used to declare importation, exportation or in transit information for each commodity item (ii.) continuation sheets to declare other commodity items and (iii.) section sheet for official use.
Note. Declaration forms are on sale at all Regional Customs offices.
Instructions to fill each box of the form.

Box No.1   Declaration Regime

Inscribe one of the following codes to identify the type of transaction the declaration is for:

Regime Code	Description
10	Exportation of domestic Goods
14	Exportation under a drawback regime
20	Temporary Exportation
35	Re-Exportation
40	Importation of goods for Home consumption.
4A	Importation of goods for diplomatic use, returning residents, and humanitarian assistance; samples, educational materials and certain religious articles.
4B	Goods ex-warehoused to duty free shops

4C	Goods ex-warehoused for exportation out of Lao PDR
45	Home Consumption of Goods after temporary admission
47	Home Consumption of Goods entered under a warehousing regime
50	Temporary Importation
62	Re-Importation of Goods Exported temporarily
70	Warehousing of Goods
80	Transit

Office Codes.

Enter the code of the office where the declaration is presented. See Annex I for a list of all customs offices and their codes.

Manifest /Airway bill number.

Enter the cargo control number from the air waybill if the goods arrive or leave by air or from the manifest if goods arrive or leave by any other mode of transport.
Declaration Number and Date.

Customs will assign the declaration number and the date when the declaration is presented and registered with customs.

Box No.2   Exporter and Address

If you enter goods for exportation, indicate your name and address as well as the taxpayer identification number (TIN) issued by the Tax Department. If you have not yet been issued a TIN please obtain a number from the nearest tax office and use it on all subsequent customs declarations. Also include your office telephone number. For diplomatic and personal exportations, leave the number field blank.

Box No.3   Gross Mass Kg.

Indicate the gross weight in kilograms of the entire consignment of goods as declared on the manifest or air waybill.

Box No.4   Items

Indicate the total number of items as shown on the invoice.

Box No.5   Total Packages.

Indicate the total number of packages as declared on the manifest or airway bill. In case of bulk cargo, indicate BULK only.

Box No. 6   Importer and Address

If you enter goods for importation, indicate your name and address as well as the taxpayer identification number (TIN) issued by the Tax Department. If you have not been issued a TIN please obtain a number from the nearest tax office and use it on all subsequent customs declarations. Also include your office telephone number. For diplomatic and personal importations, leave the number field blank.

Box No.7   Consignee.

If you are importing goods on behalf of another person, or the other party holds title to the good at time of importation indicate the name and address of the consignee as well as the TIN issued by the Tax Department. Please contact the nearest tax office for a number and use on all subsequent declarations, or obtain the TIN number from the consignee if one has been issued to the consignee by the tax department. For diplomatic importations, leave the number field blank.

Box No.8   Declarant.

If you are a licensed agent authorized to transact business in customs, enter the TIN issued by the Tax Department. If you do not have a TIN, contact the nearest tax office.

Box No.9   Country of Consignment/Destination.

For importation, indicate the country and the code from where the goods have been consigned. For exportation, indicate the country and the code to where the goods are exported or re-exported.

See Annex II: List of Country and Currency Codes.

Box No.10   Type of License.

Indicate the type of trade or industry license held by you.

Box. No.11   Delivery Terms.

Indicate the terms of delivery of goods either CIF for importation, or FOB for exportation.

Box No.12   Total Invoice in Foreign Currency.

For importation, indicate the total amount of the invoice in foreign currency. See list of Country and Currency Codes in Annex II.

Box No.13   Total Invoice in Local Currency.

Enter here the total value of the invoice in Kip by converting the value declared in box No. 12 with the rate of exchange indicated in box No.16. If there is only one item, this value should correspond to the value declared in box no.38. If there are many items, the total value should correspond to the total of values declared in all the boxes no.38 on the Continuation sheets.

Box No.14   Total FOB (Exports)

Indicate the FOB value of the goods in foreign currency.
(if known)
Box No. 14   Total FOB (Imports)

Enter the FOB value in foreign currency. (if known)

Box No.15   Total FOB Ncy (Import/Export)

For import, leave blank.
For export, indicate the FOB value of the goods in Kip.

Box No.16   Rate of Exchange.

Indicate the rate of exchange of the foreign currency to the Kip and the code of the foreign currency. (The exchange rate shall be that which is in force at time of importation, unless otherwise advised).

Box No.17   Mode of Transport.

Indicate the mode of transport, the voyage number. Also the country code of the nationality of the aircraft, truck or ship.
(if known)

The codes for mode of transport are:

SEA	1
RAIL	2
ROAD	3
AIR	4

Box No.18   Port of Loading/Unloading.

For imports indicate the name and the code of the foreign country where goods are loaded,
For exports, indicate the name and the code of the foreign country where goods are destined.

See Annex II for a list of Country Codes.

Box No.19   Place of Shipping/ Landing.

For imports, indicate the place in Lao PDR where goods have arrived. At export, or re-export, indicate the place in Lao PDR from where the goods are exported or re-exported.

Box No.20   Entry/Exit Office.

Indicate the code of the Lao customs office where the declaration is presented for clearance.

In a transit operation, indicate the code of the customs office where the transit operation commences. Also indicate the code of the exit customs office where the transit operations is to be terminated.

Box No.21   Identification Warehouse (Leave blank until bonded warehouses are established)

Indicate the code of the bonded warehouse where goods are to be warehoused or ex-warehoused.

Box No.22   Financial and Banking Data.

Indicate the terms of payment of the transaction, as well as the name of the bank and the branch where payment for the commercial transaction is made.

Box No.23   Attached Documents.

Indicate the codes of attached documents, which support your declaration. (Documents must be originals or certified as true copies).

1		Invoice
2		Manifest
3		Airway bill
4		Packing List
5		Certificate of Origin (If required)
6		Phytosanitary Certificate (If required)
7		Import Permit from Ministry of Trade (If required)
8		Import permit from Ministry of Agriculture (If required)
9		Import Permit from Ministry of Heath (If required)
10		Authorization from Department of Transport (If required)
11		If claiming duty and tax exemptions, documents authorizing such exemptions must be presented with the declaration.

Box No.24   Marks, Numbers and Description of Goods

Indicate the marks and numbers of the packages as shown on the manifest or airway bill.

If goods arrive or leave by containers, indicate the container number as shown on the manifest.

The total number of packages should correspond to the total number of packages indicated in box No.5.

Give a detailed description of the goods. Avoid, as far as possible, trade names. Except in the case of vehicles and electronic devices, provide make and model.

Box No.25   No. of Items.

Indicate the number of items on the invoice.

Box No.26   Tariff Code

Indicate the classification code of the commodity imported. This classification code in based on the AHTN and must be eight digits.

Box No.27   Customs Procedure Codes.
(Leave blank at this time)

Box No.28   Country of Origin/Destination

For imports, indicate the code of the country of origin of the goods imported, if the country of origin of the goods is different from the country where the goods have been consigned.

Box No.29   Zone.
It the goods originate from ASEAN member countries and are supported by a certificate of origin enter ASEAN. For other countries enter GEN. At export enter XPT.

Box No.30   Valuation Code

Indicate the code of the valuation method used to determine the customs value for duty.

There are six valuation methods and coded as follows:

	VALUATION METHOD	Code	
	Transaction Method	1	
	Identical Goods Method	2	
	Similar Goods Method	3	
	Deductive Method	4	
	Computed Method	5	
	Flexible Method	6	

Note: The transaction valuation method must be used as the primary method for valuation if possible.

Box No.31   Gross Mass.

Enter the gross weight in kilograms for the item on the first page only. The total weight of all items on the continuation sheets in the declaration should be equal to the weight declared in box no.3 of the general segment.

Box No.32   Net Mass.

Enter the net weight of the goods in kilograms for each item declared. If a continuation sheet is used a net mass must be inscribed for each item.

Box No.33   FOB Foreign Currency.

Enter the FOB value of the item in foreign currency (if known).

Box No.34   FOB Local Currency, only if transport and insurance are not prepaid by exporter. If prepaid, enter the value that includes transportation and insurance.

Enter the FOB value of the item in Kips, only if transport and insurance are not prepaid by exporter. If prepaid, enter the value that includes transportation and insurance.

Box No. 35   Freight.

Enter the amount of freight paid or payable for the item in Kip. For a shipment of various items, the freight charges are apportioned according to freight paid or payable and by weight. If freight is prepaid by exporter and included in the value, mark the box "Prepaid".

Box No.36   Insurance.

Enter the amount of insurance in Kip for the item.

For a shipment of various items, the insurance paid or payable is to be apportioned.

If the insurance is prepaid by the exporter and included in the value, mark the box "prepaid"

Box No.37   Other Costs.

Enter other costs and expenses incurred for the import of goods and paid to the exporter for the imported goods.

Box No.38   Customs Value in Local Currency.

Enter the customs value for the item, which is the total of values of boxes 33, 34, 35 and 36.

Box No. 39   Supplementary Unit/Quantity.

Some of the most common international units of quantity are as follows:

	Unit	Code	
	Cubic Metre	MTQ	
	Gigawatt-hour	GWH	
	Hundred	CEN	
	Kilogram	KGM	
	Litre	LTR	
	Metre	MTR	
	Number	NMB	
	Number of packs	NMP	
	Square Metre	MTK	
	Ten	TEN	
	Ten Pairs	TPR	
	Thousand	MIL	
	Tonne	TNE	

Enter any of the code, which describes the unit quantity of goods imported/exported. If the units of imports or exports are not included in this list, consult a customs officer for more detailed lists.

Box No.40   Duty Payable.

Enter the amount of duties and taxes payable for the item declared per category of duty, tax and excise.

Enter also the taxable base for each category of duty, tax and excise. Duty rate is calculated on the Customs value. The tax is calculated on the customs value plus the duty payable. The excise tax is calculated on the customs value plus duty payable plus tax payable.

For other items of the declaration, on the continuation sheets enter the duty, tax and excise payable.

Box No.41   Permit Numbers.

Enter permit number and date of issue for the shipment, if required.

For additional analytical, business and investment opportunities information, please contact Global Investment & Business Center, USA at (703) 370-8082. Fax: (703) 370-8083. E-mail: ibpusa3@gmail.com Global Business and Investment Info Databank - www.ibpus.com

Box No.42   Previous Declaration.

If the declaration refers to a previous declaration, the registration number and date of the previous declaration is entered here.

Present a copy of the previous declaration with the declaration you have just prepared.

Responsibility of Declaration

You must enter your full name, indicate the capacity in which you are acting. And sign the declaration.

You must also indicate the mode of payment by which duty and taxes are to be paid.

After you have completed your declaration, trader can now lodge it at the designated customs office where your goods are held.

After customs review and approval of the declaration, please make the payment of all applicable duties and taxes, and present a copy of the payment receipt to the customs office where the declaration was presented.

On receipt of the customs release note, present the release note to the warehouse keeper for delivery of the imported goods and sign for receipt of the goods or have the carrier sign for receipt.

LAOS GLOSSARY

Asian Development Bank

Established in 1967, the bank assists in economic development and promotes growth and cooperation in developing member countries. The bank is owned by its forty-seven member governments, which include both developed and developing countries in Asia and developed countries in the West.

Association of Southeast Asian Nations (ASEAN)

Founded in 1967 primarily for economic cooperation and consisting of Brunei (since 1984), Indonesia, Malaysia, the Philippines, Singapore, and Thailand. Laos has had observer status since 1992 and applied for membership in July 1994.

ban

Village; grouped administratively into *tasseng* (q.v.) and *muang* (q.v.).

dharma

Buddhist teaching or moral law; laws of nature, all that exists, real or imaginary.

fiscal year (FY)

October 1 to September 30.

gross domestic product (GDP)

A value measure of the flow of domestic goods and services produced by an economy over a period of time, such as a year. Only output values of goods for final consumption and intermediate production are assumed to be included in the final prices. GDP is sometimes aggregated and shown at market prices, meaning that indirect taxes and subsidies are included; when these indirect taxes and subsidies have been eliminated, the result is GDP at factor cost. The word *gross* indicates that deductions for depreciation of physical assets have not been made. Income arising from investments and possessions owned abroad is not included, only domestic production. Hence, the use of the word *domestic* to distinguish GDP from gross national product (*q.v.*).

gross national product (GNP)

The gross domestic product (GDP--*q.v.*) plus net income or loss stemming from transactions with foreign countries, including income received from abroad by residents and subtracting payments remitted abroad to nonresidents. GNP is the broadest measurement of the output of goods and services by an economy. It can be calculated at market prices, which include indirect taxes and subsidies. Because indirect taxes and subsidies are only transfer payments, GNP is often calculated at factor cost by removing indirect taxes and subsidies.

Hmong

Largest Lao Sung (*q.v.*) ethnic group of northern Laos. This tribal group dwells at higher elevations than other ethnic groups. During the period of the Royal Lao Government (RLG) (*q.v.*), the Hmong were referred to as Meo.

International Monetary Fund (IMF)

Established on July 22, 1944, the IMF began operating along with the World Bank (*q.v.*) on December 27, 1945. The IMF is a specialized agency affiliated with the United Nations that takes responsibility for stabilizing international exchange rates and payments. The IMF's main business is the provision of loans to its members when they experience balance of payments difficulties. These loans often carry conditions that require substantial internal economic adjustments by the recipients. In 1994 the IMF had 179 members.

karma

Buddhist concept of the sum of one's past actions, which affect one's current life and future reincarnations.

khoueng

Province; first order administrative division.

kip(k)

Lao currency. In June 1994, US$1=R721.

Lao Issara

Free Laos. Movement formed in 1945 to resist any attempt to return to French colonial status.

Lao Loum

Literally translated as the valley Laotian. Inclusive term for people of Tai stock living in Laos, including lowland Lao and upland Tai. Group of lowland peoples comprising the majority population of Laos; generally used to refer to ethnic Lao, the country's dominant ethnic group (approximately 66 percent of the population according to the 1985 census), and speaking Tai-Kadai languages, including Lao, Lue, Tai Dam (Black Tai), and Tai Deng (Red Tai).

Lao Patrocitic Front (LPF) (Neo Lao Hak Xat)

Sucessor to Neo Lao Issara (*q.v.*), the political arm of the Pathrt Liberation Army (*q.v.*)--formerly known as the Pathet Lao (q.v.)--is its milituary arm.

Lao People's Army

Formed in 1976 when the Lao People's Liberation Army (LPLA-- *q.v.*) was restructured after the establishment of the Lao People's Democratic Republic in December 1975.

Lao People's Liberation Army (LPLA)

Official title of Pathet Lao armed forces, more commonly known as the communist revolutionaries, or guerrilla forces. The LPLA originated with the Latsavong detachment, formed in January 1949 by Kaysone Phomvihan, and steadily increased in number to an estimated 8,000 guerrillas in 1960 and an estimated 48,000 troops between 1962 and 1970.

Lao People's Revolutionary Party (LPRP) (Phak Pasason Pativat Lao)

Founded secretly in 1955 as the Phak Pasason Lao (Lao People's Party--LPP); name changed in 1972. Seized full power and became the ruling (communist) party of Laos in 1975. The LPRP Central Committee formulates party policy; it is dominated by the Political Bureau (Politburo) and the Secretariat and maintains control by placing its members in key institutions throughout the government and the army.

Lao Sung

Literally translated as the Laotian of the mountain top--those who traditionally live in the high altitudes in northern Laos. In official use, term denotes a category of ethnic groups that speak Tibeto-Burmese, Miao-Yao languages; chiefly the Hmong (*q.v.*) (Meo) group of highland or upland minorities but also the Mien (Yao) and Akha. According to the 1985 census, these groups make up approximately 10 percent of the population.

Lao Theung

Literally, Laotian of the mountain slopes; group--including Kammu, Loven, and Lamet--that traditionally lives in medium altitudes, practices swidden, or slash-and-burn-agriculture, and speaks Mon-Khmer languages and dialects. According to the 1985 census, approximately 24 percent of the population. Regarded as original inhabitants of Laos, formally referred to by ethnic Lao as *kha*, or slave.

mandala

Indian geopolitical term referring to a variable circle of power centered on a ruler, his palace, and the religious center from which he drew his legitimization.

***muang* (*muong*)**

Administrative district; also an independent principality; comprises several *tasseng* (*q.v.*), second order administrative divisions.

Lao Patriotic Front (LPF) (Neo Lao Hak Xat)

Successor to Neo Lao Issara (*q.v.*), the political arm of the Pathet Lao (*q.v.*) during the Indochina Wars (1946- 75). The Lao People's Liberation Army (*q.v.*)--formerly known as the Pathet Lao (*q.v.*)--is its military arm.

Neo Lao Issara

Free Laos Front--organization established by former Lao Issara (Free Laos) (*q.v.*) to continue anti-French resistance movement with the Viet Minh (*q.v.*); succeeded by Neo Lao Hak Xat (Lao Patriotic Front--LPF) (*q.v.*) in 1956.

net material product

Gross material output minus depreciation on capital and excluding "unproductive services." According to the World Bank (*q.v.*), net material product is "a socialist concept of national accounts."

Nonaligned Movement

Established in September 1961 with the aim of promoting political and military cooperation apart from the traditional East and West blocs. As of 1994, there were 107 members (plus the Palestine Liberation Organization), twenty-one observers, and twenty-one "guests."

Pathet Lao (Lao Nation)

Literally, land of the Lao. Until October 1965, the name for the Lao People's Liberation Army (*q.v.*), the military arm of the Lao Patriotic Front (*q.v.*).

Royal Lao Government (RLG)

The ruling authority in Laos from 1947 until the communist seizure of power in December 1975 and the proclamation of the Lao People's Democratic Republic.

Sipsong Panna

Region in southern Yunnan Province, China, from which migrated many groups that now inhabit Laos.

Southeast Asia Treaty Organization (SEATO)

Established in September 1954 as a result of the 1954 Geneva Agreements to stop the spread of communism in Southeast Asia. SEATO never had an active military role and was ultimately disbanded in June 1977 following the success of the communist movements in Cambodia, Laos, and Vietnam in 1975. Original signatories to SEATO were Australia, Britain, France, New Zealand, Pakistan, the Philippines, Thailand, and the United States.

tasseng

Administrative unit; territorial subdivision of *muang* (*q.v.*), subdistrict grouping of ten to twenty villages.

That Luang

Most sacred Buddhist stupa in Vientiane and site of annual festival on the full moon of the twelfth month.

Theravada Buddhism

Predominant branch of Buddhism practiced in Laos, Cambodia, Sri Lanka, and Thailand.

United Nations Children's Fund (UNICEF)

Acronym retained from predecessor organization, United Nations International Children's Emergency Fund, established in December 1946. Provides funds for establishing child health and welfare services.

United Nations Development Programme (UNDP)

Created by the United Nations in 1965, the UNDP is the world's largest channel for multilateral technical and preinvestment assistance to low-income countries. It functions as an overall programming, financing, and monitoring agency. The actual fieldwork is done by other UN agencies.

United Nations High Commissioner for Refugees (UNHCR)

Established by the United Nations in 1949, it did not become effective until 1951. The first world institution to aid refugees, the UNHCR seeks to ensure the humanitarian treatment of refugees and find a permanent solution to refugee problems. The agency deals with the international protection of refugees and problems arising from mass movements of people forced to seek refuge.

Viet Minh

Coalition of Vietnamese national elements formed in May 1941 and dominated by the communists in their movement calling for an uprising against the French colonial government.

World Bank

Informal name used to designate a group of four affiliated international institutions: the International Bank for Reconstruction and Development (IBRD), the International Development Association (IDA), the International Finance Corporation (IFC), and the Multilateral Investment Guarantee Agency (MIGA). The IBRD, established in 1945, has as its primary purpose the provision of loans at market-related rates of interest to developing countries at more advanced stages of development. The IDA, a legally separate loan fund but administered by the staff of the IBRD, was set up in 1960 to furnish credits to the poorest developing countries on much easier terms than those of conventional IBRD loans. The IFC, founded in 1956, supplements the activities of the IBRD through loans and assistance designed specifically to encourage the growth of productive private enterprises in the less developed countries. The MIGA, founded in 1988, insures private foreign investment in developing countries against various noncommercial risk. The president and certain senior officers of the IBRD hold the same positions in the IFC. The four institutions are owned by the governments of the countries that subscribe their capital. To participate in the World Bank group, member states must first belong to the Intentional Monetary Fund (IMF--*q.v.*).

SELECTED TOUR OPERATORS IN LAOS

The following list is issued by the National Tourism Authority of Lao PDR. This is not an exhaustive list of travel companies. You are advised to contact the travel company directly for their up-to-date itineraries and prices.

Dafi Travel Co., Ltd 093/4 Samsenthai St,	P.O. Box 5351, Vientiane	**Lao Tourism Co., Ltd** 08/02 Lane Xang Ave,

P.O. Box 2511,
Vientiane

Luang Prabang Tourism Co., Ltd
P.O. Box 356,
Sisavangvong Rd,
Luang Prabang.

Phathanakhet Phoudoi Travel Co., Ltd
Phonxay Rd,

P.O. Box 5796,
Vientiane

Phathana Saysomboune Travel & Tour Co., Ltd
Km 5, 13 South Rd,
12/G Chommanytai
Xaysetha DTR,
P.O. Box 7117,
Vientiane

Chackavane Travel & Tour

92 Thongkankham Rd,
P.O. Box 590,
Vientiane

Raja Tour
03 Heng boon St,
P.O. Box 3655,
Vientiane

Sode Tour
114 Quai Fa Ngum,
P.O. Box 70,
Vientiane

LAO PDR EMBASSIES AND CONSULATES-GENERAL

Country	Address
Brunei Darussalam	Embassy of the Lao PDR Tel : 673-2-345 666 Fax : 456-888
Cambodia	Embassy of the Lao PDR 15-17 Mao Tse Tung Boulvard P.O. Box 19 Phnom Penh Tel : 855-23-982 632 Fax : 720 907
Indonesia	Embassy of the Lao PDR Jl. Patra Kuningan XIV No.1.A Kuningan Jakarta Selatan - 12950 Tel : 62-21-522 9602, 522 7862 Fax : 522 9601
Malaysia	Embassy of the Lao PDR I Lorong Damai Tiga Kuala Lumpur 55000 Tel : 60-3-248 3895, Residence: 245 6023 HP : 60-012 218 0075 Fax : 60-3- 242 0344
Myanmar	Embassy of the Lao PDR NA I Diplomatic Quarters Franser Road Yangon Tel : 95-1-222 482, 227 445 Fax : 227 446
The Philippines	Embassy of the Lao PDR N. 34 Lapu-Lapu Street Magallences Village

	Makati City, Manila Tel & Fax : 63-2-833 5759
Singapore	Embassy of the Lao PDR 179-B Gold Hill Centre Thomson Road Tel : 65-250 6044 Fax : 65-250 6214
Thailand	Embassy of the Lao PDR 520-502/ 1-3 Soi Ramkhamheng 39 Bangkapi Bangkok 10310 Tel : 539 6667 Fax : 66-2-539 6678 Consulate General of the Lao PDR Khonkaen Tel : 66-43-223 698, 223 473, 221 961 Fax : 223 849
Vietnam	Embassy of the Lao PDR 22 Rue Tran Bing Trong Hanoi Tel : 84-4-8- 25 4576, 29 6746 Fax : 22 8414 Consulate General of the LAO PDR 93 Larteur ST, District 1 Ho Chi Minh City Tel : 84-8-8- 29 7667, 29 9275 Fax : 29 9272 Consulate General of the LAO PDR 12 Tran Quy-Cap Danang Tel : 84-51-8- 21 208, 24 101 Fax : 22 628
Australia	Embassy of the Lao PDR I Dalman Crescent O' Malley Canberra ACT 2606 Tel : 61-2- 6286 4595, 6286 6933 Fax : 6290 1910
China	Embassy of the Lao PDR 11 Salitun Dongsie Jie Bejing 100 600 IfsTel : 86-1- 6532 1224 Fax : 6532 6748 Consulate General of the Lao PDR Room 3226 Camellia Hotel 154 East Dong Feng Road Kunming 650041 Tel : 86-871- 317 6623, 317 6624 Fax : 317 8556

For additional analytical, business and investment opportunities information, please contact Global Investment & Business Center, USA at (703) 370-8082. Fax: (703) 370-8083. E-mail: ibpusa3@gmail.com Global Business and Investment Info Databank - www.ibpus.com

France	Embassy of the Lao PDR 74 Ave Raymond Poincare 75116 Paris Tel : 33-1- 4553 0298, 4553 7047 Fax : 4727 5789
Germany	Embassy of the Lao PDR Am Lessing 6 53639 Koeningswinter Tel : 49- 2223 21501 Fax : 2223 3065
India	Embassy of the Lao PDR E53 Panchsheel Park New Delhi-17 Tel : 91-11-642 7447 Fax : 642 8588
Japan	Embassy of the Lao PDR 3-3-22 Nishi-Azabu Minato-Ku Tokyo 106 Tel : 81-3-5411 2291, 5411 2292 Fax : 5411 2293
Russia	Embassy of the Lao PDR Ul Katchalova 18 Moscow 121 069 Tel : 7-095-203 1454, 291 8966 Fax : 290 4246, 291 7218
Sweden	Embassy of the Lao PDR Badstrandvagen 11 11265 Stockholm Tel : 46-8-618 2010, 695 0160 Fax : 618 2001
United States of America	Embassy of the Lao PDR 2222 S Street NW Washington DC 10022 Tel : 1-202- 332 6416, 332 6417 Fax : 332 4923 Permanent Mission of the Lao PDR 317 East 51st Street New York, NY 10022 Tel : 1-212- 832 2734 Fax : 750 0039

For additional analytical, business and investment opportunities information,
please contact Global Investment & Business Center, USA
at (703) 370-8082. Fax: (703) 370-8083. E-mail: ibpusa3@gmail.com
Global Business and Investment Info Databank - www.ibpus.com

BASIC TITLE FOR LAOS

IMPORTANT!
All publications are updated annually!
Please contact IBP, Inc. at ibpusa3@gmail.com for the latest ISBNs and additional information
Global Business and Investment Info Databank: www.ibpus.com

TITLE
Lao People's Dem. Rep. Fishing and Aquaculture Industry Handbook - Strategic Information, Regulations, Opportunities
Lao People's Democratic Republic Traders and Investors Handbook
Lao People's Democratic Republic Investment, Trade Strategy and Agreements Handbook - Strategic Information and Basic Agreements
Lao People's Democratic Republic Traders and Investors Handbook
Laos A "Spy" Guide - Strategic Information and Developments
Laos A Spy" Guide"
Laos Business and Investment Opportunities Yearbook
Laos Business and Investment Opportunities Yearbook
Laos Business and Investment Opportunities Yearbook Volume 1 Strategic Information and Opportunities
Laos Business Intelligence Report - Practical Information, Opportunities, Contacts
Laos Business Intelligence Report - Practical Information, Opportunities, Contacts
Laos Business Law Handbook - Strategic Information and Basic Laws
Laos Business Law Handbook - Strategic Information and Basic Laws
Laos Business Law Handbook - Strategic Information and Basic Laws
Laos Business Law Handbook - Strategic Information and Basic Laws
Laos Business Law Handbook Volume 1 Strategic Information and Basic Laws
Laos Business Success Guide - Basic Practical Information and Contacts
Laos Clothing & Textile Industry Handbook
Laos Clothing & Textile Industry Handbook
Laos Company Laws and Regulations Handbook
Laos Country Study Guide - Strategic Information and Developments
Laos Country Study Guide - Strategic Information and Developments
Laos Country Study Guide - Strategic Information and Developments Volume 1 Strategic Information and Developments
Laos Country Study Guide Volume 1 Strategic Information and Developments
Laos Country Study Guide Volume 1 Strategic Information and Developments - Everything you need to know about the country - Geography, history, politics, economy, business, etc.
Laos Criminal Laws, Regulations and Procedures Handbook - Strategic Information, Regulations, Procedures
Laos Customs, Trade Regulations and Procedures Handbook
Laos Customs, Trade Regulations and Procedures Handbook
Laos Diplomatic Handbook - Strategic Information and Developments
Laos Diplomatic Handbook - Strategic Information and Developments
Laos Ecology & Nature Protection Handbook
Laos Ecology & Nature Protection Handbook

For additional analytical, business and investment opportunities information,
please contact Global Investment & Business Center, USA
at (703) 370-8082. Fax: (703) 370-8083. E-mail: ibpusa3@gmail.com
Global Business and Investment Info Databank - www.ibpus.com

TITLE
Laos Ecology & Nature Protection Laws and Regulation Handbook
Laos Economic & Development Strategy Handbook
Laos Economic & Development Strategy Handbook
Laos Education System and Policy Handbook
Laos Electoral, Political Parties Laws and Regulations Handbook - Strategic Information, Regulations, Procedures
Laos Energy Policy, Laws and Regulation Handbook
Laos Export-Import Trade and Business Directory
Laos Export-Import Trade and Business Directory
Laos Foreign Policy and Government Guide
Laos Foreign Policy and Government Guide
Laos Industrial and Business Directory
Laos Industrial and Business Directory
Laos Internet and E-Commerce Investment and Business Guide - Strategic and Practical Information: Regulations and Opportunities
Laos Internet and E-Commerce Investment and Business Guide - Strategic and Practical Information: Regulations and Opportunities
Laos Investment and Business Guide - Strategic and Practical Information
Laos Investment and Business Guide - Strategic and Practical Information
Laos Investment and Business Guide - Strategic and Practical Information
Laos Investment and Business Guide - Strategic and Practical Information
Laos Investment and Business Guide Volume 1 Strategic and Practical Information
Laos Investment and Business Profile - Basic Information and Contacts for Succesful investment and Business Activity
Laos Investment and Trade Laws and Regulations Handbook
Laos Justice System and National Police Handbook
Laos Justice System and National Police Handbook
Laos Medical & Pharmaceutical Industry Handbook
Laos Medical & Pharmaceutical Industry Handbook
Laos Mineral & Mining Sector Investment and Business Guide - Strategic and Practical Information
Laos Mineral, Mining Sector Investment and Business Guide - Strategic and Practical Information
Laos Mining Laws and Regulations Handbook
Laos Recent Economic and Political Developments Yearbook
Laos Recent Economic and Political Developments Yearbook
Laos Recent Economic and Political Developments Yearbook
Laos Research & Development Policy Handbook
Laos Research & Development Policy Handbook
Laos Research & Development Policy Handbook
Laos Social Security System, Policies, Laws and Regulations Handbook - Strategic Information and Basic Laws
Laos Starting Business (Incorporating) in....Guide
Laos Tax Guide Volume 1 Strategic Information and Basic Regulations
Laos Taxation Laws and Regulations Handbook
Laos Telecom Laws and Regulations Handbook

TITLE
Laos Telecommunication Industry Business Opportunities Handbook
Laos Telecommunication Industry Business Opportunities Handbook
Laos Traders Manual: Export-Import, Trade, Investment
Laos Transportation Policy and Regulations Handbook
Laos: Doing Business and Investing in ... Guide Volume 1 Strategic, Practical Information, Regulations, Contacts
Laos: How to Invest, Start and Run Profitable Business in Laos Guide - Practical Information, Opportunities, Contacts

BASIC LAWS AND REGULATIONS AFFECTING BUSINESS[4]

COUTRY	LAW TITLE
Lao DPR	Constitution of the Lao PDR
Lao DPR	Decree on Commercial Banks
Lao DPR	Decree On Organization and Activities of the National Statistical System
Lao DPR	Decree on Procurement
Lao DPR	Decree on the Organization and Activities of the Bank Of Lao PDR
Lao DPR	Forest Law
Lao DPR	Intellectual Property Law
Lao DPR	Law governing the Management of Foreign Exchange and Precious Metals
Lao DPR	Law on Agriculture
Lao DPR	Law on Anti-Corruption
Lao DPR	Law on Bankruptcy on Enterprises
Lao DPR	Law on Civil Aviation
Lao DPR	Law on Civil Procedure
Lao DPR	Law on Commercial Banks
Lao DPR	Law on Contract
Lao DPR	Law on Court Fees
Lao DPR	Law on Criminal Procedure
Lao DPR	Law on Customs
Lao DPR	Law on Development and Protection of Women
Lao DPR	Law on Drugs and Medical Products
Lao DPR	Law on Electricity
Lao DPR	Law on Enterprise
Lao DPR	Law on Enterprise Accounting
Lao DPR	Law on Environmental Protection
Lao DPR	Law on Family
Lao DPR	Law on Family Registration
Lao DPR	Law on Food
Lao DPR	Law on Health Care

[4] For ordering texts of specific laws in English, French, or otehr languages, please contact Global Investment Center USA at ibpusa3@gmail.com

Lao DPR	Law on Heritage and Basis of Inheritance
Lao DPR	Law on Hygiene, Disease Prevention and Health Promotion
Lao DPR	Law on Industrial Processing
Lao DPR	Law on Insurance
Lao DPR	Law on Judgment Enforcement
Lao DPR	Law on Labor
Lao DPR	Law on Land
Lao DPR	Law on Land Traffic
Lao DPR	Law on Land Transport
Lao DPR	Law on Lao Nationality
Lao DPR	Law on Local Administration
Lao DPR	Law on Mining
Lao DPR	Law on National Defense Obligations
Lao DPR	Law on National Heritage
Lao DPR	Law on Notary Offices
Lao DPR	Law on Postal Services
Lao DPR	Law on Property
Lao DPR	Law on Public Roads
Lao DPR	Law on Resolution of Economic Disputes
Lao DPR	Law on Resolution of Economic Disputes
Lao DPR	Law on Secured Transactions
Lao DPR	Law on State Assets
Lao DPR	Law on State Budget
Lao DPR	Law on Tax
Lao DPR	Law on Telecommunications
Lao DPR	Law on the Bank of the Lao PDR
Lao DPR	Law on the Election of Members of the National Assembly
Lao DPR	Law on the Government of the Lao People's Democratic Republic
Lao DPR	Law on the Handling of Petitions
Lao DPR	Law on the National Assembly
Lao DPR	Law on the People's Court
Lao DPR	Law on the Promotion of Domestic Investment
Lao DPR	Law on the Promotion of Foreign Investment
Lao DPR	Law on the Promotion of Investment
Lao DPR	Law on the Protection of the Rights and Interests of Children
Lao DPR	Law on Tort
Lao DPR	Law on Tourism
Lao DPR	Law on Urban Plans
Lao DPR	Law on Value Added Tax
Lao DPR	Law on Water and Water Resources
Lao DPR	Mining Law
Lao DPR	Penal Law
Lao DPR	Wildlife and Aquatic Law

For additional analytical, business and investment opportunities information, please contact Global Investment & Business Center, USA at (703) 370-8082. Fax: (703) 370-8083. E-mail: ibpusa3@gmail.com Global Business and Investment Info Databank - www.ibpus.com

INFORMATION STRATEGY, INTERNET AND E-COMMERCE DEVELOPMENT HANDBOOKS LIBRARY

Price: $99.95 Each

World Business Information Catalog: http://www.ibpus.com

TITLE
Albania Information Strategy, Internet and E-Commerce Development Handbook - Strategic Information, Programs, Regulations
Algeria Information Strategy, Internet and E-Commerce Development Handbook - Strategic Information, Programs, Regulations
Angola Information Strategy, Internet and E-Commerce Development Handbook - Strategic Information, Programs, Regulations
Argentina Information Strategy, Internet and E-Commerce Development Handbook - Strategic Information, Programs, Regulations
Armenia Information Strategy, Internet and E-Commerce Development Handbook - Strategic Information, Programs, Regulations
Australia Information Strategy, Internet and E-Commerce Development Handbook - Strategic Information, Programs, Regulations
Austria Information Strategy, Internet and E-Commerce Development Handbook - Strategic Information, Programs, Regulations
Azerbaijan Information Strategy, Internet and E-Commerce Development Handbook - Strategic Information, Programs, Regulations
Bangladesh Information Strategy, Internet and E-Commerce Development Handbook - Strategic Information, Programs, Regulations
Belarus Information Strategy, Internet and E-Commerce Development Handbook - Strategic Information, Programs, Regulations
Belgium Information Strategy, Internet and E-Commerce Development Handbook - Strategic Information, Programs, Regulations
Bermuda Information Strategy, Internet and E-Commerce Development Handbook - Strategic Information, Programs, Regulations
Bolivia Information Strategy, Internet and E-Commerce Development Handbook - Strategic Information, Programs, Regulations
Bosnia and Herzegovina Information Strategy, Internet and E-Commerce Development Handbook - Strategic Information, Programs, Regulations
Botswana Information Strategy, Internet and E-Commerce Development Handbook - Strategic Information, Programs, Regulations
Brazil Information Strategy, Internet and E-Commerce Development Handbook - Strategic Information, Programs, Regulations
Bulgaria Information Strategy, Internet and E-Commerce Development Handbook - Strategic Information, Programs, Regulations
Cambodia Information Strategy, Internet and E-Commerce Development Handbook - Strategic Information, Programs, Regulations
Cameroon Information Strategy, Internet and E-Commerce Development Handbook - Strategic Information, Programs, Regulations
Canada Information Strategy, Internet and E-Commerce Development Handbook - Strategic Information, Programs, Regulations
Chile Information Strategy, Internet and E-Commerce Development Handbook - Strategic Information, Programs,

TITLE
Regulations
China Information Strategy, Internet and E-Commerce Development Handbook - Strategic Information, Programs, Regulations
Colombia Information Strategy, Internet and E-Commerce Development Handbook - Strategic Information, Programs, Regulations
Cook Islands Information Strategy, Internet and E-Commerce Development Handbook - Strategic Information, Programs, Regulations
Costa Rica Information Strategy, Internet and E-Commerce Development Handbook - Strategic Information, Programs, Regulations
Croatia Information Strategy, Internet and E-Commerce Development Handbook - Strategic Information, Programs, Regulations
Cuba Information Strategy, Internet and E-Commerce Development Handbook - Strategic Information, Programs, Regulations
Cyprus Information Strategy, Internet and E-Commerce Development Handbook - Strategic Information, Programs, Regulations
Czech Republic Information Strategy, Internet and E-Commerce Development Handbook - Strategic Information, Programs, Regulations
Denmark Information Strategy, Internet and E-Commerce Development Handbook - Strategic Information, Programs, Regulations
Dominican Republic Information Strategy, Internet and E-Commerce Development Handbook - Strategic Information, Programs, Regulations
Dubai Information Strategy, Internet and E-Commerce Development Handbook - Strategic Information, Programs, Regulations
Ecuador Information Strategy, Internet and E-Commerce Development Handbook - Strategic Information, Programs, Regulations
Egypt Information Strategy, Internet and E-Commerce Development Handbook - Strategic Information, Programs, Regulations
El Salvador Information Strategy, Internet and E-Commerce Development Handbook - Strategic Information, Programs, Regulations
Equatorial Guinea Information Strategy, Internet and E-Commerce Development Handbook - Strategic Information, Programs, Regulations
Estonia Information Strategy, Internet and E-Commerce Development Handbook - Strategic Information, Programs, Regulations
Fiji Information Strategy, Internet and E-Commerce Development Handbook - Strategic Information, Programs, Regulations
Finland Information Strategy, Internet and E-Commerce Development Handbook - Strategic Information, Programs, Regulations
France Information Strategy, Internet and E-Commerce Development Handbook - Strategic Information, Programs, Regulations
Georgia Republic Information Strategy, Internet and E-Commerce Development Handbook - Strategic Information, Programs, Regulations
Germany Information Strategy, Internet and E-Commerce Development Handbook - Strategic Information, Programs, Regulations
Greece Information Strategy, Internet and E-Commerce Development Handbook - Strategic Information, Programs, Regulations
Guatemala Information Strategy, Internet and E-Commerce Development Handbook - Strategic Information, Programs, Regulations
Guernsey Information Strategy, Internet and E-Commerce Development Handbook - Strategic Information, Programs, Regulations
Guyana Information Strategy, Internet and E-Commerce Development Handbook - Strategic Information, Programs, Regulations
Haiti Information Strategy, Internet and E-Commerce Development Handbook - Strategic Information, Programs, Regulations
Honduras Information Strategy, Internet and E-Commerce Development Handbook - Strategic Information, Programs, Regulations
Hungary Information Strategy, Internet and E-Commerce Development Handbook - Strategic Information, Programs, Regulations
Iceland Information Strategy, Internet and E-Commerce Development Handbook - Strategic Information, Programs, Regulations
India Information Strategy, Internet and E-Commerce Development Handbook - Strategic Information, Programs, Regulations

TITLE
Indonesia Information Strategy, Internet and E-Commerce Development Handbook - Strategic Information, Programs, Regulations
Iran Information Strategy, Internet and E-Commerce Development Handbook - Strategic Information, Programs, Regulations
Iraq Information Strategy, Internet and E-Commerce Development Handbook - Strategic Information, Programs, Regulations
Ireland Information Strategy, Internet and E-Commerce Development Handbook - Strategic Information, Programs, Regulations
Israel Information Strategy, Internet and E-Commerce Development Handbook - Strategic Information, Programs, Regulations
Italy Information Strategy, Internet and E-Commerce Development Handbook - Strategic Information, Programs, Regulations
Jamaica Information Strategy, Internet and E-Commerce Development Handbook - Strategic Information, Programs, Regulations
Japan Information Strategy, Internet and E-Commerce Development Handbook - Strategic Information, Programs, Regulations
Jordan Information Strategy, Internet and E-Commerce Development Handbook - Strategic Information, Programs, Regulations
Kazakhstan Information Strategy, Internet and E-Commerce Development Handbook - Strategic Information, Programs, Regulations
Kenya Information Strategy, Internet and E-Commerce Development Handbook - Strategic Information, Programs, Regulations
Korea, North Information Strategy, Internet and E-Commerce Development Handbook - Strategic Information, Programs, Regulations
Korea, South Information Strategy, Internet and E-Commerce Development Handbook - Strategic Information, Programs, Regulations
Kuwait Information Strategy, Internet and E-Commerce Development Handbook - Strategic Information, Programs, Regulations
Kyrgyzstan Information Strategy, Internet and E-Commerce Development Handbook - Strategic Information, Programs, Regulations
Laos Information Strategy, Internet and E-Commerce Development Handbook - Strategic Information, Programs, Regulations
Latvia Information Strategy, Internet and E-Commerce Development Handbook - Strategic Information, Programs, Regulations
Lebanon Information Strategy, Internet and E-Commerce Development Handbook - Strategic Information, Programs, Regulations
Libya Information Strategy, Internet and E-Commerce Development Handbook - Strategic Information, Programs, Regulations
Lithuania Information Strategy, Internet and E-Commerce Development Handbook - Strategic Information, Programs, Regulations
Macao Information Strategy, Internet and E-Commerce Development Handbook - Strategic Information, Programs, Regulations
Macedonia, Republic Information Strategy, Internet and E-Commerce Development Handbook - Strategic Information, Programs, Regulations
Madagascar Information Strategy, Internet and E-Commerce Development Handbook - Strategic Information, Programs, Regulations
Malaysia Information Strategy, Internet and E-Commerce Development Handbook - Strategic Information, Programs, Regulations
Malta Information Strategy, Internet and E-Commerce Development Handbook - Strategic Information, Programs, Regulations
Mauritius Information Strategy, Internet and E-Commerce Development Handbook - Strategic Information, Programs, Regulations
Mauritius Information Strategy, Internet and E-Commerce Development Handbook - Strategic Information, Programs, Regulations
Mexico Information Strategy, Internet and E-Commerce Development Handbook - Strategic Information, Programs, Regulations
Micronesia Information Strategy, Internet and E-Commerce Development Handbook - Strategic Information, Programs, Regulations
Moldova Information Strategy, Internet and E-Commerce Development Handbook - Strategic Information, Programs, Regulations
Monaco Information Strategy, Internet and E-Commerce Development Handbook - Strategic Information,

TITLE
Programs, Regulations
Mongolia Information Strategy, Internet and E-Commerce Development Handbook - Strategic Information, Programs, Regulations
Morocco Information Strategy, Internet and E-Commerce Development Handbook - Strategic Information, Programs, Regulations
Myanmar Information Strategy, Internet and E-Commerce Development Handbook - Strategic Information, Programs, Regulations
Namibia Information Strategy, Internet and E-Commerce Development Handbook - Strategic Information, Programs, Regulations
Netherlands Information Strategy, Internet and E-Commerce Development Handbook - Strategic Information, Programs, Regulations
New Zealand Information Strategy, Internet and E-Commerce Development Handbook - Strategic Information, Programs, Regulations
Nicaragua Information Strategy, Internet and E-Commerce Development Handbook - Strategic Information, Programs, Regulations
Nigeria Information Strategy, Internet and E-Commerce Development Handbook - Strategic Information, Programs, Regulations
Norway Information Strategy, Internet and E-Commerce Development Handbook - Strategic Information, Programs, Regulations
Opportunities
Pakistan Information Strategy, Internet and E-Commerce Development Handbook - Strategic Information, Programs, Regulations
Panama Information Strategy, Internet and E-Commerce Development Handbook - Strategic Information, Programs, Regulations
Peru Information Strategy, Internet and E-Commerce Development Handbook - Strategic Information, Programs, Regulations
Philippines Information Strategy, Internet and E-Commerce Development Handbook - Strategic Information, Programs, Regulations
Poland Information Strategy, Internet and E-Commerce Development Handbook - Strategic Information, Programs, Regulations
Portugal Information Strategy, Internet and E-Commerce Development Handbook - Strategic Information, Programs, Regulations
Romania Information Strategy, Internet and E-Commerce Development Handbook - Strategic Information, Programs, Regulations
Russia Information Strategy, Internet and E-Commerce Development Handbook - Strategic Information, Programs, Regulations
Saudi Arabia Information Strategy, Internet and E-Commerce Development Handbook - Strategic Information, Programs, Regulations
Scotland Information Strategy, Internet and E-Commerce Development Handbook - Strategic Information, Programs, Regulations
Serbia Information Strategy, Internet and E-Commerce Development Handbook - Strategic Information, Programs, Regulations
Singapore Information Strategy, Internet and E-Commerce Development Handbook - Strategic Information, Programs, Regulations
Slovakia Information Strategy, Internet and E-Commerce Development Handbook - Strategic Information, Programs, Regulations
Slovenia Information Strategy, Internet and E-Commerce Development Handbook - Strategic Information, Programs, Regulations
South Africa Information Strategy, Internet and E-Commerce Development Handbook - Strategic Information, Programs, Regulations
Spain Information Strategy, Internet and E-Commerce Development Handbook - Strategic Information, Programs, Regulations
Sri Lanka Information Strategy, Internet and E-Commerce Development Handbook - Strategic Information, Programs, Regulations
Sudan Information Strategy, Internet and E-Commerce Development Handbook - Strategic Information, Programs, Regulations
Suriname Information Strategy, Internet and E-Commerce Development Handbook - Strategic Information, Programs, Regulations
Sweden Information Strategy, Internet and E-Commerce Development Handbook - Strategic Information, Programs, Regulations
Switzerland Information Strategy, Internet and E-Commerce Development Handbook - Strategic Information,

TITLE
Programs, Regulations
Syria Export Import &Business Directory
Taiwan Information Strategy, Internet and E-Commerce Development Handbook - Strategic Information, Programs, Regulations
Tajikistan Information Strategy, Internet and E-Commerce Development Handbook - Strategic Information, Programs, Regulations
Thailand Information Strategy, Internet and E-Commerce Development Handbook - Strategic Information, Programs, Regulations
Tunisia Information Strategy, Internet and E-Commerce Development Handbook - Strategic Information, Programs, Regulations
Turkey Information Strategy, Internet and E-Commerce Development Handbook - Strategic Information, Programs, Regulations
Turkmenistan Information Strategy, Internet and E-Commerce Development Handbook - Strategic Information, Programs, Regulations
Uganda Information Strategy, Internet and E-Commerce Development Handbook - Strategic Information, Programs, Regulations
Ukraine Information Strategy, Internet and E-Commerce Development Handbook - Strategic Information, Programs, Regulations
United Arab Emirates Information Strategy, Internet and E-Commerce Development Handbook - Strategic Information, Programs, Regulations
United Kingdom Information Strategy, Internet and E-Commerce Development Handbook - Strategic Information, Programs, Regulations
United States Information Strategy, Internet and E-Commerce Development Handbook - Strategic Information, Programs, Regulations
Uruguay Information Strategy, Internet and E-Commerce Development Handbook - Strategic Information, Programs, Regulations
US Information Strategy, Internet and E-Commerce Development Handbook - Strategic Information, Programs, Regulations
Uzbekistan Information Strategy, Internet and E-Commerce Development Handbook - Strategic Information, Programs, Regulations
Venezuela Information Strategy, Internet and E-Commerce Development Handbook - Strategic Information, Programs, Regulations
Vietnam Information Strategy, Internet and E-Commerce Development Handbook - Strategic Information, Programs, Regulations